Louis Menand

PRAGMATISM

Louis Menand is Professor of English at the Graduate Center of the City University of New York. He is the author of *Discovering Modernism: T. S. Eliot and His Context* and the editor of *The Future of Academic Freedom*. He has been Contributing Editor of *The New York Review of Books* since 1994 and has written regularly for that magazine, *The New Yorker*, and *The New Republic*.

PRAGMATISM

A READER

PRAGMATISM

A READER

*Edited and
with an Introduction by* Louis Menand

Vintage Books · A Division of Random House Inc. · New York

A VINTAGE ORIGINAL, OCTOBER 1997
First Edition

Copyright © 1997 by Louis Menand

Library of Congress Cataloging-in-Publication Data
Pragmatism : a reader / edited and with an introduction by Louis
Menand.
p.   cm.
Including bibliographical references and index.
ISBN 0-679-77544-7
1. Pragmatism.   I. Menand, Louis.
B832.P756   1997
144'.3—dc21   97-9328
CIP

Permissions acknowledgments may be found on pages 523–524.

Book design by Rebecca Aidlin

Random House Web address: http//www.randomhouse.com/

Printed in the United States of America
10 9 8 7 6 5 4 3 2 1

Contents

Contents

An Introduction to Pragmatism

Pragmatism is an account of the way people think. This may not seem like a terribly useful thing to have. After all, if pragmatism's account of the way people think is accurate, then we are already thinking the way pragmatists tell us we are. Why would we be in need of a description of something we do anyway without it? It is as though someone were to offer us an account of the way our hair grows with the promise that having it will give us nicer hair.

But pragmatists don't believe there is a problem with the way people think. They believe there is a problem with the way people think they think. They believe, in other words, that other accounts of the way people think are mistaken; they believe that these mistaken accounts are responsible for a large number of conceptual puzzles; and they believe that these puzzles, when they are not simply wasting the energy of the people who spend their time trying to "solve" them, actually get in the way of our everyday efforts to cope with the world.

Pragmatism is therefore an effort to unhitch human beings from what pragmatists regard as a useless structure of bad abstractions about thought. The sheer bravado of the attempt, the suggestion that all we need to do to lighten our load is drop the whole contraption over the side of a cliff and continue on doing what we want to be doing anyway, is what makes pragmatist writing so exhilarating to read. The classic pragmatist essay—Charles Sanders Peirce's "How to Make Our Ideas Clear," William James's "The Will to Believe," Oliver Wendell Holmes's "The Path of the Law," Richard Rorty's "Philosophy as a Kind of Writing"—has a kind of ground-clearing sweep to it that gives many readers the sense that a pressing but vaguely understood obligation has suddenly been lifted from their shoulders, that some final examination for which they could never possibly have felt prepared has just been canceled.

What has seemed liberating to some readers has, of course, seemed like negligence and worse to others. The nonchalance with which pragmatists tend to dispose of issues that have engaged other thinkers has always struck many people as intellectually slipshod and morally dangerous. "Pragmatism is a matter of human needs," wrote G. K. Chesterton in 1908, when international interest in pragmatism was first at its height, "and one of the first of human needs is to be something more than a pragmatist."[1] If the pragmatist account is correct, warned Bertrand Russell a year later, then "ironclads and Maxim guns must be the ultimate arbiters of metaphysical truth."[2] Pragmatists today have attracted similar sorts of hostility. They have been accused of purveying what one writer has called "a relativism-cum-aestheticism that verges on nihilism and that may ultimately subvert liberal democracy,"[3] and what another has denounced as an "abandonment of traditional standards of objectivity, truth, and rationality, [which] opens the way for an educational agenda one of whose primary purposes is to achieve social and political transformation."[4]

Pragmatists—and this, to their critics, may be the most irritating thing about them—love these objections. For as Dewey (borrowing a figure from William James) wrote of Chesterton's remark, they spill "the personal milk in the [philosopher's] cocoanut."[5] They confirm what the pragmatist has always claimed, which is that what people believe to be true is just what they think it is good to believe to be true. The critic who argues from the consequences of accepting the pragmatist account of the way we think—the critic who warns that dumping those other accounts over a cliff will lead to despair, war, illiberalism, or political correctness—has (in the pragmatist's view) already conceded the key point, which is that every account of the way people think is, at bottom, a support for those human goods the person making the account believes to be important. The whole force of a philosophical account of anything, pragmatists insist, lies in the advertised consequences of accepting it. When we say "That's the way the world is" to a child, we are not making a neutral report. We are saying that understanding the world in that way will put the child into a better relation with it, will enable him or her to cope with it more satisfactorily—even if this means recognizing how unsatisfactory, from a child's point of view (or anyone's), the world can be.

What is pragmatism's account of the way people think, and how did it arise? The term was introduced to the world by William James in a lecture called "Philosophical Conceptions and Practical Results," which he delivered on a visit to the University of California at Berkeley in 1898. In it James presented what he called "the principle of Peirce, the principle of pragmatism," which he defined as follows: "To attain perfect clearness in our thoughts of an object . . . we need only consider what effects of a conceivably practical kind the object may involve—what sensations we are to expect from it, and what reactions we must prepare. Our conception of these effects, then, is for us the whole of our conception of the object, so far as that conception has positive significance at all." James went on to suggest that this principle might be expressed "more broadly," which he proceeded to do: "The ultimate test for us of what a truth means is indeed the conduct it dictates or inspires. . . . The effective meaning of any philosophic proposition can always be brought down to some particular consequence, in our future practical experience, whether active or passive; the point lying rather in the fact that the experience must be particular, than in the fact that it must be active."[6]

What James was doing was stretching a principle of scientific inquiry to cover thinking generally. The principle of scientific inquiry is the "principle of Peirce." It states that if we want our conception of an object to be meaningful—or, as Peirce put it, "clear"—then we should limit that conception to the real-world behavior the object will exhibit under all possible conditions. To use one of Peirce's examples: what we mean when we call a substance "hard" is that it will scratch glass, resist bending, and so on; and those practical effects are all that the concept of "hardness" consists in. "Hardness" is not an abstract property or essence; it is just the sum total of what all hard things do.

James's idea was to extend this way of understanding scientific concepts to all of our beliefs. What makes any belief true? he asked. It is not, he thought, its rational self-sufficiency, its ability to stand up to logical scrutiny. It is that we find that holding the belief leads us into more useful relations with the world. James thought that philosophers had wasted huge amounts of time attempting to derive truths from general first principles, trying to prove or disprove rationally the tenets of various philosophical systems, when all they needed to do was ask what practical effects our choosing one philosophical view rather than another might have. "What is its *cash-value* in terms of practical experience?" James thought the philosopher ought to ask of any idea, "and what special difference would come into the world according as it were true or false?"[7] Or as he put it more famously, nine years later, in *Pragmatism:* "The true is the name for whatever proves itself to be good in the way of belief, and good, too, for definite and assignable reasons."[8]

Words like "practical" and "cash-value" may make James seem an advocate of materialism and science. But one of his chief purposes in introducing pragmatism into philosophy was to open a window, in what he regarded as an excessively materialistic and scientific age, for faith in God. We needn't ask, he thought, whether the existence of God can be proved; we need only ask what difference believing or disbelieving in God will make in our lives. If we wait for absolute proof that there is or is not a God, we will wait forever. We have to choose whether to believe on other criteria—that is, on pragmatic criteria. For this is, James thought, how we make all our choices. We can never hope for *absolute* proof of anything. All our decisions are bets on what the universe is today, and what it will do tomorrow.

In crediting "the principle of pragmatism" to Peirce, James was, characteristically, doing a favor for a friend. But he was also helping to establish a genealogy for pragmatism that may contain more legend than history. The attribution was a favor because in 1898 Charles Sanders Peirce was an almost wholly forgotten figure. James had known him well in the 1860s, when both were students at the Lawrence Scientific School at Harvard. Peirce was the son of a distinguished Harvard professor, the mathematician Benjamin Peirce, and he had already, when James met him, acquired a reputation as a prodigy of mathematics, science, and logic. But his career unfolded disastrously. He lost his academic appointment, at Johns Hopkins University, because of a scandal involving his remarriage. (Peirce never knew the reason for his dismissal; it was because the trustees had learned that he had begun living with the woman who would become his second wife after he had separated from but before he had legally divorced the woman who had been his first wife.) He lost his other job, working for the U.S. Coastal Survey, a government scientific agency, soon afterward. In 1898, having spent part of the decade in New York City, sleeping on the streets and cadging food from the Century Club (until he was evicted) while on the lam from creditors and assault charges, Peirce was living in poverty and neglect in Pennsylvania, on an enormous, dilapidated estate called Arisbe, which he had purchased in an ill-considered moment of financial optimism.

James, by contrast, was a Harvard professor and an international academic celebrity. The publication in 1890 of his *Principles of Psychology,* a book twelve years in the making, had secured his reputation. So an announcement by him of a new approach to philosophy was assured of attention, as was his attribution of the "principle of pragmatism" to Peirce. In his lecture James referred to an article Peirce had published twenty years before in *The Popular Science Monthly* (a more scholarly journal than the name suggests), entitled "How to Make Our Ideas Clear." The word "pragmatism" does not appear in that article (nor anywhere else before 1898); but James also mentioned that Peirce had formulated his principle and begun calling it "pragmatism" even earlier: "I first heard him enunciate it," he said, "at Cambridge in the early '70s."[9]

Within a few years of James's lecture, pragmatism became a full-fledged intellectual movement, attracting adherents and detractors around the world; and Peirce, still isolated on his Pennsylvania estate, wrote a number of papers—some published, most unfinished—in the hope, largely unmet, of being recognized as a participant in the debate. In some of the unpublished papers, composed between 1905 and 1908, Peirce amplified James's remark about the origins of the pragmatism. "It was in the earliest seventies," he wrote in one of them, "that a knot of us young men in Old Cambridge, calling ourselves half-ironically, half-defiantly, 'The Metaphysical Club' . . . used to meet, sometimes in my study, sometimes in that of William James."[10] And he listed the names of the other participants in this discussion group: Oliver Wendell Holmes, Joseph Warner, Nicholas St. John Green, Chauncey Wright, John Fiske, and Francis Ellingwood Abbot. (Holmes, Warner, and Green were lawyers; Wright, Fiske, and Abbot, like Peirce and James, were scientists and philosophers.) It was within this circle, Peirce suggested, that pragmatism developed.

This has proved an influential account, though corroboration is thin. One item that supports it is a letter written by Henry James (then in Cambridge) in January 1872, in which he reports that "my brother has just helped to found a metaphysical club, in Cambridge, (consisting of Chauncey Wright, C. Peirce etc.)."[11] A second is a letter to Henry (now in Paris) from William, dated the following November, in which he mentions that Peirce "read us an admirable introductory chapter to his book on logic the other day."[12] That book was one of many abandoned Peircean projects, but the drafts survive,[13] and they suggest that the chapter James was referring to was very likely a version of the argument Peirce did publish six years later in *The Popular Science Monthly*. Peirce himself remembered that "lest the club should be dissolved without leaving any material *souvenir* behind, I drew up a little paper expressing some of the opinions that I had been urging all along under the name of pragmatism"[14]—a paper that served as the basis, he recalled, for what he later published in *The Popular Science Monthly*.

The conclusion it has seemed natural to draw from this sketchy record is that pragmatism emerged out of discussions among James, Peirce, Holmes, and the others over the course of 1872 and achieved its first articulation in Peirce's paper that November. But the conclusion is misleading, and for several reasons. One is that Peirce's recollections, colored by time, distance, and an understandable inclination to cast his own contribution in a central role, were almost certainly imperfect. None of the several accounts of the Metaphysical Club in his own manuscripts matches, in all its details, the others: the years, the nature of the proceedings, and even the names of members vary. If the group was indeed, as the Jameses' letters suggest, convened in 1872, it could not have been a very regular affair. It is unlikely that Abbot attended at all, since he spent the entire year in Ohio. Peirce himself was in Washington most of the time, working at the Coastal Survey office. Holmes, by all accounts, including his own later recollection, was immersed in his first major scholarly project, a revision of Kent's *Commentaries on American Law*, which was published in 1873, and gave little time to anything else. Chauncey Wright went to Europe in July and did not return until November.

To make matters hazier still, there were many Metaphysical Clubs, since "metaphysical club" was simply a generic name in the nineteenth century for a philosophical discussion group. James loved philosophical discussion groups. He was forever forming and re-forming them, as well as engaging in long-running one-on-one dialogues with friends; nearly all the people named in Peirce's

accounts were, at one time or another, his philosophical inter-
locutors. So it is hard to know just how self-conscious and cohe-
sive a group the Metaphysical Club Peirce described really was for
anyone but, in retrospect, Peirce himself.

The important point, though, is not the reliability of Peirce's recollection. The important point is that James and Holmes (and, for
that matter, Chauncey Wright and Nicholas St. John Green, the
other figures whose work is associated with pragmatism) had already formulated what is distinctively pragmatic in their views before 1872. Peirce may have given James the name, but he could not
have given him the idea.

In 1872 James was emerging from a nervous collapse that had
lasted almost three years. After a wildly peripatetic education in
Europe and America, he had finally graduated from the Harvard
Medical School (the only course of study he ever completed) in
1869, at the age of twenty-seven, and immediately fallen into a
state of lassitude, depression, and chronic ill health. Whatever the
causes of his various symptoms, James seems to have explained
them to himself in intellectual terms. He treated his depression as
a kind of philosophical problem that might be relieved by coming up with a philosophical solution; and one day in 1870, in his
diary, he announced a breakthrough. "I finished the first part of
Renouvier's second 'Essais,'" he wrote (Charles Renouvier was a
nineteenth-century French philosopher),

> and see no reason why his definition of Free Will—'the sustaining
> of a thought *because I choose to* when I might have other thoughts'—
> need be the definition of an illusion. At any rate, I will assume for
> the present—until next year—that it is no illusion. My first act of
> free will shall be to believe in free will. . . . Not in maxims, not in
> *Anschauungen* [contemplations], but in accumulated *acts* of thought
> lies salvation. . . . Hitherto, when I have felt like taking a free ini-
> tiative, like daring to act originally, without carefully waiting for

> contemplation of the external world to determine all for me, sui-
> cide seemed the most manly form to put my daring into: now, I
> will go a step further with my will, not only act with it, but believe
> as well; believe in my individual reality and creative power.[15]

The breakthrough did not prove definitive; James's complaints
persisted. But this passage, with its admonition to act on beliefs
without waiting for philosophical confirmation of their validity, is
the germ of the doctrine James would announce, twenty-six years
later, in "The Will to Believe." And it is the essence of his pragmatism.

Holmes underwent his own crisis in a very different setting. In
1861, at the end of his senior year at Harvard, he enlisted in the
Union Army (something James seems scarcely to have contem-
plated doing), and he served for three years, and in some of the
bloodiest fighting of the Civil War. Although he later gave
speeches in which he glorified the soldier's blind allegiance to
duty, Holmes hated war itself. He was seriously wounded three
times; the third wound was in the foot, which he hoped would
have to be amputated so he could be discharged before his commission was up. That hope was disappointed, but Holmes did
emerge from the war purged of illusions. He thought he had paid
a high price for the privilege of losing them, and he was careful
never to acquire any again.

After his return Holmes attended Harvard Law School and then
went into practice with a Boston firm. He also developed an intimate friendship with William James. Their letters are unusually
warm and spirited, but their personal relations eventually became
strained, and Holmes was always unsympathetic to James's philosophical writings. They seemed to promote, in their spiritual
hopefulness, just the sort of sentimental idealism he had rejected:
James's "wishes led him to turn down the lights so as to give miracle a chance,"[16] he complained to a friend after James's death in
1910. Holmes had no high regard for Peirce either; he thought his
genius "overrated."[17] But although Holmes would never have

referred to himself as a pragmatist, his twentieth-century disciples have not been wrong to understand his jurisprudence as a form of pragmatism.

In 1870, when he was twenty-nine, Holmes became coeditor of the *American Law Review,* and the first paragraph of the first article he published there gives, in a very early nutshell, the pragmatist premise of his jurisprudence. "It is the merit of the common law," he wrote,

> that it decides the case first and determines the principle afterwards. Looking at the forms of logic it might be inferred that when you have a minor premise and a conclusion, there must be a major, which you are also prepared then and there to assert. But in fact lawyers, like other men, frequently see well enough how they ought to decide on a given state of facts without being very clear as to the *ratio decidendi* [the ground of the decision]. Lord Mansfield's often-quoted advice to the business man who was suddenly appointed judge, that he should state his conclusions and not give his reasons, as his judgment would probably be right and the reasons wrong, is not without application to more educated courts.[18]

Holmes's target in these sentences was legal formalism, the theory that the law has an internal logical consistency and consists of general doctrines—such as "a person shall not use his property in a way that injures the property of another"—which guide the outcomes of particular cases. Holmes devoted his career as a judge and a jurisprudential thinker to demolishing this view of the law—pointing out, for example, that people use their property legally to injure the property of others all the time, as when they set up a shop with the intention of putting the shop owner down the street out of business.

Holmes's insight into the insufficiency of general principles left him with an obvious question, which is, if general principles don't decide cases, what does? His answer was unveiled in the opening paragraph of *The Common Law* (1881), in what is possibly the most famous sentence in American legal thought: "The life of the law has not been logic; it has been experience."[19] Holmes did not mean that there is no logic in the law. He meant that what guides the direction of the law, from case to case over time, is not immutable reason but changing experience. This assertion has sometimes been misinterpreted to mean that what ultimately determines a judge's decision is his personal background and taste— what he ate for breakfast. But that is not what Holmes meant by experience. He was not referring to the life history of the individual lawmaker or judge; he was referring to the life history of society. Experience, for him, was the name for everything that arises out of the interaction of the human organism with its environment: beliefs, values, intuitions, customs, prejudices—what he called "the felt necessities of the time."[20] Our word for it is "culture."

For when we think judicially—when we try to determine what would be the just outcome in a legal dispute—Holmes believed that we think the same way we do when we have to make a practical decision of any sort. We don't do whatever feels pleasant or convenient to us at the moment (since experience teaches that this is rarely a wise basis for making a decision). But we don't reason logically from abstract principles either. Yet our decision, when we are happy with it, never feels subjective or irrational: how could we be pleased if we knew it to be arbitrary? It just feels like the decision we *had* to reach, and this is because its rightness is a function of its "fit" with the whole inchoate set of cultural assumptions of our world, the assumptions that give the moral weight—much greater moral weight than logic or taste could ever give—to every judgment we make. This is why, so often, we know we're right before we know why we're right. We decide, then we deduce.

Philosophies and theories and formal methodologies are part of our culture, but they are, in Holmes's view, the dinner jacket and bow tie we instinctively take off when it is time to change the tires. "All the pleasure of life is in general ideas," he wrote to a

correspondent in 1899. "But all the use of life is in specific solutions—which cannot be reached through generalities any more
than a picture can be painted by knowing some rules of method.
They are reached by insight, tact and specific knowledge."[21] Or as
he put it many years later, with more kindness to speculative
thought, in a letter to the philosopher Morris Cohen: "Philosophy as a fellow once said to me is only thinking. Thinking is an instrument of adjustment to the conditions of life—but it becomes
an end in itself."[22]

The one self-proclaimed pragmatist whose writings Holmes admired (and Holmes was not a man ordinarily given to admiration
for the views of other people) was John Dewey. In the final chapter of *Experience and Nature* (1925), the work of the widest philosophical scope among his many books, Dewey praised Holmes as
"one of our greatest American philosophers"[23] and went on to
quote a long passage from Holmes's essay "Natural Law" (1918).
Holmes read the book several times with growing pleasure (what
was there, after all, not to like?), and his reaction sums up the reaction many of his contemporaries had both to Dewey's wisdom
and to Dewey's style: "It seemed to me . . . to have a feeling of intimacy with the inside of the cosmos that I found unequaled. So
methought God would have spoken had He been inarticulate but
keenly desirous to tell you how it was."[24]

Dewey's influence in his own long lifetime—he was born in
1859, the year of *On the Origin of Species,* and died in 1952, the year
of the hydrogen bomb—touched many fields. He was a psychologist, a philosopher, a political activist, a public intellectual, and a
social reformer. But his most lasting contribution was in education, and although pragmatism, once he took it up, underwrote
everything Dewey did, it is his work as an educator that shows its
consequences most dramatically.

Dewey began his career as an absolute idealist. He was trained at
Hopkins, when Peirce was on the faculty, by George Sylvester

Morris, a Hegelian, and he wrote his first books under the influence of Hegel. His work began turning in a pragmatist direction after he read James's *Principles of Psychology* in 1890. In 1894 he accepted a position as chair of the philosophy department at the newly founded University of Chicago. In 1896 he established the Laboratory School there, an experiment in progressive education run by the Department of Pedagogy (of which he was also the chair), and began to write the works on education for which he quickly became famous around the world: *The School and Society* (1899), *The Child and the Curriculum* (1902), *How We Think* (1910), *Democracy and Education* (1916). The first of these, *The School and Society,* is one of the most influential educational treatises ever written. Its argument for the importance of the practical and of "learning by doing" in education was adopted (and possibly partly formulated) by Dewey's close friend Jane Addams as the blueprint for the educational programs at Hull House, her pioneering social welfare institution in Chicago, at the turn of the century. And the book itself has never gone out of print.

Dewey regarded *Democracy and Education,* when it appeared, as the summa of his thought, and it is easy to see why, for the book is an integration of his theory of politics, his theory of knowledge, and his theory of education. The theory of politics is democratic; the theory of knowledge is holistic; the theory of education is progressive. Dewey believed that philosophers had invented an invidious distinction between knowing and doing, a distinction that had had the intellectually pernicious effect of producing a series of pseudoproblems about the relations between the mind and reality, and the socially pernicious effect of elevating a leisure class of speculative thinkers above the world's workers and doers. There was, Dewey thought, no such distinction. Knowing and doing are indivisible aspects of the same process, which is the business of adaptation. We learn, in the progressivist phrase, by doing: we take a piece of acquired knowledge into a concrete situation, and the results we get constitute a new piece of knowledge, which we carry over into our next encounter with our environment. When we hypostatize knowledge by embalming it in a textbook, we cut thought off from experience, and we damage our relations with the world. Knowledge is not a mental copy of a reality external to us, Dewey said; "it is an instrument or organ of successful action."[25]

What is democratic about Dewey's theory is that it conceives of learning as a collaborative activity. Dewey thought of the school as a "miniature community,"[26] a kind of training camp for life in a democracy. "The only way to prepare for social life," as he put it, "is to engage in social life";[27] and this emphasis on the associated nature of human existence is crucial to most of what he wrote about politics and social reform. He believed that individual fulfillment could be achieved only through participation in the collective life; for outside of the collectivity no such thing as an individual is possible. "The non-social individual," he wrote in one of his earliest essays, "is an abstraction arrived at by imagining what man would be if all his human qualities were taken away."[28]

The emphasis on the community as the ground for our conduct and beliefs echoes Holmes's conception of "experience" (a term Dewey used, in *Experience and Nature,* in the same sense Holmes had: as a name for culture). And it echoes Peirce as well, for Peirce regarded truth as a matter of community consensus rather than individual belief (one of the points on which he was at odds with James). But the thinker Dewey credited with introducing this way of thinking into his own work was George Herbert Mead, whom he met at the University of Michigan in the 1880s and with whom he continued to work after moving to Chicago, where Mead joined him. "From the nineties on," Dewey said in 1939, eight years after Mead's death, "the influence of Mead ranked with that of James."[29]

Mead was a physiologist and psychologist, and his method was to apply a Darwinian model to those areas of inquiry. He explained physiological development in adaptive terms, as something that happens as a result of the interaction of the human being with its environment. And he explained consciousness, including the sense of individual identity, in the same manner, as something that happens as a result of the interaction of the human being with other human beings. "The process out of which the self arises is a social process which implies [the] interaction of individuals in the group, implies the pre-existence of the group,"[30] he wrote. Even our innermost thoughts, in Mead's view, are social. For we think, as we act, relationally: we talk to ourselves. "Inner consciousness," as he put it, "is socially organized by the importation of the social organization of the outer world."[31] The field he developed was social psychology, and its influence on twentieth-century thought extends well beyond pragmatism. *Dewey pollutes his pragmatism with an idealist illusion.*

It is common today to speak of a revival of pragmatism, a phenomenon usually dated from the publication of Richard Rorty's *Philosophy and the Mirror of Nature* in 1979. The implication is that after the generation of Peirce, James, Holmes, Dewey, Addams, and Mead, pragmatism went into eclipse, and that only in the last fifteen years has it reemerged as a distinctively American style of thought with wide appeal. This notion is not entirely false. Pragmatism after Dewey did go into relative eclipse, and twentieth-century intellectuals have been more likely to identify themselves with other schools of thought—Marxism, psychoanalysis, existentialism, structuralism—than to think of themselves as pragmatists.

But the notion that pragmatism was eclipsed by other schools of thought in the twentieth century is also a little misleading, and the reason is that it is part of the nature of pragmatism to decline the honor of becoming a "school of thought." Pragmatists have always been wary of the danger that pragmatism will turn into a discipline, that it will become just another one of the things professional thinkers "do." James presented pragmatism, after all, not as a philosophy but as a way of doing philosophy, and Peirce, in the beginning (for his pragmatism became in later years quite technical), described it as a method for making ideas clear and not as a place to look for ideas themselves. Pragmatism, in the most basic sense, is about how we think, not what we think.

If we locate pragmatism within the broader picture of intellectual life around 1900, we can see it as a kind of knot in the tapestry, a pulling together of threads that reach into many other areas of thought, with many other consequences—threads that, running back into the nineteenth century, include the emergence of theories of cultural pluralism and political progressivism; the fascination with pure science and the logic of scientific inquiry; the development of probability theory as a means for coping with randomness and uncertainty; the spread of historicist approaches to the study of culture; the rapid assimilation of the Darwinian theory of evolution; and the Emersonian suspicion of institutional authority. None of these developments is "pragmatist," but pragmatism was one of the places where they came into focus.

The threads that lead out of the pragmatist knot and into twentieth-century thought are as various as the threads that lead into it. Pragmatism served as a kind of philosophical tonic for many twentieth-century thinkers whom it would seem beside the point to call pragmatists. One of the most striking effects of the contemporary pragmatist revival is that a whole array of American (and non-American) writers has suddenly been placed in a new shared context. Cornel West, in *The American Evasion of Philosophy* (1989), used pragmatism to show what people like James, W. E. B. Du Bois, Reinhold Niebuhr, and Lionel Trilling have in common, just as Rorty, in *Philosophy and the Mirror of Nature* and *Consequences of Pragmatism* (1982), used pragmatism to show what people like Dewey, Martin Heidegger, Ludwig Wittgenstein, and Jacques Derrida have in common, and Richard Poirier, in *Poetry and Pragmatism* (1992), used it to show what Emerson, Robert Frost, and Gertrude Stein have in common. A complete list of American writers who acknowledged the stimulus of pragmatism would be varied and long, and would include, besides those just named, Wallace Stevens, Learned Hand, Benjamin Cardozo,

Kenneth Burke, Sidney Hook, C. Wright Mills, Arthur Schlesinger, Jr., Tom Hayden, and Harold Bloom.

Of the various strands emerging from the pragmatism of James and Dewey, four in particular lead into the cluster of concerns that have helped to animate the contemporary resurgence of interest in pragmatism. One is the development of theories of cultural pluralism in response to the xenophobia induced by the turn-of-the-century waves of immigration and exacerbated by America's entry into the First World War. Three figures whose writing was seminal to this development were students of James and Dewey. Horace Kallen, whose essay "Democracy *versus* the Melting Pot" (1915) is often cited as the founding document of cultural pluralism, regarded himself as an heir of James, with whom he had studied at Harvard, and as a disciple of Dewey (though Dewey himself had reservations about Kallen's enthusiasm for diversity). Alain Locke, who delivered his groundbreaking lectures on "Race Contacts and Interracial Relations" at Howard University in 1915 and 1916 (and later summarized their argument in the essay "The Concept of Race as Applied to Culture" [1924]), had also been a student of James at Harvard. And Randolph Bourne, whose essay "Trans-National America" appeared in 1916, had been a student of Dewey at Columbia—though he later broke with his teacher over American involvement in the war.

As the term suggests, cultural pluralism owes most, in the pragmatist tradition, to James's *A Pluralistic Universe* (1909). One of the consequences of the pragmatic way of thinking, for James, was that the universe is better thought of as a "multi-verse," something that is never completed, never synthesized into a stable whole. Things are strung together, James argued, but their differences are never—as absolutists, or monists, believe—completely transcended. "Monism thinks that the all-form or collective-unit is the only form that is rational," said James. "Pluralism lets things really exist in the each-form or distributively."[32] It is the corollary of a view he had expressed two years earlier in *Pragmatism:* "All 'homes' are in finite experience; finite experience as such is homeless. Nothing outside of the flux secures the issue of it."[33]

James drew no particular political conclusions from his pluralism (though it undoubtedly had some connection with his impassioned antiimperialism). But Kallen, Locke, and Bourne saw that if the universe is multiple and unfinished, then society—particularly an ethnically heterogeneous society like the United States in 1915—might be understood as multiple, too. Of the three, Locke's argument involved the subtlest pragmatism: it was that although race has no real basis in biology, and although racial pride is, in itself, socially divisive, the only way to overcome social divisiveness was to foster racial pride—to encourage the different ethnic groups in American society to take satisfaction in their different cultural practices. This is, Locke said, "only apparently paradoxical. It is not paradoxical when it is worked out in practice, because . . . the very stimulation to collective activity which race pride or racial self-respect may give will issue into the qualification test and the aim to meet that qualification test, which, of course, must be in terms of the common standard."[34] The desire to be recognized as like everyone else—to meet the common standard—flows from the desire to be recognized as different from everyone else. You want to prove that your group is as good as every other group. Cultural pluralism is the recipe for civil cohesion; and the pragmatic beauty of the formulation is that neither human sameness nor human difference is made to seem essential.

A second consequence of turn-of-the-century pragmatism was the revolution in American law and legal thinking inspired by the writings, and to some extent the personality, of Holmes. Holmes in old age—he was sixty-one when he was appointed to the Supreme Court, in 1902, and served until he was ninety—became a hero to progressive political writers. Holmes was himself a progressive only in a neutral sense. He didn't believe that social and economic reform could do more than shift a few burdens incrementally in one direction or another; he considered economic relations to be more or less fixed. But he saw no constitutional barrier to legislative attempts to move those burdens, by imposing taxes, passing health and safety regulations, or protecting unions; and this endeared him to progressives who *did* believe in the reformative powers of reform.

Holmes's belief in society's right to try out new forms of self-regulation followed from his belief, shared by all pragmatists, in the virtues of experimentation. If we learn by doing, we have to keep doing new things, since that is how knowledge progresses—or, at least, adapts. And this was the rationale for Holmes's most celebrated opinion as a judge, his dissent in *Abrams v. United States* (1919), in which he rejected state efforts to punish political opinion as a foreclosing of social possibilities. Even the Constitution, he said, "is an experiment, as all life is an experiment. Every year if not every day we have to wager our salvation upon some prophecy based upon imperfect knowledge. While that experiment is part of our system I think that we should be eternally vigilant against attempts to check the expression of opinions that we loathe and believe to be fraught with death."[35]

Holmes's vibrant dissents in cases involving the regulation of business and the suppression of opinion bore fruit after his death in the judicial acceptance of New Deal economic policies and in the establishment of the constitutional law of free speech. The argument of his jurisprudential writings—that law is not merely a system of abstract doctrines but a response to changing conditions—helped give rise to a series of fresh approaches to the law. These include the legal pragmatism of Roscoe Pound and Benjamin Cardozo, which emphasized the social aspect of legal reasoning and the experimental nature of judicial decision making; the legal realism of Karl Llewellyn and Jerome Frank, which regarded law sociologically and as an instrument of reform; Critical Legal Studies, which considers law as both a form of rhetoric and a form of politics; and the "law and economics" jurisprudence of

Richard Posner, which proposes cost-benefit analysis as a basis for judicial decision making. All these ways of thinking about the law can be said to have grown from seeds planted in Holmes's 1897 essay "The Path of the Law."

A third strand that has recently reemerged from early pragmatist thought involves the educational philosophy developed around the turn of the century by John Dewey. That philosophy—the theory that children "learn by doing"—established itself long ago in the field of early childhood education, but until the 1980s its relevance to undergraduate education seemed remote. Then, in an essay called "Toward Pragmatic Liberal Education" in 1995,[36] the historian Bruce A. Kimball argued that trends in undergraduate education since the 1960s reflect a move toward a pragmatic educational philosophy. For a century, American higher education was dominated by the model of knowledge that obtains in research universities, where learning is split up among separate scholarly disciplines, or departments; where the emphasis is on "knowledge for its own sake"; where a distinction between "facts" and "values" is rigorously observed; and where education is divorced from practical affairs. Kimball maintained that in smaller liberal arts colleges across the country, educators have been quietly abandoning the research model, and have been adopting curricula in which learning is oriented toward values, toward citizenship, toward the recognition of cultural diversity, and toward the Deweyan virtue of "doing." This new model stresses "general education"— that is, education designed for all students, rather than for future specialists in an academic field of inquiry—and "liberal education"—the education of temperament and sensibility. Whether the educators responsible for this shift in the paradigm of the college experience ever thought of themselves as pragmatists, it is clear that the developments Kimball traced are consistent with the pragmatic, particularly the Deweyan, tradition, and that if this

movement ever becomes coherent and self-conscious enough to
acquire a philosophical label, "pragmatist" is an obvious choice.

Not at all. It's flabbiness rather than flexibility
"Many things go" is pluralism, "anything goes" is another
form of absolutism

The final strand connecting turn-of-the-century pragmatism with
its late-twentieth-century avatar may seem the most obvious, but
it is in fact the oddest. This is the strand that runs through philosophy itself. James and Dewey regarded themselves as philosophers;
but it is not hard to see how their dismissal of the traditional problems of philosophy made them seem, to many professional
philosophers, enemies of the discipline. Pragmatism is antiformal-
ist: it represents a principle of endless assault on every tendency to
erect contingent knowledge into a formal system. To the extent
that philosophy is an effort to erect what we know about how we
know into a formal system, pragmatism cannot help acting the
role of termite—undermining foundations, collapsing distinctions, deflating abstractions, suggesting that the real work of the
world is being done somewhere other than in philosophy departments.

In spite of this, not only did James and Dewey think of themselves as philosophers but they were, in their day, builders of philosophy departments—James at Harvard and Dewey at Chicago
and then Columbia. So there has been, ever since James's lecture
"Philosophical Conceptions and Practical Results" in 1898, a tradition of professional pragmatist philosophy, begun by students
and colleagues of James and Dewey, such as James Tufts, C. I.
Lewis, Ralph Barton Perry, Charles W. Morris, and Sidney Hook,
and running into the present, in the work of philosophers such as
John J. McDermott, Sandra B. Rosenthal, and Karl-Otto Apel.

Yet this line of philosophical pragmatists is not the line that
connects James with Rorty and the contemporary pragmatist revival. That line runs, paradoxically, through the philosophical tradition that is usually regarded as the antagonist of pragmatism, and
as the tradition that won the battle for the control of modern

philosophy departments: analytic philosophy. "Analytic philosophy" is an overbroad term that embraces a number of philosophical movements since the time of Bertrand Russell, including
logical atomism, logical positivism, and the philosophy of language. The differences among these movements are, of course,
important to their practitioners; but from the point of view of
pragmatism, the notion they all share is that there is a distinctively
philosophical method of analysis that can be used to get to the
bottom of problems about mind, knowledge, meaning, truth, and
so on.

This is the tradition in which Rorty (though he was trained, by
his teachers at the University of Chicago, and at Yale, where he attended graduate school, primarily in the history of philosophy)
found himself working when he began teaching philosophy in the
1950s. And although *Philosophy and the Mirror of Nature* can seem,
from one point of view, an all-out attack on analytic philosophy, it
was actually intended as the culmination of the whole tradition.
"The aim of the book," Rorty explained, "is to undermine the
reader's confidence in 'the mind' as something about which one
should have a 'philosophical' view, in 'knowledge' as something
about which there ought to be a 'theory' and which has 'foundations,' and in 'philosophy' as it has been conceived since Kant."
But, he continued, this argument was "parasitic upon the constructive efforts of the very analytic philosophers whose frame of
reference I am trying to put into question. . . . I hope to convince
the reader that the dialectic within analytic philosophy . . . needs
to be carried a few steps further. These additional steps will, I
think, put us into a position to criticize the very notion of 'analytic philosophy,' and indeed of 'philosophy' itself."[37]

Rorty thus proceeded to construct a kind of staircase out of analytic philosophy, made up of works that questioned a succession
of fundamental tenets of the analytic approach—principal among
them Willard Van Orman Quine's "Two Dogmas of Empiricism"
(1951), Wilfrid Sellars's attack on the "Myth of the Given" in *Sci-*

ence, Perception and Reality (1963), Donald Davidson's "On the Very Notion of a Conceptual Scheme" (1974), and Hilary Putnam's rejection of "metaphysical realism" in *Realism and Reason* (1977). (This tactic of manufacturing the explosive out of the very stuff to be demolished was adopted soon after by the literary critics Steven Knapp and Walter Benn Michaels, who, in an essay called "Against Theory" [1982], argued on pragmatist grounds that a genuine theory of literary interpretation is impossible, and efforts to design one ought therefore to be abandoned. Readers of poems, argued Knapp and Michaels, just don't think the way theorists of inter pretation think they think.)

If Rorty had stopped there, it is unlikely that a pragmatist revival would have followed, for *Philosophy and the Mirror of Nature* is, technically, just a piece of professional philosophy. And merely showing the way out of the reigning philosophical paradigm left him with no obvious paradigm within which to work next. (He did toy briefly, at the end of the book, with the idea that hermeneutics might become the new discipline.) Accepting the pragmatist analysis and seeing how it leads to different ways of conceiving of the traditional problems of analytic philosophy was a path chosen by one philosopher, Hilary Putnam, who has developed a philosophy he has called "pragmatic realism." But it was not the path chosen by Rorty.

The alternative to operating within a paradigm is to rely on your genius; and although Rorty has not ceased to repeat his analytic argument about the poverty of professional philosophy, since professional philosophers have not ceased to criticize it, he turned, after the publication of *Philosophy and the Mirror of Nature,* to an unexpectedly imaginative engagement with literature, critical theory, political thought, and social commentary. He transformed himself, in short, from a philosopher into an intellectual. In this his model has clearly been Dewey (though Rorty has been involved in a running debate with other Deweyites, among them the political philosopher Richard J. Bernstein, over the accuracy of his understanding of Dewey). But Rorty is a far more exciting writer than Dewey, and his work has served for many people as a model for the kind of wide-ranging engagement with art, ideas, and public affairs that pragmatism might make possible.

As James discovered during his mental crisis of 1870, pragmatism can encourage us to trust, without ever assuming them to be infallible, our own judgments—to have faith that if we do what is right, the metaphysics will take care of themselves. What pragmatism cannot do, though, is explain where our judgments come from. The easy answer to that question today is to say that our decisions are determined by the cultural "rules" of the social group we happen to belong to. No doubt the cultural rules explain a great deal of what people do, but different individuals in the same group make different judgments—if they didn't, there would be nothing that needed explaining—and, as Holmes concluded, we can't say in any determinate way how we make our choices. They seem to arise, in the end, out of the mysteries of personality, which are a scandal to theory. All we can say is that we seem to have, as naturally associated beings, a powerful social incentive to rationalize and justify the choices we make.

It is sometimes complained that pragmatism is a bootstrap theory—that it cannot tell us where we should want to go or how we can get there. The answer to this is that theory can never tell us where to go; only we can tell us where to go. Theories are just one of the ways we make sense of our needs. We wake up one morning and find ourselves in a new place, and then we build a ladder to explain how we got there. The pragmatist is the person who asks whether this is a good place to be. The nonpragmatist is the person who admires the ladder.

A Note on the Selections

This volume tries to provide, in a reasonable and affordable number of pages, the essentials of pragmatist thought. Major statements are reprinted, for the most part, unabridged; the entries introduced by the word "from" are excerpted from longer essays or books. Annotations have been made with the general reader in mind, and with a view to pointing him or her to connections among the selections and toward further reading. All the original footnotes have been retained in the unabridged entries; a few footnotes in the excerpted entries have been silently dropped. Unless otherwise noted, all ellipses that are not within quotation marks and all material inside square brackets that are not within parentheses are the editor's.

There are more writers associated with pragmatism, in both its early and contemporary periods, than could be represented here. The selection in the first section has been guided by what a reader interested in pragmatism now would find it most useful to know—these are the texts most commonly referred to today—and in the second by a sense of the writers who, in their various fields, have had the greatest influence. Still, readers should keep in mind that the meaning and application of pragmatism are always being debated. People who are drawn to pragmatism tend, after all, to be the kind of people who are reluctant to regard someone else's word on a subject as final. The bibliography lists some of the places in which these debates can be found. A pragmatic attitude towards the perversion of Pragmatism is to reject the Authorities' conclusion that multi-cultural equality is pluralism It is the pragmatic version of truth that philosophies don't inevitably lead to perversion (because leading to inaction) — a useful truth would be that the perverters are enemy agents

The First Generation

3

Charles Sanders Peirce

Peirce was born in Cambridge, Massachusetts, in 1839. He graduated from Harvard College and in 1863 received a degree in chemistry from the Lawrence Scientific School, where he met William James. In 1861 he began working for the United States Coastal Survey, a government scientific agency. From 1879 to 1884 he was Lecturer in Logic at Johns Hopkins University, where John Dewey was a graduate student. His contract with Hopkins was not renewed because of a scandal involving his divorce and remarriage, and in 1891 he was forced to resign from the Coastal Survey. After the failure of a number of business ventures, he retired to Arisbe, his home in Milford, Pennsylvania, where he spent his last years in poverty and illness, supported in part by the charity of James and producing an enormous quantity of unfinished and unpublished manuscripts. He died of cancer in 1914.

from Some Consequences
of Four Incapacities

(1868)

DESCARTES IS THE FATHER of modern philosophy, and the spirit of Cartesianism—that which principally distinguishes it from the scholasticism which it displaced—may be compendiously stated as follows:

1. It teaches that philosophy must begin with universal doubt; whereas scholasticism had never questioned fundamentals.

2. It teaches that the ultimate test of certainty is to be found in the individual consciousness; whereas scholasticism had rested on the testimony of sages and of the Catholic Church.

3. The multiform argumentation of the middle ages is replaced by a single thread of inference depending often upon inconspicuous premises.

4. Scholasticism had its mysteries of faith, but undertook to explain all created things. But there are many acts which Cartesianism not only does not explain, but renders absolutely inexplicable, unless to say that "God makes them so" is to be regarded as an explanation.

In some, or all of these respects, most modern philosophers have been, in effect, Cartesians. Now without wishing to return to scholasticism, it seems to me that modern science and modern logic require us to stand upon a very different platform from this.

1. We cannot begin with complete doubt. We must begin with all the prejudices which we actually have when we enter upon the study of philosophy. These prejudices are not to be dispelled by a maxim, for they are things which it does not occur to us *can* be

questioned. Hence this initial scepticism will be a mere self-deception, and not real doubt; and no one who follows the Cartesian method will ever be satisfied until he has formally recovered all those beliefs which in form he has given up. It is, therefore, as useless a preliminary as going to the North Pole would be in order to get to Constantinople by coming down regularly upon a meridian. A person may, it is true, in the course of his studies, find reason to doubt what he began by believing; but in that case he doubts because he has a positive reason for it, and not on account of the Cartesian maxim. Let us not pretend to doubt in philosophy what we do not doubt in our hearts.

2. The same formalism appears in the Cartesian criterion, which amounts to this: "Whatever I am clearly convinced of, is true." If I were really convinced, I should have done with reasoning, and should require no test of certainty. But thus to make single individuals absolute judges of truth is most pernicious. The result is that metaphysicians will all agree that metaphysics has reached a pitch of certainty far beyond that of the physical sciences;—only they can agree upon nothing else. In sciences in which men come to agreement, when a theory has been broached, it is considered to be on probation until this agreement is reached. After it is reached, the question of certainty becomes an idle one, because there is no one left who doubts it. We individually cannot reasonably hope to attain the ultimate philosophy which we pursue; we can only seek it, therefore, for the *community* of philosophers. Hence, if disciplined and candid minds carefully examine a theory and refuse to accept it, this ought to create doubts in the mind of the author of the theory himself.

3. Philosophy ought to imitate the successful sciences in its methods, so far as to proceed only from tangible premises which can be subjected to careful scrutiny, and to trust rather to the multitude and variety of its arguments than to the conclusiveness of any one. Its reasoning should not form a chain which is no stronger than its weakest link, but a cable whose fibres may be ever

so slender, provided they are sufficiently numerous and intimately connected.

4. Every unidealistic philosophy supposes some absolutely inexplicable, unanalyzable ultimate; in short, something resulting from mediation itself not susceptible of mediation. Now that anything *is* thus inexplicable can only be known by reasoning from signs. But the only justification of an inference from signs is that the conclusion explains the fact. To suppose the fact absolutely inexplicable, is not to explain it, and hence this supposition is never allowable.

The Fixation of Belief

(1877)

I

FEW PERSONS CARE to study logic, because everybody conceives himself to be proficient enough in the art of reasoning already. But I observe that this satisfaction is limited to one's own ratiocination, and does not extend to that of other men.

We come to the full possession of our power of drawing inferences the last of all our faculties, for it is not so much a natural gift as a long and difficult art. The history of its practice would make a grand subject for a book. The mediæval schoolmen, following the Romans, made logic the earliest of a boy's studies after grammar, as being very easy. So it was, as they understood it. Its fundamental principle, according to them, was, that all knowledge rests on either authority or reason; but that whatever is deduced by reason depends ultimately on a premise derived from authority. Accordingly, as soon as a boy was perfect in the syllogistic procedure, his intellectual kit of tools was held to be complete.

To Roger Bacon,[1] that remarkable mind who in the middle of the thirteenth century was almost a scientific man, the schoolmen's conception of reasoning appeared only an obstacle to truth. He saw that experience alone teaches anything—a proposition which to us seems easy to understand, because a distinct conception of experience has been handed down to us from former generations: which to him also seemed perfectly clear, because its difficulties had not yet unfolded themselves. Of all kinds of experience, the best, he thought, was interior illumination, which teaches many things about Nature which the external senses could never discover, such as the transubstantiation of bread.

Four centuries later, the more celebrated Bacon, in the first book of his *Novum Organum,* gave his clear account of experience as something which must be open to verification and reexamination. But, superior as Lord Bacon's conception is to earlier notions, a modern reader who is not in awe of his grandiloquence is chiefly struck by the inadequacy of his view of scientific procedure. That we have only to make some crude experiments, to draw up briefs of the results in certain blank forms, to go through these by rule, checking off everything disproved and setting down the alternatives, and that thus in a few years physical science would be finished up—what an idea! "He wrote on science like a Lord Chancellor,"[2] indeed.

The early scientists, Copernicus, Tycho Brahe, Kepler, Galileo, and Gilbert, had methods more like those of their modern brethren. Kepler undertook to draw a curve through the places of Mars;[3] and his greatest service to science was in impressing on men's minds that this was the thing to be done if they wished to improve astronomy; that they were not to content themselves with inquiring whether one system of epicycles was better than another, but that they were to sit down to the figures and find out what the curve, in truth, was. He accomplished this by his incomparable energy and courage, blundering along in the most inconceivable way (to us), from one irrational hypothesis to another, until, after trying twenty-two of these, he fell, by the mere exhaustion of his invention, upon the orbit which a mind well furnished with the weapons of modern logic would have tried almost at the outset.

In the same way, every work of science great enough to be remembered for a few generations affords some exemplification of the defective state of the art of reasoning of the time when it was written; and each chief step in science has been a lesson in logic. It was so when Lavoisier[4] and his contemporaries took up the study of chemistry. The old chemist's maxim had been, *"Lege, lege, lege, labora, ora, et relege."*[5] Lavoisier's method was not to read and pray, not to dream that some long and complicated chemical process would have a certain effect, to put it into practice with dull patience, after its inevitable failure to dream that with some modification it would have another result, and to end by publishing the last dream as a fact: his way was to carry his mind into his laboratory, and to make of his alembics and cucurbits instruments of thought, giving a new conception of reasoning, as something which was to be done with one's eyes open, by manipulating real things instead of words and fancies.

The Darwinian controversy is, in large part, a question of logic. Mr. Darwin proposed to apply the statistical method to biology. The same thing had been done in a widely different branch of science, the theory of gases. Though unable to say what the movements of any particular molecule of a gas would be on a certain hypothesis regarding the constitution of this class of bodies, Clausius and Maxwell[6] were yet able, by the application of the doctrine of probabilities, to predict that in the long run such and such a proportion of the molecules would, under given circumstances, acquire such and such velocities; that there would take place, every second, such and such a number of collisions, etc.; and from these propositions were able to deduce certain properties of gases, especially in regard to their heat-relations. In like manner, Darwin, while unable to say what the operation of variation and natural selection in any individual case will be, demonstrates that in the long run they will adapt animals to their circumstances. Whether or not existing animal forms are due to such action, or what position the theory ought to take, forms the subject of a discussion in which questions of fact and questions of logic are curiously interlaced.

II

The object of reasoning is to find out, from the consideration of what we already know, something else which we do not know. Consequently, reasoning is good if it be such as to give a true conclusion from true premises, and not otherwise. Thus, the question of its validity is purely one of fact and not of thinking. A being the premises and B the conclusion, the question is, whether these facts are really so related that if A is B is. If so, the inference is valid; if not, not. It is not in the least the question whether, when the premises are accepted by the mind, we feel an impulse to accept the conclusion also. It is true that we do generally reason correctly by nature. But that is an accident; the true conclusion would remain true if we had no impulse to accept it; and the false one would remain false, though we could not resist the tendency to believe in it.

We are, doubtless, in the main logical animals, but we are not perfectly so. Most of us, for example, are naturally more sanguine and hopeful than logic would justify. We seem to be so constituted that in the absence of any facts to go upon we are happy and self-satisfied; so that the effect of experience is continually to contract our hopes and aspirations. Yet a lifetime of the application of this corrective does not usually eradicate our sanguine disposition. Where hope is unchecked by any experience, it is likely that our optimism is extravagant. Logicality in regard to practical matters is the most useful quality an animal can possess, and might, therefore, result from the action of natural selection; but outside of these it is probably of more advantage to the animal to have his mind filled with pleasing and encouraging visions, independently of their truth; and thus, upon unpractical subjects, natural selection might occasion a fallacious tendency of thought.

That which determines us, from given premises, to draw one inference rather than another, is some habit of mind, whether it be constitutional or acquired. The habit is good or otherwise, according as it produces true conclusions from true premises or not; and an inference is regarded as valid or not, without reference to the truth or falsity of its conclusion specially, but according as the habit which determines it is such as to produce true conclusions in general or not. The particular habit of mind which governs this or that inference may be formulated in a proposition whose truth de-

depends on their relevance and sufficiency

pends on the validity of the inferences which the habit determines; and such a formula is called a *guiding principle* of inference.
Suppose, for example, that we observe that a rotating disk of copper quickly comes to rest when placed between the poles of a
magnet, and we infer that this will happen with every disk of copper. The guiding principle is, that what is true of one piece of
copper is true of another. Such a guiding principle with regard to
copper would be much safer than with regard to many other substances—brass, for example.

A book might be written to signalize all the most important of
these guiding principles of reasoning. It would probably be, we
must confess, of no service to a person whose thought is directed
wholly to practical subjects, and whose activity moves along thoroughly beaten paths. The problems which present themselves to
such a mind are matters of routine which he has learned once for
all to handle in learning his business. But let a man venture into an
unfamiliar field, or where his results are not continually checked
by experience, and all history shows that the most masculine intellect will ofttimes lose his orientation and waste his efforts in directions which bring him no nearer to his goal, or even carry him
entirely astray. He is like a ship in the open sea, with no one on
board who understands the rules of navigation. And in such a case
some general study of the guiding principles of reasoning would
be sure to be found useful.

The subject could hardly be treated, however, without being
first limited; since almost any fact may serve as a guiding principle.
But it so happens that there exists a division among facts, such that
in one class are all those which are absolutely essential as guiding
principles, while in the others are all which have any other interest as objects of research. This division is between those which are
necessarily taken for granted in asking whether a certain conclusion follows from certain premises, and those which are not implied in that question. A moment's thought will show that a
variety of facts are already assumed when the logical question is
first asked. It is implied, for instance, that there are such states of

mind as doubt and belief—that a passage from one to the other is possible, the object of thought remaining the same, and that this transition is subject to some rules which all minds are alike bound by. As these are facts which we must already know before we can have any clear conception of reasoning at all, it cannot be supposed to be any longer of much interest to inquire into their truth or falsity. On the other hand, it is easy to believe that those rules of reasoning which are deduced from the very idea of the process are the ones which are the most essential; and, indeed, that so long as it conforms to these it will, at least, not lead to false conclusions from true premises. In point of fact, the importance of what may be deduced from the assumptions involved in the logical question turns out to be greater than might be supposed, and this for reasons which it is difficult to exhibit at the outset. The only one which I shall here mention is, that conceptions which are really products of logical reflection, without being readily seen to be so, mingle with our ordinary thoughts, and are frequently the causes of great confusion. This is the case, for example, with the conception of quality. A quality as such is never an object of observation. We can see that a thing is blue or green, but the quality of being blue and the quality of being green are not things which we see; they are products of logical reflection. The truth is, that common-sense, or thought as it first emerges above the level of the narrowly practical, is deeply imbued with that bad logical quality to which the epithet *metaphysical* is commonly applied; and nothing can clear it up but a severe course of logic.

III

We generally know when we wish to ask a question and when we wish to pronounce a judgment, for there is a dissimilarity between the sensation of doubting and that of believing.

But this is not all which distinguishes doubt from belief. There is a practical difference. Our beliefs guide our desires and shape our actions. The Assassins, or followers of the Old Man of the Mountain, used to rush into death at his least command, because they believed that obedience to him would insure everlasting felicity. Had they doubted this, they would not have acted as they did. So it is with every belief, according to its degree. The feeling of believing is a more or less sure indication of there being established in our nature some habit which will determine our actions. Doubt never has such an effect.

Nor must we overlook a third point of difference. Doubt is an uneasy and dissatisfied state from which we struggle to free ourselves and pass into the state of belief; while the latter is a calm and satisfactory state which we do not wish to avoid, or to change to a belief in anything else.[7] On the contrary, we cling tenaciously, not merely to believing, but to believing just what we do believe.

Thus, both doubt and belief have positive effects upon us, though very different ones. Belief does not make us act at once, but puts us into such a condition that we shall behave in a certain way, when the occasion arises. Doubt has not the least effect of this sort, but stimulates us to action until it is destroyed. This reminds us of the irritation of a nerve and the reflex action produced thereby; while for the analogue of belief, in the nervous system, we must look to what are called nervous associations—for example, to that habit of the nerves in consequence of which the smell of a peach will make the mouth water.

IV

The irritation of doubt causes a struggle to attain a state of belief. I shall term this struggle *inquiry*, though it must be admitted that this is sometimes not a very apt designation.

The irritation of doubt is the only immediate motive for the struggle to attain belief. It is certainly best for us that our beliefs should be such as may truly guide our actions so as to satisfy our desires; and this reflection will make us reject any belief which does not seem to have been so formed as to insure this result. But it will only do so by creating a doubt in the place of that belief.

With the doubt, therefore, the struggle begins, and with the cessation of doubt it ends. Hence, the sole object of inquiry is the settlement of opinion. We may fancy that this is not enough for us, and what we seek, not merely an opinion, but a true opinion. But put this fancy to the test, and it proves groundless; for as soon as a firm belief is reached we are entirely satisfied, whether the belief be true or false. And it is clear that nothing out of the sphere of our knowledge can be our object, for nothing which does not affect the mind can be the motive for a mental effort. The most that can be maintained is, that we seek for a belief that we shall *think* to be true. But we think each one of our beliefs to be true, and, indeed, it is mere tautology to say so.

That the settlement of opinion is the sole end of inquiry is a very important proposition. It sweeps away, at once, various vague and erroneous conceptions of proof. A few of these may be noticed here.

1. Some philosophers have imagined that to start an inquiry it was only necessary to utter a question or set it down upon paper, and have even recommended us to begin our studies with questioning everything! But the mere putting of a proposition into the interrogative form does not stimulate the mind to any struggle after belief. There must be a real and living doubt, and without this all discussion is idle.

2. It is a very common idea that a demonstration must rest on some ultimate and absolutely indubitable propositions. These, according to one school, are first principles of a general nature; according to another, are first sensations. But, in point of fact, an inquiry, to have that completely satisfactory result called demonstration, has only to start with propositions perfectly free from all actual doubt. If the premises are not in fact doubted at all, they cannot be more satisfactory than they are.

3. Some people seem to love to argue a point after all the world is fully convinced of it. But no further advance can be made. When doubt ceases, mental action on the subject comes to an end; and, if it did go on, it would be without a purpose.

V

If the settlement of opinion is the sole object of inquiry, and if belief is of the nature of a habit, why should we not attain the desired end, by taking any answer to a question which we may fancy, and constantly reiterating it to ourselves, dwelling on all which may conduce to that belief, and learning to turn with contempt and hatred from anything which might disturb it? This simple and direct method is really pursued by many men. I remember once being entreated not to read a certain newspaper lest it might change my opinion upon free-trade. "Lest I might be entrapped by its fallacies and misstatements," was the form of expression. "You are not," my friend said, "a special student of political economy. You might, therefore, easily be deceived by fallacious arguments upon the subject. You might, then, if you read this paper, be led to believe in protection. But you admit that free-trade is the true doctrine; and you do not wish to believe what is not true." I have often known this system to be deliberately adopted. Still oftener, the instinctive dislike of an undecided state of mind, exaggerated into a vague dread of doubt, makes men cling spasmodically to the views they already take. The man feels that, if he only holds to his belief without wavering, it will be entirely satisfactory. Nor can it be denied that a steady and immovable faith yields great peace of mind. It may, indeed, give rise to inconveniences, as if a man should resolutely continue to believe that fire would not burn him, or that he would be eternally damned if he received his *ingesta* otherwise than through a stomach-pump. But then the man who adopts this method will not allow that its inconveniences are greater than its advantages. He will say, "I hold steadfastly to the truth, and the truth is always wholesome." And in many cases it may very well be that the pleasure he derives from his calm faith overbalances any inconveniences resulting from its deceptive character. Thus, if it be true that death is annihilation, then the man who believes that he will certainly go straight to heaven when he dies, provided he have fulfilled certain simple observances in this life, has a cheap pleasure which will not be followed by the least disappointment. A similar consideration seems to have weight with many persons in religious topics, for we frequently hear it said, "Oh, I could not believe so-and-so, because I should be wretched if I did." When an ostrich buries its head in the sand as danger approaches, it very likely takes the happiest course. It hides the danger, and then calmly says there is no danger; and, if it feels perfectly sure there is none, why should it raise its head to see? A man may go through life, systematically keeping out of view all that might cause a change in his opinions, and if he only suc-ceeds—basing his method, as he does, on two fundamental psy-chological laws—I do not see what can be said against his doing so. It would be an egotistical impertinence to object that his pro-cedure is irrational, for that only amounts to saying that his method of settling belief is not ours. He does not propose to him-self to be rational, and, indeed, will often talk with scorn of man's weak and illusive reason. So let him think as he pleases.

But this method of fixing belief, which may be called the method of tenacity, will be unable to hold its ground in practice. The social impulse is against it. The man who adopts it will find that other men think differently from him, and it will be apt to oc-cur to him, in some saner moment, that their opinions are quite as good as his own, and this will shake his confidence in his belief. This conception, that another man's thought or sentiment may be equivalent to one's own, is a distinctly new step, and a highly im-portant one. It arises from an impulse too strong in man to be sup-pressed, without danger of destroying the human species. Unless we make ourselves hermits, we shall necessarily influence each other's opinions; so that the problem becomes how to fix belief, not in the individual merely, but in the community.

Let the will of the state act, then, instead of that of the individ-ual. Let an institution be created which shall have for its object to keep correct doctrines before the attention of the people, to reit-erate them perpetually, and to teach them to the young; having at the same time power to prevent contrary doctrines from being taught, advocated, or expressed. Let all possible causes of a change of mind be removed from men's apprehensions. Let them be kept ignorant, lest they should learn of some reason to think otherwise than they do. Let their passions be enlisted, so that they may regard private and unusual opinions with hatred and horror. Then, let all men who reject the established belief be terrified into silence. Let the people turn out and tar-and-feather such men, or let inquisitions be made into the manner of thinking of suspected persons, and, when they are found guilty of forbidden beliefs, let them be subjected to some signal punishment. When complete agreement could not otherwise be reached, a general massacre of all who have not thought in a certain way has proved a very effective means of settling opinion in a country. If the power to do this be wanting, let a list of opinions be drawn up, to which no man of the least independence of thought can assent, and let the faithful be required to accept all these propositions, in order to segregate them as radically as possible from the influence of the rest of the world.

This method has, from the earliest times, been one of the chief means of upholding correct theological and political doctrines, and of preserving their universal or catholic character. In Rome, especially, it has been practiced from the days of Numa Pompilius to those of Pius Nonus.[8] This is the most perfect example in history; but wherever there is a priesthood—and no religion has been without one—this method has been more or less made use of. Wherever there is an aristocracy, or a guild, or any association of a class of men whose interests depend or are supposed to depend on certain propositions, there will be inevitably found some traces of this natural product of social feeling. Cruelties always accompany this system; and when it is consistently carried out, they become atrocities of the most horrible kind in the eyes of any rational man. Nor should this occasion surprise, for the officer of a society does not feel justified in surrendering the interests of that society for the sake of mercy, as he might his own private interests. It is natural, therefore, that sympathy and fellowship should thus produce a most ruthless power.

In judging this method of fixing belief, which may be called the method of authority, we must, in the first place, allow its immeasurable mental and moral superiority to the method of tenacity. Its success is proportionately greater; and, in fact, it has over and over again worked the most majestic results. The mere structures of stone which it has caused to be put together—in Siam, for example, in Egypt, and in Europe—have many of them a sublimity hardly more than rivaled by the greatest works of Nature. And, except the geological epochs, there are no periods of time so vast as those which are measured by some of these organized faiths. If we scrutinize the matter closely, we shall find that there has not been one of their creeds which has remained always the same; yet the change is so slow as to be imperceptible during one person's life, so that individual belief remains sensibly fixed. For the mass of mankind, then, there is perhaps no better method than this. If it is their highest impulse to be intellectual slaves, then slaves they ought to remain.

But no institution can undertake to regulate opinions upon every subject. Only the most important ones can be attended to, and on the rest men's minds must be left to the action of natural causes. This imperfection will be no source of weakness so long as men are in such a state of culture that one opinion does not influence another—that is, so long as they cannot put two and two together. But in the most priestridden states some individuals will be found who are raised above that condition. These men possess a wider sort of social feeling; they see that men in other countries and in other ages have held to very different doctrines from those which they themselves have been brought up to believe; and they cannot help seeing that it is the mere accident of their having been taught as they have, and of their having been surrounded with the manners and associations they have, that has caused them to believe as they do and not far differently. And their candor cannot resist the reflection that there is no reason to rate their own views at a higher value than those of other nations and other centuries; and this gives rise to doubts in their minds.

They will further perceive that such doubts as these must exist in their minds with reference to every belief which seems to be determined by the caprice either of themselves or of those who originated the popular opinions. The willful adherence to a belief, and the arbitrary forcing of it upon others, must, therefore, both be given up, and a new method of settling opinions must be adopted, which shall not only produce an impulse to believe, but shall also decide what proposition it is which is to be believed. Let the action of natural preferences be unimpeded, then, and under their influence let men, conversing together and regarding matters in different lights, gradually develop beliefs in harmony with natural causes. This method resembles that by which conceptions of art have been brought to maturity. The most perfect example of it is to be found in the history of metaphysical philosophy. Systems of this sort have not usually rested upon any observed facts, at least not in any great degree. They have been chiefly adopted because their fundamental propositions seemed "agreeable to reason." This is an apt expression; it does not mean that which agrees with experience, but that which we find ourselves inclined to believe. Plato, for example, finds it agreeable to reason that the distances of the celestial spheres from one another should be proportional to the different lengths of strings which produce harmonious chords. Many philosophers have been led to their main conclusions by considerations like this; but this is the lowest and least developed form which the method takes, for it is clear that another man might find Kepler's theory, that the celestial spheres are proportional to the inscribed and circumscribed spheres of the different regular solids, more agreeable to *his* reason. But the shock of opinions will soon lead men to rest on preferences of a far more universal nature. Take, for example, the doctrine that man only acts selfishly—that is, from the consideration that acting in one way will afford him more pleasure than acting in another. This rests on no fact in the world, but it has a wide acceptance as being the only reasonable theory.

This method is far more intellectual and respectable from the point of view of reason than either of the others which we have noticed. But its failure has been the most manifest. It makes of inquiry something similar to the development of taste; but taste, unfortunately, is always more or less a matter of fashion, and accordingly metaphysicians have never come to any fixed agreement, but the pendulum has swung backward and forward between a more material and a more spiritual philosophy, from the earliest times to the latest. And so from this, which has been called the *a priori* method, we are driven, in Lord Bacon's phrase, to a true induction. We have examined into this *a priori* method as something which promised to deliver our opinions from their accidental and capricious element. But development, while it is a process which eliminates the effect of some casual circumstances, only magnifies that of others. This method, therefore, does not differ in a very essential way from that of authority. The government may not have lifted its finger to influence my convictions; I may have been left outwardly quite free to choose, we will say, between monogamy and polygamy, and, appealing to my conscience only, I may have concluded that the latter practice is in itself licentious. But when I come to see that the chief obstacle to the spread of Christianity among a people of as high culture as the Hindoos has been a conviction of the immorality of our way of treating women, I cannot help seeing that, though governments do not interfere, sentiments in their development will be very greatly determined by accidental causes. Now, there are some people, among whom I must suppose that my reader is to be found, who, when they see that any belief of theirs is determined by any circumstance extraneous to the facts, will from that moment not merely admit in words that that belief is doubtful, but will experience a real doubt of it, so that it ceases to be a belief.

To satisfy our doubts, therefore, it is necessary that a method should be found by which our beliefs may be caused by nothing human, but by some external permanency—by something upon which our thinking has no effect. Some mystics imagine that they have such a method in a private inspiration from on high. But that is only a form of the method of tenacity, in which the conception of truth as something public is not yet developed. Our external permanency would not be external, in our sense, if it was restricted in its influence to one individual. It must be something which affects, or might affect, every man. And, though these affections are necessarily as various as are individual conditions, yet the method must be such that the ultimate conclusion of every man shall be the same. Such is the method of science. Its fundamental hypothesis, restated in more familiar language, is this: There are real things, whose characters are entirely independent of our opinions about them; those realities affect our senses according to regular laws, and, though our sensations are as different as our relations to the objects, yet, by taking advantage of the laws of perception, we can ascertain by reasoning how things really are, and any man, if he have sufficient experience and reason enough about it, will be led to the one true conclusion. The new conception here involved is that of reality. It may be asked how I know that there are any realities. If this hypothesis is the sole support of my method of inquiry, my method of inquiry must not be used to support my hypothesis. The reply is this: 1. If investigation cannot be regarded as proving that there are real things, it at least does not lead to a contrary conclusion; but the method and the conception on which it is based remain ever in harmony. No doubts of the method, therefore, necessarily arise from its practice, as is the case with all the others. 2. The feeling which gives rise to any method of fixing belief is a dissatisfaction at two repugnant propositions. But here already is a vague concession that there is some *one* thing to which a proposition should conform. Nobody, therefore, can really doubt that there are realities, or, if he did, doubt would not be a source of dissatisfaction. The hypothesis, therefore, is one which every mind admits. So that the social impulse does not cause me to doubt it. 3. Everybody uses the scientific method about a great many things, and only ceases to use it when he does not know how to apply it. 4. Experience of the method has not led me to doubt it, but, on the contrary, scientific investigation has had the most wonderful triumphs in the way of settling opinion. These afford the explanation of my not doubting the method or the hypothesis which it supposes; and not having any doubt, nor believing that anybody else whom I could influence has, it would be the merest babble for me to say more about it. If there be anybody with a living doubt upon the subject, let him consider it.

To describe the method of scientific investigation is the object of this series of papers.[9] At present I have only room to notice some points of contrast between it and other methods of fixing belief.

This is the only one of the four methods which presents any distinction of a right and a wrong way. If I adopt the method of tenacity and shut myself out from all influences, whatever I think necessary to doing this is necessary according to that method. So with the method of authority: the state may try to put down heresy by means which, from a scientific point of view, seem very ill-calculated to accomplish its purposes; but the only test *on that method* is what the state thinks, so that it cannot pursue the method wrongly. So with the *a priori* method. The very essence of it is to think as one is inclined to think. All metaphysicians will be sure to do that, however they may be inclined to judge each other to be perversely wrong. The Hegelian system recognizes every natural tendency of thought as logical, although it be certain to be abolished by counter-tendencies. Hegel thinks there is a regular system in the succession of these tendencies, in consequence of which, after drifting one way and the other for a long time, opinion will at last go right. And it is true that metaphysicians get the right ideas at last; Hegel's system of Nature represents tolerably the science of that day; and one may be sure that whatever scientific investigation has put out of doubt will presently receive *a priori* demonstration on the part of the metaphysicians. But with the scientific method the case is different. I may start with known and

observed facts to proceed to the unknown; and yet the rules which
I follow in doing so may not be such as investigation would ap-
prove. The test of whether I am truly following the method is not
an immediate appeal to my feelings and purposes, but, on the contrary, itself involves the application of the method. Hence it is that
bad reasoning as well as good reasoning is possible; and this fact is
the foundation of the practical side of logic. *Don't they really proceed by hunches?*

It is not to be supposed that the first three methods of settling
opinion present no advantage whatever over the scientific method.
On the contrary, each has some peculiar convenience of its own.
The *a priori* method is distinguished for its comfortable conclusions. It is the nature of the process to adopt whatever belief we
are inclined to, and there are certain flatteries to the vanity of man
which we all believe by nature, until we are awakened from our
pleasing dream by some rough facts. The method of authority will
always govern the mass of mankind; and those who wield the various forms of organized force in the state will never be convinced
that dangerous reasoning ought not to be suppressed in some way.
If liberty of speech is to be untrammeled from the grosser forms
of constraint, then uniformity of opinion will be secured by a
moral terrorism to which the respectability of society will give its
thorough approval. Following the method of authority is the path
of peace. Certain non-conformities are permitted; certain others
(considered unsafe) are forbidden. These are different in different
countries and in different ages; but, wherever you are, let it be
known that you seriously hold a tabooed belief, and you may be
perfectly sure of being treated with a cruelty less brutal but more
refined than hunting you like a wolf. Thus, the greatest intellectual
benefactors of mankind have never dared, and dare not now, to
utter the whole of their thought; and thus a shade of *prima facie*
doubt is cast upon every proposition which is considered essential
to the security of society. Singularly enough, the persecution does
not all come from without; but a man torments himself and is of-
tentimes most distressed at finding himself believing propositions
which he has been brought up to regard with aversion. The peaceful

and sympathetic man will, therefore, find it hard to resist the temptation to submit his opinions to authority. But most of all I admire the method of tenacity for its strength, simplicity, and directness. Men who pursue it are distinguished for their decision of character, which becomes very easy with such a mental rule. They do not waste time in trying to make up their minds what they want, but, fastening like lightning upon whatever alternative comes first, they hold to it to the end, whatever happens, without an instant's irresolution. This is one of the splendid qualities which generally accompany brilliant, unlasting success. It is impossible not to envy the man who can dismiss reason, although we know how it must turn out at last.

Such are the advantages which the other methods of settling opinion have over scientific investigation. A man should consider well of them; and then he should consider that, after all, he wishes his opinions to coincide with the fact, and that there is no reason why the results of these three methods should do so. To bring about this effect is the prerogative of the method of science. Upon such considerations he has to make his choice—a choice which is far more than the adoption of any intellectual opinion, which is one of the ruling decisions of his life, to which, when once made, he is bound to adhere. The force of habit will sometimes cause a man to hold on to old beliefs, after he is in a condition to see that they have no sound basis. But reflection upon the state of the case will overcome these habits, and he ought to allow reflection its full weight. People sometimes shrink from doing this, having an idea that beliefs are wholesome which they cannot help feeling rest on nothing. But let such persons suppose an analogous though different case from their own. Let them ask themselves what they would say to a reformed Mussulman who should hesitate to give up his old notions in regard to the relations of the sexes; or to a reformed Catholic who should still shrink from reading the Bible. Would they not say that these persons ought to consider the matter fully, and clearly understand the new doctrine, and then ought to embrace it, in its entirety? But, above all, let it be considered that what is more wholesome than any particular belief is integrity of belief, and that to avoid looking into the support of any belief from a fear that it may turn out rotten is quite as immoral as it is disadvantageous. The person who confesses that there is such a thing as truth, which is distinguished from falsehood simply by this, that if acted on it will carry us to the point we aim at and not astray, and then, though convinced of this, dares not know the truth and seeks to avoid it, is in a sorry state of mind indeed.

Yes, the other methods do have their merits: a clear logical conscience does cost something—just as any virtue, just as all that we cherish, costs us dear. But we should not desire it to be otherwise. The genius of a man's logical method should be loved and reverenced as his bride, whom he has chosen from all the world. He need not contemn the others; on the contrary, he may honor them deeply, and in doing so he only honors her the more. But she is the one that he has chosen, and he knows that he was right in making that choice. And having made it, he will work and fight for her, and will not complain that there are blows to take, hoping that there may be as many and as hard to give, and will strive to be the worthy knight and champion of her from the blaze of whose splendors he draws his inspiration and his courage.

How to Make Our Ideas Clear

(1878)

I

WHOEVER HAS LOOKED into a modern treatise on logic of the common sort, will doubtless remember the two distinctions between *clear* and *obscure* conceptions, and between *distinct* and *confused* conceptions. They have lain in the books now for nigh two centuries, unimproved and unmodified, and are generally reckoned by logicians as among the gems of their doctrine.

A clear idea is defined as one which is so apprehended that it will be recognized wherever it is met with, and so that no other will be mistaken for it. If it fails of this clearness, it is said to be obscure.

This is rather a neat bit of philosophical terminology; yet, since it is clearness that they were defining, I wish the logicians had made their definition a little more plain. Never to fail to recognize an idea, and under no circumstances to mistake another for it, let it come in how recondite a form it may, would indeed imply such prodigious force and clearness of intellect as is seldom met with in this world. On the other hand, merely to have such an acquaintance with the idea as to have become familiar with it, and to have lost all hesitancy in recognizing it in ordinary cases, hardly seems to deserve the name of clearness of apprehension, since after all it only amounts to a subjective feeling of mastery which may be entirely mistaken. I take it, however, that when the logicians speak of "clearness," they mean nothing more than such a familiarity with an idea, since they regard the quality as but a small merit, which needs to be supplemented by another, which they call *distinctness.*

A distinct idea is defined as one which contains nothing which is not clear. This is technical language; by the *contents* of an idea logicians understand whatever is contained in its definition. So that an idea is *distinctly* apprehended, according to them, when we can give a precise definition of it, in abstract terms. Here the professional logicians leave the subject; and I would not have troubled the reader with what they have to say, if it were not such a striking example of how they have been slumbering through ages of intellectual activity, listlessly disregarding the enginery of modern thought, and never dreaming of applying its lessons to the improvement of logic. It is easy to show that the doctrine that familiar use and abstract distinctness make the perfection of apprehension has its only true place in philosophies which have long been extinct; and it is now time to formulate the method of attaining to a more perfect clearness of thought, such as we see and admire in the thinkers of our own time.

When Descartes set about the reconstruction of philosophy, his first step was to (theoretically) permit skepticism and to discard the practice of the schoolmen of looking to authority as the ultimate source of truth. That done, he sought a more natural fountain of true principles, and professed to find it in the human mind; thus passing, in the directest way, from the method of authority to that of apriority, as described in my first paper.[1] Self-consciousness was to furnish us with our fundamental truths, and to decide what was agreeable to reason. But since, evidently, not all ideas are true, he was led to note, as the first condition of infallibility, that they must be clear. The distinction between an idea *seeming* clear and really being so, never occurred to him. Trusting to introspection, as he did, even for a knowledge of external things, why should he question its testimony in respect to the contents of our own minds? But then, I suppose, seeing men, who seemed to be quite clear and positive, holding opposite opinions upon fundamental principles, he was further led to say that clearness of ideas is not sufficient, but that they need also to be distinct, i.e., to have nothing unclear about them. What he probably meant by this (for he did not explain himself with precision) was, that they must sustain the test of dialectical examination; that they must not only seem clear

at the outset, but that discussion must never be able to bring to
light points of obscurity connected with them.

Such was the distinction of Descartes, and one sees that it was
precisely on the level of his philosophy. It was somewhat developed by Leibnitz. This great and singular genius was as remarkable
for what he failed to see as for what he saw. That a piece of mechanism could not do work perpetually without being fed with
power in some form, was a thing perfectly apparent to him; yet he
did not understand that the machinery of the mind can only transform knowledge, but never originate it, unless it be fed with facts
of observation. He thus missed the most essential point of the
Cartesian philosophy, which is, that to accept propositions which
seem perfectly evident to us is a thing which, whether it be logical or illogical, we cannot help doing. Instead of regarding the matter in this way, he sought to reduce the first principles of science to
formulas which cannot be denied without self-contradiction, and
was apparently unaware of the great difference between his position and that of Descartes. So he reverted to the old formalities of
logic, and, above all, abstract definitions played a great part in his
philosophy. It was quite natural, therefore, that on observing that
the method of Descartes labored under the difficulty that we may
seem to ourselves to have clear apprehensions of ideas which in
truth are very hazy, no better remedy occurred to him than to require an abstract definition of every important term. Accordingly,
in adopting the distinction of *clear* and *distinct* notions, he described the latter quality as the clear apprehension of everything
contained in the definition; and the books have ever since copied
his words. There is no danger that his chimerical scheme will ever
again be over-valued. Nothing new can ever be learned by analyzing definitions. Nevertheless, our existing beliefs can be set in order by this process, and order is an essential element of intellectual
economy, as of every other. It may be acknowledged, therefore,
that the books are right in making familiarity with a notion the
first step toward clearness of apprehension, and the defining of it
the second. But in omitting all mention of any higher perspicuity

of thought, they simply mirror a philosophy which was exploded a hundred years ago. That much-admired "ornament of logic"— the doctrine of clearness and distinctness—may be pretty enough, but it is high time to relegate to our cabinet of curiosities the antique *bijou,* and to wear about us something better adapted to modern uses.

The very first lesson that we have a right to demand that logic shall teach us is, how to make our ideas clear; and a most important one it is, depreciated only by minds who stand in need of it. To know what we think, to be masters of our own meaning, will make a solid foundation for great and weighty thought. It is most easily learned by those whose ideas are meagre and restricted; and far happier they than such as wallow helplessly in a rich mud of conceptions. A nation, it is true, may, in the course of generations, overcome the disadvantage of an excessive wealth of language and its natural concomitant, a vast, unfathomable deep of ideas. We may see it in history, slowly perfecting its literary forms, sloughing at length its metaphysics, and, by virtue of the untirable patience which is often a compensation, attaining great excellence in every branch of mental acquirement. The page of history is not yet unrolled which is to tell us whether such a people will or will not in the long-run prevail over one whose ideas (like the words of their language) are few, but which possesses a wonderful mastery over those which it has. For an individual, however, there can be no question that a few clear ideas are worth more than many confused ones. A young man would hardly be persuaded to sacrifice the greater part of his thoughts to save the rest; and the muddled head is the least apt to see the necessity of such a sacrifice. Him we can usually only commiserate, as a person with a congenital defect. Time will help him, but intellectual maturity with regard to clearness comes rather late, an unfortunate arrangement of Nature, inasmuch as clearness is of less use to a man settled in life, whose errors have in great measure had their effect, than it would be to one whose path lies before him. It is terrible to see how a single unclear idea, a single formula without meaning, lurking in a young man's head, will sometimes act like an obstruction of inert matter in an artery, hindering the nutrition of the brain, and condemning its victim to pine away in the fullness of his intellectual vigor and in the midst of intellectual plenty. Many a man has cherished for years as his hobby some vague shadow of an idea, too meaningless to be positively false; he has, nevertheless, passionately loved it, has made it his companion by day and by night, and has given to it his strength and his life, leaving all other occupations for its sake, and in short has lived with it and for it, until it has become, as it were, flesh of his flesh and bone of his bone; and then he has waked up some bright morning to find it gone, clean vanished away like the beautiful Melusina of the fable, and the essence of his life gone with it. I have myself known such a man;[2] and who can tell how many histories of circle-squarers, metaphysicians, astrologers, and what not, may not be told in the old German story?

II

The principles set forth in the first of these papers lead, at once, to a method of reaching a clearness of thought of a far higher grade than the "distinctness" of the logicians. We have there found that the action of thought is excited by the irritation of doubt, and ceases when belief is attained; so that the production of belief is the sole function of thought. All these words, however, are too strong for my purpose. It is as if I had described the phenomena as they appear under a mental microscope. Doubt and Belief, as the words are commonly employed, relate to religious or other grave discussions. But here I use them to designate the starting of any question, no matter how small or how great, and the resolution of it. If, for instance, in a horse-car, I pull out my purse and find a five-cent nickel and five coppers, I decide, while my hand is going to the purse, in which way I will pay my fare. To call such a question Doubt, and my decision Belief, is certainly to use words very disproportionate to the occasion. To speak of such a doubt as causing an irritation which needs to be appeased, suggests a temper

which is uncomfortable to the verge of insanity. Yet, looking at
the matter minutely, it must be admitted that, if there is the least
hesitation as to whether I shall pay the five coppers or the nickel
(as there will be sure to be, unless I act from some previously con-
tracted habit in the matter), though irritation is too strong a word,
yet I am excited to such small mental activity as may be necessary
to deciding how I shall act. Most frequently doubts arise from
some indecision, however momentary, in our action. Sometimes it
is not so. I have, for example, to wait in a railway-station, and to
pass the time I read the advertisements on the walls, I compare the
advantages of different trains and different routes which I never
expect to take, merely fancying myself to be in a state of hesitancy,
because I am bored with having nothing to trouble me. Feigned
hesitancy, whether feigned for mere amusement or with a lofty
purpose, plays a great part in the production of scientific inquiry.
However the doubt may originate, it stimulates the mind to an activity which may be slight or energetic, calm or turbulent. Images
pass rapidly through consciousness, one incessantly melting into
another, until at last, when all is over—it may be in a fraction of a
second, in an hour, or after long years—we find ourselves decided
as to how we should act under such circumstances as those which
occasioned our hesitation. In other words, we have attained belief.

In this process we observe two sorts of elements of consciousness, the distinction between which may best be made clear by
means of an illustration. In a piece of music there are the separate
notes, and there is the air. A single tone may be prolonged for an
hour or a day, and it exists as perfectly in each second of that time
as in the whole taken together; so that, as long as it is sounding, it
might be present to a sense from which everything in the past was
as completely absent as the future itself. But it is different with the
air, the performance of which occupies a certain time, during the
portions of which only portions of it are played. It consists in an
orderliness in the succession of sounds which strike the ear at different times; and to perceive it there must be some continuity of
consciousness which makes the events of a lapse of time present

to us. We certainly only perceive the air by hearing the separate
notes; yet we cannot be said to directly hear it, for we hear only
what is present at the instant, and an orderliness of succession cannot exist in an instant. These two sorts of objects, what we are *immediately* conscious of and what we are *mediately* conscious of, are
found in all consciousness. Some elements (the sensations) are
completely present at every instant so long as they last, while others (like thought) are actions having beginning, middle, and end,
and consist in a congruence in the succession of sensations which
flow through the mind. They cannot be immediately present to
us, but must cover some portion of the past or future. Thought is
a thread of melody running through the succession of our sensations.

We may add that just as a piece of music may be written in
parts, each part having its own air, so various systems of relationship of succession subsist together between the same sensations.
These different systems are distinguished by having different motives, ideas, or functions. Thought is only one such system, for its
sole motive, idea, and function, is to produce belief, and whatever
does not concern that purpose belongs to some other system of
relations. The action of thinking may incidentally have other results; it may serve to amuse us, for example, and among *dilettanti* it
is not rare to find those who have so perverted thought to the purposes of pleasure that it seems to vex them to think that the questions upon which they delight to exercise it may ever get finally
settled; and a positive discovery which takes a favorite subject out
of the arena of literary debate is met with ill-concealed dislike.
This disposition is the very debauchery of thought. But the soul
and meaning of thought, abstracted from the other elements
which accompany it, though it may be voluntarily thwarted, can
never be made to direct itself toward anything but the production
of belief. Thought in action has for its only possible motive the attainment of thought at rest; and whatever does not refer to belief
is no part of the thought itself.

And what, then, is belief? It is the demi-cadence which closes a musical phrase in the symphony of our intellectual life. We have seen that it has just three properties: First, it is something that we are aware of; second, it appeases the irritation of doubt; and, third, it involves the establishment in our nature of a rule of action, or, say for short, a *habit*. As it appeases the irritation of doubt, which is the motive for thinking, thought relaxes and comes to rest for a moment when belief is reached. But, since belief is a rule for action, the application of which involves further doubt and further thought, at the same time that it is a stopping-place, it is also a new starting-place for thought. That is why I have permitted myself to call it thought at rest, although thought is essentially an action. The *final* upshot of thinking is the exercise of volition, and of this thought no longer forms a part; but belief is only a stadium of mental action, an effect upon our nature due to thought, which will influence future thinking.

The essence of belief is the establishment of a habit, and different beliefs are distinguished by the different modes of action to which they give rise. If beliefs do not differ in this respect, if they appease the same doubt by producing the same rule of action, then no mere differences in the manner of consciousness of them can make them different beliefs, any more than playing a tune in different keys is playing different tunes. Imaginary distinctions are often drawn between beliefs which differ only in their mode of expression;—the wrangling which ensues is real enough, however. To believe that any objects are arranged as in Figure 1, and to believe that they are arranged in Figure 2, are one and the same belief;[3] yet it is conceivable that a man should assert one proposition and deny the other. Such false distinctions do as much harm as the confusion of beliefs really different, and are among the pitfalls of which we ought constantly to beware, especially when we are upon metaphysical ground. One singular deception of this sort, which often occurs, is to mistake the sensation produced by our own unclearness of thought for a character of the object we are thinking. Instead of perceiving that the obscurity is purely subjective, we fancy that we contemplate a quality of the object which

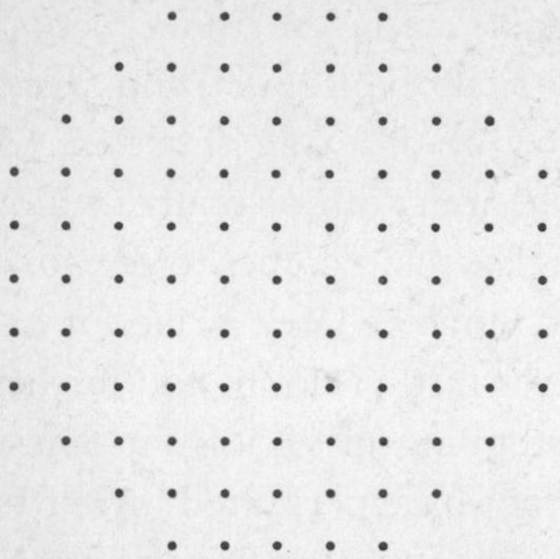

Figure 1 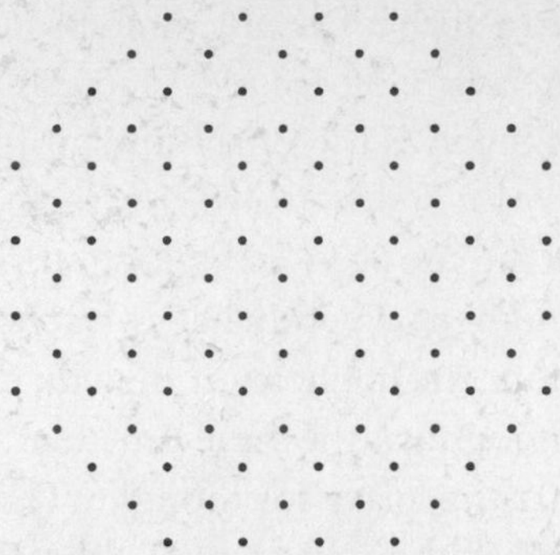   Figure 2

is essentially mysterious; and if our conception be afterward presented to us in a clear form we do not recognize it as the same,
owing to the absence of the feeling of unintelligibility. So long as
this deception lasts it obviously puts an impassable barrier in the
way of perspicuous thinking; so that it equally interests the opponents of rational thought to perpetuate it, and its adherents to
guard against it.

Another such deception is to mistake a mere difference in the
grammatical construction of two words for a distinction between
the ideas they express. In this pedantic age, when the general mob
of writers attend so much more to words than to things, this error
is common enough. When I just said that thought is an *action,* and
that it consists in a *relation,* although a person performs an action
but not a relation, which can only be the result of an action, yet
there was no inconsistency in what I said, but only a grammatical
vagueness.

From all these sophisms we shall be perfectly safe so long as we
reflect that the whole function of thought is to produce habits of
action; and that whatever there is connected with a thought, but
irrelevant to its purpose, is an accretion to it, but no part of it. If
there be a unity among our sensations which has no reference to

how we shall act on a given occasion, as when we listen to a piece of music, why we do not call that thinking. To develop its meaning, we have, therefore, simply to determine what habits it produces, for what a thing means is simply what habits it involves. Now, the identity of a habit depends on how it might lead us to act, not merely under such circumstances as are likely to arise, but under such as might possibly occur, no matter how improbable they may be. What the habit is depends on *when* and *how* it causes us to act. As for the *when,* every stimulus to action is derived from perception; as for the *how,* every purpose of action is to produce some sensible result. Thus, we come down to what is tangible and practical, as the root of every real distinction of thought, no matter how subtle it may be; and there is no distinction of meaning so fine as to consist in anything but a possible difference of practice.

To see what this principle leads to, consider in the light of it such a doctrine as that of transubstantiation. The Protestant churches generally hold that the elements of the sacrament are flesh and blood only in a tropical[4] sense; they nourish our souls as meat and the juice of it would our bodies. But the Catholics maintain that they are literally just that; although they possess all the sensible qualities of wafer-cakes and diluted wine. But we can have no conception of wine except what may enter into a belief, either—

1. That this, that, or the other, is wine; or,
2. That wine possesses certain properties.

Such beliefs are nothing but self-notifications that we should, upon occasion, act in regard to such things as we believe to be wine according to the qualities which we believe wine to possess. The occasion of such action would be some sensible perception, the motive of it to produce some sensible result. Thus our action has exclusive reference to what affects the senses, our habit has the same bearing as our action, our belief the same as our habit, our conception the same as our belief; and we can consequently mean nothing by wine but what has certain effects, direct or indirect, upon our senses; and to talk of something as having all the sensible characters of wine, yet being in reality blood, is senseless jargon. Now, it is not my object to pursue the theological question; and having used it as a logical example I drop it, without caring to anticipate the theologian's reply. I only desire to point out how impossible it is that we should have an idea in our minds which relates to anything but conceived sensible effects of things. Our idea of anything *is* our idea of its sensible effects; and if we fancy that we have any other we deceive ourselves, and mistake a mere sensation accompanying the thought for a part of the thought itself. It is absurd to say that thought has any meaning unrelated to its only function. It is foolish for Catholics and Protestants to fancy themselves in disagreement about the elements of the sacrament, if they agree in regard to all their sensible effects, here or hereafter.

It appears, then, that the rule for attaining the third grade of clearness of apprehension is as follows: Consider what effects, which might conceivably have practical bearings, we conceive the object of our conception to have. Then, our conception of these effects is the whole of our conception of the object.

III

Let us illustrate this rule by some examples; and, to begin with the simplest one possible, let us ask what we mean by calling a thing *hard*. Evidently that it will not be scratched by many other substances. The whole conception of this quality, as of every other, lies in its conceived effects. There is absolutely no difference between a hard thing and a soft thing so long as they are not brought to the test. Suppose, then, that a diamond could be crystallized in the midst of a cushion of soft cotton, and should remain there until it was finally burned up. Would it be false to say that that diamond was soft? This seems a foolish question, and would be so, in fact, except in the realm of logic. There such questions are often of the greatest utility as serving to bring logical principles into sharper relief than real discussions ever could. In studying logic we must not put them aside with hasty answers, but must consider them with attentive care, in order to make out the principles involved. We may, in the present case, modify our question, and ask what prevents us from saying that all hard bodies remain perfectly soft until they are touched, when their hardness increases with the pressure until they are scratched. Reflection will show that the reply is this: there would be no *falsity* in such modes of speech. They would involve a modification of our present usage of speech with regard to the words hard and soft, but not of their meanings. For they represent no fact to be different from what it is; only they involve arrangements of facts which would be exceedingly maladroit. This leads us to remark that the question of what would occur under circumstances which do not actually arise is not a question of fact, but only of the most perspicuous arrangement of them. For example, the question of free-will and fate in its simplest form, stripped of verbiage, is something like this: I have done something of which I am ashamed; could I, by an effort of the will, have resisted the temptation, and done otherwise? The philosophical reply is, that this is not a question of fact, but only of the arrangement of facts. Arranging them so as to exhibit what is particularly pertinent to my question—namely, that I ought to blame myself for having done wrong—it is perfectly true to say that, if I had willed to do otherwise than I did, I should have done otherwise. On the other hand, arranging the facts so as to exhibit another important consideration, it is equally true that, when a temptation has once been allowed to work, it will, if it has a certain force, produce its effect, let me struggle how I may. There is no objection to a contradiction in what would result from a false supposition. The *reductio ad absurdum* consists in showing that contradictory results would follow from a hypothesis which is consequently judged to be false. Many questions are involved in the free-will discussion, and I am far from desiring to say that both sides are equally right. On the contrary, I am of opinion that one side denies important facts, and that the other does not. But what I do say is, that the above single question was the origin of the whole doubt; that, had it not been for this question, the controversy would never have arisen; and that this question is perfectly solved in the manner which I have indicated.

Let us next seek a clear idea of Weight. This is another very easy case. To say that a body is heavy means simply that, in the absence of opposing force, it will fall. This (neglecting certain specifications of how it will fall, etc., which exist in the mind of the physicist who uses the word) is evidently the whole conception of weight. It is a fair question whether some particular facts may not *account* for gravity; but what we mean by the force itself is completely involved in its effects.

This leads us to undertake an account of the idea of Force in general. This is the great conception which, developed in the early part of the seventeenth century from the rude idea of a cause, and constantly improved upon since, has shown us how to explain all the changes of motion which bodies experience, and how to think about all physical phenomena; which has given birth to modern science, and changed the face of the globe; and which, aside from its more special uses, has played a principal part in directing the course of modern thought, and in furthering modern social development. It is, therefore, worth some pains to comprehend it. According to our rule, we must begin by asking what is the immediate use of thinking about force; and the answer is, that we thus account for changes of motion. If bodies were left to themselves, without the intervention of forces, every motion would continue unchanged both in velocity and in direction. Furthermore, change of motion never takes place abruptly; if its direction is changed, it is always through a curve without angles; if its velocity alters, it is by degrees. The gradual changes which are constantly taking place are conceived by geometers to be compounded together according to the rules of the parallelogram of forces. If the reader does not already know what this is, he will find it, I hope, to his advantage to endeavor to follow the following explanation; but if mathematics are insupportable to him, pray let him skip three paragraphs rather than that we should part company here.

A *path* is a line whose beginning and end are distinguished. Two paths are considered to be equivalent, which, beginning at the same point, lead to the same point. Thus in Figure 3 the two paths, *ABCDE* and *AFGHE,* are equivalent. Paths which do *not* begin at the same point are considered to be equivalent, provided that, on moving either of them without turning it, but keeping it always parallel to its original position, when its beginning coincides with that of the other path, the ends also coincide. Paths are considered as geometrically added together, when one begins where the other ends; thus the path *AE* is conceived to be a sum of *AB, BC, CD,* and *DE.* In the parallelogram of Figure 4 the diagonal *AC* is the sum of *AB* and *BC;* or, since *AD* is geometrically equivalent to *BC, AC* is the geometrical sum of *AB* and *AD.*

All this is purely conventional. It simply amounts to this: that we choose to call paths having the relations I have described equal or added. But, though it is a convention, it is a convention with a good reason. The rule for geometrical addition may be applied not only to paths, but to any other things which can be represented by paths. Now, as a path is determined by the varying direction and distance of the point which moves over it from the starting-point, it follows that anything which from its beginning to its end is determined by a varying direction and a varying magnitude is capable of being represented by a line. Accordingly, *velocities* may be represented by lines, for they have only directions and rates. The

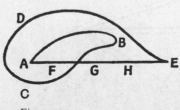

Figure 3

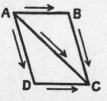

Figure 4

same thing is true of *accelerations,* or changes of velocities. This is evident enough in the case of velocities; and it becomes evident for accelerations if we consider that precisely what velocities are to positions—namely, states of change of them—that accelerations are to velocities.

The so-called "parallelogram of forces" is simply a rule for compounding accelerations. The rule is, to represent the accelerations by paths, and then to geometrically add the paths. The geometers, however, not only use the "parallelogram of forces" to compound different accelerations, but also to resolve one acceleration into a sum of several. Let *AB* (Figure 5) be the path which represents a certain acceleration—say, such a change in the motion of a body that at the end of one second the body will, under the influence of that change, be in a position different from what it would have had if its motion had continued unchanged such that a path equivalent to *AB* would lead from the latter position to the former. This acceleration may be considered as the sum of the accelerations represented by *AC* and *CB*. It may also be considered as the sum of the very different accelerations represented by *AD* and *DB,* where *AD* is almost the opposite of *AC*. And it is clear that there is an immense variety of ways in which *AB* might be resolved into the sum of two accelerations.

After this tedious explanation, which I hope, in view of the extraordinary interest of the conception of force, may not have exhausted the reader's patience, we are prepared at last to state the

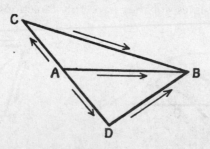

Figure 5

grand fact which this conception embodies. This fact is that if the actual changes of motion which the different particles of bodies experience are each resolved in its appropriate way, each component acceleration is precisely such as is prescribed by a certain law of Nature, according to which bodies in the relative positions which the bodies in question actually have at the moment,[5] always receive certain accelerations, which, being compounded by geometrical addition, give the acceleration which the body actually experiences.

This is the only fact which the idea of force represents, and whoever will take the trouble clearly to apprehend what this fact is, perfectly comprehends what force is. Whether we ought to say that a force *is* an acceleration, or that it *causes* an acceleration, is a mere question of propriety of language, which has no more to do with our real meaning than the difference between the French idiom *"Il fait froid"* and its English equivalent *"It is cold."* Yet it is surprising to see how this simple affair has muddled men's minds. In how many profound treatises is not force spoken of as a "mysterious entity," which seems to be only a way of confessing that the author despairs of ever getting a clear notion of what the word means! In a recent admired work on "Analytic Mechanics"[6] it is stated that we understand precisely the effect of force, but what force itself is we do not understand! This is simply a self-contradiction. The idea which the word force excites in our minds has no other function than to affect our actions, and these actions can have no reference to force otherwise than through its effects. Consequently, if we know what the effects of force are, we are acquainted with every fact which is implied in saying that a force exists, and there is nothing more to know. The truth is, there is some vague notion afloat that a question may mean something which the mind cannot conceive; and when some hair-splitting philosophers have been confronted with the absurdity of such a view, they have invented an empty distinction between positive and negative conceptions, in the attempt to give their non-idea a form not obviously nonsensical. The nullity of it is sufficiently plain from the considerations given a few pages back; and, apart from those considerations, the quibbling character of the distinction must have struck every mind accustomed to real thinking.

IV

Let us now approach the subject of logic, and consider a conception which particularly concerns it, that of *reality*. Taking clearness in the sense of familiarity, no idea could be clearer than this. Every child uses it with perfect confidence, never dreaming that he does not understand it. As for clearness in its second grade, however, it would probably puzzle most men, even among those of a reflective turn of mind, to give an abstract definition of the real. Yet such a definition may perhaps be reached by considering the points of difference between reality and its opposite, fiction. A figment is a product of somebody's imagination; it has such characters as his thought impresses upon it. That whose characters are independent of how you or I think is an external reality. There are, however, phenomena within our own minds, dependent upon our thought, which are at the same time real in the sense that we really think them. But though their characters depend on how we think, they do not depend on what we think those characters to be. Thus, a dream has a real existence as a mental phenomenon, if somebody has really dreamt it; that he dreamt so and so, does not depend on what anybody thinks was dreamt, but is completely independent of all opinion on the subject. On the other hand, considering, not the fact of dreaming, but the thing dreamt, it retains its peculiarities by virtue of no other fact than that it was dreamt to possess them. Thus we may define the real as that whose characters are independent of what anybody may think them to be.

But, however satisfactory such a definition may be found, it would be a great mistake to suppose that it makes the idea of reality perfectly clear. Here, then, let us apply our rules. According to them, reality, like every other quality, consists in the peculiar sensible effects which things partaking of it produce. The only effect which real things have is to cause belief, for all the sensations which they excite emerge into consciousness in the form of beliefs. The question therefore is, how is true belief (or belief in the real) distinguished from false belief (or belief in fiction). Now, as we have seen in the former paper,[7] the ideas of truth and falsehood, in their full development, appertain exclusively to the scientific method of settling opinion. A person who arbitrarily chooses the propositions which he will adopt can use the word truth only to emphasize the expression of his determination to hold on to his choice. Of course, the method of tenacity never prevailed exclusively; reason is too natural to men for that. But in the literature of the dark ages we find some fine examples of it. When Scotus Erigena is commenting upon a poetical passage in which hellebore is spoken of as having caused the death of Socrates, he does not hesitate to inform the inquiring reader that Helleborus and Socrates were two eminent Greek philosophers, and that the latter having been overcome in argument by the former took the matter to heart and died of it! What sort of an idea of truth could a man have who could adopt and teach, without the qualification of a perhaps, an opinion taken so entirely at random? The real spirit of Socrates, who I hope would have been delighted to have been "overcome in argument," because he would have learned something by it, is in curious contrast with the naïve idea of the glossist, for whom discussion would seem to have been simply a struggle. When philosophy began to awake from its long slumber, and before theology completely dominated it, the practice seems to have been for each professor to seize upon any philosophical position he found unoccupied and which seemed a strong one, to intrench himself in it, and to sally forth from time to time to give battle to the others. Thus, even the scanty records we possess of those disputes enable us to make out a dozen or more opinions held by different teachers at one time concerning the question of nominalism and realism. Read the opening part of the

"Historia Calamitatum" of Abelard, who was certainly as philosophical as any of his contemporaries, and see the spirit of com-
bat which it breathes. For him, the truth is simply his particular
stronghold. When the method of authority prevailed, the truth
meant little more than the Catholic faith. All the efforts of the
scholastic doctors are directed toward harmonizing their faith in
Aristotle and their faith in the Church, and one may search their
ponderous folios through without finding an argument which
goes any further. It is noticeable that where different faiths flourish side by side, renegades are looked upon with contempt even by
the party whose belief they adopt; so completely has the idea of
loyalty replaced that of truth-seeking. Since the time of Descartes,
the defect in the conception of truth has been less apparent. Still,
it will sometimes strike a scientific man that the philosophers have
been less intent on finding out what the facts are, than on inquiring what belief is most in harmony with their system. It is hard to
convince a follower of the *a priori* method by adducing facts; but
show him that an opinion he is defending is inconsistent with
what he has laid down elsewhere, and he will be very apt to retract
it. These minds do not seem to believe that disputation is ever to
cease; they seem to think that the opinion which is natural for one
man is not so for another, and that belief will, consequently, never
be settled. In contenting themselves with fixing their own opinions by a method which would lead another man to a different
result, they betray their feeble hold of the conception of what
truth is.

On the other hand, all the followers of science are fully persuaded that the processes of investigation, if only pushed far
enough, will give one certain solution to every question to which
they can be applied. One man may investigate the velocity of light
by studying the transits of Venus and the aberration of the stars;
another by the oppositions of Mars and the eclipses of Jupiter's
satellites; a third by the method of Fizeau; a fourth by that of Foucault; a fifth by the motions of the curves of Lissajous;[8] a sixth, a

seventh, an eighth, and a ninth, may follow the different methods of comparing the measures of statical and dynamical electricity. They may at first obtain different results, but, as each perfects his method and his processes, the results will move steadily together toward a destined centre. So with all scientific research. Different minds may set out with the most antagonistic views, but the progress of investigation carries them by a force outside of themselves to one and the same conclusion. This activity of thought by which we are carried, not where we wish, but to a foreordained goal, is like the operation of destiny. No modification of the point of view taken, no selection of other facts for study, no natural bent of mind even, can enable a man to escape the predestinate opinion. This great law is embodied in the conception of truth and reality. The opinion which is fated[9] to be ultimately agreed to by all who investigate, is what we mean by the truth, and the object represented in this opinion is the real. That is the way I would explain reality.

But it may be said that this view is directly opposed to the abstract definition which we have given of reality, inasmuch as it makes the characters of the real to depend on what is ultimately thought about them. But the answer to this is that, on the one hand, reality is independent, not necessarily of thought in general, but only of what you or I or any finite number of men may think about it; and that, on the other hand, though the object of the final opinion depends on what that opinion is, yet what that opinion is does not depend on what you or I or any man thinks. Our perversity and that of others may indefinitely postpone the settlement of opinion; it might even conceivably cause an arbitrary proposition to be universally accepted as long as the human race should last. Yet even that would not change the nature of the belief, which alone could be the result of investigation carried sufficiently far; and if, after the extinction of our race, another should arise with faculties and disposition for investigation, that true opinion must be the one which they would ultimately come to.

"Truth crushed to earth shall rise again,"[10] and the opinion which would finally result from investigation does not depend on how anybody may actually think. But the reality of that which is real does depend on the real fact that investigation is destined to lead, at last, if continued long enough, to a belief in it.

But I may be asked what I have to say to all the minute facts of history, forgotten never to be recovered, to the lost books of the ancients, to the buried secrets.

> Full many a gem of purest ray serene
>   The dark, unfathomed caves of ocean bear;
> Full many a flower is born to blush unseen.
>   And waste its sweetness on the desert air.[11]

Do these things not really exist because they are hopelessly beyond the reach of our knowledge? And then, after the universe is dead (according to the prediction of some scientists), and all life has ceased forever, will not the shock of atoms continue though there will be no mind to know it? To this I reply that, though in no possible state of knowledge can any number be great enough to express the relation between the amount of what rests unknown to the amount of the known, yet it is unphilosophical to suppose that, with regard to any given question (which has any clear meaning), investigation would not bring forth a solution of it, if it were carried far enough. Who would have said, a few years ago, that we could ever know of what substances stars are made whose light may have been longer in reaching us than the human race has existed? Who can be sure of what we shall not know in a few hundred years? Who can guess what would be the result of continuing the pursuit of science for ten thousand years, with the activity of the last hundred? And if it were to go on for a million, or a billion, or any number of years you please, how is it possible to say that there is any question which might not ultimately be solved?

But it may be objected, "Why make so much of these remote considerations, especially when it is your principle that only practical distinctions have a meaning?" Well, I must confess that it makes very little difference whether we say that a stone on the bottom of the ocean, in complete darkness, is brilliant or not— that is to say, that it *probably* makes no difference, remembering always that that stone *may* be fished up to-morrow. But that there are gems at the bottom of the sea, flowers in the untraveled desert, etc., are propositions which, like that about a diamond being hard when it is not pressed, concern much more the arrangement of our language than they do the meaning of our ideas.

It seems to me, however, that we have, by the application of our rule, reached so clear an apprehension of what we mean by reality, and of the fact which the idea rests on, that we should not, perhaps, be making a pretension so presumptuous as it would be singular, if we were to offer a metaphysical theory of existence for universal acceptance among those who employ the scientific method of fixing belief. However, as metaphysics is a subject much more curious than useful, the knowledge of which, like that of a sunken reef, serves chiefly to enable us to keep clear of it, I will not trouble the reader with any more Ontology at this moment. I have already been led much further into that path than I should have desired; and I have given the reader such a dose of mathematics, psychology, and all that is most abstruse, that I fear he may already have left me, and that what I am now writing is for the compositor and proof-reader exclusively. I trusted to the importance of the subject. There is no royal road to logic, and really valuable ideas can only be had at the price of close attention. But I know that in the matter of ideas the public prefer the cheap and nasty: and in my next paper[12] I am going to return to the easily intelligible, and not wander from it again. The reader who has been at the pains of wading through this month's paper, shall be rewarded in the next one by seeing how beautifully what has been developed in this tedious way can be applied to the ascertainment of the rules of scientific reasoning.

We have, hitherto, not crossed the threshold of scientific logic. It is certainly important to know how to make our ideas clear, but they may be ever so clear without being true. How to make them so, we have next to study. How to give birth to those vital and pro-creative ideas which multiply into a thousand forms and diffuse themselves everywhere, advancing civilization and making the dignity of man, is an art not yet reduced to rules, but of the secret of which the history of science affords some hints.

from **A Guess at the Riddle**

(ca. 1890)

AMONG OTHER REGULAR FACTS that have to be explained is Law or regularity itself. We enormously exaggerate the part that law plays in the universe. It is by means of regularities that we understand what little we do understand of the world, and thus there is a sort of mental perspective which brings regular phenomena to the foreground. We say that every event is determined by causes according to law. But apart from the fact that this must not be regarded as absolutely true, it does not mean so much as it seems to do. We do not mean, for example, that if a man and his antipode both sneeze at the same instant, that event comes under any general law. That is merely what we call a coincidence. But what we mean is there was a cause for the first man's sneezing, and another cause for the second man's sneezing; and the aggregate of these two events make up the first event about which we began by inquiring. The doctrine is that the events of the physical universe are merely motions of matter, and that these obey the laws of dynamics. But this only amounts to saying that among the countless systems of relationship existing among things we have found one that is universal and at the same time is subject to law. There is nothing except this singular character which makes this particular system of relationship any more important than the others. From this point of view, uniformity is seen to be really a highly exceptional phenomenon. But we pay no attention to irregular relationships, as having no interest for us.

We are brought, then, to this: conformity to law exists only within a limited range of events and even there is not perfect, for an element of pure spontaneity or lawless originality mingles, or at least, must be supposed to mingle, with law everywhere. Moreover, conformity with law is a fact requiring to be explained; and since Law in general cannot be explained by any law in particular, the explanation must consist in showing how law is developed out of pure chance, irregularity, and indeterminacy.

To this problem we are bound to address ourselves; and it is particularly needful to do so in the present state of science. The theory of the molecular constitution of matter has now been carried as far as there are clear indications to direct us, and we are now in the mists. To develop the mathematical consequences of any hypothesis as to the nature and laws of the minute parts of matter, and then to test it by physical experiment, will take fifty years; and out of the innumerable hypotheses that might be framed, there seems to be nothing to make one more antecedently probable than another. At this rate how long will it take to make any decided advance? We need some hint as to how molecules may be expected to behave; whether for instance, they would be likely to attract or repel one another inversely as the fifth power of the distance, so that we may be saved from many false suppositions, if we are not at once shown the way to the true one. Tell us how the laws of nature came about, and we may distinguish in some measure between laws that might and laws that could not have resulted from such a process of development.

To find that out is our task. I will begin the work with this guess. Uniformities in the modes of action of things have come about by their taking habits. At present, the course of events is approximately determined by law. In the past that approximation was less perfect; in the future it will be more perfect. The tendency to obey laws has always been and always will be growing. We look back toward a point in the infinitely distant past when there was no law but mere indeterminacy; we look forward to a point in the infinitely distant future when there will be no indeterminacy or chance but a complete reign of law. But at any assignable date in the past, however early, there was already some tendency toward uniformity; and at any assignable date in the future there will be some slight aberrancy from law. Moreover, all things have a tendency to take habits. For atoms and their parts, molecules and groups of molecules, and in short every conceivable real object, there is a greater probability of acting as on a former like occasion than otherwise. This tendency itself constitutes a regularity, and is continually on the increase. In looking back into the past we are looking towards periods when it was a less and less decided tendency. But its own essential nature is to grow. It is a generalizing tendency; it causes actions in the future to follow some generalization of past actions; and this tendency is itself something capable of similar generalization; and thus, it is self-generative. We have therefore only to suppose the smallest spur of it in the past, and that germ would have been bound to develop into a mighty and over-ruling principle, until it supersedes itself by strengthening habits into absolute laws regulating the action of all things in every respect in the indefinite future.

According to this, three elements are active in the world, first, chance; second, law; and third, habit-taking.

Such is our guess of the secret of the sphynx.

from **Evolutionary Love**

(1893)

THE MOVEMENT OF LOVE is circular, at one and the same impulse projecting creations into independency and drawing them into harmony. This seems complicated when stated so; but it is fully summed up in the simple formula we call the Golden Rule. This does not, of course, say, Do everything possible to gratify the egoistic impulses of others, but it says, Sacrifice your own perfection to the perfectionment of your neighbor. Nor must it for a moment be confounded with the Benthamite, or Helvetian, or, Beccarian motto, Act for the greatest good of the greatest number.[1] Love is not directed to abstractions but to persons; not to persons we do not know, nor to numbers of people, but to our own dear ones, our family and neighbors. "Our neighbor," we remember, is one whom we live near, not locally perhaps, but in life and feeling. *Why nationalism is natural, and globalism even more destructive*

Everybody can see that the statement of St. John[2] is the formula of an evolutionary philosophy, which teaches that growth comes only from love, from—I will not say self-*sacrifice,* but from the ardent impulse to fulfil another's highest impulse. Suppose, for example, that I have an idea that interests me. It is my creation. It is my creature; . . . it is a little person. I love it; and I will sink myself in perfecting it. It is not by dealing out cold justice to the circle of my ideas that I can make them grow, but by cherishing and tending them as I would the flowers in my garden. The philosophy we draw from John's gospel is that this is the way mind develops; and as for the cosmos, only so far as it yet is mind, and so has life, is it capable of further evolution. Love, recognising germs of loveliness in the hateful, gradually warms it into life, and makes it lovely.

That is the sort of evolution which every careful student of my essay "The Law of Mind" must see that *synechism*[3] calls for.

The nineteenth century is now fast sinking into the grave, and
we all begin to review its doings and to think what character it is
destined to bear as compared with other centuries in the minds of
future historians. It will be called, I guess, the Economical Century; for political economy has more direct relations with all the
branches of its activity than has any other science. Well, political
economy has its formula of redemption, too. It is this: Intelligence
in the service of greed ensures the justest prices, the fairest con
tracts, the most enlightened conduct of all the dealings between
men, and leads to the *summum bonum,* food in plenty and perfect
comfort. Food for whom? Why, for the greedy master of intelligence. I do not mean to say that this is one of the legitimate conclusions of political economy, the scientific character of which I
fully acknowledge. But the study of doctrines, themselves true,
will often temporarily encourage generalisations extremely false,
as the study of physics has encouraged necessitarianism. What I
say, then, is that the great attention paid to economical questions
during our century has induced an exaggeration of the beneficial
effects of greed and of the unfortunate results of sentiment, until
there has resulted a philosophy which comes unwittingly to this,
that greed is the great agent in the elevation of the human race
and in the evolution of the universe. He dropped intelligence *[handwritten annotation: He dropped intelligence from the argument]*

The economists accuse those to whom the enunciation of their
atrocious villainies communicates a thrill of horror of being *sentimentalists.* It may be so: I willingly confess to having some tincture
of sentimentalism in me, God be thanked! Ever since the French
Revolution brought this leaning of thought into ill-repute,—and
not altogether undeservedly, I must admit, true, beautiful, and
good as that great movement was,—it has been the tradition to
picture sentimentalists as persons incapable of logical thought and
unwilling to look facts in the eyes. This tradition may be classed
with the French tradition that an Englishman says *godam* at every
second sentence, the English tradition that an American talks

[handwritten annotation at bottom: Greed by the incompetent is the problem.]

about "Britishers," and the American tradition that a Frenchman carries forms of etiquette to an inconvenient extreme, in short with all those traditions which survive simply because the men who use their eyes and ears are few and far between. Doubtless some excuse there was for all those opinions in days gone by; and sentimentalism, when it was the fashionable amusement to spend one's evenings in a flood of tears over a woeful performance on a candle-litten stage, sometimes made itself a little ridiculous. But what after all is sentimentalism? It is an *ism,* a doctrine, namely, the doctrine that great respect should be paid to the natural judgments of the sensible heart. This is what sentimentalism precisely is; and I entreat the reader to consider whether to contemn it is not of all blasphemies the most degrading. Yet the nineteenth century has steadily contemned it, because it brought about the Reign of Terror. That it did so is true. Still, the whole question is one of *how much.* The reign of terror was very bad; but now the Gradgrind banner has been this century long flaunting in the face of heaven, with an insolence to provoke the very skies to scowl and rumble. Soon a flash and quick peal will shake economists quite out of their complacency, too late. The twentieth century, in its latter half, shall surely see the deluge-tempest burst upon the social order,— to clear upon a world as deep in ruin as that greed-philosophy has long plunged it into guilt. No post-thermidorian high jinks then!

So a miser is a beneficent power in a community, is he? With the same reason precisely, only in a much higher degree, you might pronounce the Wall Street sharp to be a good angel, who takes money from heedless persons not likely to guard it properly, who wrecks feeble enterprises better stopped, and who administers wholesome lessons to unwary scientific men, by passing worthless checks upon them,—as you did, the other day, to me, my millionaire Master in glomery, when you thought you saw your way to using my process without paying for it, and of so bequeathing to your children something to boast of their father about,—and who by a thousand wiles puts money at the service of intelligent greed, in his own person.[4] Bernard Mandeville, in his

But the other extreme is doing good for bad people.

Fable of the Bees, maintains that private vices of all descriptions are public benefits, and proves it, too, quite as cogently as the economist proves his point concerning the miser. He even argues, with no slight force, that but for vice civilisation would never have existed. In the same spirit, it has been strongly maintained and is today widely believed that all acts of charity and benevolence, private and public, go seriously to degrade the human race.

The *Origin of Species* of Darwin merely extends politico-economical views of progress to the entire realm of animal and vegetable life. The vast majority of our contemporary naturalists hold the opinion that the true cause of those exquisite and marvellous adaptations of nature for which, when I was a boy, men used to extol the divine wisdom, is that creatures are so crowded together that those of them that happen to have the slightest advantage force those less pushing into situations unfavorable to multiplication or even kill them before they reach the age of reproduction. Among animals, the mere mechanical individualism is vastly reënforced as a power making for good by the animal's ruthless greed. As Darwin puts it on his title-page, it is the struggle for existence; and he should have added for his motto: Every individual for himself, and the Devil take the hindmost! Jesus, in his Sermon on the Mount, expressed a different opinion.

Here, then, is the issue. The gospel of Christ says that progress comes from every individual merging his individuality in sympathy with his neighbors. On the other side, the conviction of the nineteenth century is that progress takes place by virtue of every individual's striving for himself with all his might and trampling his neighbor under foot whenever he gets a chance to do so. This may accurately be called the Gospel of Greed.

Much is to be said on both sides. I have not concealed, I could not conceal, my own passionate predilection. Such a confession will probably shock my scientific brethren. Yet the strong feeling is in itself, I think an argument of some weight in favor of the agapastic theory of evolution,[5]—so far as it may be presumed to bespeak the normal judgment of the Sensible Heart.

Why do animals still live animals if their system is so progressive?

A Definition of Pragmatism

(ca. 1904)

NO CRITICISM OF SUCH A BOOK,[1] no characterization of it, not even as slight a one as that here to be attempted, can have any meaning until the standpoint of the critic's observations be recognized. Our standpoint will be pragmatism; but this word has been so loosely used,[2] that a partial explanation of its nature is needful, with some indications of the intricate process by which those who hold it become assured of its truth. If philosophy is ever to become a sound science, its students must submit themselves to that same ethics of terminology that students of chemistry and taxonomic biology observe; and when a word has been invented for the declared purpose of conveying a precisely defined meaning, they must give up their habit of using it for every other purpose that may happen to hit their fancy at the moment. The word *pragmatism* was invented to express a certain maxim of logic, which, as was shown at its first enouncement, involves a whole system of philosophy. The maxim is intended to furnish a method for the analysis of concepts. A concept is something having the mode of being of a general type which is, or may be made, the rational part of the purport of a word. A more precise or fuller definition cannot here be attempted. The method prescribed in the maxim is to trace out in the imagination the conceivable practical consequences,—that is, the consequences for deliberate, self-controlled conduct,—of the affirmation or denial of the concept; and the assertion of the maxim is that herein lies the *whole* of the purport of the word, the *entire* concept. The sedulous exclusion from this statement of all reference to sensation is specially to be remarked. Such a distinction as that between red and blue is held to form no part of the concept. This maxim is put forth neither as a handy tool to serve so far as it may be found serviceable, nor as a self-evident truth, but as a far-reaching theorem solidly grounded upon an elaborate study of the nature of signs. Every thought, or cognitive representation, is of the nature of a sign. "Representation" and "sign" are synonyms. The whole purpose of a sign is that it shall be interpreted in another sign; and its whole purport lies in the special character which it imparts to that interpretation. When a sign determines an interpretation of itself in another sign, it produces an effect external to itself, a physical effect, though the sign producing the effect may itself be not an existent object but merely a type. It produces this effect, not in this or that metaphysical sense, but in an indisputable sense. As to this, it is to be remarked that actions beyond the reach of self-control are not subjects of blame. Thinking is a kind of action, and reasoning is a kind of deliberate action; and to call an argument illogical, or a proposition false, is a special kind of moral judgment, and as such is inapplicable to what we cannot help. This does not deny that what cannot be conceived today may be conceivable tomorrow. But just as long as we cannot help adopting a mode of thought, so long it must be thoroughly accepted as true. Any doubt of it is idle make-believe and irredeemable paper. Now we all do regard, and cannot help regarding, signs as *affecting* their interpretant signs. It is by a patient examination of the various modes (some of them quite disparate) of interpretations of signs, and of the connections between these (an exploration in which one ought, if possible, to provide himself with a guide, or, if that cannot be, to prepare his courage to see one conception that will have to be mastered peering over the head of another, and soon another peering over that, and so on, until he shall begin to think there is to be no end of it, or that life will not be long enough to complete the study) that the pragmatist has at length, to his great astonishment, emerged from the disheartening labyrinth with this simple maxim in his hand. In distrust of so surprising a result he has searched for some flaw in its method, and for some case in which it should break down, but

after every deep-laid plot for disproving it that long-working ingenuity could devise has recoiled upon his own head, and all
doubts he could start have been exhausted, he has been forced at
last to acknowledge its truth. This maxim once accepted,—intelligently accepted, in the light of the evidence of its truth,—speedily sweeps all metaphysical rubbish out of one's house. Each
abstraction is either pronounced to be gibberish or is provided
with a plain, practical definition. The general leaning of the results
is toward what the idealists call the naïve, toward common sense,
toward anthropomorphism. Thus, for example, the *real* becomes
that which is such as it is regardless of what you or I or any of our
folks may think it to be. The *external* becomes that element which
is such as it is regardless of what somebody thinks, feels, or does,
whether about that external object or about anything else. Accordingly, the external is necessarily real, while the real may or
may not be external; nor is anything absolutely external nor absolutely devoid of externality. Every assertory proposition refers to
something external, and even a dream withstands us sufficiently
for one description to be true of it and another not. The *existent* is
that which reacts against other things. Consequently, the external
world, (that is, the world that is comparatively external) does not
consist of existent objects merely, nor merely of these and their reactions; but on the contrary, its most important reals have the
mode of being of what the nominalist calls "mere" words, that is,
general types and would-bes. The nominalist is right in saying that
they are substantially of the nature of words; but his "mere" reveals a complete misunderstanding of what our everyday world
consists of.

William James

James was born in New York City in 1842, the first of the five children of Henry and Mary James. He received a peripatetic education in Europe and America, ending up at Harvard, where he became close friends with both Charles Sanders Peirce and Oliver Wendell Holmes. In 1869 he earned a degree from the Harvard Medical School, his only academic credential. From 1869 to 1872 he suffered from depression and illness but in 1872 accepted a position at Harvard, where he spent the remainder of his career, teaching physiology, psychology, and, eventually, philosophy. His reputation was established by *The Principles of Psychology* (1890). Later books include *The Will to Believe* (1897), *The Varieties of Religious Experience* (1902), *Pragmatism* (1907), *A Pluralistic Universe* (1909), and *The Meaning of Truth* (1909). In 1898 he began suffering from a weakened heart; he died in 1910.

from **Habit**

in *The Principles of Psychology* (1890)

WHEN WE LOOK at living creatures from an outward point of view, one of the first things that strike us is that they are bundles of habits. In wild animals, the usual round of daily behavior seems a necessity implanted at birth; in animals domesticated, and especially in man, it seems, to a great extent, to be the result of education. The habits to which there is an innate tendency are called instincts; some of those due to education would by most persons be called acts of reason. It thus appears that habit covers a very large part of life, and that one engaged in studying the objective manifestations of mind is bound at the very outset to define clearly just what its limits are.

The moment one tries to define what habit is, one is led to the fundamental properties of matter. The laws of Nature are nothing but the immutable habits which the different elementary sorts of matter follow in their actions and reactions upon each other. In the organic world, however, the habits are more variable than this. Even instincts vary from one individual to another of a kind; and are modified in the same individual . . . to suit the exigencies of the case. The habits of an elementary particle of matter cannot change (on the principles of the atomistic philosophy), because the particle is itself an unchangeable thing; but those of a compound mass of matter can change, because they are in the last instance due to the structure of the compound, and either outward forces or inward tensions can, from one hour to another, turn that structure into something different from what it was. That is, they can do so if the body be plastic enough to maintain its integrity, and be not disrupted when its structure yields. The change of structure here spoken of need not involve the outward shape; it may be invisible and molecular, as when a bar of iron becomes magnetic or crystalline through the action of certain outward causes, or India-rubber becomes friable, or plaster "sets." All these changes are rather slow; the material in question opposes a certain resistance to the modifying cause, which it takes time to over-come, but the gradual yielding whereof often saves the material from being disintegrated altogether. When the structure has yielded, the same inertia becomes a condition of its comparative perma-nence in the new form, and of the new habits the body then man-ifests. *Plasticity,* then, in the wide sense of the word, means the possession of a structure weak enough to yield to an influence, but strong enough not to yield all at once. Each relatively stable phase of equilibrium in such a structure is marked by what we may call a new set of habits. Organic matter, especially nervous tissue, seems endowed with a very extraordinary degree of plasticity of this sort; so that we may without hesitation lay down as our first proposition the following, that *the phenomena of habit in living beings are due to the plasticity of the organic materials of which their bodies are composed.* . . .

If habits are due to the plasticity of materials to outward agents, we can immediately see to what outward influences, if to any, the brain-matter is plastic. Not to mechanical pressures, not to thermal changes, not to any of the forces to which all the other organs of our body are exposed; for Nature has carefully shut up our brain and spinal cord in bony boxes, where no influences of this sort can get at them. She has floated them in fluid so that only the severest shocks can give them a concussion, and blanketed and wrapped them about in an altogether exceptional way. The only impres-sions that can be made upon them are through the blood, on the one hand, and through the sensory nerve-roots, on the other; and it is to the infinitely attenuated currents that pour in through these latter channels that the hemispherical cortex shows itself to be so peculiarly susceptible. The currents, once in, must find a way out. In getting out they leave their traces in the paths which they take.

The only thing they *can* do, in short, is to deepen old paths or to make new ones; and the whole plasticity of the brain sums itself up in two words when we call it an organ in which currents pouring in from the sense-organs make with extreme facility paths which do not easily disappear. For, of course, a simple habit, like every other nervous event—the habit of snuffling, for example, or of putting one's hands into one's pockets, or of biting one's nails—is, mechanically, nothing but a reflex discharge; and its anatomical substratum must be a path in the system. The most complex habits, as we shall presently see more fully, are, from the same point of view, nothing but *concatenated* discharges in the nerve-centres, due to the presence there of systems of reflex paths, so organized as to wake each other up successively—the impression produced by one muscular contraction serving as a stimulus to provoke the next, until a final impression inhibits the process and closes the chain. The only difficult mechanical problem is to explain the formation *de novo* of a simple reflex or path in a pre-existing nervous system., Here, as in so many other cases, it is only the *premier pas qui coûte.*[1] For the entire nervous system *is* nothing but a system of paths between a sensory *terminus a quo* and a muscular, glandular, or other *terminus ad quem*. A path once traversed by a nerve-current might be expected to follow the law of most of the paths we know, and to be scooped out and made more permeable than before, and this ought to be repeated with each new passage of the current. Whatever obstructions may have kept it at first from being a path should then, little by little, and more and more, be swept out of the way, until at last it might become a natural drainage-channel. This is what happens where either solids or liquids pass over a path; there seems no reason why it should not happen where the thing that passes is a mere wave of rearrangement in matter that does not displace itself, but merely changes chemically or turns itself round in place, or vibrates across the line.

"Habit a second nature! Habit is ten times nature," the Duke of Wellington is said to have exclaimed; and the degree to which this is true no one can probably appreciate as well as one who is a veteran soldier himself. The daily drill and the years of discipline end by fashioning a man completely over again, as to most of the possibilities of his conduct.

Riderless cavalry-horses, at many a battle, have been seen to come together and go through their customary evolutions at the sound of the bugle-call. Most trained domestic animals, dogs and oxen, and omnibus- and car-horses, seem to be machines almost pure and simple, undoubtingly, unhesitatingly doing from minute to minute the duties they have been taught, and giving no sign that the possibility of an alternative ever suggests itself to their mind. Men grown old in prison have asked to be readmitted after being once set free. In a railroad accident to a travelling menagerie in the United States some time in 1884, a tiger, whose cage had broken open, is said to have emerged, but presently crept back again, as if too much bewildered by his new responsibilities, so that he was without difficulty secured.

Habit is thus the enormous fly-wheel of society, its most precious conservative agent. It alone is what keeps us all within the bounds of ordinance, and saves the children of fortune from the envious uprisings of the poor. It alone prevents the hardest and most repulsive walks of life from being deserted by those brought up to tread therein. It keeps the fisherman and the deck-hand at sea through the winter; it holds the miner in his darkness, and nails the countryman to his log-cabin and his lonely farm through all the months of snow; it protects us from invasion by the natives of the desert and the frozen zone. It dooms us all to fight out the battle of life upon the lines of our nurture or our early choice, and to make the best of a pursuit that disagrees, because there is no other for which we are fitted, and it is too late to begin again. It keeps different social strata from mixing. Already at the age of twenty-five you see the professional mannerism settling down on the young commercial traveller, on the young doctor, on the young minister, on the young counsellor-at-law. You see the little lines of cleavage running through the character, the tricks of thought, the prejudices, the ways of the "shop," in a word, from which the man can by-and-by no more escape than his coat-sleeve can suddenly fall into a new set of folds. On the whole, it is best he should not escape. It is well for the world that in most of us, by the age of thirty, the character has set like plaster, and will never soften again.

If the period between twenty and thirty is the critical one in the formation of intellectual and professional habits, the period below twenty is more important still for the fixing of *personal* habits, properly so called, such as vocalization and pronunciation, gesture, motion, and address. Hardly ever is a language learned after twenty spoken without a foreign accent; hardly ever can a youth transferred to the society of his betters unlearn the nasality and other vices of speech bred in him by the associations of his growing years. Hardly ever, indeed, no matter how much money there be in his pocket, can he even learn to *dress* like a gentleman-born. The merchants offer their wares as eagerly to him as to the veriest "swell," but he simply *cannot* buy the right things. An invisible law, as strong as gravitation, keeps him within his orbit, arrayed this year as he was the last; and how his better-bred acquaintances contrive to get the things they wear will be for him a mystery till his dying day.

The great thing, then, in all education, is to *make our nervous system our ally instead of our enemy.* It is to fund and capitalize our acquisitions, and live at ease upon the interest of the fund. *For this we must make automatic and habitual, as early as possible, as many useful actions as we can,* and guard against the growing into ways that are likely to be disadvantageous to us, as we should guard against the plague. The more of the details of our daily life we can hand over to the effortless custody of automatism, the more our higher powers of mind will be set free for their own proper work. There is no more miserable human being than one in whom nothing is habitual but indecision, and for whom the lighting of every cigar, the drinking of every cup, the time of rising and going to bed every day, and the beginning of every bit of work, are subjects of express volitional deliberation. Full half the time of such a man goes to the deciding, or regretting, of matters which ought to be so ingrained in him as practically not to exist for his consciousness at all. If there be such daily duties not yet ingrained in any one of my readers, let him begin this very hour to set the matter right.

In Professor Bain's chapter on "The Moral Habits"[2] there are some admirable practical remarks laid down. Two great maxims emerge from his treatment. The first is that in the acquisition of a new habit, or the leaving off of an old one, we must take care to *launch ourselves with as strong and decided an initiative as possible.* Accumulate all the possible circumstances which shall re-enforce the right motives; put yourself assiduously in conditions that encourage the new way; make engagements incompatible with the old; take a public pledge, if the case allows; in short, envelop your resolution with every aid you know. This will give your new beginning such a momentum that the temptation to break down will not occur as soon as it otherwise might; and every day during which a breakdown is postponed adds to the chances of its not occurring at all.

The second maxim is: *Never suffer an exception to occur till the new habit is securely rooted in your life.* Each lapse is like the letting fall of a ball of string which one is carefully winding up; a single slip undoes more than a great many turns will wind again. *Continuity* of training is the great means of making the nervous system act infallibly right. . . .

A third maxim may be added to the preceding pair: *Seize the very first possible opportunity to act on every resolution you make, and on every emotional prompting you may experience in the direction of the habits you aspire to gain.* It is not in the moment of their forming, but in the moment of their producing *motor effects,* that resolves and aspirations communicate the new "set" to the brain. . . .

No matter how full a reservoir of *maxims* one may possess, and no matter how good one's *sentiments* may be, if one has not taken advantage of every concrete opportunity to *act,* one's character may remain entirely unaffected for the better. With mere good intentions, hell is proverbially paved. And this is an obvious consequence of the principles we have laid down. A "character," as J. S. Mill says, "is a completely fashioned will";[3] and a will, in the sense in which he means it, is an aggregate of tendencies to act in a firm and prompt and definite way upon all the principal emergencies of life. A tendency to act only becomes effectively ingrained in us in proportion to the uninterrupted frequency with which the actions actually occur, and the brain "grows" to their use. Every time a resolve or a fine glow of feeling evaporates without bearing practical fruit is worse than a chance lost; it works so as positively to hinder future resolutions and emotions from taking the normal path of discharge. There is no more contemptible type of human character than that of the nerveless sentimentalist and dreamer, who spends his life in a weltering sea of sensibility and emotion, but who never does a manly concrete deed. Rousseau, inflaming all the mothers of France, by his eloquence, to follow Nature and nurse their babies themselves, while he sends his own children to the foundling hospital, is the classical example of what I mean. But every one of us in his measure, whenever, after glowing for an abstractly formulated Good, he practically ignores some actual case, among the squalid "other particulars" of which that same Good lurks disguised, treads straight on Rousseau's path. All Goods are disguised by the vulgarity of their concomitants, in this work-a-day world; but woe to him who can only recognize them when he thinks them in their pure and abstract form! The habit of excessive novel-reading and theatre-going will produce true monsters in this line. The weeping of a Russian lady over the fictitious personages in the play, while her coachman is freezing to death on his seat outside, is the sort of thing that everywhere happens on a less glaring scale. Even the habit of excessive indulgence in music, for those who are neither performers themselves nor musically gifted enough to take it in a purely intellectual way, has probably a relaxing effect upon the character. One becomes filled with emotions which habitually pass without prompting to any deed, and so the inertly sentimental condition is kept up. The remedy would be, never to suffer one's self to have an emotion at a concert, without expressing it afterwards in *some* active way. Let the expression be the least thing in the world—speaking genially to one's aunt, or giving up one's seat in a horse-car, if nothing more heroic offers— but let it not fail to take place.

These latter cases make us aware that it is not simply *particular lines* of discharge, but also *general forms* of discharge, that seem to be grooved out by habit in the brain. Just as, if we let our emotions evaporate, they get into a way of evaporating; so there is reason to suppose that if we often flinch from making an effort, before we know it the effort-making capacity will be gone; and that, if we suffer the wandering of our attention, presently it will wander all the time. Attention and effort are . . . but two names for the same psychic fact. To what brain-processes they correspond we do not know. The strongest reason for believing that they do depend on brain-processes at all, and are not pure acts of the spirit, is just this fact, that they seem in some degree subject to the law of habit, which is a material law. As a final practical maxim, relative to these habits of the will, we may, then, offer something like this: *Keep the faculty of effort alive in you by a little gratuitous exercise every day.* That is, be systematically ascetic or heroic in little unnecessary points, do every day or two something for no other reason than that you would rather not do it, so that when the hour of dire need draws nigh, it may find you not unnerved and untrained to stand the test. Asceticism of this sort is like the insurance which a man pays on his house and goods. The tax does him no good at the time, and possibly may never bring him a return. But if the fire *does* come, his having paid it will be his salvation from ruin. So with the man who has daily inured himself to habits of concentrated attention, energetic volition, and self-denial in unnecessary things. He will stand like a tower when everything rocks around him, and when his softer fellow-mortals are winnowed like chaff in the blast.

The physiological study of mental conditions is thus the most powerful ally of hortatory ethics. The hell to be endured hereafter, of which theology tells, is no worse than the hell we make for ourselves in this world by habitually fashioning our characters in the wrong way. Could the young but realize how soon they will become mere walking bundles of habits, they would give more heed to their conduct while in the plastic state. We are spinning our own fates, good or evil, and never to be undone. Every smallest stroke of virtue or of vice leaves its never so little scar. The drunken Rip Van Winkle, in Jefferson's play,[4] excuses himself for every fresh dereliction by saying, "I won't count this time!" Well! he may not count it, and a kind Heaven may not count it; but it is being counted none the less. Down among his nerve-cells and fibres the molecules are counting it, registering and storing it up to be used against him when the next temptation comes. Nothing we ever do is, in strict scientific literalness, wiped out. Of course, this has its good side as well as its bad one. As we become permanent drunkards by so many separate drinks, so we become saints in the moral, and authorities and experts in the practical and scientific spheres, by so many separate acts and hours of work. Let no youth have any anxiety about the upshot of his education, whatever the line of it may be. If he keep faithfully busy each hour of the working-day, he may safely leave the final result to itself. He can with perfect certainty count on waking up some fine morning, to find himself one of the competent ones of his generation, in whatever pursuit he may have singled out. Silently, between all the details of his business, the *power of judging* in all that class of matter will have built itself up within him as a possession that will never pass away. Young people should know this truth in advance. The ignorance of it has probably engendered more discouragement and faint-heartedness in youths embarking on arduous careers than all other causes put together.

The Will to Believe

(1896)

IN THE RECENTLY PUBLISHED Life by Leslie Stephen of his brother, Fitz-James,[1] there is an account of a school to which the latter went when he was a boy. The teacher, a certain Mr. Guest, used to converse with his pupils in this wise: "Gurney, what is the difference between justification and sanctification?—Stephen, prove the omnipotence of God!" etc. In the midst of our Harvard freethinking and indifference we are prone to imagine that here at your good old orthodox College conversation continues to be somewhat upon this order; and to show you that we at Harvard have not lost all interest in these vital subjects, I have brought with me to-night something like a sermon on justification by faith to read to you,—I mean an essay in justification *of* faith, a defence of our right to adopt a believing attitude in religious matters, in spite of the fact that our merely logical intellect may not have been co-erced. "The Will to Believe," accordingly, is the title of my paper.

I have long defended to my own students the lawfulness of voluntarily adopted faith; but as soon as they have got well imbued with the logical spirit, they have as a rule refused to admit my contention to be lawful philosophically, even though in point of fact they were personally all the time chock-full of some faith or other themselves. I am all the while, however, so profoundly convinced that my own position is correct, that your invitation has seemed to me a good occasion to make my statements more clear. Perhaps your minds will be more open than those with which I have hitherto had to deal. I will be as little technical as I can, though I must begin by setting up some technical distinctions that will help us in the end.

I

Let us give the name of *hypothesis* to anything that may be proposed to our belief; and just as the electricians speak of live and dead wires, let us speak of any hypothesis as either *live* or *dead*. A live hypothesis is one which appeals as a real possibility to him to whom it is proposed. If I ask you to believe in the Mahdi, the notion makes no electric connection with your nature,—it refuses to scintillate with any credibility at all. As an hypothesis it is completely dead. To an Arab, however (even if he be not one of the Mahdi's followers), the hypothesis is among the mind's possibilities: it is alive. This shows that deadness and liveness in an hypothesis are not intrinsic properties, but relations to the individual thinker. They are measured by his willingness to act. The maximum of liveness in an hypothesis means willingness to act irrevocably. Practically, that means belief; but there is some believing tendency wherever there is willingness to act at all.

Next, let us call the decision between two hypotheses an *option*. Options may be of several kinds. They may be—1, *living* or *dead;* 2, *forced* or *avoidable;* 3, *momentous* or *trivial;* and for our purposes we may call an option a *genuine* option when it is of the forced, living, and momentous kind.

1. A living option is one in which both hypotheses are live ones. If I say to you: "Be a theosophist or be a Mohammedan," it is probably a dead option, because for you neither hypothesis is likely to be alive. But if I say: "Be an agnostic or be a Christian," it is otherwise: trained as you are, each hypothesis makes some appeal, however small, to your belief.

2. Next, if I say to you: "Choose between going out with your umbrella or without it," I do not offer you a genuine option, for it is not forced. You can easily avoid it by not going out at all. Similarly, if I say, "Either love me or hate me," "Either call my theory true or call it false," your option is avoidable. You may remain indifferent to me, neither loving nor hating, and you may decline to offer any judgment as to my theory. But if I say, "Either accept this

truth or go without it," I put on you a forced option, for there is no standing place outside of the alternative. Every dilemma based on a complete logical disjunction, with no possibility of not choosing, is an option of this forced kind.

3. Finally, if I were Dr. Nansen and proposed to you to join my North Pole expedition,[2] your option would be momentous; for this would probably be your only similar opportunity, and your choice now would either exclude you from the North Pole sort of immortality altogether or put at least the chance of it into your hands. He who refuses to embrace a unique opportunity loses the prize as surely as if he tried and failed. *Per contra,* the option is trivial when the opportunity is not unique, when the stake is insignificant, or when the decision is reversible if it later prove unwise. Such trivial options abound in the scientific life. A chemist finds an hypothesis live enough to spend a year in its verification: he believes in it to that extent. But if his experiments prove inconclusive either way, he is quit for his loss of time, no vital harm being done.

It will facilitate our discussion if we keep all these distinctions well in mind.

II

The next matter to consider is the actual psychology of human opinion. When we look at certain facts, it seems as if our passional and volitional nature lay at the root of all our convictions. When we look at others, it seems as if they could do nothing when the intellect had once said its say. Let us take the latter facts up first.

Does it not seem preposterous on the very face of it to talk of our opinions being modifiable at will? Can our will either help or hinder our intellect in its perceptions of truth? Can we, by just willing it, believe that Abraham Lincoln's existence is a myth, and that the portraits of him in McClure's Magazine are all of some one else? Can we, by any effort of our will, or by any strength of wish that it were true, believe ourselves well and about when we are roaring with rheumatism in bed, or feel certain that the sum of the two one-dollar bills in our pocket must be a hundred dollars? We can *say* any of these things, but we are absolutely impotent to believe them; and of just such things is the whole fabric of the truths that we do believe in made up,—matters of fact, immediate or remote, as Hume said, and relations between ideas, which are either there or not there for us if we see them so, and which if not there cannot be put there by any action of our own.[3]

In Pascal's Thoughts[4] there is a celebrated passage known in literature as Pascal's wager. In it he tries to force us into Christianity by reasoning as if our concern with truth resembled our concern with the stakes in a game of chance. Translated freely his words are these: You must either believe or not believe that God is—which will you do? Your human reason cannot say. A game is going on between you and the nature of things which at the day of judgment will bring out either heads or tails. Weigh what your gains and your losses would be if you should stake all you have on heads, or God's existence: if you win in such case, you gain eternal beatitude; if you lose, you lose nothing at all. If there were an infinity of chances, and only one for God in this wager, still you ought to stake your all on God; for though you surely risk a finite loss by this procedure, any finite loss is reasonable, even a certain one is reasonable, if there is but the possibility of infinite gain. Go, then, and take holy water, and have masses said; belief will come and stupefy your scruples,—*Cela vous fera croire et vous abêtira.*[5] Why should you not? At bottom, what have you to lose?

You probably feel that when religious faith expresses itself thus, in the language of the gaming-table, it is put to its last trumps. Surely Pascal's own personal belief in masses and holy water had far other springs; and this celebrated page of his is but an argument for others, a last desperate snatch at a weapon against the hardness of the unbelieving heart. We feel that a faith in masses and holy water adopted wilfully after such a mechanical calculation would lack the inner soul of faith's reality; and if we were ourselves in the place of the Deity, we should probably take particular pleasure in cutting off believers of this pattern from their infinite reward. It is evident that unless there be some pre-existing tendency to believe in masses, and holy water, the option offered to the will by Pascal is not a living option. Certainly no Turk ever took to masses and holy water on its account; and even to us Protestants these means of salvation seem such foregone impossibilities that Pascal's logic, invoked for them specifically, leaves us unmoved. As well might the Mahdi write to us, saying, "I am the Expected One whom God has created in his effulgence. You shall be infinitely happy if you confess me; otherwise you shall be cut off from the light of the sun. Weigh, then, your infinite gain if I am genuine against your finite sacrifice if I am not!" His logic would be that of Pascal; but he would vainly use it on us, for the hypothesis he offers us is dead. No tendency to act on it exists in us to any degree.

The talk of believing by our volition seems, then, from one point of view, simply silly. From another point of view it is worse than silly, it is vile. When one turns to the magnificent edifice of the physical sciences, and sees how it was reared; what thousands of disinterested moral lives of men lie buried in its mere foundations; what patience and postponement, what choking down of preference, what submission to the icy laws of outer fact are wrought into its very stones and mortar; how absolutely impersonal it stands in its vast augustness,—then how besotted and contemptible seems every little sentimentalist who comes blowing his voluntary smoke-wreaths, and pretending to decide things from out of his private dream! Can we wonder if those bred in the rugged and manly school of science should feel like spewing such subjectivism out of their mouths? The whole system of loyalties which grow up in the schools of science go dead against its toleration; so that it is only natural that those who have caught the scientific fever should pass over to the opposite extreme, and write sometimes as if the incorruptibly truthful intellect ought positively to prefer bitterness and unacceptableness to the heart in its cup.

> It fortifies my soul to know
> That, though I perish, Truth is so——[6]

sings Clough, while Huxley exclaims: "My only consolation lies
in the reflection that, however bad our posterity may become, so
far as they hold by the plain rule of not pretending to believe what
they have no reason to believe, because it may be to their advantage so to pretend [the word "pretend" is surely here redundant],
they will not have reached the lowest depth of immorality."[7] And
that delicious *enfant terrible* Clifford writes: "Belief is desecrated
when given to unproved and unquestioned statements for the solace and private pleasure of the believer. . . . Whoso would deserve well of his fellows in this matter will guard the purity of·his
belief with a very fanaticism of jealous care, lest at any time it
should rest on an unworthy object, and catch a stain which can
never be wiped away. . . . If [a] belief has been accepted on insufficient evidence [even though the belief be true, as Clifford on the
same page explains] the pleasure is a stolen one. . . . It is sinful because it is stolen in defiance of our duty to mankind. That duty is
to guard ourselves from such beliefs as from a pestilence which
may shortly master our own body and then spread to the rest of
the town. . . . It is wrong always, everywhere, and for every one,
to believe anything upon insufficient evidence."[8]

III

All this strikes one as healthy, even when expressed, as by Clifford,
with somewhat too much of robustious pathos in the voice. Free-
will and simple wishing do seem, in the matter of our credences,
to be only fifth wheels to the coach. Yet if any one should thereupon assume that intellectual insight is what remains after wish
and will and sentimental preference have taken wing, or that pure
reason is what then settles our opinions, he would fly quite as directly in the teeth of the facts.

It is only our already dead hypotheses that our willing nature is unable to bring to life again. But what has made them dead for us is for the most part a previous action of our willing nature of an antagonistic kind. When I say "willing nature," I do not mean only such deliberate volitions as may have set up habits of belief that we cannot now escape from,—I mean all such factors of belief as fear and hope, prejudice and passion, imitation and partisanship, the circumpressure of our caste and set. As a matter of fact we find ourselves believing, we hardly know how or why. Mr. Balfour gives the name of "authority" to all those influences, born of the intellectual climate, that make hypotheses possible or impossible for us, alive or dead.[9] Here in this room, we all of us believe in molecules and the conservation of energy, in democracy and necessary progress, in Protestant Christianity and the duty of fighting for "the doctrine of the immortal Monroe," all for no reasons worthy of the name. We see into these matters with no more inner clearness, and probably with much less, than any disbeliever in them might possess. His unconventionality would probably have some grounds to show for its conclusions; but for us, not insight, but the *prestige* of the opinions, is what makes the spark shoot from them and light up our sleeping magazines of faith. Our reason is quite satisfied, in nine hundred and ninety-nine cases out of every thousand of us, if it can find a few arguments that will do to recite in case our credulity is criticised by some one else. Our faith is faith in some one else's faith, and in the greatest matters this is most the case. Our belief in truth itself, for instance, that there is a truth, and that our minds and it are made for each other,—what is it but a passionate affirmation of desire, in which our social system backs us up? We want to have a truth; we want to believe that our experiments and studies and discussions must put us in a continually better and better position towards it; and on this line we agree to fight out our thinking lives. But if a pyrrhonistic sceptic asks us *how we know* all this, can our logic find a reply? No! certainly it cannot. It is just one volition against another,—we willing to go in for life upon a trust or assumption which he, for his part, does not care to make.[10]

As a rule we disbelieve all facts and theories for which we have no use. Clifford's cosmic emotions find no use for Christian feelings. Huxley belabors the bishops because there is no use for sacerdotalism in his scheme of life. Newman, on the contrary, goes over to Romanism, and finds all sorts of reasons good for staying there, because a priestly system is for him an organic need and delight.[11] Why do so few "scientists" even look at the evidence for telepathy, so called? Because they think, as a leading biologist, now dead, once said to me, that even if such a thing were true, scientists ought to band together to keep it suppressed and concealed. It would undo the uniformity of Nature and all sorts of other things without which scientists cannot carry on their pursuits. But if this very man had been shown something which as a scientist he might *do* with telepathy, he might not only have examined the evidence, but even have found it good enough. This very law which the logicians would impose upon us—if I may give the name of logicians to those who would rule out our willing nature here—is based on nothing but their own natural wish to exclude all elements for which they, in their professional quality of logicians, can find no use.

Evidently, then, our non-intellectual nature does influence our convictions. There are passional tendencies and volitions which run before and others which come after belief, and it is only the latter that are too late for the fair; and they are not too late when the previous passional work has been already in their own direction. Pascal's argument, instead of being powerless, then seems a regular clincher, and is the last stroke needed to make our faith in masses and holy water complete. The state of things is evidently far from simple; and pure insight and logic, whatever they might do ideally, are not the only things that really do produce our creeds.

Ad hominem could give the key to questioning their conclusions and looking for omission of other data. Also their historical record makes them

IV

Our next duty, having recognized this mixed-up state of affairs, is to ask whether it be simply reprehensible and pathological, or

untrustworthy "We were stupid to think that, but the latest data overturns it, so now we're smart."

whether, on the contrary, we must treat it as a normal element in making up our minds. The thesis I defend is, briefly stated, this: *Our passional nature not only lawfully may, but must, decide an option between propositions, whenever it is a genuine option that cannot by its nature be decided on intellectual grounds; for to say, under such circumstances, "Do not decide, but leave the question open," is itself a passional decision,—just like deciding yes or no,—and is attended with the same risk of losing the truth.* The thesis thus abstractly expressed will, I trust, soon become quite clear. But I must first indulge in a bit more of preliminary work.

V

It will be observed that for the purposes of this discussion we are on "dogmatic" ground,—ground, I mean, which leaves systematic philosophical scepticism altogether out of account. The postulate that there is truth, and that it is the destiny of our minds to attain it, we are deliberately resolving to make, though the sceptic will not make it. We part company with him, therefore, absolutely, at this point. But the faith that truth exists, and that our minds can find it, may be held in two ways. We may talk of the *empiricist* way and of the *absolutist* way of believing in truth. The absolutists in this matter say that we not only can attain to knowing truth, but we can *know when* we have attained to knowing it; while the empiricists think that although we may attain it, we cannot infallibly know when. To *know* is one thing, and to know for certain *that* we know is another. One may hold to the first being possible without the second; hence the empiricists and the absolutists, although neither of them is a sceptic in the usual philosophic sense of the term, show very different degrees of dogmatism in their lives.

If we look at the history of opinions, we see that the empiricist tendency has largely prevailed in science, while in philosophy the absolutist tendency has had everything its own way. The characteristic sort of happiness, indeed, which philosophies yield has mainly consisted in the conviction felt by each successive school or system that by it bottom-certitude had been attained. "Other philosophies are collections of opinions, mostly false; *my* philoso- phy gives standing-ground forever,"—who does not recognize in this the key-note of every system worthy of the name? A system, to be a system at all, must come as a *closed* system, reversible in this or that detail, perchance, but in its essential features never!

Scholastic orthodoxy, to which one must always go when one wishes to find perfectly clear statement, has beautifully elaborated this absolutist conviction in a doctrine which it calls that of "ob- jective evidence." If, for example, I am unable to doubt that I now exist before you, that two is less than three, or that if all men are mortal then I am mortal too, it is because these things illumine my intellect irresistibly. The final ground of this objective evidence possessed by certain propositions is the *adæquatio intellectûs nostri cum rê.*[12] The certitude it brings involves an *aptitudinem ad ex- torquendum certum assensum*[13] on the part of the truth envisaged, and on the side of the subject a *quietem in cognitione,*[14] when once the object is mentally received, that leaves no possibility of doubt behind; and in the whole transaction nothing operates but the *en- titas ipsa*[15] of the object and the *entitas ipsa* of the mind. We slouchy modern thinkers dislike to talk in Latin,—indeed, we dis- like to talk in set terms at all; but at bottom our own state of mind is very much like this whenever we uncritically abandon ourselves: You believe in objective evidence, and I do. Of some things we feel that we are certain: we know, and we know that we do know. There is something that gives a click inside of us, a bell that strikes twelve, when the hands of our mental clock have swept the dial and meet over the meridian hour. The greatest empiricists among us are only empiricists on reflection: when left to their instincts, they dogmatize like infallible popes. When the Cliffords tell us how sinful it is to be Christians on such "insufficient evidence," insufficiency is really the last thing they have in mind. For them the evidence is absolutely sufficient, only it makes the other way. They believe so completely in an anti-Christian order of the universe that there is no living option: Christianity is a dead hypothesis from the start.

VI

But now, since we are all such absolutists by instinct, what in our quality of students of philosophy ought we to do about the fact? Shall we espouse and indorse it? Or shall we treat it as a weakness of our nature from which we must free ourselves, if we can?

I sincerely believe that the latter course is the only one we can follow as reflective men. Objective evidence and certitude are doubtless very fine ideals to play with, but where on this moonlit and dream-visited planet are they found? I am, therefore, myself a complete empiricist so far as my theory of human knowledge goes. I live, to be sure, by the practical faith that we must go on experiencing and thinking over our experience, for only thus can our opinions grow more true; but to hold any one of them—I absolutely do not care which—as if it never could be reinterpretable or corrigible, I believe to be a tremendously mistaken attitude, and I think that the whole history of philosophy will bear me out. There is but one indefectibly certain truth, and that is the truth that pyrrhonistic scepticism itself leaves standing,—the truth that the present phenomenon of consciousness exists. That, however, is the bare starting-point of knowledge, the mere admission of a stuff to be philosophized about. The various philosophies are but so many attempts at expressing what this stuff really is. And if we repair to our libraries what disagreement do we discover! Where is a certainly true answer found? Apart from abstract propositions of comparison (such as two and two are the same as four), propositions which tell us nothing by themselves about concrete reality, we find no proposition ever regarded by any one as evidently certain that has not either been called a falsehood, or at least had its truth sincerely questioned by some one else. The transcending of the axioms of geometry, not in play but in earnest, by certain of our contemporaries (as Zöllner and Charles H. Hinton),[16] and the rejection of the whole Aristotelian logic by the Hegelians, are striking instances in point.

No concrete test of what is really true has ever been agreed upon. Some make the criterion external to the moment of perception, putting it either in revelation, the *consensus gentium*,[17] the instincts of the heart, or the systematized experience of the race. Others make the perceptive moment its own test,—Descartes, for instance, with his clear and distinct ideas guaranteed by the veracity of God; Reid with his "common-sense"; and Kant with his forms of synthetic judgment *a priori*. The inconceivability of the opposite; the capacity to be verified by sense; the possession of complete organic unity or self-relation, realized when a thing is its own other,—are standards which, in turn, have been used. The much lauded objective evidence is never triumphantly there; it is a mere aspiration or *Grenzbegriff*,[18] marking the infinitely remote ideal of our thinking life. To claim that certain truths now possess it, is simply to say that when you think them true and they *are* true, then their evidence is objective, otherwise it is not. But practically one's conviction that the evidence one goes by is of the real objective brand, is only one more subjective opinion added to the lot. For what a contradictory array of opinions have objective evidence and absolute certitude been claimed! The world is rational through and through,—its existence is an ultimate brute fact; there is a personal God,—a personal God is inconceivable; there is an extra-mental physical world immediately known,—the mind can only know its own ideas; a moral imperative exists,— obligation is only the resultant of desires; a permanent spiritual principle is in every one,—there are only shifting states of mind; there is an endless chain of causes,—there is an absolute first cause; an eternal necessity,—a freedom; a purpose,—no purpose; a primal One,—a primal Many; a universal continuity,—an essential discontinuity in things; an infinity,—no infinity. There is this,— there is that; there is indeed nothing which some one has not thought absolutely true, while his neighbor deemed it absolutely false; and not an absolutist among them seems ever to have considered that the trouble may all the time be essential, and that the intellect, even with truth directly in its grasp, may have no infallible signal for knowing whether it be truth or no. When, indeed, one remembers that the most striking practical application to life of the doctrine of objective certitude has been the conscientious labors of the Holy Office of the Inquisition, one feels less tempted than ever to lend the doctrine a respectful ear.

But please observe, now, that when as empiricists we give up the doctrine of objective certitude, we do not thereby give up the quest or hope of truth itself. We still pin our faith on its existence, and still believe that we gain an ever better position towards it by systematically continuing to roll up experiences and think. Our great difference from the scholastic lies in the way we face. The strength of his system lies in the principles, the origin, the *terminus a quo* of his thought; for us the strength is in the outcome, the upshot, the *terminus ad quem*. Not where it comes from but what it leads to is to decide. It matters not to an empiricist from what quarter an hypothesis may come to him: he may have acquired it by fair means or by foul; passion may have whispered or accident suggested it; but if the total drift of thinking continues to confirm it, that is what he means by its being true.

VII

One more point, small but important, and our preliminaries are done. There are two ways of looking at our duty in the matter of opinion,—ways entirely different, and yet ways about whose difference the theory of knowledge seems hitherto to have shown very little concern. We must *know the truth;* and *we must avoid error,*—these are our first and great commandments as would-be knowers; but they are not two ways of stating an identical commandment, they are two separable laws. Although it may indeed happen that when we believe the truth *A,* we escape as an incidental consequence from believing the falsehood *B,* it hardly ever happens that by merely disbelieving B we necessarily believe A. We may in escaping B fall into believing other falsehoods, C or D, just as bad as B; or we may escape B by not believing anything at all, not even A.

Believe truth! Shun error!—these, we see, are two materially different laws; and by choosing between them we may end by coloring differently our whole intellectual life. We may regard the chase for truth as paramount, and the avoidance of error as secondary; or we may, on the other hand, treat the avoidance of error as more imperative, and let truth take its chance. Clifford, in the instructive passage which I have quoted, exhorts us to the latter course. Believe nothing, he tells us, keep your mind in suspense forever, rather than by closing it on insufficient evidence incur the awful risk of believing lies. You, on the other hand, may think that the risk of being in error is a very small matter when compared with the blessings of real knowledge, and be ready to be duped many times in your investigation rather than postpone indefinitely the chance of guessing true. I myself find it impossible to go with Clifford. We must remember that these feelings of our duty about either truth or error are in any case only expressions of our passional life. Biologically considered, our minds are as ready to grind out falsehood as veracity, and he who says, "Better go without belief forever than believe a lie!" merely shows his own preponderant private horror of becoming a dupe. He may be critical of many of his desires and fears, but this fear he slavishly obeys. He cannot imagine any one questioning its binding force. For my own part, I have also a horror of being duped; but I can believe that worse things than being duped may happen to a man in this world: so Clifford's exhortation has to my ears a thoroughly fantastic sound. It is like a general informing his soldiers that it is better to keep out of battle forever than to risk a single wound. Not so are victories either over enemies or over nature gained. Our errors are surely not such awfully solemn things. In a world where we are so certain to incur them in spite of all our caution, a certain lightness of heart seems healthier than this excessive nervousness on their behalf. At any rate, it seems the fittest thing for the empiricist philosopher.

VIII

And now, after all this introduction, let us go straight at our question. I have said, and now repeat it, that not only as a matter of fact do we find our passional nature influencing us in our opinions, but that there are some options between opinions in which this influence must be regarded both as an inevitable and as a lawful determinant of our choice.

I fear here that some of you, my hearers, will begin to scent danger, and lend an inhospitable ear. Two first steps of passion you have indeed had to admit as necessary,—we must think so as to avoid dupery, and we must think so as to gain truth; but the surest path to those ideal consummations, you will probably consider, is from now onwards to take no further passional step.

Well, of course, I agree as far as the facts will allow. Wherever the option between losing truth and gaining it is not momentous, we can throw the chance of *gaining truth* away, and at any rate save ourselves from any chance of *believing falsehood*, by not making up our minds at all till objective evidence has come. In scientific questions, this is almost always the case; and even in human affairs in general, the need of acting is seldom so urgent that a false belief to act on is better than no belief at all. Law courts, indeed, have to decide on the best evidence attainable for the moment, because a judge's duty is to make law as well as to ascertain it, and (as a learned judge once said to me) few cases are worth spending much time over: the great thing is to have them decided on *any* acceptable principle, and got out of the way. But in our dealings with objective nature we obviously are recorders, not makers, of the truth; and decisions for the mere sake of deciding promptly and getting on to the next business would be wholly out of place. Throughout the breadth of physical nature facts are what they are quite independently of us, and seldom is there any such hurry about them that the risks of being duped by believing a premature theory need be faced. The questions here are always trivial options, the hypotheses are hardly living (at any rate not living for us spectators), the choice between believing truth or falsehood is seldom forced. The attitude of sceptical balance is therefore the absolutely wise one if we would escape mistakes. What difference, indeed, does it make to most of us whether we have or have not a theory of the Röntgen rays, whether we believe or not in mind-stuff, or have a conviction about the causality of conscious states? It makes no difference. Such options are not forced on us. On every account it is better not to make them, but still keep weighing reasons *pro et contra* with an indifferent hand.

I speak, of course, here of the purely judging mind. For purposes of discovery such indifference is to be less highly recommended, and science would be far less advanced than she is if the passionate desires of individuals to get their own faiths confirmed had been kept out of the game. See for example the sagacity which Spencer and Weismann now display.[19] On the other hand, if you want an absolute duffer in an investigation, you must, after all, take the man who has no interest whatever in its results: he is the warranted incapable, the positive fool. The most useful investigator, because the most sensitive observer, is always he whose eager interest in one side of the question is balanced by an equally keen nervousness lest he become deceived.[20] Science has organized this nervousness into a regular *technique,* her so-called method of verification; and she has fallen so deeply in love with the method that one may even say she has ceased to care for truth by itself at all. It is only truth as technically verified that interests her. The truth of truths might come in merely affirmative form, and she would decline to touch it. Such truth as that, she might repeat with Clifford, would be stolen in defiance of her duty to mankind. Human passions, however, are stronger than technical rules. "Le cœur a ses raisons," as Pascal says, "que la raison ne connaît pas;"[21] and however indifferent to all but the bare rules of the game the umpire, the abstract intellect, may be, the concrete play-

ers who furnish him the materials to judge of are usually, each one
of them, in love with some pet "live hypothesis" of his own. Let
us agree, however, that wherever there is no forced option, the
dispassionately judicial intellect with no pet hypothesis, saving us,
as it does, from dupery at any rate, ought to be our ideal.

The question next arises: Are there not somewhere forced options in our speculative questions, and can we (as men who may be
interested at least as much in positively gaining truth as in merely
escaping dupery) always wait with impunity till the coercive evidence shall have arrived? It seems *a priori* improbable that the truth
should be so nicely adjusted to our needs and powers as that. In the
great boarding-house of nature, the cakes and the butter and the
syrup seldom come out so even and leave the plates so clean. Indeed, we should view them with scientific suspicion if they did.

IX

Moral questions immediately present themselves as questions whose
solution cannot wait for sensible proof. A moral question is a question not of what sensibly exists, but of what is good, or would be
good if it did exist. Science can tell us what exists; but to compare
the *worths,* both of what exists and of what does not exist we must
consult not science, but what Pascal calls our heart. Science herself
consults her heart when she lays it down that the infinite ascertainment of fact and correction of false belief are the supreme
goods for man. Challenge the statement, and science can only repeat it oracularly, or else prove it by showing that such ascertainment and correction bring man all sorts of other goods which
man's heart in turn declares. The question of having moral beliefs
at all or not having them is decided by our will. Are our moral
preferences true or false, or are they only odd biological phenomena, making things good or bad for *us,* but in themselves indifferent? How can your pure intellect decide? If your heart does not
want a world of moral reality, your head will assuredly never make
you believe in one. Mephistophelian scepticism, indeed, will

satisfy the head's play-instincts much better than any rigorous idealism can. Some men (even at the student age) are so naturally cool-hearted that the moralistic hypothesis never has for them any pungent life, and in their supercilious presence the hot young moralist always feels strangely ill at ease. The appearance of knowingness is on their side, of *naïveté* and gullibility on his. Yet, in the inarticulate heart of him, he clings to it that he is not a dupe, and that there is a realm in which (as Emerson says)[22] all their wit and intellectual superiority is no better than the cunning of a fox. Moral scepticism can no more be refuted or proved by logic than intellectual scepticism can. When we stick to it that there *is* truth (be it of either kind), we do so with our whole nature, and resolve to stand or fall by the results. The sceptic with his whole nature adopts the doubting attitude; but which of us is the wiser, Omniscience only knows.

Turn now from these wide questions of good to a certain class of questions of fact, questions concerning personal relations, states of mind between one man and another. *Do you like me or not?*—for example. Whether you do or not depends, in countless instances, on whether I meet you half-way, am willing to assume that you must like me, and show you trust and expectation. The previous faith on my part in your liking's existence is in such cases what makes your liking come. But if I stand aloof, and refuse to budge an inch until I have objective evidence, until you shall have done something apt, as the absolutists say, *ad extorquendum assensum meum,*[23] ten to one your liking never comes. How many women's hearts are vanquished by the mere sanguine insistence of some man that they *must* love him! He will not consent to the hypothesis that they cannot. The desire for a certain kind of truth here brings about that special truth's existence; and so it is in innumerable cases of other sorts. Who gains promotions, boons, appointments, but the man in whose life they are seen to play the part of live hypotheses, who discounts them, sacrifices other things for their sake before they have come, and takes risks for them in advance? His faith acts on the powers above him as a claim, and creates its own verification.

A social organism of any sort whatever, large or small, is what it is because each member proceeds to his own duty with a trust that the other members will simultaneously do theirs. Wherever a desired result is achieved by the co-operation of many independent persons, its existence as a fact is a pure consequence of the precursive faith in one another of those immediately concerned. A government, an army, a commercial system, a ship, a college, an athletic team, all exist on this condition, without which not only is nothing achieved, but nothing is even attempted. A whole train of passengers (individually brave enough) will be looted by a few highwaymen, simply because the latter can count on one another, while each passenger fears that if he makes a movement of resistance, he will be shot before any one else backs him up. If we believed that the whole car-full would rise at once with us, we should each severally rise, and train-robbing would never even be attempted. There are, then, cases where a fact cannot come at all unless a preliminary faith exists in its coming. *And where faith in a fact can help create the fact,* that would be an insane logic which should say that faith running ahead of scientific evidence is the "lowest kind of immorality" into which a thinking being can fall. Yet such is the logic by which our scientific absolutists pretend to regulate our lives!

X

In truths dependent on our personal action, then, faith based on desire is certainly a lawful and possibly an indispensable thing.

But now, it will be said, these are all childish human cases, and have nothing to do with great cosmical matters, like the question of religious faith. Let us then pass on to that. Religions differ so much in their accidents that in discussing the religious question we must make it very generic and broad. What then do we now mean by the religious hypothesis? Science says things are; morality says some things are better than other things; and religion says essentially two things.

First, she says that the best things are the more eternal things, the overlapping things, the things in the universe that throw the last stone, so to speak, and say the final word. "Perfection is eternal,"[24]—this phrase of Charles Secrétan seems a good way of putting this first affirmation of religion, an affirmation which obviously cannot yet be verified scientifically at all.

The second affirmation of religion is that we are better off even now if we believe her first affirmation to be true.

Now, let us consider what the logical elements of this situation are *in case the religious hypothesis in both its branches be really true.* (Of course, we must admit that possibility at the outset. If we are to discuss the question at all, it must involve a living option. If for any of you religion be a hypothesis that cannot, by any living possibility be true, then you need go no farther. I speak to the "saving remnant" alone.) So proceeding, we see, first, that religion offers itself as a *momentous* option. We are supposed to gain, even now, by our belief, and to lose by our non-belief, a certain vital good. Secondly, religion is a *forced* option, so far as that good goes. We cannot escape the issue by remaining sceptical and waiting for more light, because, although we do avoid error in that way *if religion be untrue,* we lose the good, *if it be true,* just as certainly as if we positively chose to disbelieve. It is as if a man should hesitate indefinitely to ask a certain woman to marry him because he was not perfectly sure that she would prove an angel after he brought her home. Would he not cut himself off from that particular angel-possibility as decisively as if he went and married some one else? Scepticism, then, is not avoidance of option; it is option of a certain particular kind of risk. *Better risk loss of truth than chance of error,*—that is your faith-vetoer's exact position. He is actively playing his stake as much as the believer is; he is backing the field against the religious hypothesis, just as the believer is backing the religious hypothesis against the field. To preach scepticism to us as

a duty until "sufficient evidence" for religion be found, is tantamount therefore to telling us, when in presence of the religious
hypothesis, that to yield to our fear of its being error is wiser and
better than to yield to our hope that it may be true. It is not intellect against all passions, then; it is only intellect with one passion
laying down its law. And by what, forsooth, is the supreme wisdom of this passion warranted? Dupery for dupery, what proof is
there that dupery through hope is so much worse than dupery
through fear? I, for one, can see no proof; and I simply refuse obedience to the scientist's command to imitate his kind of option, in
a case where my own stake is important enough to give me the
right to choose my own form of risk. If religion be true and the
evidence for it be still insufficient, I do not wish, by putting your
extinguisher upon my nature (which feels to me as if it had after
all some business in this matter), to forfeit my sole chance in life
of getting upon the winning side,—that chance depending, of
course, on my willingness to run the risk of acting as if my passional need of taking the world religiously might be prophetic and
right.

All this is on the supposition that it really may be prophetic and
right, and that, even to us who are discussing the matter, religion
is a live hypothesis which may be true. Now, to most of us religion
comes in a still further way that makes a veto on our active faith
even more illogical. The more perfect and more eternal aspect of
the universe is represented in our religions as having personal
form. The universe is no longer a mere *It* to us, but a *Thou,* if we
are religious; and any relation that may be possible from person to
person might be possible here. For instance, although in one sense
we are passive portions of the universe, in another we show a curious autonomy, as if we were small active centres on our own account. We feel, too, as if the appeal of religion to us were made to
our own active good-will, as if evidence might be forever with-
held from us unless we met the hypothesis half-way. To take a trivial illustration: just as a man who in a company of gentlemen made
no advances, asked a warrant for every concession, and believed

no one's worth without proof, would cut himself off by such churlishness from all the social rewards that a more trusting spirit would earn,—so here, one who should shut himself up in snarling logicality and try to make the gods extort his recognition willy-nilly, or not get it at all, might cut himself off forever from his only opportunity of making the gods' acquaintance. This feeling, forced on us we know not whence, that by obstinately believing that there are gods (although not to do so would be so easy both for our logic and our life) we are doing the universe the deepest service we can, seems part of the living essence of the religious hypothesis. If the hypothesis *were* true in all its parts, including this one, then pure intellectualism, with its veto on our making willing advances, would be an absurdity; and some participation of our sympathetic nature would be logically required. I, therefore, for one, cannot see my way to accepting the agnostic rules for truth-seeking, or wilfully agree to keep my willing nature out of the game. I cannot do so for this plain reason, that *a rule of thinking which would absolutely prevent me from acknowledging certain kinds of truth if those kinds of truth were really there, would be an irrational rule.* That for me is the long and short of the formal logic of the situation, no matter what the kinds of truth might materially be.

I confess I do not see how this logic can be escaped. But sad experience makes me fear that some of you may still shrink from radically saying with me, *in abstracto,* that we have the right to believe at our own risk any hypothesis that is live enough to tempt our will. I suspect, however, that if this is so, it is because you have got away from the abstract logical point of view altogether, and are thinking (perhaps without realizing it) of some particular religious hypothesis which for you is dead. The freedom to "believe what we will" you apply to the case of some patent superstition; and the faith you think of is the faith defined by the schoolboy when he said, "Faith is when you believe something that you know ain't true." I can only repeat that this is misapprehension. *In concreto,* the freedom to believe can only cover living options which the intellect of the individual cannot by itself resolve; and living options never seem absurdities to him who has them to consider. When I look at the religious question as it really puts itself to concrete men, and when I think of all the possibilities which both practically and theoretically it involves, then this command that we shall put a stopper on our heart, instincts, and courage, and *wait*—acting of course meanwhile more or less as if religion were *not* true[25]—till doomsday, or till such time as our intellect and senses working together may have raked in evidence enough, this command, I say, seems to me the queerest idol ever manufactured in the philosophic cave. Were we scholastic absolutists, there might be more excuse. If we had an infallible intellect with its objective certitudes, we might feel ourselves disloyal to such a perfect organ of knowledge in not trusting to it exclusively, in not waiting for its releasing word. But if we are empiricists, if we believe that no bell in us tolls to let us know for certain when truth is in our grasp, then it seems a piece of idle fantasticality to preach so solemnly our duty of waiting for the bell. Indeed we *may* wait if we will,— I hope you do not think that I am denying that,—but if we do so, we do so at our peril as much as if we believed. In either case we *act,* taking our life in our hands. No one of us ought to issue vetoes to the other, nor should we bandy words of abuse. We ought, on the contrary, delicately and profoundly to respect one another's mental freedom: then only shall we bring about the intellectual republic; then only shall we have that spirit of inner tolerance without which all our outer tolerance is soulless, and which is empiricism's glory; then only shall we live and let live, in speculative as well as in practical things.

I began by a reference to Fitzjames Stephen; let me end by a quotation from him. "What do you think of yourself? What do you think of the world? . . . These are questions with which all must deal as it seems good to them. They are riddles of the Sphinx, and in some way or other we must deal with them. . . . In all important transactions of life we have to take a leap in the dark. . . . If we decide to leave the riddles unanswered, that is a choice; if we waver in our answer, that, too, is a choice: but whatever choice we make, we make it at our peril. If a man chooses to turn his back altogether on God and the future, no one can prevent him; no one can show beyond reasonable doubt that he is mistaken. If a man thinks otherwise and acts as he thinks, I do not see that any one can prove that *he* is mistaken. Each must act as he thinks best; and if he is wrong, so much the worse for him. We stand on a mountain pass in the midst of whirling snow and blinding mist, through which we get glimpses now and then of paths which may be deceptive. If we stand still we shall be frozen to death. If we take the wrong road we shall be dashed to pieces. We do not certainly know whether there is any right one. What must we do? 'Be strong and of a good courage.' Act for the best, hope for the best, and take what comes. . . . If death ends all, we cannot meet death better."[26]

What Pragmatism Means

in *Pragmatism* (1907)

SOME YEARS AGO, being with a camping party in the mountains, I returned from a solitary ramble to find everyone engaged in a ferocious metaphysical dispute. The *corpus* of the dispute was a squirrel—a live squirrel supposed to be clinging to one side of a tree-trunk; while over against the tree's opposite side a human being was imagined to stand. This human witness tries to get sight of the squirrel by moving rapidly round the tree, but no matter how fast he goes, the squirrel moves as fast in the opposite direction, and always keeps the tree between himself and the man, so that never a glimpse of him is caught. The resultant metaphysical problem now is this: *Does the man go round the squirrel or not?* He goes round the tree, sure enough, and the squirrel is on the tree; but does he go round the squirrel? In the unlimited leisure of the wilderness, discussion had been worn threadbare. Everyone had taken sides, and was obstinate; and the numbers on both sides were even. Each side, when I appeared, therefore appealed to me to make it a majority. Mindful of the scholastic adage that whenever you meet a contradiction you must make a distinction, I immediately sought and found one, as follows: "Which party is right," I said, "depends on what you *practically mean* by 'going round' the squirrel. If you mean passing from the north of him to the east, then to the south, then to the west, and then to the north of him again, obviously the man does go round him, for he occupies these successive positions. But if on the contrary you mean being first in front of him, then on the right of him, then behind him, then on his left, and finally in front again, it is quite as obvious that the man fails to go round him, for by the compensating movements the squirrel makes, he keeps his belly turned towards the man all the time, and his back turned away. Make the distinction, and there is no occasion for any farther dispute. You are both right and both wrong according as you conceive the verb 'to go round' in one practical fashion or the other."

Altho one or two of the hotter disputants called my speech a shuffling evasion, saying they wanted no quibbling or scholastic hair-splitting, but meant just plain honest English "round," the majority seemed to think that the distinction had assuaged the dispute.

I tell this trivial anecdote because it is a peculiarly simple example of what I wish now to speak of as *the pragmatic method*. The pragmatic method is primarily a method of settling metaphysical disputes that otherwise might be interminable. Is the world one or many?—fated or free?—material or spiritual?—here are notions either of which may or may not hold good of the world; and disputes over such notions are unending. The pragmatic method in such cases is to try to interpret each notion by tracing its respective practical consequences. What difference would it practically make to anyone if this notion rather than that notion were true? If no practical difference whatever can be traced, then the alternatives mean practically the same thing, and all dispute is idle. Whenever a dispute is serious, we ought to be able to show some practical difference that must follow from one side or the other's being right.

A glance at the history of the idea will show you still better what pragmatism means. The term is derived from the same Greek word πράγμα, meaning action, from which our words "practice" and "practical" come. It was first introduced into philosophy by Mr. Charles Peirce in 1878. In an article entitled "How to Make Our Ideas Clear," in the *Popular Science Monthly* for January of that year[1] Mr. Peirce, after pointing out that our beliefs are really rules for action, said that, to develop a thought's meaning, we need only determine what conduct it is fitted to produce: that conduct is for us its sole significance. And the tangible fact at the root of all our thought-distinctions, however subtle, is that there is no one of them so fine as to consist in anything but a possible difference of practice. To attain perfect clearness in our thoughts of an object, then, we need only consider what conceivable effects of a practical kind the object may involve—what sensations we are to expect from it, and what reactions we must prepare. Our conception of these effects, whether immediate or remote, is then for us the whole of our conception of the object, so far as that conception has positive significance at all.

This is the principle of Peirce, the principle of pragmatism. It lay entirely unnoticed by anyone for twenty years, until I, in an address before Professor Howison's philosophical union at the university of California, brought it forward again and made a special application of it to religion.[2] By that date (1898) the time seemed ripe for its reception. The word "pragmatism" spread, and at present it fairly spots the pages of the philosophic journals. On all hands we find the "pragmatic movement" spoken of, sometimes with respect, sometimes with contumely, seldom with clear understanding. It is evident that the term applies itself conveniently to a number of tendencies that hitherto have lacked a collective name, and that it has "come to stay."

To take in the importance of Peirce's principle, one must get accustomed to applying it to concrete cases. I found a few years ago that Ostwald, the illustrious Leipzig chemist, had been making perfectly distinct use of the principle of pragmatism in his lectures on the philosophy of science, tho he had not called it by that name.

"All realities influence our practice," he wrote me, "and that influence is their meaning for us. I am accustomed to put questions to my classes in this way: In what respects would the world be different if this alternative or that were true? If I can find nothing that would become different, then the alternative has no sense."

That is, the rival views mean practically the same thing, and meaning, other than practical, there is for us none. Ostwald in a published lecture gives this example of what he means. Chemists have long wrangled over the inner constitution of certain bodies called "tautomerous." Their properties seemed equally consistent with the notion that an instable hydrogen atom oscillates inside of them, or that they are instable mixtures of two bodies. Controversy raged; but never was decided. "It would never have begun," says Ostwald, "if the combatants had asked themselves what particular experimental fact could have been made different by one or the other view being correct. For it would then have appeared that no difference of fact could possible ensue; and the quarrel was as unreal as if, theorizing in primitive times about the raising of dough by yeast, one party should have invoked a 'brownie,' while another insisted on an 'elf' as the true cause of the phenomenon."[3]

It is astonishing to see how many philosophical disputes collapse into insignificance the moment you subject them to this simple test of tracing a concrete consequence. There can *be* no difference anywhere that doesn't *make* a difference elsewhere—no difference in abstract truth that doesn't express itself in a difference in concrete fact and in conduct consequent upon that fact, imposed on somebody, somehow, somewhere and somewhen. The whole function of philosophy ought to be to find out what definite difference it will make to you and me, at definite instants of our life, if this world-formula or that world-formula be the true one.

There is absolutely nothing new in the pragmatic method. Socrates was an adept at it. Aristotle used it methodically. Locke, Berkeley and Hume made momentous contributions to truth by its means. Shadworth Hodgson[4] keeps insisting that realities are only what they are "known-as." But these forerunners of pragmatism used it in fragments: they were preluders only. Not until in our time has it generalized itself, become conscious of a universal mission, pretended to a conquering destiny. I believe in that destiny, and I hope I may end by inspiring you with my belief.

Pragmatism represents a perfectly familiar attitude in philosophy, the empiricist attitude, but it represents it, as it seems to me, both in a more radical and in a less objectionable form than it has ever yet assumed. A pragmatist turns his back resolutely and once for all upon a lot of inveterate habits dear to professional philosophers. He turns away from abstraction and insufficiency, from verbal solutions, from bad *a priori* reasons, from fixed principles, closed systems, and pretended absolutes and origins. He turns towards concreteness and adequacy, towards facts, towards action, and towards power. That means the empiricist temper regnant, and the rationalist temper sincerely given up. It means the open air and possibilities of nature, as against dogma, artificiality and the pretence of finality in truth.

At the same time it does not stand for any special results. It is a method only. But the general triumph of that method would mean an enormous change in what I called in my last lecture the "temperament" of philosophy. Teachers of the ultra-rationalistic type would be frozen out, much as the courtier type is frozen out in republics, as the ultramontane type of priest is frozen out in protestant lands. Science and metaphysics would come much nearer together, would in fact work absolutely hand in hand.

Metaphysics has usually followed a very primitive kind of quest. You know how men have always hankered after unlawful magic, and you know what a great part, in magic, *words* have always played. If you have his name, or the formula of incantation that binds him, you can control the spirit, genie, afrite, or whatever the power may be. Solomon knew the names of all the spirits, and having their names, he held them subject to his will. So the universe has always appeared to the natural mind as a kind of enigma, of which the key must be sought in the shape of some illuminating or power-bringing word or name. That word names the universe's *principle,* and to possess it is, after a fashion, to possess the universe itself. "God," "Matter," "Reason," "the Absolute," "Energy'" are so many solving names. You can rest when you have them. You are at the end of your metaphysical quest.

But if you follow the pragmatic method, you cannot look on any such word as closing your quest. You must bring out of each

word its practical cash-value, set it at work within the stream of
your experience. It appears less as a solution, then, than as a program for more work, and more particularly as an indication of the
ways in which existing realities may be *changed.*

*Theories thus become instruments, not answers to enigmas, in which we
can rest.* We don't lie back upon them, we move forward, and, on
occasion, make nature over again by their aid. Pragmatism unstiffens all our theories, limbers them up and sets each one at work.
Being nothing essentially new, it harmonizes with many ancient
philosophic tendencies. It agrees with nominalism for instance, in
always appealing to particulars; with utilitarianism in emphasizing
practical aspects; with positivism in its disdain for verbal solutions,
useless questions, and metaphysical abstractions.

All these, you see, are *anti-intellectualist* tendencies. Against rationalism as a pretension and a method, pragmatism is fully armed
and militant. But, at the outset, at least, it stands for no particular
results. It has no dogmas, and no doctrines save its method. As the
young Italian pragmatist Papini[5] has well said, it lies in the midst of
our theories, like a corridor in a hotel. Innumerable chambers
open out of it. In one you may find a man writing an atheistic volume; in the next someone on his knees praying for faith and
strength; in a third a chemist investigating a body's properties. In a
fourth a system of idealistic metaphysics is being excogitated; in a
fifth the impossibility of metaphysics is being shown. But they all
own the corridor, and all must pass through it if they want a practicable way of getting into or out of their respective rooms.

No particular results then, so far, but only an attitude of orientation, is what the pragmatic method means. *The attitude of looking
away from first things, principles, "categories," supposed necessities; and of
looking towards last things, fruits, consequences, facts.*

So much for the pragmatic method! You may say that I have
been praising it rather than explaining it to you, but I shall
presently explain it abundantly enough by showing how it works
on some familiar problems. Meanwhile the word pragmatism has
come to be used in a still wider sense, as meaning also a certain *the-*

ory of truth. I mean to give a whole lecture[6] to the statement of that theory, after first paving the way, so I can be very brief now. But brevity is hard to follow, so I ask for your redoubled attention for a quarter of an hour. If much remains obscure, I hope to make it clearer in the later lectures.

One of the most successfully cultivated branches of philosophy in our time is what is called inductive logic, the study of the conditions under which our sciences have evolved. Writers on this subject have begun to show a singular unanimity as to what the laws of nature and elements of fact mean, when formulated by mathematicians, physicists and chemists. When the first mathematical, logical and natural uniformities, the first *laws,* were discovered, men were so carried away by the clearness, beauty and simplification that resulted, that they believed themselves to have deciphered authentically the eternal thoughts of the Almighty. His mind also thundered and reverberated in syllogisms. He also thought in conic sections, squares and roots and ratios, and geometrized like Euclid. He made Kepler's laws for the planets to follow; he made velocity increase proportionally to the time in falling bodies; he made the law of the sines for light to obey when refracted; he established the classes, orders, families and genera of plants and animals, and fixed the distances between them. He thought the archetypes of all things, and devised their variations; and when we rediscover any one of these his wondrous institutions, we seize his mind in its very literal intention.

But as the sciences have developed farther, the notion has gained ground that most, perhaps all, of our laws are only approximations. The laws themselves, moreover, have grown so numerous that there is no counting them; and so many rival formulations are proposed in all the branches of science that investigators have become accustomed to the notion that no theory is absolutely a transcript of reality, but that any one of them may from some point of view be useful. Their great use is to summarize old facts and to lead to new ones. They are only a man-made language, a conceptual shorthand, as someone calls them, in which we write our reports of nature; and languages, as is well known, tolerate much choice of expression and many dialects.

Thus human arbitrariness has driven divine necessity from scientific logic. If I mention the names of Sigwart, Mach, Ostwald, Pearson, Milhaud, Poincaré, Duhem, Ruyssen,[7] those of you who are students will easily identify the tendency I speak of, and will think of additional names.

Riding now on the front of this wave of scientific logic Messrs. Schiller[8] and Dewey appear with their pragmatistic account of what truth everywhere signifies. Everywhere, these teachers say, "truth" in our ideas and beliefs means the same thing that it means in science. It means, they say, nothing but this, *that ideas (which themselves are but parts of our experience) become true just in so far as they help us to get into satisfactory relation with other parts of our experience,* to summarize them and get about among them by conceptual short-cuts instead of following the interminable succession of particular phenomena. Any idea upon which we can ride, so to speak; any idea that will carry us prosperously from any one part of our experience to any other part, linking things satisfactorily, working securely, simplifying, saving labor; is true for just so much, true in so far forth, true *instrumentally.* This is the "instrumental" view of truth taught so successfully at Chicago,[9] the view that truth in our ideas means their power to "work," promulgated so brilliantly at Oxford.

Messrs. Dewey, Schiller and their allies, in reaching this general conception of all truth, have only followed the example of geologists, biologists and philologists. In the establishment of these other sciences, the successful stroke was always to take some simple process actually observable in operation—as denudation by weather, say, or variation from parental type, or change of dialect by incorporation of new words and pronunciations—and then to generalize it, making it apply to all times, and produce great results by summating its effects through the ages.

The observable process which Schiller and Dewey particularly singled out for generalization is the familiar one by which any individual settles into *new opinions*. The process here is always the same. The individual has a stock of old opinions already, but he meets a new experience that puts them to a strain. Somebody contradicts them; or in a reflective moment he discovers that they contradict each other; or he hears of facts with which they are incompatible; or desires arise in him which they cease to satisfy. The result is an inward trouble to which his mind till then had been a stranger, and from which he seeks to escape by modifying his previous mass of opinions. He saves as much of it as he can, for in this matter of belief we are all extreme conservatives. So he tries to change first this opinion, and then that (for they resist change very variously), until at last some new idea comes up which he can graft upon the ancient stock with a minimum of disturbance of the latter, some idea that mediates between the stock and the new experience and runs them into one another most felicitously and expediently.

This new idea is then adopted as the true one. It preserves the older stock of truths with a minimum of modification, stretching them just enough to make them admit the novelty, but conceiving that in ways as familiar as the case leaves possible. An *outré* explanation, violating all our preconceptions, would never pass for a true account of a novelty. We should scratch round industriously till we found something less eccentric. The most violent revolutions in an individual's beliefs leave most of his old order standing. Time and space, cause and effect, nature and history, and one's own biography remain untouched. New truth is always a go-between, a smoother-over of transitions. It marries old opinion to new fact so as ever to show a minimum of jolt, a maximum of continuity. We hold a theory true just in proportion to its success in solving this "problem of maxima and minima." But success in solving this problem is eminently a matter of approximation. We say this theory solves it on the whole more satisfactorily than that theory; but that means more satisfactorily to ourselves, and individuals will emphasize their points of satisfaction differently. To a certain degree, therefore, everything here is plastic.

The point I now urge you to observe particularly is the part played by the older truths. Failure to take account of it is the source of much of the unjust criticism leveled against pragmatism. Their influence is absolutely controlling. Loyalty to them is the first principle—in most cases it is the only principle; for by far the most usual way of handling phenomena so novel that they would make for a serious rearrangement of our preconceptions is to ignore them altogether, or to abuse those who bear witness for them.

You doubtless wish examples of this process of truth's growth, and the only trouble is their superabundance. The simplest case of new truth is of course the mere numerical addition of new kinds of facts, or of new single facts of old kinds, to our experience—an addition that involves no alteration in the old beliefs. Day follows day, and its contents are simply added. The new contents themselves are not true, they simply *come* and *are*. Truth is *what we say about* them, and when we say that they have come, truth is satisfied by the plain additive formula.

But often the day's contents oblige a rearrangement. If I should now utter piercing shrieks and act like a maniac on this platform, it would make many of you revise your ideas as to the probable worth of my philosophy. "Radium" came the other day as part of the day's content, and seemed for a moment to contradict our ideas of the whole order of nature, that order having come to be identified with what is called the conservation of energy. The mere sight of radium paying heat away indefinitely out of its own pocket seemed to violate that conservation. What to think? If the radiations from it were nothing but an escape of unsuspected "potential" energy, pre-existent inside of the atoms, the principle of conservation would be saved. The discovery of "helium" as the radiation's outcome, opened a way to this belief. So Ramsay's[10] view is generally held to be true, because, altho it extends our old ideas of energy, it causes a minimum of alteration in their nature.

I need not multiply instances. A new opinion counts as "true" just in proportion as it gratifies the individual's desire to assimilate

the novel in his experience to his beliefs in stock. It must both lean
on old truth and grasp new fact; and its success (as I said a moment
ago) in doing this, is a matter for the individual's appreciation.
When old truth grows, then, by new truth's addition, it is for subjective reasons. We are in the process and obey the reasons. That
new idea is truest which performs most felicitously its function of
satisfying our double urgency. It makes itself true, gets itself classed
as true, by the way it works; grafting itself then upon the ancient
body of truth, which thus grows much as a tree grows by the activity of a new layer of cambium.

Now Dewey and Schiller proceed to generalize this observation
and to apply it to the most ancient parts of truth. They also once
were plastic. They also were called true for human reasons. They
also mediated between still earlier truths and what in those days
were novel observations. Purely objective truth, truth in whose establishment the function of giving human satisfaction in marrying
previous parts of experience with newer parts played no rôle
whatever, is nowhere to be found. The reasons why we call things
true is the reason why they *are* true, for "to be true" *means* only to
perform this marriage-function.

The trail of the human serpent is thus over everything. Truth
independent; truth that we *find* merely; truth no longer malleable
to human need; truth incorrigible, in a word; such truth exists indeed superabundantly—or is supposed to exist by rationalistically
minded thinkers; but then it means only the dead heart of the living tree, and its being there means only that truth also has its pale-
ontology and its "prescription," and may grow stiff with years of
veteran service and petrified in men's regard by sheer antiquity.
But how plastic even the oldest truths nevertheless really are has
been vividly shown in our day by the transformation of logical
and mathematical ideas, a transformation which seems even to be
invading physics. The ancient formulas are reinterpreted as special
expressions of much wider principles, principles that our ancestors
never got a glimpse of in their present shape and formulation.

Mr. Schiller still gives to all this view of truth the name of

The old ways seem to obstruct progress instead.

"Humanism," but, for this doctrine too, the name of pragmatism seems fairly to be in the ascendant, so I will treat it under the name of pragmatism in these lectures.

Such then would be the scope of pragmatism—first, a method; and second, a genetic theory of what is meant by truth. And these two things must be our future topics.

What I have said of the theory of truth will, I am sure, have appeared obscure and unsatisfactory to most of you by reason of its brevity. I shall make amends for that hereafter. In a lecture on "common sense" I shall try to show what I mean by truths grown petrified by antiquity. In another lecture I shall expatiate on the idea that our thoughts become true in proportion as they successfully exert their go-between function. In a third I shall show how hard it is to discriminate subjective from objective factors in Truth's development.[11] You may not follow me wholly in these lectures; and if you do, you may not wholly agree with me. But you will, I know, regard me at least as serious, and treat my effort with respectful consideration.

You will probably be surprised to learn, then, that Messrs. Schiller's and Dewey's theories have suffered a hailstorm of contempt and ridicule. All rationalism has risen against them. In influential quarters Mr. Schiller, in particular, has been treated like an impudent schoolboy who deserves a spanking. I should not mention this, but for the fact that it throws so much sidelight upon that rationalistic temper to which I have opposed the temper of pragmatism. Pragmatism is uncomfortable away from facts. Rationalism is comfortable only in the presence of abstractions. This pragmatist talk about truths in the plural, about their utility and satisfactoriness, about the success with which they "work," etc., suggests to the typical intellectualist mind a sort of coarse lame second-rate makeshift article of truth. Such truths are not real truth. Such tests are merely subjective. As against this, objective truth must be something non-utilitarian, haughty, refined, remote, august, exalted. It must be an absolute correspondence of our thoughts with an equally absolute reality. It must be what we *ought* to think, unconditionally. The conditioned ways in which we *do* think are so much irrelevance and matter for psychology. Down with psychology, up with logic, in all this question!

See the exquisite contrast of the types of mind! The pragmatist clings to facts and concreteness, observes truth at its work in particular cases, and generalizes. Truth, for him, becomes a classname for all sorts of definite working-values in experience. For the rationalist it remains a pure abstraction, to the bare name of which we must defer. When the pragmatist undertakes to show in detail just *why* we must defer, the rationalist is unable to recognize the concretes from which his own abstraction is taken. He accuses us of *denying* truth; whereas we have only sought to trace exactly why people follow it and always ought to follow it. Your typical ultra-abstractionist fairly shudders at concreteness: other things equal, he positively prefers the pale and spectral. If the two universes were offered, he would always choose the skinny outline rather than the rich thicket of reality. It is so much purer, clearer, nobler.

I hope that as these lectures go on, the concreteness and closeness to facts of the pragmatism which they advocate may be what approves itself to you as its most satisfactory peculiarity. It only follows here the example of the sister-sciences, interpreting the unobserved by the observed. It brings old and new harmoniously together. It converts the absolutely empty notion of a static relation of "correspondence" (what that may mean we must ask later) between our minds and reality, into that of a rich and active commerce (that anyone may follow in detail and understand) between particular thoughts of ours, and the great universe of other experiences in which they play their parts and have their uses.

But enough of this at present? The justification of what I say must be postponed. I wish now to add a word in further explanation of the claim I made at our last meeting, that pragmatism may be a happy harmonizer of empiricist ways of thinking, with the more religious demands of human beings.

Men who are strongly of the fact-loving temperament, you may remember me to have said, are liable to be kept at a distance by the small sympathy with facts which that philosophy from the present-day fashion of idealism offers them. It is far too intellectualistic. Old fashioned theism was bad enough, with its notion of God as an exalted monarch, made up of a lot of unintelligible or preposterous "attributes"; but, so long as it held strongly by the argument from design, it kept some touch with concrete realities. Since, however, Darwinism has once for all displaced design from the minds of the "scientific," theism has lost that foothold; and some kind of an immanent or pantheistic deity working *in* things rather than above them is, if any, the kind recommended to our contemporary imagination. Aspirants to a philosophic religion turn, as a rule, more hopefully nowadays towards idealistic pantheism than towards the other dualistic theism, in spite of the fact that the latter still counts able defenders.

But, as I said in my first lecture, the brand of pantheism offered is hard for them to assimilate if they are lovers of facts, or empirically minded. It is the absolutistic brand, spurning the dust and reared upon pure logic. It keeps no connexion whatever with concreteness. Affirming the Absolute Mind, which is its substitute for God, to be the rational presupposition of all particulars of fact, whatever they may be, it remains supremely indifferent to what the particular facts in our world actually are. Be they what they may, the Absolute will father them. Like the sick lion in Esop's fable, all footprints lead into his den, but *nulla vestigia retrorsum*.[12] You cannot redescend into the world of particulars by the Absolute's aid, or deduce any necessary consequences of detail important for your life from your idea of his nature. He gives you indeed the assurance that all is well with *Him,* and for his eternal way of thinking; but thereupon he leaves you to be finitely saved by your own temporal devices.

Far be it from me to deny the majesty of this conception, or its capacity to yield religious comfort to a most respectable class of minds. But from the human point of view, no one can pretend that it doesn't suffer from the faults of remoteness and abstractness. It is eminently a product of what I have ventured to call the rationalistic temper. It disdains empiricism's needs. It substitutes a pallid outline for the real world's richness. It is dapper; it is noble in the bad sense, in the sense in which to be noble is to be inapt for humble service. In this real world of sweat and dirt, it seems to me that when a view of things is "noble," that ought to count as a presumption against its truth, and as a philosophic disqualification. The prince of darkness may be a gentleman, as we are told he is, but whatever the God of earth and heaven is, he can surely be no gentleman. His menial services are needed in the dust of our human trials, even more than his dignity is needed in the empyrean.

Now pragmatism, devoted tho she be to facts, has no such materialistic bias as ordinary empiricism labors under. Moreover, she has no objection whatever to the realizing of abstractions, so long as you get about among particulars with their aid and they actually carry you somewhere. Interested in no conclusions but those which our minds and our experiences work out together, she has no *a priori* prejudices against theology. *If theological ideas prove to have a value for concrete life, they will be true, for pragmatism, in the sense of being good for so much. For how much more they are true, will depend entirely on their relations to the other truths that also have to be acknowledged.*

What I said just now about the Absolute of transcendental idealism is a case in point. First, I called it majestic and said it yielded religious comfort to a class of minds, and then I accused it of remoteness and sterility. But so far as it affords such comfort, it surely is not sterile; it has that amount of value; it performs a concrete function. As a good pragmatist, I myself ought to call the Absolute true "in so far forth," then; and I unhesitatingly now do so.

But what does *true in so far forth* mean in this case? To answer, we need only apply the pragmatic method. What do believers in the Absolute mean by saying that their belief affords them comfort? They mean that since in the Absolute finite evil is "overruled" already, we may, therefore, whenever we wish, treat the temporal as if it were potentially the eternal, be sure that we can trust its outcome, and, without sin, dismiss our fear and drop the worry of our finite responsibility. In short, they mean that we have a right ever and anon to take a moral holiday, to let the world wag in its own way, feeling that its issues are in better hands than ours and are none of our business.

The universe is a system of which the individual members may relax their anxieties occasionally, in which the don't-care mood is also right for men, and moral holidays in order—that, if I mistake not, is part, at least, of what the Absolute is "known-as," that is the great difference in our particular experiences which his being true makes for us, that is part of his cash-value when he is pragmatically interpreted. Farther than that the ordinary lay-reader in philosophy who thinks favorably of absolute idealism does not venture to sharpen his conceptions. He can use the Absolute for so much, and so much is very precious. He is pained at hearing you speak incredulously of the Absolute, therefore, and disregards your criticisms because they deal with aspects of the conception that he fails to follow.

If the Absolute means this, and means no more than this, who can possibly deny the truth of it? To deny it would be to insist that men should never relax, and that holidays are never in order.

I am well aware how odd it must seem to some of you to hear me say that an idea is "true" so long as to believe it is profitable to our lives. That it is *good,* for as much as it profits, you will gladly admit. If what we do by its aid is good, you will allow the idea itself to be good in so far forth, for we are the better for possessing it. But is it not a strange misuse of the word "truth," you will say, to call ideas also "true" for this reason?

To answer this difficulty fully is impossible at this stage of my account. You touch here upon the very central point of Messrs.

Schiller's, Dewey's and my own doctrine of truth, which I cannot discuss with detail until my sixth lecture.[13] Let me now say only this, that truth is *one species of good,* and not, as is usually supposed, a category distinct from good, and co-ordinate with it. *The true is the name of whatever proves itself to be good in the way of belief, and good, too, for definite, assignable reasons.* Surely you must admit this, that if there were *no* good for life in true ideas, or if the knowledge of them were positively disadvantageous and false ideas the only useful ones, then the current notion that truth is divine and precious, and its pursuit a duty, could never have grown up or become a dogma. In a world like that, our duty would be to *shun* truth, rather. But in this world, just as certain foods are not only agreeable to our taste, but good for our teeth, our stomach and our tissues; so certain ideas are not only agreeable to think about, or agreeable as supporting other ideas that we are fond of, but they are also helpful in life's practical struggles. If there be any life that it is really better we should lead, and if there be any idea which, if believed in, would help us to lead that life, then it would be really *better for us* to believe in that idea, *unless, indeed, belief in it incidentally clashed with other greater vital benefits.*

"What would be better for us to believe"! This sounds very like a definition of truth. It comes very near to saying "what we *ought* to believe": and in *that* definition none of you would find any oddity. Ought we ever not to believe what it is *better for us* to believe? And can we then keep the notion of what is better for us, and what is true for us, permanently apart?

Pragmatism says no, and I fully agree with her. Probably you also agree, so far as the abstract statement goes, but with a suspicion that if we practically did believe everything that made for good in our own personal lives, we should be found indulging all kinds of fancies about this world's affairs, and all kinds of sentimental superstitions about a world hereafter. Your suspicion here is undoubtedly well founded, and it is evident that something happens when you pass from the abstract to the concrete, that complicates the situation.

I said just now that what is better for us to believe is true *unless the belief incidentally clashes with some other vital benefit.* Now in real life what vital benefits is any particular belief of ours most liable to clash with? What indeed except the vital benefits yielded by *other beliefs* when these prove incompatible with the first ones? In other words, the greatest enemy of any one of our truths may be the rest of our truths. Truths have once for all this desperate instinct of self-preservation and of desire to extinguish whatever contradicts them. My belief in the Absolute, based on the good it does me, must run the gauntlet of all my other beliefs. Grant that it may be true in giving me a moral holiday. Nevertheless, as I conceive it,— and let me speak now confidentially, as it were, and merely in my own private person,—it clashes with other truths of mine whose benefits I hate to give up on its account. It happens to be associated with a kind of logic of which I am the enemy, I find that it entangles me in metaphysical paradoxes that are inacceptable, etc., etc. But as I have enough trouble in life already without adding the trouble of carrying these intellectual inconsistencies, I personally just give up the Absolute. I just *take* my moral holidays; or else as a professional philosopher, I try to justify them by some other principle.

If I could restrict my notion of the Absolute to its bare holiday-giving value, it wouldn't clash with my other truths. But we cannot easily thus restrict our hypotheses. They carry supernumerary features, and these it is that clash so. My disbelief in the Absolute means then disbelief in those other supernumerary features, for I fully believe in the legitimacy of taking moral holidays.

You see by this what I meant when I called pragmatism a mediator and reconciler and said, borrowing the word from Papini, that she "unstiffens" our theories. She has in fact no prejudices whatever, no obstructive dogmas, no rigid canons of what shall count as proof. She is completely genial. She will entertain any hypothesis, she will consider any evidence. It follows that in the religious field she is at a great advantage both over positivistic empiricism, with its anti-theological bias, and over religious rationalism, with its exclusive interest in the remote, the noble, the simple, and the abstract in the way of conception.

In short, she widens the field of search for God. Rationalism sticks to logic and the empyrean. Empiricism sticks to the external senses. Pragmatism is willing to take anything, to follow either logic or the senses, and to count the humblest and most personal experiences. She will count mystical experiences if they have practical consequences. She will take a God who lives in the very dirt of private fact—if that should seem a likely place to find him.

Her only test of probable truth is what works best in the way of leading us, what fits every part of life best and combines with the collectivity of experience's demands, nothing being omitted. If theological ideas should do this, if the notion of God, in particular, should prove to do it, how could pragmatism possibly deny God's existence? She could see no meaning in treating as "not true" a notion that was pragmatically so successful. What other kind of truth could there be, for her, than all this agreement with concrete reality?

In my last lecture I shall return again to the relations of pragmatism with religion. But you see already how democratic she is. Her manners are as various and flexible, her resources as rich and endless, and her conclusions as friendly as those of mother nature.

Pragmatism's Conception of Truth

in *Pragmatism* (1907)

WHEN CLERK MAXWELL[1] WAS A CHILD it is written that he had a mania for having everything explained to him, and that when people put him off with vague verbal accounts of any phenomenon he would interrupt them impatiently by saying, "Yes; but I want you to tell me the *particular go* of it!" Had his question been about truth, only a pragmatist could have told him the particular go of it. I believe that our contemporary pragmatists, especially Messrs. Schiller[2] and Dewey, have given the only tenable account of this subject. It is a very ticklish subject, sending subtle rootlets into all kinds of crannies, and hard to treat in the sketchy way that alone befits a public lecture. But the Schiller-Dewey view of truth has been so ferociously attacked by rationalistic philosophers, and so abominably misunderstood, that here, if anywhere, is the point where a clear and simple statement should be made.

I fully expect to see the pragmatist view of truth run through the classic stages of a theory's career. First, you know, a new theory is attacked as absurd; then it is admitted to be true, but obvious and insignificant; finally it is seen to be so important that its adversaries claim that they themselves discovered it. Our doctrine of truth is at present in the first of these three stages, with symptoms of the second stage having begun in certain quarters. I wish that this lecture might help it beyond the first stage in the eyes of many of you.

Truth, as any dictionary will tell you, is a property of certain of our ideas. It means their "agreement," as falsity means their disagreement, with "reality." Pragmatists and intellectualists both accept this definition as a matter of course. They begin to quarrel only after the question is raised as to what may precisely be meant by the term "agreement," and what by the term "reality," when reality is taken as something for our ideas to agree with.

In answering these questions the pragmatists are more analytic and painstaking, the intellectualists more offhand and irreflective. The popular notion is that a true idea must copy its reality. Like other popular views, this one follows the analogy of the most usual experience. Our true ideas of sensible things do indeed copy them. Shut your eyes and think of yonder clock on the wall, and you get just such a true picture or copy of its dial. But your idea of its "works" (unless you are a clock-maker) is much less of a copy, yet it passes muster, for it in no way clashes with the reality. Even tho it should shrink to the mere word "works," that word still serves you truly; and when you speak of the "time-keeping function" of the clock, or of its spring's "elasticity," it is hard to see exactly what your ideas can copy.

You perceive that there is a problem here. Where our ideas cannot copy definitely their object, what does agreement with that object mean? Some idealists seem to say that they are true whenever they are what God means that we ought to think about that object. Others hold the copy-view all through, and speak as if our ideas possessed truth just in proportion as they approach to being copies of the Absolute's eternal way of thinking.

These views, you see, invite pragmatistic discussion. But the great assumption of the intellectualists is that truth means essentially an inert static relation. When you've got your true idea of anything, there's an end of the matter. You're in possession; you *know;* you have fulfilled your thinking destiny. You are where you ought to be mentally; you have obeyed your categorical imperative; and nothing more need follow on that climax of your rational destiny. Epistemologically you are in stable equilibrium.

Pragmatism, on the other hand, asks its usual question. "Grant an idea or belief to be true," it says, "what concrete difference will its being true make in anyone's actual life? How will the truth be realized? What experiences will be different from those which would obtain if the belief were false? What, in short, is the truth's cash-value in experiential terms?"

The moment pragmatism asks this question, it sees the answer: *True ideas are those that we can assimilate, validate, corroborate and verify. False ideas are those that we cannot.* That is the practical difference it makes to us to have true ideas; that, therefore, is the meaning of truth, for it is all that truth is known-as.

This thesis is what I have to defend. The truth of an idea is not a stagnant property inherent in it. Truth *happens* to an idea. It *becomes* true, is *made* true by events. Its verity *is* in fact an event, a process: the process namely of its verifying itself, its veri-*fication.* Its validity is the process of its valid-*ation.*

But what do the words verification and validation themselves pragmatically mean? They again signify certain practical consequences of the verified and validated idea. It is hard to find any one phrase that characterizes these consequences better than the ordinary agreement-formula—just such consequences being what we have in mind whenever we say that our ideas "agree" with reality. They lead us, namely, through the acts and other ideas which they instigate, into or up to, or towards, other parts of experience with which we feel all the while—such feeling being among our potentialities—that the original ideas remain in agreement. The connexions and transitions come to us from point to point as being progressive, harmonious, satisfactory. This function of agreeable leading is what we mean by an idea's verification. Such an account is vague and it sounds at first quite trivial, but it has results which it will take the rest of my hour to explain.

Let me begin by reminding you of the fact that the possession of true thoughts means everywhere the possession of invaluable instruments of action; and that our duty to gain truth, so far from being a blank command from out of the blue, or a "stunt" self-imposed by our intellect, can account for itself by excellent practical reasons.

The importance to human life of having true beliefs about matters of fact is a thing too notorious. We live in a world of realities
that can be infinitely useful or infinitely harmful. Ideas that tell us
which of them to expect count as the true ideas in all this primary
sphere of verification, and the pursuit of such ideas is a primary
human duty. The possession of truth, so far from being here an
end in itself, is only a preliminary means towards other vital satisfactions. If I am lost in the woods and starved, and find what looks
like a cow-path, it is of the utmost importance that I should think
of a human habitation at the end of it, for if I do so and follow it,
I save myself. The true thought is useful here because the house
which is its object is useful. The practical value of true ideas is thus
primarily derived from the practical importance of their objects to
us. Their objects are, indeed, not important at all times. I may on
another occasion have no use for the house; and then my idea of
it, however verifiable, will be practically irrelevant, and had better
remain latent. Yet since almost any object may some day become
temporarily important, the advantage of having a general stock of
extra truths, of ideas that shall be true of merely possible situations,
is obvious. We store such extra truths away in our memories, and
with the overflow we fill our books of reference. Whenever such
an extra truth becomes practically relevant to one of our emergencies, it passes from cold-storage to do work in the world, and
our belief in it grows active. You can say of it then either that "it
is useful because it is true" or that "it is true because it is useful."
Both these phrases mean exactly the same thing, namely that here
is an idea that gets fulfilled and can be verified. True is the name
for whatever idea starts the verification-process, useful is the name
for its completed function in experience. True ideas would never
have been singled out as such, would never have acquired a classname, least of all a name suggesting value, unless they had been
useful from the outset in this way.

From this simple cue pragmatism gets her general notion of
truth as something essentially bound up with the way in which
one moment in our experience may lead us towards other moments

which it will be worth while to have been led to. Primarily, and on the common-sense level, the truth of a state of mind means this function of *a leading that is worth while.* When a moment in our experience, of any kind whatever, inspires us with a thought that is true, that means that sooner or later we dip by that thought's guidance into the particulars of experience again and make advantageous connexion with them. This is a vague enough statement, but I beg you to retain it, for it is essential.

Our experience meanwhile is all shot through with regularities. One bit of it can warn us to get ready for another bit, can "intend" or be "significant of" that remoter object. The object's advent is the significance's verification. Truth, in these cases, meaning nothing but eventual verification, is manifestly incompatible with waywardness on our part. Woe to him whose beliefs play fast and loose with the order which realities follow in his experience: they will lead him nowhere or else make false connexions.

By "realities" or "objects" here, we mean either things of common sense, sensibly present, or else common-sense relations, such as dates, places, distances, kinds, activities. Following our mental image of a house along the cow-path, we actually come to see the house; we get the image's full verification. *Such simply and fully verified leadings are certainly the originals and prototypes of the truth-process.* Experience offers indeed other forms of truth-process, but they are all conceivable as being primary verifications arrested, multiplied or substituted one for another.

Take, for instance, yonder object on the wall. You and I consider it to be a "clock," altho no one of us has seen the hidden works that make it one. We let our notion pass for true without attempting to verify. If truths mean verification-process essentially, ought we then to call such unverified truths as this abortive? No, for they form the overwhelmingly large number of the truths we live by. Indirect as well as direct verifications pass muster. Where circumstantial evidence is sufficient, we can go without eye-witnessing. Just as we here assume Japan to exist without ever having been there, because it *works* to do so, everything we know conspiring with the belief, and nothing interfering, so we assume that thing to be a clock. We *use* it as a clock, regulating the length of our lecture by it. The verification of the assumption here means its leading to no frustration or contradiction. Verifi*ability* of wheels and weights and pendulum is as good as verification. For one truth-process completed there are a million in our lives that function in this state of nascency. They turn us *towards* direct verification; lead us into the *surroundings* of the objects they envisage; and then, if everything runs on harmoniously, we are so sure that verification is possible that we omit it, and are usually justified by all that happens.

Truth lives, in fact, for the most part on a credit system. Our thoughts and beliefs "pass," so long as nothing challenges them, just as bank-notes pass so long as nobody refuses them. But this all points to direct face-to-face verifications somewhere, without which the fabric of truth collapses like a financial system with no cash-basis whatever. You accept my verification of one thing, I yours of another. We trade on each other's truth. But beliefs verified concretely by *somebody* are the posts of the whole super-structure.

Another great reason—beside economy of time—for waiving complete verification in the usual business of life is that all things exist in kinds and not singly. Our world is found once for all to have that peculiarity. So that when we have once directly verified our ideas about one specimen of a kind, we consider ourselves free to apply them to other specimens without verification. A mind that habitually discerns the kind of thing before it, and acts by the law of the kind immediately, without pausing to verify, will be a "true" mind in ninety-nine out of a hundred emergencies, proved so by its conduct fitting everything it meets, and getting no refutation.

Indirectly or only potentially verifying processes may thus be true as well as full verification-processes. They work as true processes would work, give us the same advantages, and claim our recognition for the same reasons. All this on the common-sense level of matters of fact, which we are alone considering.

But matters of fact are not our only stock in trade. *Relations among purely mental ideas* form another sphere where true and false beliefs obtain, and here the beliefs are absolute, or unconditional. When they are true they bear the name either of definitions or of principles. It is either a principle or a definition that 1 and 1 make 2, that 2 and 1 make 3, and so on; that white differs less from gray than it does from black; that when the cause begins to act the effect also commences. Such propositions hold of all possible "ones," of all conceivable "whites" and "grays" and "causes." The objects here are mental objects. Their relations are perceptually obvious at a glance, and no sense-verification is necessary. Moreover, once true, always true, of those same mental objects. Truth here has an "eternal" character. If you can find a concrete thing anywhere that is "one" or "white" or "gray," or an "effect," then your principles will everlastingly apply to it. It is but a case of ascertaining the kind, and then applying the law of its kind to the particular object. You are sure to get truth if you can but name the kind rightly, for your mental relations hold good of everything of that kind without exception. If you then, nevertheless, failed to get truth concretely, you would say that you had classed your real objects wrongly.

In this realm of mental relations, truth again is an affair of leading. We relate one abstract idea with another, framing in the end great systems of logical and mathematical truth, under the respective terms of which the sensible facts of experience eventually arrange themselves, so that our eternal truths hold good of realities also. This marriage of fact and theory is endlessly fertile. What we say is here already true in advance of special verification, *if we have subsumed our objects rightly.* Our ready-made ideal framework for all sorts of possible objects follows from the very structure of our thinking. We can no more play fast and loose with these abstract relations than we can do so with our sense-experiences. They coerce us; we must treat them consistently, whether or not we like the results. The rules of addition apply to our debts as rigorously as to our assets. The hundredth decimal of π, the ratio of the circumference to its diameter, is predetermined ideally now, tho no one may have computed it. If we should ever need the figure in our dealings with an actual circle we should need to have it given rightly, calculated by the usual rules; for it is the same kind of truth that those rules elsewhere calculate.

Between the coercions of the sensible order and those of the ideal order, our mind is thus wedged tightly. Our ideas must agree with realities, be such realities concrete or abstract, be they facts or be they principles, under penalty of endless inconsistency and frustration.

So far, intellectualists can raise no protest. They can only say that we have barely touched the skin of the matter.

Realities mean, then, either concrete facts, or abstract kinds of things and relations perceived intuitively between them. They furthermore and thirdly mean, as things that new ideas of ours must no less take account of, the whole body of other truths already in our possession. But what now does "agreement" with such three-fold realities mean?—to use again the definition that is current.

Here it is that pragmatism and intellectualism begin to part company. Primarily, no doubt, to agree means to copy, but we saw that the mere word "clock" would do instead of a mental picture of its works, and that of many realities our ideas can only be symbols and not copies. "Past time," "power," "spontaneity"—how can our mind copy such realities?

To "agree" in the widest sense with a reality, *can only mean to be guided either straight up to it or into its surroundings, or to be put into such working touch with it as to handle either it or something connected with it better than if we disagreed.* Better either intellectually or practically!

And often agreement will only mean the negative fact that nothing contradictory from the quarter of that reality comes to interfere with the way in which our ideas guide us elsewhere. To copy a reality is, indeed, one very important way of agreeing with it, but it is far from being essential. The essential thing is the process of being guided. Any idea that helps us to *deal,* whether practically or intellectually, with either the reality or its belongings, that doesn't entangle our progress in frustrations, that *fits,* in fact, and adapts our life to the reality's whole setting, will agree sufficiently to meet the requirement. It will hold true of that reality.

Thus, *names* are just as "true" or "false" as definite mental pictures are. They set up similar verification-processes, and lead to fully equivalent practical results.

All human thinking gets discursified; we exchange ideas; we lend and borrow verifications, get them from one another by means of social intercourse. All truth thus gets verbally built out, stored up, and made available for everyone. Hence, we must *talk* consistently just as we must *think* consistently: for both in talk and thought we deal with kinds. Names are arbitrary, but once understood they must be kept to. We mustn't now call Abel "Cain" or Cain "Abel." If we do, we ungear ourselves from the whole book of Genesis, and from all its connexions with the universe of speech and fact down to the present time. We throw ourselves out of whatever truth that entire system of speech and fact may embody.

The overwhelming majority of our true ideas admit of no direct or face-to-face verification—those of past history, for example, as of Cain and Abel. The stream of time can be remounted only verbally, or verified indirectly by the present prolongations or effects of what the past harbored. Yet if they agree with these verbalities and effects, we can know that our ideas of the past are true. *As true as past time itself was,* so true was Julius Caesar, so true were antediluvian monsters, all in their proper dates and settings. That past time itself was, is guaranteed by its coherence with everything that's present. True as the present *is,* the past *was* also.

Agreement thus turns out to be essentially an affair of leading—leading that is useful because it is into quarters that contain objects that are important. True ideas lead us into useful verbal and conceptual quarters as well as directly up to useful sensible termini. They lead to consistency, stability and flowing human intercourse. They lead away from excentricity and isolation, from foiled and barren thinking. The untrammeled flowing of the leading-process, its general freedom from clash and contradiction, passes for its indirect verification; but all roads lead to Rome, and in the end and eventually, all true processes must lead to the fact of directly verifying sensible experiences *somewhere,* which somebody's ideas have copied.

Such is the large loose way in which the pragmatist interprets the word agreement. He treats it altogether practically. He lets it cover any process of conduction from a present idea to a future terminus, provided only it run prosperously. It is only thus that "scientific" ideas, flying as they do beyond common sense, can be said to agree with their realties. It is, as I have already said, *as if* reality were made of ether, atoms or electrons, but we mustn't think so literally. The term "energy" doesn't even pretend to stand for anything "objective." It is only a way of measuring the surface of phenomena so as to string their changes on a simple formula.

Yet in the choice of these man-made formulas we cannot be capricious with impunity any more than we can be capricious on the common-sense practical level. We must find a theory that will *work;* and that means something extremely difficult; for our theory must mediate between all previous truths and certain new experiences. It must derange common sense and previous belief as little as possible, and it must lead to some sensible terminus or other that can be verified exactly. To "work" means both these things; and the squeeze is so tight that there is little loose play for any hypothesis. Our theories are wedged and controlled as nothing else is. Yet sometimes alternative theoretic formulas are equally compatible with all the truths we know, and then we choose between them for subjective reasons. We choose the kind of theory to which we are already partial; we follow "elegance" or "economy." Clerk Maxwell somewhere says it would be "poor scientific taste"[3] to choose the more complicated of two equally well-evidenced conceptions; and you will all agree with him. Truth in science is what gives us the maximum possible sum of satisfactions, taste included, but consistency both with previous truth and with novel fact is always the most imperious claimant.

I have led you through a very sandy desert. But now, if I may be allowed so vulgar an expression, we begin to taste the milk in the cocoanut. Our rationalist critics here discharge their batteries upon us, and to reply to them will take us out from all this dryness into full sight of a momentous philosophical alternative.

Our account of truth is an account of truths in the plural, or processes of leading, realized *in rebus,*[4] and having only this quality in common, that they *pay.* They pay by guiding us into or towards some part of a system that dips at numerous points into sense-percepts, which we may copy mentally or not, but with which at any rate we are now in the kind of commerce vaguely designated as verification. Truth for us is simply a collective name for verification-processes, just as health, wealth, strength, etc., are names for other processes connected with life, and also pursued because it pays to pursue them. Truth is *made,* just as health, wealth and strength are made, in the course of experience.

Here rationalism is instantaneously up in arms against us. I can imagine a rationalist to talk as follows:

"Truth is not made," he will say; "it absolutely obtains, being a unique relation that does not wait upon any process, but shoots straight over the head of experience, and hits its reality every time. Our belief that yon thing on the wall is a clock is true already, altho no one in the whole history of the world should verify it. The bare quality of standing in that transcendent relation is what makes any thought true that possesses it, whether or not there be verification. You pragmatists put the cart before the horse in making truth's being reside in verification-processes. These are merely signs of its being, merely our lame ways of ascertaining after the fact, which of our ideas already has possessed the wondrous quality. The quality itself is timeless, like all essences and natures. Thoughts partake of it directly, as they partake of falsity or of irrelevancy. It can't be analyzed away into pragmatic consequences."

The whole plausibility of this rationalist tirade is due to the fact to which we have already paid so much attention. In our world, namely, abounding as it does in things of similar kinds and similarly associated, one verification serves for others of its kind, and one great use of knowing things is to be led not so much to them as to their associates, especially to human talk about them. The quality of truth, obtaining *ante rem,*[5] pragmatically means, then, the fact that in such a world innumerable ideas work better by their indirect or possible than by their direct and actual verification. Truth *ante rem* means only verifiability, then; or else it is a case of the stock rationalist trick of treating the *name* of a concrete phenomenal reality as an independent prior entity, and placing it behind the reality as its explanation. Professor Mach quotes somewhere an epigram of Lessings's:

> Sagt Hänschen Schlau zu Vetter Fritz,
> "Wie kommt es, Vetter Fritzen,
> Dass grad' die Reichsten in der Welt,
> Das meiste Geld besitzen?"[6]

Hänschen Schlau here treats the principle "wealth" as something distinct from the facts noted by the man's being rich. It antedates them; the facts become only a sort of secondary coincidence with the rich man's essential nature.

In the case of "wealth" we all see the fallacy. We know that wealth is but a name for concrete processes that certain men's lives play a part in, and not a natural excellence found in Messrs. Rockefeller and Carnegie, but not in the rest of us.

Like wealth, health also lives *in rebus*. It is a name for processes, as digestion, circulation, sleep, etc., that go on happily, tho in this instance we are more inclined to think of it as a principle and to say the man digests and sleeps so well· *because* he is so healthy.

With "strength" we are, I think, more rationalistic still, and decidedly inclined to treat it as an excellence pre-existing in the man and explanatory of the herculean performances of his muscles.

With "truth" most people go over the border entirely, and treat the rationalistic account as self-evident. But really all these words in *th* are exactly similar. Truth exists *ante rem* just as much and as little as the other things do.

The scholastics, following Aristotle, made much of the distinction between habit and act. Health *in actu*[7] means, among other things, good sleeping and digesting. But a healthy man need not always be sleeping, or always digesting, any more than a wealthy man need be always handling money, or a strong man always lifting weights. All such qualities sink to the status of "habits" between their times of exercise; and similarly truth becomes a habit of certain of our ideas and beliefs in their intervals of rest from their verifying activities. But those activities are the root of the whole matter, and the condition of there being any habit to exist in the intervals.

"The time," to put it very briefly, is only the expedient in the way of our thinking, just as "the right" is only the expedient in the way of our behaving. Expedient in almost any fashion; and expedient in the long run and on the whole of course; for what meets expediently all the experience in sight won't necessarily meet all farther experiences equally satisfactorily. Experience, as we know, has ways of *boiling over,* and making us correct our present formulas.

The "absolutely" true, meaning what no farther experience will ever alter, is that ideal vanishing-point towards which we imagine that all our temporary truths will some day converge. It runs on all fours with the perfectly wise man, and with the absolutely complete experience; and, if these ideals are ever realized, they will all be realized together. Meanwhile we have to live today by what truth we can get to-day, and be ready to-morrow to call it falsehood. Ptolemaic astronomy, euclidean space, aristotelian logic, scholastic metaphysics, were expedient for centuries, but human experience has boiled over those limits, and we now call these things only relatively true, or true within those borders of experience. "Absolutely" they are false; for we know that those limits were casual, and might have been transcended by past theorists just as they are by present thinkers.

When new experiences lead to retrospective judgments, using the past tense, what these judgments utter *was* true, even tho no past thinker had been led there. We live forwards, a Danish thinker[8] has said, but we understand backwards. The present sheds a backward light on the world's previous processes. They may have been truth-processes for the actors in them. They are not so for one who knows the later revelations of the story.

This regulative notion of a potential better truth to be established later, possibly to be established some day absolutely and having powers of retroactive legislation, turns its face, like all pragmatist notions, towards concreteness of fact, and towards the future. Like the half-truths, the absolute truth will have to be *made,* made as a relation incidental to the growth of a mass of verification-experience, to which the half-true ideas are all along contributing their quota.

I have already insisted on the fact that truth is made largely out of previous truths. Men's beliefs at any time are so much experience *funded*. But the beliefs are themselves parts of the sum total of the world's experience, and become matter, therefore, for the next day's funding operations. So far as reality means experience-able reality, both it and the truths men gain about it are everlastingly in process of mutation—mutation towards a definite goal, it may be—but still mutation.

Mathematicians can solve problems with two variables. On the Newtonian theory, for instance, acceleration varies with distance, but distance also varies with acceleration. In the realm of truth-processes facts come independently and determine our beliefs provisionally. But these beliefs make us act, and as fast as they do so, they bring into sight or into existence new facts which re-determine the beliefs accordingly. So the whole coil and ball of truth, as it rolls up, is the product of a double influence. Truths emerge from facts; but they dip forward into facts again and add to them; which facts again create or reveal new truth (the word is in-different) and so on indefinitely. The "facts" themselves mean-while are not *true*. They simply *are*. Truth is the function of the beliefs that start and terminate among them.

The case is like a snowball's growth, due as it is to the distribu-tion of the snow on the one hand, and to the successive pushes of the boys on the other, with these factors co-determining each other incessantly.

The most fateful point of difference between being a rationalist and being a pragmatist is now fully in sight. Experience is in mutation, and our psychological ascertainments of truth are in mutation—so much rationalism will allow; but never that either reality itself or truth itself is mutable. Reality stands complete and ready-made from all eternity, rationalism insists, and the agree-ment of our ideas with it is that unique unanalyzable virtue in them of which she has already told us. As that intrinsic excellence, their truth has nothing to do with our experiences. It adds noth-ing to the content of experience. It makes no difference to reality itself; it is supervenient, inert, static, a reflexion merely. It doesn't *exist*, it *holds* or *obtains*, it belongs to another dimension from that of either facts or fact-relations, belongs, in short, to the epistemo-logical dimension—and with that big word rationalism closes the discussion.

Thus, just as pragmatism faces forward to the future, so does ra-tionalism here again face backward to a past eternity. True to her inveterate habit, rationalism reverts to "principles," and thinks that when an abstraction once is named, we own an oracular solution.

The tremendous pregnancy in the way of consequences for life of this radical difference of outlook will only become apparent in my later lectures. I wish meanwhile to close this lecture by showing that rationalism's sublimity does not save it from inanity.

When, namely, you ask rationalists, instead of accusing pragmatism of desecrating the notion of truth, to define it themselves by saying exactly what *they* understand by it, the only positive attempts I can think of are these two:

1. "Truth is just the system of propositions which have an unconditional claim to be recognized as valid."[9]

2. "Truth is a name for all those judgments which we find ourselves under obligation to make by a kind of imperative duty."[10]

The first thing that strikes one in such definitions is their unutterable triviality. They are absolutely true, of course, but absolutely insignificant until you handle them pragmatically. What do you mean by "claim" here, and what do you mean by "duty"? As summary names for the concrete reasons why thinking in true ways is overwhelmingly expedient and good for mortal men, it is all right to talk of claims on reality's part to be agreed with, and of obligations on our part to agree. We feel both the claims and the obligations, and we feel them for just those reasons.

But the rationalists who talk of claim and obligation *expressly say that they have nothing to do with our practical interests or personal reasons.* Our reasons for agreeing are psychological facts, they say, relative to each thinker, and to the accidents of his life. They are his evidence merely, they are no part of the life of truth itself. That life transacts itself in a purely logical or epistemological, as distinguished from a psychological, dimension, and its claims antedate and exceed all personal motivations whatsoever. Tho neither man nor God should ever ascertain truth, the word would still have to be defined as that which *ought* to be ascertained and recognized.

There never was a more exquisite example of an idea abstracted from the concretes of experience and then used to oppose and negate what it was abstracted from.

Philosophy and common life abound in similar instances. The "sentimentalist fallacy" is to shed tears over abstract justice and generosity, beauty, etc., and never to know these qualities when you meet them in the street, because there the circumstances make them vulgar. Thus I read in the privately printed biography of an eminently rationalistic mind: "It was strange that with such admiration for beauty in the abstract, my brother had no enthusiasm for fine architecture, for beautiful painting, or for flowers." And in almost the last philosophic work I have read, I find such passages as the following: "Justice is ideal, solely ideal. Reason conceives that it ought to exist, but experience shows that it cannot. . . . Truth, which ought to be, cannot be. . . . Reason is deformed by experience. As soon as reason enters experience, it becomes contrary to reason."

The rationalist's fallacy here is exactly like the sentimentalist's. Both extract a quality from the muddy particulars of experience, and find it so pure when extracted that they contrast it with each and all its muddy instances as an opposite and higher nature. All the while it is *their* nature. It is the nature of truths to be validated, verified. It pays for our ideas to be validated. Our obligation to seek truth is part of our general obligation to do what pays. The payments true ideas bring are the sole why of our duty to follow them.

Identical whys exist in the case of wealth and health. Truth makes no other kind of claim and imposes no other kind of ought than health and wealth do. All these claims are conditional; the concrete benefits we gain are what we mean by calling the pursuit a duty. In the case of truth, untrue beliefs work as perniciously in the long run as true beliefs work beneficially. Talking abstractly, the quality "true" may thus be said to grow absolutely precious, and the quality "untrue" absolutely damnable: the one may be called good, the other bad, unconditionally. We ought to think the true, we ought to shun the false, imperatively.

But if we treat all this abstraction literally and oppose it to its mother soil in experience, see what a preposterous position we work ourselves into.

We cannot then take a step forward in our actual thinking. When shall I acknowledge this truth and when that? Shall the acknowledgment be loud?—or silent? If sometimes loud, sometimes silent, which *now?* When may a truth go into cold-storage in the encyclopedia? and when shall it come out for battle? Must I constantly be repeating the truth "twice two are four" because of its eternal claim on recognition? or is it sometimes irrelevant? Must my thoughts dwell night and day on my personal sins and blemishes, because I truly have them?—or may I sink and ignore them in order to be a decent social unit, and not a mass of morbid melancholy and apology?

It is quite evident that our obligation to acknowledge truth, so far from being unconditional, is tremendously conditioned. Truth with a big T, and in the singular, claims abstractly to be recognized of course, but concrete truths in the plural need to be recognized only when their recognition is expedient. A truth must always be preferred to a falsehood when both relate to the situation; but when neither does, truth is as little of a duty as falsehood. If you ask me what o'clock it is and I tell you that I live at 95 Irving Street, my answer may indeed be true, but you don't see why it is my duty to give it. A false address would be as much to the purpose.

With this admission that there are conditions that limit the application of the abstract imperative, *the pragmatistic treatment of truth sweeps back upon us in its fulness.* Our duty to agree with reality is seen to be grounded in a perfect jungle of concrete expediences.

When Berkeley had explained what people meant by matter, people thought that he denied matter's existence. When Messrs. Schiller and Dewey now explain what people mean by truth, they are accused of denying *its* existence. These pragmatists destroy all objective standards, critics say, and put foolishness and wisdom on one level. A favorite formula for describing Mr. Schiller's doctrines and mine is that we are persons who think that by saying whatever you find it pleasant to say and calling it truth you fulfil every pragmatistic requirement.

I leave it to you to judge whether this be not an impudent slander. Pent in, as the pragmatist more than anyone else sees himself to be, between the whole body of funded truths squeezed from the past and the coercions of the world of sense about him, who so well as he feels the immense pressure of objective control under which our minds perform their operations? If anyone imagines that this law is lax, let him keep its commandment one day, says Emerson.[11] We have heard much of late of the uses of the imagination in science. It is high time to urge the use of a little imagination in philosophy. The unwillingness of some of our critics to read any but the silliest of possible meanings into our statements is as discreditable to their imaginations as anything I know in recent philosophic history. Schiller says the true is that which "works." Thereupon he is treated as one who limits verification to the lowest material utilities. Dewey says truth is what gives "satisfaction." He is treated as one who believes in calling everything true which, if it were true, would be pleasant.

Our critics certainly need more imagination of realities. I have honestly tried to stretch my own imagination and to read the best possible meaning into the rationalist conception, but I have to confess that it still completely baffles me. The notion of a reality calling on us to "agree" with it, and that for no reasons, but simply because its claim is "unconditional" or "transcendent," is one that I can make neither head nor tail of. I try to imagine myself as the sole reality in the world, and then to imagine what more I would "claim" if I were allowed to. If you suggest the possibility of my claiming that a mind should come into being from out of the void inane and stand and *copy* me, I can indeed imagine what the copying might mean, but I can conjure up no motive. What good it would do me to be copied, or what good it would do that mind to copy me, if farther consequences are expressly and in principle ruled out as motives for the claim (as they are by our rationalist authorities) I cannot fathom. When the Irishman's admirers ran him along to the place of banquet in a sedan chair with no bottom, he said, "Faith, if it wasn't for the honor of the thing, I might as well have come on foot." So here: but for the honor of the thing, I might as well have remained uncopied. Copying is one genuine mode of knowing (which for some strange reason our contemporary transcendentalists seem to be tumbling over each other to repudiate); but when we get beyond copying, and fall back on unnamed forms of agreeing that are expressly denied to be either copyings or leadings or fittings, or any other processes pragmatically definable, the *what* of the "agreement" claimed becomes as unintelligible as the why of it. Neither content nor motive can be imagined for it. It is an absolutely meaningless abstraction.[12]

Surely in this field of truth it is the pragmatists and not the rationalists who are the more genuine defenders of the universe's rationality.

from **A Pluralistic Universe**

(1909)

BUT WHAT AT BOTTOM is meant by calling the universe many or by calling it one?

Pragmatically interpreted, pluralism or the doctrine that it is many means only that the sundry parts of reality *may be externally related*. Everything you can think of, however vast or inclusive, has on the pluralistic view a genuinely "external" environment of some sort or amount. Things are "with" one another in many ways, but nothing includes everything, or dominates over everything. The word "and" trails along after every sentence. Something always escapes. "Ever not quite"[1] has to be said of the best attempts made anywhere in the universe at attaining all-inclusiveness. The pluralistic world is thus more like a federal republic than like an empire or a kingdom. However much may be collected, however much may report itself as present at any effective centre of consciousness or action, something else is self-governed and absent and unreduced to unity.

Monism, on the other hand, insists that when you come down to reality as such, to the reality of realities, everything is present to *everything* else in one vast instantaneous co-implicated completeness—nothing can in *any* sense, functional or substantial, be really absent from anything else, all things interpenetrate and telescope together in the great total conflux.

For pluralism, all that we are required to admit as the constitution of reality is what we ourselves find empirically realized in every minimum of finite life. Briefly it is this, that nothing real is absolutely simple, that every smallest bit of experience is a *multum in parvo*[2] plurally related, that each relation is one aspect, character,

Oliver Wendell Holmes

Holmes was born in Boston in 1841. He left Harvard College in his senior year to enlist in the Union Army, serving from 1861 to 1864. He was seriously wounded in battle three times. After the war he attended Harvard Law School and practiced law briefly, forming, for a period, a close friendship with William James. He became an editor of the *American Law Review* in 1870. His lectures *The Common Law* were published in 1881, and the following year he joined the faculty of Harvard Law School. In 1882 he left Harvard abruptly to become associate justice of the Supreme Judicial Court of Massachusetts; he was made chief justice in 1899. In 1902 Theodore Roosevelt appointed him to the United States Supreme Court, where he sat until 1932. He wrote, in his fifty years on the bench, over two thousand opinions, probably a record for judges sitting in courts of last resort. He was also a formidable correspondent, and the various editions of his letters fill many volumes. He died in Washington, D.C., in 1935.

or function, way of its being taken, or way of its taking something else; and that a bit of reality when actively engaged in one of these relations is not *by that very fact* engaged in all the other relations simultaneously. The relations are not *all* what the French call *solidaires* with one another. Without losing its identity a thing can either take up or drop another thing, like the log I spoke of,[3] which by taking up new careers and dropping old ones can travel anywhere with a light escort.

For monism, on the contrary, everything, whether we realize it or not, drags the whole universe along with itself and drops nothing. The log starts and arrives with all its carriers supporting it. If a thing were once disconnected, it could never be connected again, according to monism. The pragmatic difference between the two systems is thus a definite one. It is just thus, that if *a* is once out of sight of *b* or out of touch with it, or, more briefly, "out" of it at all, then, according to monism, it must always remain so, they can never get together; whereas pluralism admits that on another occasion they may work together, or in some way be connected again. Monism allows for no such things as "other occasions" in reality—in *real* or absolute reality, that is.

The difference I try to describe amounts, you see, to nothing more than the difference between . . . the each-form and the all-form of reality. Pluralism lets things really exist in the each-form or distributively. Monism thinks that the all-form or collective-unit form is the only form that is rational. The all-form allows of no taking up and dropping of connexions, for in the all the parts are essentially and eternally co-implicated. In the each-form, on the contrary, a thing may be connected by intermediary things, with a thing with which it has no immediate or essential connexion. It is thus at all times in many possible connexions which are not necessarily actualized at the moment. They depend on which actual path of intermediation it may functionally strike into: the word "or" names a genuine reality. Thus, as I speak here, I may look ahead *or* to the right *or* to the left, and in either case the intervening space and air and aether unable me to see the faces of a different portion of this audience. My being here is independent of any one set of these faces.

If the each-form be the eternal form of reality no less than it is the form of temporal appearance, we still have a coherent world, and not an incarnate incoherence, as is charged by so many absolutists. Our "multiverse" still makes a "universe"; for every part, tho it may not be in actual or immediate connexion, is nevertheless in some possible or mediated connexion, with every other part however remote, through the fact that each part hangs together with its very next neighbors in inextricable interfusion. The type of union, it is true, is different here from the monistic type of *alleinheit*.[4] It is not a universal co-implication, or integration of all things *durcheinander*.[5] It is what I call the strung-along type, the type of continuity, contiguity, or concatenation. If you prefer Greek words, you may call it the synechistic type.[6] At all events, you see that it forms a definitely conceivable alternative to the through-and-through unity of all things at once, which is the type opposed to it by monism. You see also that it stands or falls with the notion . . . of the through-and-through union of adjacent minima of experience, of the confluence of every passing moment of concretely felt experience with its immediately next neighbors. The recognition of this fact of coalescence of next with next in concrete experience, so that all the insulating cuts we make there are artificial products of the conceptualizing faculty, is what distinguishes the empiricism which I call "radical,"[7] from the bugaboo empiricism of the traditional rationalist critics, which (rightly or wrongly) is accused of chopping up experience into atomistic sensations, incapable of union with one another until a purely intellectual principle has swooped down upon them from on high and folded them in its own conjunctive categories.

Here, then, you have the plain alternative, and the full mystery of the difference between pluralism and monism, as clearly as I can set it forth on this occasion. It packs up into a nutshell:—Is the manyness-in-oneness that indubitably characterizes the world we inhabit, a property only of the absolute whole of things, so that

you must postulate that one-enormous-whole indivisibly as the *prius*[8] of there being any many at all—in other words, start with the rationalistic block-universe, entire, unmitigated, and complete?—or can the finite elements have their own aboriginal forms of manyness-in-oneness, and where they have no immediate oneness still be continued into one another by intermediary terms—each one of these terms being one with its next neighbors, and yet the total "oneness" never getting absolutely complete?

The alternative is definite. It seems to me, moreover, that the two horns of it make pragmatically different ethical appeals—at least they *may* do so, to certain individuals. But if you consider the pluralistic horn to be intrinsically irrational, self-contradictory, and absurd, I can now say no more in its defence. Having done what I could in my earlier lectures to break the edge of the intellectualistic *reductiones ad absurdum,* I must leave the issue in your hands. Whatever I may say, each of you will be sure to take pluralism or leave it, just as your own sense of rationality moves and inclines. The only thing I emphatically insist upon is that it is a fully coordinate hypothesis with monism. This world *may,* in the last resort, be a block-universe; but on the other hand it *may* be a universe only strung-along, not rounded in and closed. Reality *may* exist distributively just as it sensibly seems to, after all. On that possibility I do insist.

[handwritten note:] This attacks the journalistic fallacy of "get the facts straight and everything else will fall into place." They neglect relevant facts; clutter with irrelevancies just because they are "true"; and, most of all, jump to conclusions, grabbing at the most simplistic deductions

from **Lecture I: Early Forms of Liability**

in *The Common Law* (1881)

THE OBJECT of this book is to present a general view of the Common Law. To accomplish the task, other tools are needed besides logic. It is something to show that the consistency of a system requires a particular result, but it is not all. The life of the law has not been logic; it has been experience. The felt necessities of the time, the prevalent moral and political theories, intuitions of public policy, avowed or unconscious, even the prejudices which judges share with their fellow-men, have had a good deal more to do than the syllogism in determining the rules by which men should be governed. The law embodies the story of a nation's development through many centuries, and it cannot be dealt with as if it contained only the axioms and corollaries of a book of mathematics. In order to know what it is, we must know what it has been, and what it tends to become. We must alternately consult history and existing theories of legislation. But the most difficult labor will be to understand the combination of the two into new products at every stage. The substance of the law at any given time pretty nearly corresponds, so far as it goes, with what is then understood to be convenient; but its form and machinery, and the degree to which it is able to work out desired results, depend very much upon its past.

In Massachusetts to-day, while, on the one hand, there are a great many rules which are quite sufficiently accounted for by their manifest good sense, on the other, there are some which can only be understood by reference to the infancy of procedure among the German tribes, or to the social condition of Rome under the Decemvirs.

I shall use the history of our law so far as it is necessary to explain a conception or to interpret a rule, but no further. In doing so there are two errors equally to be avoided both by writer and reader. One is that of supposing, because an idea seems very familiar and natural to us, that it has always been so. Many things which we take for granted have had to be laboriously fought out or thought out in past times. The other mistake is the opposite one of asking too much of history. We start with man full grown. It may be assumed that the earliest barbarian whose practices are to be considered, had a good many of the same feelings and passions as ourselves.

from Lecture III: Torts— Trespass and Negligence

in *The Common Law* (1881)

WHEN A CASE ARISES in which the standard of conduct, pure and simple, is submitted to the jury, the explanation is plain. It is that the court, not entertaining any clear view of public policy applicable to the matter, derives the rule to be applied from daily experience, as it has been agreed that the great body of the law of tort has been derived. But the court further feels that it is not itself possessed of sufficient practical experience to lay down the rule intelligently. It conceives that twelve men taken from the practical part of the community can aid its judgment. Therefore it aids its conscience by taking the opinion of the jury.

But supposing a state of facts often repeated in practice, is it to be imagined that the court is to go on leaving the standard to the jury forever? Is it not manifest, on the contrary, that if the jury is, on the whole, as fair a tribunal as it is represented to be, the lesson which can be got from that source will be learned? Either the court will find that the fair teaching of experience is that the conduct complained of usually is or is not blameworthy, and therefore, unless explained, is or is not a ground of liability; or it will find the jury oscillating to and fro, and will see the necessity of making up its mind for itself. There is no reason why any other such question should not be settled, as well as that of liability for stairs with smooth strips of brass upon their edges. The exceptions would mainly be found where the standard was rapidly changing, as, for instance, in some questions of medical treatment.

If this be the proper conclusion in plain cases, further

consequences ensue. Facts do not often exactly repeat themselves in practice; but cases with comparatively small variations from each other do. A judge who has long sat at *nisi prius*[1] ought gradually to acquire a fund of experience which enables him to represent the common sense of the community in ordinary instances far better than an average jury. He should be able to lead and to instruct them in detail, even where he thinks it desirable, on the whole, to take their opinion. Furthermore, the sphere in which he is able to rule without taking their opinion at all should be continually growing.

It has often been said, that negligence is pure matter of fact, or that, after the court has declared the evidence to be such that negligence *may* be inferred from it, the jury are always to decide whether the inference shall be drawn. But it is believed that the courts, when they lay down this broad proposition, are thinking of cases where the conduct to be passed upon is not proved directly, and the main or only question is what that conduct was, not what standard shall be applied to it after it is established.

Most cases which go to the jury on a ruling that there is evidence from which they may find negligence, do not go to them principally on account of a doubt as to the standard, but of a doubt as to the conduct. . . . Legal, like natural divisions, however clear in their general outline, will be found on exact scrutiny to end in a penumbra or debatable land. This is the region of the jury, and only cases falling on this doubtful border are likely to be carried far in court. Still, the tendency of the law must always be to narrow the field of uncertainty. That is what analogy, as well as the decisions on this very subject, would lead us to expect.

The growth of the law is very apt to take place in this way. Two widely different cases suggest a general distinction, which is a clear one when stated broadly. But as new cases cluster around the opposite poles, and begin to approach each other, the distinction becomes more difficult to trace; the determinations are made one way or the other on a very slight preponderance of feeling, rather than of articulate reason; and at last a mathematical line is arrived at by the contact of contrary decisions, which is so far arbitrary that it might equally well have been drawn a little farther to the one side or to the other, but which must have been drawn somewhere in the neighborhood of where it falls.[2]

from Privilege, Malice, and Intent

(1894)

IN SOME CASES, a man is not liable for a very manifest danger unless he actually intends to do the harm complained of. In some cases, he even may intend to do the harm and yet not have to answer for it: and, as I think, in some cases of this latter sort, at least, actual malice may make him liable when without it he would not have been. In this connection I mean by malice a malevolent motive for action, without reference to any hope of a remoter benefit to oneself to be accomplished by the intended harm to another. The question whether malice in this sense has any effect upon the extent of a defendant's rights and liabilities, has arisen in many forms. It is familiar in regard to the use of land in some way manifestly harmful to a neighbor. It has been suggested, and brought to greater prominence, by boycotts, and other combinations for more or less similar purposes, although in such cases the harm inflicted is only a means, and the end sought to be attained generally is some benefit to the defendant. . . .

It will be noticed that I assume that we have got past the question which is answered by the test of the external standard.[1] There is no dispute that the manifest tendency of the defendant's act is to inflict temporal damage upon the plaintiff. Generally, that result is expected, and often at least it is intended. And the first question that presents itself is why the defendant is not liable without going further. The answer is suggested by the commonplace, that the intentional infliction of temporal damage, or the doing of an act manifestly likely to inflict such damage and inflicting it, is actionable if done without just cause. When the defendant escapes, the court is of opinion that he has acted with just cause. There are various justifications. In these instances, the justification is that the defendant is privileged knowingly to inflict the damage complained of.

But whether, and how far, a privilege shall be allowed is a question of policy. Questions of policy are legislative questions, and judges are shy of reasoning from such grounds. Therefore, decisions for or against the privilege, which really can stand only upon such grounds, often are presented as hollow deductions from empty general propositions like *sic utere tuo ut alienum non laedas,*[2] which teaches nothing but a benevolent yearning, or else are put as if they themselves embodied a postulate of the law and admitted of no further deduction, as when it is said that, although there is temporal damage, there is no wrong; whereas, the very thing to be found out is whether there is a wrong or not, and if not, why not.

When the question of policy is faced it will be seen to be one which cannot be answered by generalities, but must be determined by the particular character of the case, even if everybody agrees what the answer should be. I do not try to mention or to generalize all the facts which have to be taken into account; but plainly the worth of the result, or the gain from allowing the act to be done, has to be compared with the loss which it inflicts. Therefore, the conclusion will vary, and will depend on different reasons according to the nature of the affair.

For instance, a man has a right to set up a shop in a small village which can support but one of the kind, although he expects and intends to ruin a deserving widow who is established there already. He has a right to build a house upon his land in such a position as to spoil the view from a far more valuable house hard by. He has a right to give honest answers to inquiries about a servant, although he intends thereby to prevent his getting a place. But the reasons for these several privileges are different. The first rests on the economic postulate that free competition is worth more to society than it costs. The next, upon the fact that a line must be drawn between the conflicting interests of adjoining owners, which necessarily will restrict the freedom of each; upon the unavoidable philistinism which prefers use to beauty when considering the most profitable way of administering the land in the jurisdiction taken as one whole; upon the fact that the defendant does not go outside his own boundary; and upon other reasons. . . . The third, upon the proposition that the benefit of free access to information, in some cases and within some limits, outweighs the harm to an occasional unfortunate. I do not know whether the principle has been applied in favor of a servant giving a character to a master.

Not only the existence but the extent or degree of the privilege will vary with the case. . . .

Perhaps one of the reasons why judges do not like to discuss questions of policy, or to put a decision in terms upon their views as law-makers, is that the moment you leave the path of merely logical deduction you lose the illusion of certainty which makes legal reasoning seem like mathematics. But the certainty is only an illusion, nevertheless. Views of policy are taught by experience of the interests of life. Those interests are fields of battle. Whatever decisions are made must be against the wishes and opinion of one party, and the distinctions on which they go will be distinctions of degree.

The Path of the Law

(1897)

WHEN WE STUDY LAW we are not studying a mystery but a well-known profession. We are studying what we shall want in or- der to appear before judges, or to advise people in such a way as to keep them out of court. The reason why it is a profession, why people will pay lawyers to argue for them or to advise them, is that in societies like ours the command of the public force is intrusted to the judges in certain cases, and the whole power of the state will be put forth, if necessary, to carry out their judgments and de- crees. People want to know under what circumstances and how far they will run the risk of coming against what is so much stronger than themselves, and hence it becomes a business to find out when this danger is to be feared. The object of our study, then, is pre- diction, the prediction of the incidence of the public force through the instrumentality of the courts.

The means of the study are a body of reports, of treatises, and of statutes, in this country and in England, extending back for six hundred years, and now increasing annually by hundreds. In these sibylline leaves are gathered the scattered prophecies of the past upon the cases in which the axe will fall. These are what properly have been called the oracles of the law. Far the most important and pretty nearly the whole meaning of every new effort of legal thought is to make these prophecies more precise, and to general- ize them into a thoroughly connected system. The process is one, from a lawyer's statement of a case, eliminating as it does all the dramatic elements with which his client's story has clothed it, and retaining only the facts of legal import, up to the final analyses and abstract universals of theoretic jurisprudence. The reason why a lawyer does not mention that his client wore a white hat when he made a contract, while Mrs. Quickly would be sure to dwell upon it along with the parcel gilt goblet and the sea-coal fire, is that he foresees that the public force will act in the same way whatever his client had upon his head. It is to make the prophecies easier to be remembered and to be understood that the teachings of the decisions of the past are put into general propositions and gathered into text-books, or that statutes are passed in a general form. The primary rights and duties with which jurisprudence busies itself again are nothing but prophecies. One of the many evil effects of the confusion between legal and moral ideas, about which I shall have something to say in a moment, is that theory is apt to get the cart before the horse, and to consider the right or the duty as something existing apart from and independent of the consequences of its breach, to which certain sanctions are added afterward. But, as I shall try to show, a legal duty so called is nothing but a prediction that if a man does or omits certain things he will be made to suffer in this or that way by judgment of the court; and so of a legal right.

The number of our predictions when generalized and reduced to a system is not unmanageably large. They present themselves as a finite body of dogma which may be mastered within a reasonable time. It is a great mistake to be frightened by the ever-increasing number of reports. The reports of a given jurisdiction in the course of a generation take up pretty much the whole body of the law, and restate it from the present point of view. We could reconstruct the corpus from them if all that went before were burned. The use of the earlier reports is mainly historical, a use about which I shall have something to say before I have finished.

I wish, if I can, to lay down some first principles for the study of this body of dogma or systematized prediction which we call the law, for men who want to use it as the instrument of their business to enable them to prophesy in their turn, and, as bearing upon the study, I wish to point out an ideal which as yet our law has not attained.

The first thing for a business-like understanding of the matter is to understand its limits, and therefore I think it desirable at once to point out and dispel a confusion between morality and law, which sometimes rises to the height of conscious theory, and more often and indeed constantly is making trouble in detail without reaching the point of consciousness. You can see very plainly that a bad man has as much reason as a good one for wishing to avoid an encounter with the public force, and therefore you can see the practical importance of the distinction between morality and law. A man who cares nothing for an ethical rule which is believed and practised by his neighbors is likely nevertheless to care a good deal to avoid being made to pay money, and will want to keep out of jail if he can.

I take it for granted that no hearer of mine will misinterpret what I have to say as the language of cynicism. The law is the witness and external deposit of our moral life. Its history is the history of the moral development of the race. The practice of it, in spite of popular jests, tends to make good citizens and good men. When I emphasize the difference between law and morals I do so with reference to a single end, that of learning and understanding the law. For that purpose you must definitely master its specific marks, and it is for that I ask you for the moment to imagine yourselves indifferent to other and greater things.

I do not say that there is not a wider point of view from which the distinction between law and morals becomes of secondary or no importance, as all mathematical distinctions vanish in presence of the infinite. But I do say that that distinction is of the first importance for the object which we are here to consider—a right study and mastery of the law as a business with well understood limits, a body of dogma enclosed within definite lines. I have just shown the practical reason for saying so. If you want to know the law and nothing else, you must look at it as a bad man, who cares only for the material consequences which such knowledge enables him to predict, not as a good one, who finds his reasons for conduct, whether inside the law or outside of it, in the vaguer sanctions of conscience. The theoretical importance of the distinction is no less, if you would reason on your subject aright. The law is full of phraseology drawn from morals, and by the mere force of language continually invites us to pass from one domain to the other without perceiving it, as we are sure to do unless we have the boundary constantly before our minds. The law talks about rights, and duties, and malice, and intent, and negligence, and so forth, and nothing is easier, or, I may say, more common in legal reasoning, than to take these words in their moral sense, at some stage of the argument, and so to drop into fallacy. For instance, when we speak of the rights of man in a moral sense, we mean to mark the limits of interference with individual freedom which we think are prescribed by conscience, or by our ideal, however reached. Yet it is certain that many laws have been enforced in the past, and it is likely that some are enforced now, which are condemned by the most enlightened opinion of the time, or which at all events pass the limit of interference as many consciences would draw it. Manifestly, therefore, nothing but confusion of thought can result from assuming that the rights of man in a moral sense are equally rights in the sense of the Constitution and the law. No doubt simple and extreme cases can be put of imaginable laws which the statute-making power would not dare to enact, even in the absence of written constitutional prohibitions, because the community would rise in rebellion and fight; and this gives some plausibility to the proposition that the law, if not a part of morality, is limited by it. But this limit of power is not coextensive with any system of morals. For the most part it falls far within the lines of any such system, and in some cases may extend beyond them, for reasons drawn from the habits of a particular people at a particular time. I once heard the late Professor Agassiz[1] say that a German population would rise if you added two cents to the price of a glass of beer. A statute in such a case would be empty words, not because it was wrong, but because it could not be enforced. No one will deny that wrong statutes can be and are enforced, and we should not all agree as to which were the wrong ones.

The confusion with which I am dealing besets confessedly legal conceptions. Take the fundamental question, What constitutes the law? You will find some text writers telling you that it is something different from what is decided by the courts of Massachusetts or England, that it is a system of reason, that it is a deduction from principles of ethics or admitted axioms or what not, which may or may not coincide with the decisions. But if we take the view of our friend the bad man we shall find that he does not care two straws for the axioms or deductions, but that he does want to know what the Massachusetts or English courts are likely to do in fact. I am much of his mind. The prophecies of what the courts will do in fact, and nothing more pretentious, are what I mean by the law.

Take again a notion which as popularly understood is the widest conception which the law contains—the notion of legal duty, to which already I have referred. We fill the word with all the content which we draw from morals. But what does it mean to a bad man? Mainly, and in the first place, a prophecy that if he does certain things he will be subjected to disagreeable consequences by way of imprisonment or compulsory payment of money. But from his point of view, what is the difference between being fined and being taxed a certain sum for doing a certain thing? That his point of view is the test of legal principles is shown by the many discussions which have arisen in the courts on the very question whether a given statutory liability is a penalty or a tax. On the answer to this question depends the decision whether conduct is legally wrong or right, and also whether a man is under compulsion or free. Leaving the criminal law on one side, what is the difference between the liability under the mill acts[2] or statutes authorizing a taking by eminent domain and the liability for what we call a wrongful conversion of property[3] where restoration is out of the question. In both cases the party taking another man's property has to pay its fair value as assessed by a jury, and no more. What significance is there in calling one taking right and another wrong from the point of view of the law? It does not matter, so far as the given consequence, the compulsory payment, is concerned, whether the act to which it is attached is described in terms of praise or in terms of blame, or whether the law purports to prohibit it or to allow it. If it matters at all, still speaking from the bad man's point of view, it must be because in one case and not in the other some further disadavantages, or at least some further consequences, are attached to the act by the law. The only other disadvantages thus attached to it which I ever have been able to think of are to be found in two somewhat insignificant legal doctrines, both of which might be abolished without disturbance. One is, that a contract to do a prohibited act is unlawful, and the other, that, if one of two or more joint wrongdoers has to pay all the damages, he cannot recover contribution from his fellows. And that I believe is all. You see how the vague circumference of the notion of duty shrinks and at the same time grows more precise when we wash it with cynical acid and expel everything except the object of our study, the operations of the law.

Nowhere is the confusion between legal and moral ideas more manifest than in the law of contract. Among other things here again the so called primary rights and duties are invested with a mystic significance beyond what can be assigned and explained. The duty to keep a contract at common law means a prediction that you must pay damages if you do not keep it—and nothing else. If you commit a tort,[4] you are liable to pay a compensatory sum. If you commit a contract, you are liable to pay a compensatory sum unless the promised event comes to pass, and that is all the difference. But such a mode of looking at the matter stinks in the nostrils of those who think it advantageous to get as much ethics into the law as they can. It was good enough for Lord Coke,[5] however, and here, as in many other cases, I am content to abide with him. In *Bromage v. Genning,*[6] a prohibition was sought in the King's Bench against a suit in the marches of Wales for the specific performance of a covenant[7] to grant a lease, and Coke said that it would subvert the intention of the covenantor, since he intends it to be at his election either to lose the damages or to make the lease. Sergeant Harris for the plaintiff confessed that he moved the matter against his conscience, and a prohibition was granted. This goes further than we should go now, but it shows what I venture to say has been the common law point of view from the beginning, although Mr. Harriman, in his very able little book upon Contracts has been misled, as I humbly think, to a different conclusion.

I have spoken only of the common law, because there are some cases in which a logical justification can be found for speaking of civil liabilities as imposing duties in an intelligible sense. These are the relatively few in which equity[8] will grant an injunction, and will enforce it by putting the defendant in prison or otherwise punishing him unless he complies with the order of the court. But I hardly think it advisable to shape general theory from the exception, and I think it would be better to cease troubling ourselves about primary rights and sanctions altogether, than to describe our prophecies concerning the liabilities commonly imposed by the law in those inappropriate terms.

I mentioned, as other examples of the use by the law of words drawn from morals, malice, intent, and negligence. It is enough to take malice as it is used in the law of civil liability for wrongs— what we lawyers call the law of torts—to show that it means something different in law from what it means in morals, and also to show how the difference has been obscured by giving to principles which have little or nothing to do with each other the same name. Three hundred years ago a parson preached a sermon and told a story out of Fox's *Book of Martyrs* of a man who had assisted at the torture of one of the saints, and afterward died, suffering compensatory inward torment. It happened that Fox was wrong. The man was alive and chanced to hear the sermon, and thereupon he sued the parson. Chief Justice Wray instructed the jury that the defendant was not liable, because the story was told innocently, without malice. He took malice in the moral sense, as importing a malevolent motive. But nowadays no one doubts that a man may be liable, without any malevolent motive at all, for false statements manifestly calculated to inflict temporal damage. In stating the case in pleading, we still should call the defendant's conduct malicious; but, in my opinion at least, the word means nothing about motives, or even about the defendant's attitude toward the future, but only signifies that the tendency of his conduct under the known circumstances was very plainly to cause the plaintiff temporal harm.[9]

In the law of contract the use of moral phraseology has led to equal confusion, as I have shown in part already, but only in part. Morals deal with the actual internal state of the individual's mind, what he actually intends. From the time of the Romans down to now, this mode of dealing has affected the language of the law as to contract, and the language used has reacted upon the thought. We talk about a contract as a meeting of the minds of the parties, and thence it is inferred in various cases that there is no contract because their minds have not met; that is, because they have intended different things or because one party has not known of the assent of the other. Yet nothing is more certain than that parties may be bound by a contract to things which neither of them intended, and when one does not know of the other's assent. Suppose a contract is executed in due form and in writing to deliver a lecture, mentioning no time. One of the parties thinks that the promise will be construed to mean at once, within a week. The other thinks that it means when he is ready. The court says that it means within a reasonable time. The parties are bound by the contract as it is interpreted by the court, yet neither of them meant what the court declares that they have said. In my opinion no one will understand the true theory of contract or be able even to discuss some fundamental questions intelligently until he has understood that all contracts are formal, that the making of a contract depends not on the agreement of two minds in one intention, but on the agreement of two sets of external signs—not on the parties' having *meant* the same thing but on their having *said* the same thing. Furthermore, as the signs may be addressed to one sense or another—to sight or to hearing—on the nature of the sign will depend the moment when the contract is made. If the sign is tangible, for instance, a letter, the contract is made when the letter of acceptance is delivered. If it is necessary that the minds of the parties meet, there will be no contract until the acceptance can be read—none, for example, if the acceptance be snatched from the hand of the offerer by a third person. *None aren't → All are*

This is not the time to work out a theory in detail, or to answer many obvious doubts and questions which are suggested by these general views. I know of none <u>which</u> are not easy to answer, but what I am trying to do now is only by a series of hints to throw some light on the narrow path of legal doctrine, and upon two *that?* pitfalls <u>which,</u> as it seems to me, lie perilously near to it. Of the first of these I have said enough. I hope that my illustrations have shown the danger, both to speculation and to practice, of confounding morality with law, and the trap which legal language lays for us on that side of our way. For my own part, I often doubt whether it would not be a gain if every word of moral significance could be banished from the law altogether, and other words adopted <u>which</u> should convey legal ideas uncolored by anything outside the law. We should lose the fossil records of a good deal of history and the majesty got from ethical associations, but by ridding ourselves of an unnecessary confusion we should gain very much in the clearness of our thought. *Knowing English would help too*

So much for the limits of the law. The next thing which I wish to consider is what are the forces which determine its content and its growth. You may assume, with Hobbes and Bentham and Austin, that all law emanates from the sovereign, even when the first human beings to enunciate it are the judges, or you may think that law is the voice of the Zeitgeist, or what you like. It is all one to my present purpose. Even if every decision required the sanction of an emperor with <u>despotic power</u> and a whimsical turn of *Supreme* <u>mind,</u> we should be interested none the less, still with a view to *Court* prediction, in discovering some order, some rational explanation, and some principle of growth for the rules which he laid down. In every system there are such explanations and principles to be found. It is with regard to them that a second fallacy comes in, which I think it important to expose.

The fallacy to which I refer is the notion that the only force at work in the development of the law is logic. In the broadest sense, indeed, that notion would be true. The postulate on which we think about the universe is that there is a fixed quantitative relation between every phenomenon and its antecedents and consequents. If there is such a thing as a phenomenon without these fixed quantitative relations, it is a miracle. It is outside the law of cause and effect, and as such transcends our power of thought, or at least is something to or from which we cannot reason. The condition of our thinking about the universe is that it is capable of being thought about rationally, or, in other words, that every part of it is effect and cause in the same sense in which those parts are with which we are most familiar. So in the broadest sense it is true that the law is a logical development, like everything else. The danger of which I speak is not the admission that the principles governing other phenomena also govern the law, but the notion that a given system, ours, for instance, can be worked out like mathematics from some general axioms of conduct. This is the natural error of the schools, but it is not confined to them. I once heard a very eminent judge say that he never let a decision go until he was absolutely sure that it was right. So judicial dissent often is blamed, as if it meant simply that one side or the other were not doing their sums right, and, if they would take more trouble, agreement inevitably would come.

This mode of thinking is entirely natural. The training of lawyers is a training in logic. The processes of analogy, discrimination, and deduction are those in which they are most at home. The language of judicial decision is mainly the language of logic. And the logical method and form flatter that longing for certainty and for repose which is in every human mind. But certainty generally is illusion, and repose is not the destiny of man. Behind the logical form lies a judgment as to the relative worth and importance of competing legislative grounds, often an inarticulate and uncon-

Only cases can be judged, not laws.
Overturning a law is legislative, not judicial

scious judgment, it is true, and yet the very root and nerve of the whole proceeding. You can give any conclusion a logical form. You always can imply a condition in a contract. But why do you imply it? It is because of some belief as to the practice of the community or of a class, or because of some opinion as to policy, or, in short, because of some attitude of yours upon a matter not capable of exact quantitative measurement, and therefore not capable of founding exact logical conclusions. Such matters really are battle grounds where the means do not exist for determinations that shall be good for all time, and where the decision can do no more than embody the preference of a given body in a given time and place. We do not realize how large a part of our law is open to reconsideration upon a slight change in the habit of the public mind. No concrete proposition is self evident, no matter how ready we may be to accept it, not even Mr. Herbert Spencer's "Every man has a right to do what he wills, provided he interferes not with a like right on the part of his neighbors."[10]

Why is a false and injurious statement privileged, if it is made honestly in giving information about a servant. It is because it has been thought more important that information should be given freely, than that a man should be protected from what under other circumstances would be an actionable wrong. Why is a man at liberty to set up a business which he knows will ruin his neighbor? It is because the public good is supposed to be best subserved by free competition. Obviously such judgments of relative importance may vary in different times and places. Why does a judge instruct a jury that an employer is not liable to an employee for an injury received in the course of his employment unless he is negligent, and why do the jury generally find for the plaintiff if the case is allowed to go to them? It is because the traditional policy of our law is to confine liability to cases where a prudent man might have foreseen the injury, or at least the danger, while the inclination of a very large part of the community is to make certain classes of persons insure the safety of those with whom they deal. Since the last words were written, I have seen the requirement of such insurance put forth as part of the programme of one of the best known labor organizations. There is a concealed, half conscious battle on the question of legislative policy, and if any one thinks that it can be settled deductively, or once for all, I only can say that I think he is theoretically wrong, and that I am certain that his conclusion will not be accepted in practice *semper ubique et ab omnibus.*[11]

Indeed, I think that even now our theory upon this matter is open to reconsideration, although I am not prepared to say how I should decide if a reconsideration were proposed. Our law of torts comes from the old days of isolated, ungeneralized wrongs, assaults, slanders, and the like, where the damages might be taken to lie where they fell by legal judgment. But the torts with which our courts are kept busy to-day are mainly the incidents of certain well known businesses. They are injuries to person or property by railroads, factories, and the like. The liability for them is estimated, and sooner or later goes into the price paid by the public. The public really pays the damages, and the question of liability, if pressed far enough, is really the question how far it is desirable that the public should insure the safety of those whose work it uses. It might be said that in such cases the chance of a jury finding for the defendant is merely a chance, once in a while rather arbitrarily interrupting the regular course of recovery, most likely in the case of an unusually conscientious plaintiff, and therefore better done away with. On the other hand, the economic value even of a life to the community can be estimated, and no recovery, it may be said, ought to go beyond that amount. It is conceivable that some day in certain cases we may find ourselves imitating, on a higher plane, the tariff for life and limb which we see in the *Leges Barbarorum.*[12]

I think that the judges themselves have failed adequately to recognize their duty of weighing considerations of social advantage. The duty is inevitable, and the result of the often proclaimed judicial aversion to deal with such considerations is simply to leave the very ground and foundation of judgments inarticulate, and often unconscious, as I have said. When socialism first began to be talked about, the comfortable classes of the community were a good deal frightened. I suspect that this fear has influenced judicial action both here and in England, yet it is certain that it is not a conscious factor in the decisions to which I refer. I think that something similar has led people who no longer hope to control the legislatures to look to the courts as expounders of the Constitutions, and that in some courts new principles have been discovered outside the bodies of those instruments, which may be generalized into acceptance of the economic doctrines which prevailed about fifty years ago, and a wholesale prohibition of what a tribunal of lawyers does not think about right. I cannot but believe that if the training of lawyers led them habitually to consider more definitely and explicitly the social advantage on which the rule they lay down must be justified, they sometimes would hesitate where now they are confident, and see that really they were taking sides upon debatable and often burning questions.

So much for the fallacy of logical form. Now let us consider the present condition of the law as a subject for study, and the ideal toward which it tends. We still are far from the point of view which I desire to see reached. No one has reached it or can reach it as yet. We are only at the beginning of a philosophical reaction, and of a reconsideration of the worth of doctrines which for the most part still are taken for granted without any deliberate, conscious, and systematic questioning of their grounds. The development of our law has gone on for nearly a thousand years, like the development of a plant, each generation taking the inevitable next step, mind, like matter, simply obeying a law of spontaneous growth. It is perfectly natural and right that it should have been so. Imitation is a necessity of human nature, as has been illustrated by a remarkable French writer, M. Tarde, in an admirable book, *Les Lois de l'Imitation*. Most of the things we do, we do for no better reason than that our fathers have done them or that our neighbors do them, and the same is true of a larger part than we suspect of what we think. The reason is a good one, because our short life gives us no time for a better, but it is not the best. It does not follow, because we all are compelled to take on faith at second hand most of the rules on which we base our action and our thought, that each of us may not try to set some corner of his world in the order of reason, or that all of us collectively should not aspire to carry reason as far as it will go throughout the whole domain. In regard to the law, it is true, no doubt, that an evolutionist will hesitate to affirm universal validity for his social ideals, or for the principles which he thinks should be embodied in legislation. He is content if he can prove them best for here and now. He may be ready to admit that he knows nothing about an absolute best in the cosmos, and even that he knows next to nothing about a permanent best for men. Still it is true that a body of law is more rational and more civilized when every rule it contains is referred articulately and definitely to an end which it subserves, and when the grounds for desiring that end are stated or are ready to be stated in words.

At present, in very many cases, if we want to know why a rule of law has taken its particular shape, and more or less if we want to know why it exists at all, we go to tradition. We follow it into the Year Books, and perhaps beyond them to the customs of the Salian Franks, and somewhere in the past, in the German forests, in the needs of Norman kings, in the assumptions of a dominant class, in the absence of generalized ideas, we find out the practical motive for what now best is justified by the mere fact of its acceptance and that men are accustomed to it. The rational study of law is still to a large extent the study of history. History must be a part of the study, because without it we cannot know the precise scope of rules which it is our business to know. It is a part of the rational study, because it is the first step toward an enlightened scepticism, that is, towards a deliberate reconsideration of the worth of those rules. When you get the dragon out of his cave on to the plain and in the daylight, you can count his teeth and claws, and see just what is his strength. But to get him out is only the first step. The next is either to kill him, or to tame him and make him a useful animal. For the rational study of the law the black-letter

[handwritten: Many sports rules are anachronisms.]

man[13] may be the man of the present, but the man of the future is the man of statistics and the master of economics. It is revolting to have no better reason for a rule of law than that so it was laid down in the time of Henry IV. It is still more revolting if the grounds upon which it was laid down have vanished long since, and the rule simply persists from blind imitation of the past. I am thinking of the technical rule as to trespass *ab initio,*[14] as it is called, which I attempted to explain in a recent Massachusetts case.[15]

Let me take an illustration, which can be stated in a few words, to show how the social end which is aimed at by a rule of law is obscured and only partially attained in consequence of the fact that the rule owes its form to a gradual historical development, instead of being reshaped as a whole, with conscious articulate reference to the end in view. We think it desirable to prevent one man's property being misappropriated by another, and so we make larceny a crime. The evil is the same whether the misappropriation is made by a man into whose hands the owner has put the property, or by one who wrongfully takes it away. But primitive law in its weakness did not get much beyond an effort to prevent violence, and very naturally made a wrongful taking, a trespass, part of its definition of the crime. In modern times the judges enlarged the definition a little by holding that, if the wrong-doer gets possession by a trick or device, the crime is committed. This really was giving up the requirement of a trespass, and it would have been more logical, as well as truer to the present object of the law, to abandon the requirement altogether. That, however, would have seemed too bold, and was left to statute. Statutes were passed making embezzlement a crime. But the force of tradition caused the crime of embezzlement to be regarded as so far distinct from larceny that to this day, in some jurisdictions at least, a slip corner is kept open for thieves to contend, if indicted for larceny, that they should have been indicted for embezzlement, and if indicted for embezzlement, that they should have been indicted for larceny, and to escape on that ground.

Far more fundamental questions still await a better answer than that we do as our fathers have done. What have we better than a blind guess to show that the criminal law in its present form does more good than harm? I do not stop to refer to the effect which it has had in degrading prisoners and in plunging them further into crime, or to the question whether fine and imprisonment do not fall more heavily on a criminal's wife and children than on himself. I have in mind more far-reaching questions. Does punishment deter? Do we deal with criminals on proper principles? A modern school of Continental criminalists plumes itself on the formula, first suggested, it is said, by Gall, that we must consider the criminal rather than the crime. The formula does not carry us very far, but the inquiries which have been started look toward an answer of my questions based on science for the first time. If the typical criminal is a degenerate, bound to swindle or to murder by as deep seated an organic necessity as that which makes the rattlesnake bite, it is idle to talk of deterring him by the classical method of imprisonment. He must be got rid of; he cannot be improved, or frightened out of his structural reaction. If, on the other hand, crime, like normal human conduct, is mainly a matter of imitation, punishment fairly may be expected to help to keep it out of fashion. The study of criminals has been thought by some well known men of science to sustain the former hypothesis. The statistics of the relative increase of crime in crowded places like large cities, where example has the greatest chance to work, and in less populated parts, where the contagion spreads more slowly, have been used with great force in favor of the latter view. But there is weighty authority for the belief that, however this may be, "not the nature of the crime, but the dangerousness of the criminal, constitutes the only reasonable legal criterion to guide the inevitable social reaction against the criminal."[16]

The impediments to rational generalization, which I illustrated from the law of larceny, are shown in the other branches of the law, as well as in that of crime. Take the law of tort or civil liability for damages apart from contract and the like. Is there any general theory of such liability, or are the cases in which it exists simply to be enumerated, and to be explained each on its special ground, as is easy to believe from the fact that the right of action for certain well known classes of wrongs like trespass or slander has its special history for each class? I think that there is a general theory to be discovered, although resting in tendency rather than established and accepted. I think that the law regards the infliction of temporal damage by a responsible person as actionable, if under the circumstances known to him the danger of his act is manifest according to common experience, or according to his own experience if it is more than common, except in cases where upon special grounds of policy the law refuses to protect the plaintiff or grants a privilege to the defendant.[17] I think that commonly malice, intent, and negligence mean only that the danger was manifest to a greater or less degree, under the circumstances known to the actor, although in some cases of privilege malice may mean an actual malevolent motive, and such a motive may take away a permission knowingly to inflict harm, which otherwise would be granted on this or that ground of dominant public good. But when I stated my view to a very eminent English judge the other day, he said: "You are discussing what the law ought to be; as the law is, you must show a right. A man is not liable for negligence unless he is subject to a duty." If our difference was more than a difference in words, or with regard to the proportion between the exceptions and the rule, then, in his opinion, liability for an act cannot be referred to the manifest tendency of the act to cause temporal damage in general as a sufficient explanation, but must be referred to the special nature of the damage, or must be derived from some special circumstances outside of the tendency of the act, for which no generalized explanation exists. I think that such a view is wrong, but it is familiar, and I dare say generally is accepted in England.

Everywhere the basis of principle is tradition, to such an extent that we even are in danger of making the rôle of history more important than it is. The other day Professor Ames wrote a learned article[18] to show, among other things, that the common law did not recognize the defence of fraud in actions upon specialties,[19] and the moral might seem to be that the personal character of that defence is due to its equitable origin. But if, as I have said, all contracts are formal, the difference is not merely historical, but theoretic, between defects of form which prevent a contract from being made, and mistaken motives which manifestly could not be considered in any system that we should call rational except against one who was privy to those motives. It is not confined to specialties, but is of universal application. I ought to add that I do not suppose that Mr. Ames would disagree with what I suggest.

However, if we consider the law of contract, we find it full of history. The distinctions between debt, covenant, and assumpsit[20] are merely historical. The classification of certain obligations to pay money, imposed by the law irrespective of any bargain as quasi contracts, is merely historical. The doctrine of consideration[21] is merely historical. The effect given to a seal is to be explained by history alone. Consideration is a mere form. Is it a useful form? If so, why should it not be required in all contracts? A seal is a mere form, and is vanishing in the scroll and in enactments that a consideration must be given, seal or no seal. Why should any merely historical distinction be allowed to affect the rights and obligations of business men?

Since I wrote this discourse I have come on a very good example of the way in which tradition not only overrides rational policy, but overrides it after first having been misunderstood and having been given a new and broader scope than it had when it had a meaning. It is the settled law of England that a material alteration of a written contract by a party avoids it as against him. The doctrine is contrary to the general tendency of the law. We do not tell a jury that if a man ever has lied in one particular he is to be presumed to lie in all. Even if a man has tried to defraud, it seems no sufficient reason for preventing him from proving the truth. Objections of like nature in general go to the weight, not to the admissibility, of evidence. Moreover, this rule is irrespective of fraud, and is not confined to evidence. It is not merely that you cannot use the writing, but that the contract is at an end. What does this mean? The existence of a written contract depends on the fact that the offerer and offeree have interchanged their written expressions, not on the continued existence of those expressions. But in the case of a bond, the primitive notion was different. The contract was inseparable from the parchment. If a stranger destroyed it, or tore off the seal, or altered it, the obligee could not recover, however free from fault, because the defendant's contract, that is, the actual tangible bond which he had sealed, could not be produced in the form in which it bound him. About a hundred years ago Lord Kenyon undertook to use his reason on this tradition, as he sometimes did to the detriment of the law, and, not understanding it, said he could see no reason why what was true of a bond should not be true of other contracts.[22] His decision happened to be right, as it concerned a promissory note, where again the common law regarded the contract as inseparable from the paper on which it was written, but the reasoning was general, and soon was extended to other written contracts, and various absurd and unreal grounds of policy were invented to account for the enlarged rule.

I trust that no one will understand me to be speaking with disrespect of the law, because I criticise it so freely. I venerate the law, and especially our system of law, as one of the vastest products of the human mind. No one knows better than I do the countless number of great intellects that have spent themselves in making some addition or improvement, the greatest of which is trifling when compared with the mighty whole. It has the final title to respect that it exists, that it is not a Hegelian dream, but a part of the lives of men. But one may criticise even what one reveres. Law is the business to which my life is devoted, and I should show less than devotion if I did not do what in me lies to improve it, and, when I perceive what seems to me the ideal of its future, if I hesitated to point it out and to press toward it with all my heart.

Perhaps I have said enough to show the part which the study of history necessarily plays in the intelligent study of the law as it is to-day. In the teaching of this school and at Cambridge it is in no danger of being undervalued. Mr. Bigelow here and Mr. Ames and Mr. Thayer there have made important contributions which will not be forgotten, and in England the recent history of early English law by Sir Frederick Pollock and Mr. Maitland has lent the subject an almost deceptive charm.[23] We must beware of the pitfall of antiquarianism, and must remember that for our purposes our only interest in the past is for the light it throws upon the present. I look forward to a time when the part played by history in the explanation of dogma shall be very small, and instead of ingenious research we shall spend our energy on a study of the ends sought to be attained and the reasons for desiring them. As a step toward that ideal it seems to me that every lawyer ought to seek an understanding of economics. The present divorce between the schools of political economy and law seems to me an evidence of how much progress in philosophical study still remains to be made. In the present state of political economy, indeed, we come again upon history on a larger scale, but there we are called on to consider and weigh the ends of legislation, the means of attaining them, and the cost. We learn that for everything we have we give up something else, and we are taught to set the advantage we gain against the other advantage we lose, and to know what we are doing when we elect.

There is another study which sometimes is undervalued by the practical minded, for which I wish to say a good word, although I think a good deal of pretty poor stuff goes under that name. I mean the study of what is called jurisprudence. Jurisprudence, as I look at it, is simply law in its most generalized part. Every effort to reduce a case to a rule is an effort of jurisprudence, although the name as used in English is confined to the broadest rules and most fundamental conceptions. One mark of a great lawyer is that he sees the application of the broadest rules. There is a story of a Vermont justice of the peace before whom a suit was brought by one farmer against another for breaking a churn. The justice took time to consider, and then said that he had looked through the statutes and could find nothing about churns, and gave judgment for the defendant. The same state of mind is shown in all our common digests and text-books. Applications of rudimentary rules of contract or tort are tucked away under the head of Railroads or Telegraphs or go to swell treatises on historical subdivisions, such as Shipping or Equity, or are gathered under an arbitrary title which is thought likely to appeal to the practical mind, such as Mercantile Law. If a man goes into law it pays to be a master of it, and to be a master of it means to look straight through all the dramatic incidents and to discern the true basis for prophecy. Therefore, it is well to have an accurate notion of what you mean by law, by a right, by a duty, by malice, intent, and negligence, by ownership, by possession, and so forth. I have in my mind cases in which the highest courts seem to me to have floundered because they had no clear ideas on some of these themes. I have illustrated their importance already. If a further illustration is wished, it may be found by reading the Appendix to Sir James Stephen's *Criminal Law* on the subject of possession, and then turning to Pollock and Wright's enlightened book. Sir James Stephen is not the only writer whose attempts to analyze legal ideas have been confused by striving for a useless quintessence of all systems, instead of an accurate anatomy of one. The trouble with Austin was that he did not know enough English law. But still it is a practical advantage to master Austin, and his predecessors, Hobbes and Bentham, and his worthy successors, Holland and Pollock.[24] Sir Frederick Pollock's recent little book[25] is touched with the felicity which marks all his works, and is wholly free from the perverting influence of Roman models.

The advice of the elders to young men is very apt to be as unreal as a list of the hundred best books. At least in my day I had my share of such counsels, and high among the unrealities I place the recommendation to study the Roman law. I assume that such advice means more than collecting a few Latin maxims with which to ornament the discourse—the purpose for which Lord Coke recommended Bracton.[26] If that is all that is wanted, the title *De*

Regulis Juris Antiqui can be read in an hour. I assume that, if it is well to study the Roman Law, it is well to study it as a working system. That means mastering a set of technicalities more difficult and less understood than our own, and studying another course of history by which even more than our own the Roman Law must be explained. If any one doubts me, let him read Keller's *Der Römische Civil Process und die Actionen,* a treatise on the praetor's edict, Muirhead's most interesting *Historical Introduction to the Private Law of Rome,* and, to give him the best chance, Sohm's admirable *Institutes.* No. The way to gain a liberal view of your subject is not to read something else, but to get to the bottom of the subject itself. The means of doing that are, in the first place, to follow the existing body of dogma into its highest generalizations by the help of jurisprudence; next, to discover from history how it has come to be what it is; and, finally, so far as you can, to consider the ends which the several rules seek to accomplish, the reasons why those ends are desired, what is given up to gain them, and whether they are worth the price.

We have too little theory in the law rather than too much, especially on this final branch of study. When I was speaking of history, I mentioned larceny as an example to show how the law suffered from not having embodied in a clear form a rule which will accomplish its manifest purpose. In that case the trouble was due to the survival of forms coming from a time when a more limited purpose was entertained. Let me now give an example to show the practical importance, for the decision of actual cases, of understanding the reasons of the law, by taking an example from rules which, so far as I know, never have been explained or theorized about in any adequate way. I refer to statutes of limitation and the law of prescription.[27] The end of such rules is obvious, but what is the justification for depriving a man of his rights, a pure evil as far as it goes, in consequence of the lapse of time? Sometimes the loss of evidence is referred to, but that is a secondary matter. Sometimes the desirability of peace, but why is peace more desirable after twenty years than before? It is increasingly likely to come without the aid of legislation. Sometimes it is said that, if a man neglects to enforce his rights, he cannot complain if, after a while, the law follows his example. Now if this is all that can be said about it, you probably will decide a case I am going to put, for the plaintiff; if you take the view which I shall suggest, you possibly will decide it for the defendant. A man is sued for trespass upon land, and justifies under a right of way. He proves that he has used the way openly and adversely[28] for twenty years, but it turns out that the plaintiff had granted a license to a person whom he reasonably supposed to be the defendant's agent, although not so in fact, and therefore had assumed that the use of the way was permissive, in which case no right would be gained. Has the defendant gained a right or not? If his gaining it stands on the fault and neglect of the landowner in the ordinary sense, as seems commonly to be supposed, there has been no such neglect, and the right of way has not been acquired. But if I were the defendant's counsel, I should suggest that the foundation of the acquisition of rights by lapse of time is to be looked for in the position of the person who gains them, not in that of the loser. Sir Henry Maine has made it fashionable to connect the archaic notion of property with prescription.[29] But the connection is further back than the first recorded history. It is in the nature of man's mind. A thing which you have enjoyed and used as your own for a long time, whether property or an opinion, takes root in your being and cannot be torn away without your resenting the act and trying to defend yourself, however you came by it. The law can ask no better justification than the deepest instincts of man. It is only by way of reply to the suggestion that you are disappointing the former owner, that you refer to his neglect having allowed the gradual dissociation between himself and what he claims, and the gradual association of it with another. If he knows that another is doing acts which on their face show that he is on the way toward establishing such an association, I should argue that in justice to that other he was bound at his peril to find out whether the other was acting under his permission, to see that he was warned, and if necessary, stopped.

I have been speaking about the study of the law, and I have said next to nothing of what commonly is talked about in that connection—text-books and the case system, and all the machinery with which a student comes most immediately in contact. Nor shall I say anything about them. Theory is my subject, not practical details. The modes of teaching have been improved since my time, no doubt, but ability and industry will master the raw material with any mode. Theory is the most important part of the dogma of the law, as the architect is the most important man who takes part in the building of a house. The most important improvements of the last twenty-five years are improvements in theory. It is not to be feared as unpractical, for, to the competent, it simply means going to the bottom of the subject. For the incompetent, it sometimes is true, as has been said, that an interest in general ideas means an absence of particular knowledge. I remember in army days reading of a youth who, being examined for the lowest grade and being asked a question about squadron drill, answered that he never had considered the evolutions of less than ten thousand men. But the weak and foolish must be left to their folly. The danger is that the able and practical minded should look with indifference or distrust upon ideas the connection of which with their business is remote. I heard a story, the other day, of a man who had a valet to whom he paid high wages, subject to deduction for faults. One of his deductions was, "For lack of imagination, five dollars." The lack is not confined to valets. The object of ambition, power, generally presents itself nowadays in the form of money alone. Money is the most immediate form, and is a proper object of desire. "The fortune," said Rachel, "is the measure of the intelligence."[30] That is a good text to waken people out of a fool's paradise. But, as Hegel says,[31] "It is in the end not the appetite, but the opinion, which has to be satisfied." To an imagination of any scope the most far-reaching form of power is not money, it is the command of ideas. If you want great examples, read Mr. Leslie Stephen's *History of English Thought in the Eighteenth Century,* and see how a hundred years after his death the abstract speculations of Descartes had become a practical force controlling the conduct of men. Read the works of the great German jurists, and see how much more the world is governed to-day by Kant than by Bonaparte. We cannot all be Descartes or Kant, but we all want happiness. And happiness, I am sure from having known many successful men, cannot be won simply by being counsel for great corporations and having an income of fifty thousand dollars. An intellect great enough to win the prize needs other food besides success. The remoter and more general aspects of the law are those which give it universal interest. It is through them that you not only become a great master in your calling, but connect your subject with the universe and catch an echo of the infinite, a glimpse of its unfathomable process, a hint of the universal law.

from Ideals and Doubts

(1915)

WHEN I SAY that a thing is true, I mean that I cannot help believing it. I am stating an experience as to which there is no choice. But as there are many things that I cannot help doing that the universe can, I do not venture to assume that my inabilities in the way of thought are inabilities of the universe. I therefore define the truth as the system of my limitations, and leave absolute truth for those who are better equipped. With absolute truth I leave absolute ideals of conduct equally on one side.

But although one believes in what commonly, with some equivocation, is called necessity; that phenomena always are found to stand in quantitatively fixed relations to earlier phenomena; it does not follow that without such absolute ideals we have nothing to do but to sit still and let time run over us. As I wrote many years ago, the mode in which the inevitable comes to pass is through effort. Consciously or unconsciously we all strive to make the kind of a world that we like. And although with Spinoza we may regard criticism of the past as futile, there is every reason for doing all that we can to make a future such as we desire.

There is every reason also for trying to make our desires intelligent. The trouble is that our ideals for the most part are inarticulate, and that even if we have made them definite we have very little experimental knowledge of the way to bring them about. The social reformers of today seem to me so far to forget that we no more can get something for nothing by legislation than we can by mechanics as to be satisfied if the bill to be paid for their improvements is not presented in a lump sum. Interstitial detriments that may far outweigh the benefit promised are not bothered about. Probably I am too skeptical as to our ability to do more than shift disagreeable burdens from the shoulders of the stronger to those of the weaker. But I hold to a few articles of a creed that I do not expect to see popular in my day. I believe that the whole-sale social regeneration which so many now seem to expect, if it can be helped by conscious, coördinated human effort, cannot be affected appreciably by tinkering with the institution of property, but only by taking in hand life and trying to build a race. That would be my starting point for an ideal for the law. The notion that with socialized property we should have women free and a pi-ano for everybody seems to me an empty humbug.

To get a little nearer to the practical, our current ethics and our current satisfaction with conventional legal rules, it seems to me, can be purged to a certain extent without reference to what our final ideal may be. To rest upon a formula is a slumber that, prolonged, means death. Our system of morality is a body of imperfect social generalizations expressed in terms of emotion. To get at its truth, it is useful to omit the emotion and ask our-selves what those generalizations are and how far they are confirmed by fact accurately ascertained. So in regard to the formulas of the law, I have found it very instructive to consider what may be the postulates implied. They are generically two: that such and such a condition or result is desirable and that such and such means are appropriate to bring it about. In all debatable matters there are conflicting desires to be accomplished by in-consistent means, and the further question arises, which is entitled to prevail in the specific case? Upon such issues logic does not carry us far, and the practical solution sometimes may assume a somewhat cynical shape. But I have found it a help to clear thinking to try to get behind my conventional assumptions as a judge whose first business is to see that the game is played accord-ing to the rules whether I like them or not. To have doubted one's own first principles is the mark of a civilized man. To know what you want and why you think that such a measure will help it is the first but by no means the last step towards intelligent legal reform. The other and more difficult one is to realize what you must give up to get it, and to consider whether you are ready to pay the price.

Natural Law

(1918)

IT IS NOT ENOUGH for the knight of romance that you agree that his lady is a very nice girl—if you do not admit that she is the best that God ever made or will make, you must fight. There is in all men a demand for the superlative, so much so that the poor devil who has no other way of reaching it attains it by getting drunk. It seems to me that this demand is at the bottom of the philosopher's effort to prove that truth is absolute and of the jurist's search for criteria of universal validity which he collects under the head of natural law.

I used to say, when I was young, that truth was the majority vote of that nation that could lick all others. Certainly we may expect that the received opinion about the present war will depend a good deal upon which side wins (I hope with all my soul it will be mine), and I think that the statement was correct in so far as it implied that our test of truth is a reference to either a present or an imagined future majority in favor of our view. If, as I have suggested elsewhere, the truth may be defined as the system of any (intellectual) limitations,[1] what gives it objectivity is the fact that I find my fellow man to a greater or less extent (never wholly) subject to the same *Can't Helps.* If I think that I am sitting at a table I find that the other persons present agree with me; so if I say that the sum of the angles of a triangle is equal to two right angles. If I am in a minority of one they send for a doctor or lock me up; and I am so far able to transcend the to me convincing testimony of my senses or my reason as to recognize that if I am alone probably something is wrong with my works.

Certitude is not the test of certainty. We have been cock-sure of many things that were not so. If I may quote myself again, property, friendship, and truth have a common root in time. One can not be wrenched from the rocky crevices into which one has grown for many years without feeling that one is attacked in one's life. What we most love and revere generally is determined by early associations. I love granite rocks and barberry bushes, no doubt because with them were my earliest joys that reach back through the past eternity of my life. But while one's experience thus makes certain preferences dogmatic for oneself, recognition of how they came to be so leaves one able to see that others, poor souls, may be equally dogmatic about something else. And this again means scepticism. Not that one's belief or love does not remain. Not that we would not fight and die for it if important—we all, whether we know it or not, are fighting to make the kind of a world that we should like—but that we have learned to recognize that others will fight and die to make a different world, with equal sincerity or belief. Deep-seated preferences can not be argued about—you can not argue a man into liking a glass of beer—and therefore, when differences are sufficiently far reaching, we try to kill the other man rather than let him have his way. But that is perfectly consistent with admitting that, so far as appears, his grounds are just as good as ours.

The jurists who believe in natural law seem to me to be in that naïve state of mind that accepts what has been familiar and accepted by them and their neighbors as something that must be accepted by all men everywhere. No doubt it is true that, so far as we can see ahead, some arrangements and the rudiments of familiar institutions seem to be necessary elements in any society that may spring from our own and that would seem to us to be civilized— some form of permanent association between the sexes—some residue of property individually owned—some mode of binding oneself to specified future conduct—at the bottom of all, some protection for the person. But without speculating whether a group is imaginable in which all but the last of these might disappear and the last be subject to qualifications that most of us would abhor, the question remains as to the *Ought* of natural law.

It is true that beliefs and wishes have a transcendental basis in the sense that their foundation is arbitrary. You can not help entertaining and feeling them, and there is an end of it. As an arbitrary fact people wish to live, and we say with various degrees of certainty that they can do so only on certain conditions. To do it they must eat and drink. That necessity is absolute. It is a necessity of less degree but practically general that they should live in society. If they live in society, so far as we can see, there are further conditions. Reason working on experience does tell us, no doubt, that if our wish to live continues, we can do it only on those terms. But that seems to me the whole of the matter. I see no *a priori* duty to live with others and in that way, but simply a statement of what I must do if I wish to remain alive. If I do live with others they tell me that I must do and abstain from doing various things or they will put the screws on to me. I believe that they will, and being of the same mind as to their conduct I not only accept the rules but come in time to accept them with sympathy and emotional affirmation and begin to talk about duties and rights. But for legal purposes a right is only the hypostasis of a prophecy—the imagination of a substance supporting the fact that the public force will be brought to bear upon those who do things said to contravene it—just as we talk of the force of gravitation accounting for the conduct of bodies in space. One phrase adds no more than the other to what we know without it. No doubt behind these legal rights is the fighting will of the subject to maintain them, and the spread of his emotions to the general rules by which they are maintained; but that does not seem to me the same thing as the supposed *a priori* discernment of a duty or the assertion of a preëxisting right. A dog will fight for his bone.

The most fundamental of the supposed preëxisting rights—the right of life—is sacrificed without a scruple not only in war, but whenever the interest of society, that is, of the predominant power in the community, is thought to demand it. Whether that interest is the interest of mankind in the long run no one can tell, and as, in any event, to those who do not think with Kant and Hegel it is only an interest, the sanctity disappears. I remember a very tender-hearted judge being of opinion that closing a hatch to stop a fire and the destruction of a cargo was justified even if it was known that doing so would stifle a man below. It is idle to illustrate further, because to those who agree with me I am uttering commonplaces and to those who disagree I am ignoring the necessary foundations of thought. The *a priori* men generally call the dissentients superficial. But I do agree with them in believing that one's attitude on these matters is closely connected with one's general attitude toward the universe. Proximately, as has been suggested, it is determined largely by early associations and temperament, coupled with the desire to have an absolute guide. Men to a great extent believe what they want to—although I see in that no basis for a philosophy that tells us what we should want to want.

Now when we come to our attitude toward the universe I do not see any rational ground for demanding the superlative—for being dissatisfied unless we are assured that our truth is cosmic truth, if there is such a thing—that the ultimates of a little creature on this little earth are the last word of the unimaginable whole. If a man sees no reason for believing that significance, consciousness and ideals are more than marks of the finite, that does not justify what has been familiar in French sceptics; getting upon a pedestal and professing to look with haughty scorn upon a world in ruins. The real conclusion is that the part can not swallow the whole—that our categories are not, or may not be, adequate to formulate what we cannot know. If we believe that we come out of the universe, not it out of us, we must admit that we do not know what we are talking about when we speak of brute matter. We do know that a certain complex of energies can wag its tail and another can make syllogisms. These are among the powers of the unknown, and if, as may be, it has still greater powers that we can not understand, as Fabre in his studies of instinct would have us believe,

studies that gave Bergson one of the strongest strands for his philosophy and enabled Maeterlinck to make us fancy for a moment
that we heard a clang from behind phenomena—if this be true,
why should we not be content? Why should we employ the energy that is furnished to us by the cosmos to defy it and shake our
fist at the sky? It seems to me silly.

That the universe has in it more than we understand, that the
private soldiers have not been told the plan of campaign, or even
that there is one, rather than some vaster unthinkable to which
every predicate is an impertinence, has no bearing upon our conduct. We still shall fight—all of us because we want to live, some,
at least, because we want to realize our spontaneity and prove our
powers, for the joy of it, and we may leave to the unknown the
supposed final valuation of that which in any event has value to us.
It is enough for us that the universe has produced us and has
within it, as less than it, all that we believe and love. If we think of
our existence not as that of a little god outside, but as that of a
ganglion within, we have the infinite behind us. It gives us our
only but our adequate significance. A grain of sand has the same,
but what competent person supposes that he understands a grain
of sand? That is as much beyond our grasp as man. If our imagination is strong enough to accept the vision of ourselves as parts
inseverable from the rest, and to extend our final interest beyond
the boundary of our skins, it justifies the sacrifice even of our lives
for ends outside of ourselves. The motive, to be sure, is the common wants and ideals that we find in man. Philosophy does not
furnish motives, but it shows men that they are not fools for doing
what they already want to do. It opens to the forlorn hopes on
which we throw ourselves away, the vista of the farthest stretch of
human thought, the chords of a harmony that breathes from the
unknown.

from **Abrams v. United States**

(1919)

I DO NOT DOUBT for a moment that by the same reasoning that would justify punishing persuasion to murder, the United States constitutionally may punish speech that produces or is intended to produce a clear and imminent danger that it will bring about forthwith certain substantive evils that the United States constitutionally may seek to prevent. The power undoubtedly is greater in time of war than in time of peace because war opens dangers that do not exist at other times.

But as against dangers peculiar to war, as against others, the principle of the right to free speech is always the same. It is only the present danger of immediate evil or an intent to bring it about that warrants Congress in setting a limit to the expression of opinion where private rights are not concerned. Congress certainly cannot forbid all effort to change the mind of the country. Now nobody can suppose that the surreptitious publishing of a silly leaflet by an unknown man,[1] without more, would present any immediate danger that its opinions would hinder the success of the government arms or have any appreciable tendency to do so. Publishing those opinions for the very purpose of obstructing, however, might indicate a greater danger and at any rate would have the quality of an attempt. So I assume that the second leaflet if published for the purposes alleged in the fourth count might be punishable. But it seems pretty clear to me that nothing less than that would bring these papers within the scope of this law. An actual intent[2] . . . is necessary to constitute an attempt, where a further act of the same individual is required to complete the substantive crime. It is necessary where the success of the attempt depends upon others because if that intent is not present the actor's aim may be accomplished without bringing about the evils sought to be checked. An intent to prevent interference with the revolution in Russia might have been satisfied without any hindrance to carrying on the war in which we were engaged.

I do not see how anyone can find the intent required by the statute in any of the defendants' words. The second leaflet is the only one that affords even a foundation for the charge, and there, without invoking the hatred of German militarism expressed in the former one, it is evident from the beginning to the end that the only object of the paper is to help Russia and stop American intervention there against the popular government—not to impede the United States in the war that it was carrying on. To say that two phrases taken literally might import a suggestion of conduct that would have interference with the war as an indirect and probably undesired effect seems to me by no means enough to show an attempt to produce that effect. . . .

In this case sentences of twenty years' imprisonment have been imposed for the publishing of two leaflets that I believe the defendants had as much right to publish as the government has to publish the Constitution of the United States now vainly invoked by them. Even if I am technically wrong and enough can be squeezed from these poor and puny anonymities to turn the color of legal litmus paper—I will add even if what I think the necessary intent were shown—the most nominal punishment seems to me all that possibly could be inflicted, unless the defendants are to be made to suffer not for what the indictment alleges but for the creed that they avow—a creed that I believe to be the creed of ignorance and immaturity when honestly held, as I see no reason to doubt that it was held here, but which, although made the subject of examination at the trial, no one has a right even to consider in dealing with the charges before the Court.

Persecution for the expression of opinions seems to me perfectly logical. If you have no doubt of your premises or your power and want a certain result with all your heart you naturally express your wishes in law and sweep away all opposition. To allow opposition by speech seems to indicate that you think the speech impotent, as when a man says that he has squared the circle, or that you do not care wholeheartedly for the result, or that you doubt either your power or your premises. But when men have realized that time has upset many fighting faiths, they may come to believe even more than they believe the very foundations of their own conduct that the ultimate good desired is better reached by free trade in ideas—that the best test of truth is the power of the thought to get itself accepted in the competition of the market, and that truth is the only ground upon which their wishes safely can be carried out. That at any rate is the theory of our Constitution. It is an experiment, as all life is an experiment. Every year if not every day we have to wager our salvation upon some prophecy based upon imperfect knowledge. While that experiment is part of our system I think that we should be eternally vigilant against attempts to check the expression of opinions that we loathe and believe to be fraught with death, unless they so imminently threaten immediate interference with the lawful and pressing purposes of the law that an immediate check is required to save the country. I wholly disagree with the argument of the government that the First Amendment left the common law as to seditious libel[3] in force. History seems to me against the notion. I had conceived that the United States through many years had shown its repentance for the Sedition Act of 1798, by repaying fines that it imposed. Only the emergency that makes it immediately dangerous to leave the correction of evil counsels to time warrants making any exception to the sweeping command, "Congress shall make no law . . . abridging the freedom of speech." Of course I am speaking only of expressions of opinion and exhortations, which were all that were uttered here, but I regret that I cannot put into more impressive words my belief that in their conviction upon this indictment the defendants were deprived of their rights under the Constitution of the United States.

John Dewey

Dewey was born in Burlington, Vermont, in 1859. He attended the University of Vermont and did his graduate work at Johns Hopkins University, where Charles Sanders Peirce was on the faculty. From 1884 to 1894 he taught at the University of Michigan, where he began his long friendship with George Herbert Mead. In 1894 he joined the faculty of the University of Chicago, and in 1896 he opened the famous Laboratory School, an experiment in progressive education. He and his wife, Alice Chipman, became involved in a variety of social reform movements. Among these activities was a close association with Jane Addams's Hull House. In 1904 Dewey left Chicago for Columbia, where he spent the rest of his academic career, retiring in 1930. He published more than thirty books and lectured around the world to almost every kind of audience; he was instrumental in the establishment of, among other organizations, the American Civil Liberties Union, the American Association of University Professors, and the New School for Social Research. In 1937, when he was seventy-eight, he headed a commission that traveled to Mexico to investigate Joseph Stalin's charges against Leon Trotsky. He died in 1952.

The Ethics of Democracy

(1888)

APPARENT CONTRADICTIONS always demand attention. When the contradiction is between a manner of life seemingly becoming universal, and a theory of this manner which makes it almost worthless, it is yet more striking. Such a contradiction we have in the present status of democracy. As it gains practical extension in the affairs of society, it is getting lower theoretical appreciation. While it has never had such an actual hold on life as at present, no observer can deny, I believe, that its defenders have never been so apologetic; its detractors so aggressive and pessimistic. To them, this state of affairs is no doubt additional evidence of the truth of their position; the more men see of democracy, the less they like it. The contradiction is thus easily accounted for. But those who believe that the practical instincts of men, as witnessed in a long stretch of history and over a broad area of political existence, do not easily go wholly wrong; and that in the case of a conflict of practical life with theoretical criticism, the latter is most apt to be at fault, will be likely to demand a revision of theory. Without further inquiry into the causes of this break between the beliefs of educated men, and the actual tendencies of political organisms, I wish to make one of its recent manifestations the excuse for an examination into the basal conception, the ideal of democracy. This is Sir Henry Maine's remarkable book on *Popular Government*.[1]

This book gives the ablest and most coherent exposition of one school of political philosophy known to me, for it rests upon wide historical knowledge and is the product of keen analysis. Its examination accordingly will give not a criticism of Sir Henry Maine's individual views, but the means of coming to some conclusions

regarding the fundamental nature of democracy. The thorough-
ness of Maine's position may be got at from the fact that he sees in
democracy no historical meaning, no realization of any idea. It is
but the "product of a whole series of accidents." Its future
prospects are as uncertain as its past is brief. It is "the most fragile
and insecure" of governments; since its introduction government
is more instable than it has been since the time of the Pretorian
Guards. Judging from past experience it always "ends in producing
monstrous and morbid forms of monarchy and aristocracy." His
account of its actual tendencies is such as his summary of its past
career and vaticination of its future might lead us to expect. "Its
legislation is a wild burst of destructive wantonness; an arbitrary
overthrow of all existing institutions, followed by a longer period
in which its principles put an end to all social and political activity, and result in a dead level of ultra-conservatism," for, as he
oracularly remarks: "There can be no delusion greater than that
democracy is a progressive form of government." "The establishment of the masses in power is of blackest omen for all legislation
founded on scientific opinion." The summary of the whole matter is the dictum approvingly quoted from Strauss, "History is a
sound aristocrat."[2]

As it is his theoretical, his philosophical basis that is in question
here, these views may pass without question, although I confess
that his ideas regarding the origin of democracy seem to be based
upon a view of history which denies to it all meaning except that
arising from the accidental juxtaposition of circumstance; that his
forebodings for its future rest upon an irrelevant basis; and that the
supposed destructiveness is due to the occasional necessity of doing away with the evils engendered of aristocracy; and that the
legislative infertility attributed to it goes rather to show that in
every state except the democratic, the masses of the people are
more opposed to change and progress than the few. And so it may
well be. But the charge lies against the form of government which
breeds such a mass, not against democracy.

But leaving these considerations, we must come to Maine's

Aristocrats pretending to be liberals control
the schools and the media.

philosophy of democracy and government. Maine's fundamental position, the one which he considers indispensable to any understanding of the matter, is that "democracy is only a form of government." All views which attribute to it any significance or functions not based upon the clear insight that it is only one among various forms of government are to be ruled out. This is our starting point. The next step is as to the meaning of government. Here the view of Hobbes, as worked out by the analytic school of Bentham and Austin, is virtually adopted.[3] Government is simply that which has to do with the relation of subject to sovereign, of political superior to inferior. This is the second point. The third concerns that which is taken as the distinguishing mark of governments—that which differentiates democracy from other forms. This is quantitative or numerical. If the sovereign is one or few, the subject a multitude, we have monarchy or aristocracy. If the sovereign is the multitude, the subject a small number, we have democracy. For it is a trait of democracy that the apparent ruler is in reality the servant; the seeming subject the true ruler.

We have here in skeleton outline the main points of this school of political philosophy. But they must be expanded somewhat. Democracy is the rule of the Many, of the Mass. That is the essential point. Democracy is nothing but a numerical aggregate, a conglomeration of units. Democracy is, accordingly, the most difficult form of government. For while it is conceivable that one man or a few men should have a common will, in no intelligible sense can a multitude be said to exercise will (Maine, p. 88). All government is based on the exercise of volition, and yet a multitude cannot be said to have a common will (Maine, p. 202). It must be manufactured, however, in order to have even a semblance of government, and Maine says the only powers adequate to bring about this artificial unity are party and corruption,—means of which, as he says, one is injurious to the intellect, the other to the morals of the governing mass (Maine, p. 98). Democracy being this numerical aggregate, it follows, of course, that in it sovereignty or political power is minced into morsels and each man's portion is almost infinitesimally small (Maine, p. 29). Citizens in a democracy are "fragments of political power"; the growth of democracy is the "process of cutting up political power into petty fragments." Here we have the adequate theoretical explanation of the instability and the unprogressive character of democracy. Democracy, again, being a numerical aggregate, the multitude, although the ruler and master, is obliged to delegate his power, since being a multitude he cannot himself exercise it, to the so-called ruler (Maine, p. 81). In democracy, in short, the government is an external power formed by a process of delegation.

It will be seen accordingly, that the gist of the matter lies in the question whether democracy is adequately described as the rule of the many, whether the numerical attribute of democracy is primary and causal, or secondary and derived. From the decision of this question will flow the further answers to questions regarding, first, the nature of sovereignty, secondly, the relation of government to the state, or the adequacy of the delegation theory, and, finally, as to whether democracy is adequately described as only a form of government.

It is worth remarking that it is only superficially that Maine has the authority of Aristotle for defining democracy simply as the rule of the many. Aristotle, indeed, uses the numerical mark as the basis of his classification, but in his analysis he realizes what Maine never does: that in reality it is laws which govern the state, and that the men, whether few or many, are but the instruments of the law. Many results follow, of course, from this latter trait; it is not a matter of indifference whether few or many rule; but the essential characteristic of each state is found, after all, in its form of constitution and organic law. And certainly the whole drift of political theory since the abstract natural right philosophy of the French Revolution has been towards the conception that society is an organism, and government an expression of its organic nature. If this be so, it is no more adequately defined by any merely quantitative conception than a tree is defined by counting the number of cells which constitute it. *Rule by the few men who make and interpret the laws is not rule by law.*

What makes it more surprising that Maine should adopt the numerical aggregation, the multitude conception, is the fact that in times past he has dealt such vigorous blows against a theory which is the natural and inevitable outcome of this conception. The "Social Contract" theory of states has never been more strongly attacked than by Maine, and yet the sole source of this theory is just such a conception of society, as a mass of units, as the one Maine here adopts. The essence of the "Social Contract" theory is not the idea of the formulation of a contract; it is the idea that men are mere individuals, without any social relations *until* they form a contract. The method by which they get out of their individualistic condition is not the important matter; rather this is the fact, that they are in an individualistic condition out of which they have to be got. The notion, in short, which lay in the minds of those who proposed this theory was that men in their natural state are non-social units, are a mere multitude; and that some artifice must be devised to constitute them into political society. And this artifice they found in a contract which they entered into with one another. Maine rejects this artifice as unreal, but keeps the fundamental idea, the idea of men as a mere mass, which led to it.

The fact is, however, that the theory of the "social organism," that theory that men are not isolated non-social atoms, but are men only when in intrinsic relations to men, has wholly superseded the theory of men as an aggregate, as a heap of grains of sand needing some factitious mortar to put them into semblance of order. This, indeed, does not make it incumbent upon one to accept the one theory or to reject the other; the argument to authority is always open to question; but it does make it incumbent that one rest his case upon something more than a definition which begs the question by its very make-up. For the picture which is drawn of democracy is, in effect, simply an account of anarchy. To define democracy simply as the rule of the many, as sovereignty chopped up into mince meat, is to define it as abrogation of society, as society dissolved, annihilated. When so defined, it may be easily shown to be instable to the last degree, and so dif-

ficult that a common will must be manufactured—if not by means
of a contract, then by means of a combined action of the firm of
Party and Corruption. *Double negatives invalid.*
because of confusion, . . .   *that*

But if we do not start with a definition of democracy which
makes it equivalent to the destruction of society, it may not be
found so easy to derive all these evil consequences from it. If we
start from the conception of a social organism, the *prima facie* case
stands quite otherwise. For while in a mass, in a numerical aggregate, the ultimate reality is an individual unit, and the isolated
atoms are the "facts of the case," in an organism man is essentially
a social being. Society in its unified and structural character is the
fact of the case; the non-social individual is an abstraction arrived
at by imagining what man would be if all his human qualities were
taken away. Society, as a real whole, is the normal order, and the
mass as an aggregate of isolated units is the fiction. If this be the
case, and if democracy be a form of society, it not only does have,
but must have, a common will; for it is this unity of will which
makes it an organism. A state represents men so far as they have become organically related to one another, or are possessed of unity
of purpose and interest. But as Maine's *a priori* definition of
democracy, based upon an exploded theory of society, does not
suffice to condemn democracy, neither will a conception of it
which rests upon an accepted theory suffice to justify it. No one
can claim that any society is wholly organized, or possessed of one
interest and will to the exclusion of all struggle and opposition and
hostility. There are still classes within society, circles within the
classes and cliques within the circles. If it can be shown that
democracy more than other forms tends to multiply these subdivisions, that it tends to increase this opposition; that it strengthens
their efficiency at the expense of the working force of the organism—in short, that its tendencies are towards disintegration, towards
mere government by the mass, on the one side, and resolution into
infinitesimal fragments, on the other, the case against democracy is
amply made out. But an arbitrary definition and analysis will not
serve.

What gives the democracy more than other forms of government the appearance of being a mere rule of a mass or multitude is, without doubt, the use which it makes of individual suffrage on the one hand and majority rule on the other. Since it thus appears to decide all questions of policy and of men by mere weighing of numbers, it is easy to represent democracy as concerned for the most part with a problem in arithmetic. Analytic abstraction, having perchance already deprived men of all their qualities due to their social relations, now proceeds further to reduce them into merely numerical individuals, into ballot-projecting units. Then the mere accident of a few bare units more or less on this side or that, seems, by bare numerical preponderance, to form the will of the people in this direction or that. Such is the theoretical analysis of democracy most often presented to us. Many of its upholders have no more adequate idea of it than this, and rest for their final support on the fact that after all the numerical majority would have, in case of an appeal to arms, the brute force to coerce the minority. Such presentations come off very poorly when compared with the sketch of an ideal aristocracy, where not mere stress of numbers, but superiority in wisdom, elevation in goodness, enable the few having these qualities to guide the mass without them. All Carlyle's political writings rest their lamentation on just such a conception of democracy as this numerical one, which he has set forth in a more many-sided, vivid and forcible way than even Sir Henry Maine. And the educated men of to-day, who have been trained exclusively in the school of physical science, with its tendencies towards mechanical and mathematical abstraction, almost without exception have no notion of the meaning of democracy other than this.

But the student of society has constantly to be on his guard against the abstract and purely mechanical notions introduced from the physical sciences. If he will beware of such abstractions, he will remember that men cannot be reduced for political purposes, any more than for any other, to bare figure ones, marks to be placed in rows set over against one another. A man when he comes to vote does not put off from him, like a suit of old clothes, his character, his wealth, his social influence, his devotion to political interest, and become a naked unit. He carries with him in his voting all the influence that he should have, and if he deserves twice as much as another man, it is safe to say that he decides twice as many votes as that other man. Even if his character is corrupt, and his devotion to politics is from motives of pelf, it yet remains true that he votes, not as a mere unit, but as a representative of the social organism. It is only because society allows him, nay, grants him power on such grounds, that he can use it. His very corruption is the expression of society through him. A vote, in other words, is not an impersonal counting of one; it is a manifestation of some tendency of the social organism through a member of that organism.

But this only touches the matter. There still appears to be in majority rule an instrument for putting all on a dead level, and allowing numerical surplus to determine the outcome. But the heart of the matter is found not in the voting nor in the counting the votes to see where the majority lies. It is in the process by which the majority is formed. The minority are represented in the policy which they force the majority to accept in order to be a majority; the majority have the right to "rule" because their majority is not the mere sign of a surplus in numbers, but is the manifestation of the purpose of the social organism. Were this not so, every election would be followed by a civil war; there would be no need of writing concerning the weakness of popular government; it would be the only striking fact about democracy. I know of no one by whom this matter of majority rule is better stated than by the late Governor Tilden[4]—whose opinion is the more worth quoting in this connection because he too saw in democracy only a device for carrying on government. He calls attention to the fact that generally the difference between the minority and the majority party in a general election does not exceed five per cent of the entire vote. Instead of jumping at the conclusion that thus a small proportion of the population really determines the policy of the whole, he sees that the small numerical difference is in reality testimony to the coinciding of the two parties. "The minority," he says, "adopts enough of the ideas of the majority to attract those who are nearest to the line of division; and the majority in struggling to reclaim them makes concessions. The issue is thus constantly shifting with the wavering tide of battle, until the policy which at last prevails has become adjusted so as nearly to represent the average sense of the whole people. In shaping the policy which emerges from the conflict the minority acts a part scarcely less important than the majority." (Tilden, *Writings and Speeches,* vol. i, p. 290.) Or as he sums up the whole matter: "In trying to acquire the means to govern, the majority becomes qualified to govern."[5] When, therefore, we hear the derider of democracy discrediting it by declaring that through manhood suffrage and majority rule all are put on a level, with no quality concerned but their numerical, we may be confident that he has only the most superficial view of the matter, and that the process of finding out the policy of the majority is the process by which the social organism weighs considerations and forms its consequent judgment; that the voting of the individual represents in reality, a deliberation, a tentative opinion on the part of the whole organism.

We must now turn to the other side of the picture. The theory which makes of democratic society a mere mass, makes, on the other hand, the democratic citizen a mere minced morsel of this mass, a disorganized fragment. If, however, society be truly described as organic, the citizen is a member of the organism, and, just in proportion to the perfection of the organism, has concentrated within himself its intelligence and will. Disguise it as we may, this theory can have but one result, that of the sovereignty of the citizen. There are various theories which have served to keep this in the background, and to hide the fact that the ordinary American expression of the sovereignty of every elector is not a mere exaggerated burst of individualistic feeling, fostered through crude Fourth of July patriotism, but is the logical outcome of the organic theory of society.

If they can only vote for candidates and not on issues, voting is childish and insulting.

A cellophane vote—we get to choose the wrapper.

There is the French theory which makes sovereignty the *natural* (that is, the pre-political, even the non-political) attribute of the people; a trait inhering in the people by mere stress of their including everyone within themselves, without respect to organization. There is the German theory, which, although recognizing professedly the organic conception, rids it of its significance in this respect by giving a physiological sense to the term, by interpreting the term in analogy with the human body. Thus Bluntschli,[6] in spite of all that there is valuable in him, cannot free himself from the idea that since society is an organism it must have something corresponding to the division of sexes, to the limbs, to the trunk, and to the head. Just as the head represents the wisdom and control of the body, so the mystic attribute of sovereignty, which is diffused indeed in a vague way through the nation, gets reality only in the aureole that rests upon the monarch. The English theory, as presented by Hobbes and worked out by Austin, virtually makes it consist in irresponsible power. According to one theory, sovereignty is located in the people as a whole, one might say as a mob; according to another it is latent in the nation as a definite political body, but manifest only in the head of the nation; according to the third (the one adopted here at least by Maine) it is situated in whatever portions of the state have the power to make, alter and enforce laws without appeal. If we take the latter notion, sovereignty is simply power to do this or that. It follows that in the democratic state (according to Maine's conception of it as a multitude) this power must be divided into fragments, each citizen having simply his fractional part of the total amount of sovereignty at command. Thus the exercise of sovereignty is a question of division, just as the formation of a common will is one in addition. Given so much sovereignty, and so many citizens, how much does each member have? The individual, the ultimate unit, thus becomes an n-millionth of political power. But if we really adopt the organic conception of society, the case stands quite otherwise. The attempt to make the organic theory work only in one direction, namely, as applicable to society but not to its members, is to deny the theory. This is as much an account of the individual as it is of the whole. One who has really adopted the notion can say not less, but more than any one else, that society exists for and by individuals. But it is because he has given up the fiction of isolated unsocial units, and has realized that the individual embodies and realizes within himself the spirit and will of the whole organism.

This is not the place for an examination of the conception of organism; but it must be remembered that it is a thoroughly reciprocal conception. The animal body is not the type of an organism, because the members, the organs, have their life, after all, only as parts, conditioned by their external space relations. They indeed participate in the life of the whole, while the whole lives in them, giving them their activity. But they are absorbed in this whole. The whole has not given its life to them so freely that they can take on the appearance of independent lives, isolated in space. The organic relation is incomplete. But human society represents a more perfect organism. The whole lives truly in every member, and there is no longer the appearance of physical aggregation, or continuity. The organism manifests itself as what it truly is, an ideal or spiritual life, a unity of *will*. If then, society and the individual are really organic to each other, then the individual is society concentrated. He is not merely its image or mirror. He is the localized manifestation of its life. And if, as actually happens, society be not yet possessed of one will, but partially is one and partially has a number of fragmentary and warring wills, it yet follows that *so far* as society has a common purpose and spirit, *so far* each individual is not representative of a certain proportionate share of the sum total of will, but is its vital embodiment. And this is the theory, often crudely expressed, but none the less true in substance, that every citizen is a sovereign, the American theory, a doctrine which in grandeur has but one equal in history, and that its fellow, namely, that every man is a priest of God.

In conception, at least, democracy approaches most nearly the ideal of all social organization; that in which the individual and society are organic to each other. For this reason democracy, so far as it is really democracy, is the most stable, not the most insecure, of governments. In every other form of government there are individuals who are not organs of the common will, who are outside of the political society in which they live, and are, in effect, aliens to that which should be their own commonwealth. Not participating in the formation or expression of the common will, they do not embody it in themselves. Having no share in society, society has none in them. Such is the origin of that body of irreconcilables which Maine, with inverted logic, attributes to democracy.

We have thus far analyzed the popular numerical conception of democracy as bearing upon the notions of the common will and of sovereignty. We have now to examine it in its relation to the theory of government. From this quantitative notion it necessarily follows that government comes into being by the process stated by Maine, that of delegation. If society is only a mass or aggregate, it must call government into being by some artificial means. There then exist two classes, one of governors, one of governed, and the only question is as to which is the real master, which the real servant. Democracy, like every other form of government, has these two classes set over against each other, but it reverses the relation existing in aristocracy. But, once more, if society be organic, the notion of two classes, one of which is inferior to the other, falls to the ground. The basal conception, here, is of unity, and all distinctions must occur within and on account of this unity. The organism must have its spiritual organs; having a common will, it must express it. A national consciousness which does not give itself outward reality, which does not objectify itself, is like any other consciousness in similar plight—simply non-existent. There is, indeed, a popular but none the less superficial mode of speech which identifies the government and the state. This is as if a physiologist were to identify seeing with the eye, or even with the whole body. The eye is the body organized for seeing, and just so government is the state organized for declaring and executing its judgments. Government is to the state what language is to thought; it not only communicates the purposes of the state, but in so doing gives them for the first time articulation and generality.

The chief bearing of this upon our present discussion lies in the fact that it does away with the dualism inherent in the delegation theory. Government does not mean one class or side of society set over against the other. The government is not made up of those who hold office, or who sit in the legislature. It consists of every member of political society. And this is true of democracy, not less, but more, than of other forms. The democratic formula that government derives its powers from the consent of the governed, like the theory of the sovereignty of the political citizen, has suffered as much at the hands of its friends as of its enemies; but its true significance is not thereby destroyed. It means that in democracy, at all events, the governors and the governed are not two classes, but two aspects of the same fact—the fact of the possession by society of a unified and articulate will. It means that government is the organ of society, and is as comprehensive as society. Here, as before, we may reverse Maine's argument and say that democracy, since it more fully conforms to the ideal of society, is more stable than aristocracy. Wherever government is a matter of birth, of heredity, of wealth, of superior "social" standing, in a word, of privilege, society is still unorganized, and in so far, chaotic. There are two wills; the governors and the governed are two separate classes. Unless there is complete despotism or stagnation, there is constant clashing of the two wills contained, and a constant shifting of power. There is a condition of unstable equilibrium. What Plato said of his ideal state, we may with greater truth say of democracy: "What simplicity is this that you should use the term 'state' of any but ours! Other states may indeed be spoken of more grandiloquently and in the plural number—for they are many. Any ordinary state, however small, is indeed two states at war with each other, and in either division there are many smaller states." (*Republic* iv. 423.) And again as Plato acutely remarks: "All political changes originate in divisions of the governing power, for a government which is united, however small, cannot be moved." (*Republic* viii. 545.)

We have completed the first part of our examination. We have considered the theory of democratic government suggested by Sir Henry Maine, so far as it relates to the conception of the common will, of the individual citizen, and of the origin of government. We have now to see whether we can stop with the idea of democracy as merely a form of government, or whether it implies something more. James Russell Lowell is a man of letters, not a professed student of politics, and yet where he says of democracy that he is "speaking of a sentiment, a spirit, and not of a form of government, for this is but the outgrowth of the latter and not its cause,"[7] we must recognize that the weight of history and of politics is on his side, as it is not on that of Maine. The conception that democracy and aristocracy are expedients for reaching certain jural ends, for exercising certain police powers, for compelling obedience, and that the sole question is as to what piece of machinery can accomplish this most efficiently, and with the greatest stability and economy, is one which has no justification outside of abstract theory. It is the relic of the time when governmental polities were regarded as articles of clothing, to be cut and sewed by any acute political tailor, and fitted to any nation. It belongs to a time when it was thought that a constitution could be made *ad hoc,* and established on a *tabula rasa* of past history, also manufactured with express reference to the given case. A government springs from a vast mass of sentiments, many vague, some defined, of instincts, of aspirations, of ideas, of hopes and fears, of purposes. It is their reflex and their incorporation; their projection and outgrowth. Without this basis, it is worth nothing. A gust of prejudice, a blow of despotism, and it falls like a card house. To say that democracy is *only* a form of government is like saying that home is a more or less geometrical arrangement of bricks and mortar; that the church is a building with pews, pulpit and spire. It is true; they certainly are so much. But it is false; they are so infinitely more. Democracy, like any other polity, has been finely termed the memory of an historic past, the consciousness of a living present, the ideal of the coming future. Democracy, in a word, is a social, that is to say, an ethical conception, and upon its ethical significance is based its significance as governmental. Democracy is a form of government only because it is a form of moral and spiritual association.

But so is aristocracy. What is the difference? What distinguishes the ethical basis and ideal of one from that of the other? It may appear a roundabout way to reach a simple end, to refer to Plato and to Greek life to get data for an answer; but I know of no way in which I can so easily bring out what seems to me the truth. The Platonic Republic is a splendid and imperishable formulation of the aristocratic ideal. If it had no value for philosophical reasons, if its theory of morals, of reality and of knowledge had disappeared as utterly as the breezes which swept the grasses under the plane tree by which Plato and his disciples sat and talked, the Republic would be immortal as the summary of all that was best and most permanent in Greek life, of its ways of thinking and feeling, and of its ideals. But the Republic is more; it seizes upon the heart of the ethical problem, the relation of the individual to the universal, and states a solution. The question of the Republic is as to the ideal of men's conduct; the answer is such a development of man's nature as brings him into complete harmony with the universe of spiritual relations, or, in Platonic language, the state. This universe, in turn, is man writ large; it is the manifestation, the realization of the capacities of the individual. Such a development of the individual that he shall be in harmony with all others in the state, that is, that he shall possess as his own the unified will of the community; that is the end both of politics and of ethics. Nothing could be more aside from the mark than to say that the Platonic ideal subordinates and sacrifices the individual to the state. It does, indeed, hold that the individual can be what he ought to be, can become what, in idea, he is, only as a member of a spiritual organism, called by Plato the state, and, in losing his own individual will, acquiring that of this larger reality. But this is not loss of self-hood or personality, it is its realization. The individual is not sacrificed; he is brought to reality in the state. Heidegger + Hitler

We certainly cannot find here any ground upon which to distinguish the aristocratic from the democratic ideal. But we have not asked how this unity of the individual and the universe, this perfect man in the perfect state, is to be brought about. Here lies the distinction sought for; it is not a question of end, but of means. According to Plato (and the aristocratic idea everywhere), the multitude is incapable of forming such an ideal and of attempting to reach it. Plato is the true author of the doctrine of the "remnant." There is, in his words, "no chance of perfection either in states or in individuals until a necessity is laid upon the *small* class of caring for the state." It is to the one wise man, or to the few, that Plato looks for redemption. Once found these are to be given absolute control, and are to see to it that each individual is placed in such a position in the state that he may make perfect harmony with the others, and at the same time perform that for which he is best fitted, and thus realize the goal of life—"Justice," in Plato's word.

Such is the barest outline of the most perfect picture of the aristocratic ideal which history affords. The few best, the aristoi; these know and are fitted for rule; but they are to rule not in their own interests but in that of society as a whole, and, therefore, in that of every individual in society. They do not bear rule *over* the others; they show them what they can best do, and guide them in doing it. There is no need to dwell upon the charm, upon the attractiveness of the aristocratic ideal. The best witness to it is in the long line of great men who have reiterated with increasing emphasis that all will go wrong, until the few who know and are strong, are put in power, while others, foregoing the assertion of their individuality, submit to superior wisdom and goodness.

But history has been making the other way. If history be, as Strauss said, a sound aristocrat, then history is committing suicide. It is working towards something which is not history. The aristocratic ideal, spite of all its attractions, is not equal to reality; it is not equal to the actual forces animating men as they work in history. It has failed because it is found that the practical consequence of giving the few wise and good power is that they cease to remain wise and good. They become ignorant of the needs and requirement of the many; they leave the many outside the pale with no real share in the commonwealth. Perchance they even wilfully use their wisdom and strength for themselves, for the assertion of privilege and status and to the detriment of the common good. The aristocratic society always limits the range of men who are regarded as participating in the state, in the unity of purpose and destiny; and it always neglects to see that those theoretically included really obtain their well being. Every forward democratic movement is followed by the broadening of the circle of the state, and by more effective oversight that every citizen may be insured the rights belonging to him.

But even were it possible to find men so wise as not to ignore the misery and degradation beyond their immediate ken, men so good as to use their power only for the community, there is another fact which is the condemnation of the aristocratic theory. The ethical ideal is not satisfied merely when all men sound the note of harmony with the highest social good, so be it that they have not worked it out for themselves. Were it granted that the rule of the aristoi would lead to the highest external development of society and the individual, there would still be a fatal objection. Humanity cannot be content with a good which is procured from without, however high and otherwise complete that good. The aristocratic idea implies that the mass of men are to be inserted by wisdom, or, if necessary, thrust by force, into their proper positions in the social organism. It is true, indeed, that when an individual has found that place in society for which he is best fitted and is exercising the function proper to that place, he has obtained his completest development, but it is also true (and this is the truth omitted by aristocracy, emphasized by democracy) that he must find this place and assume this work in the main for himself.

Democracy does not differ from aristocracy in its goal. The end is not mere assertion of the individual will as individual; it is not disregard of law, of the universal; it is complete realization of the law, namely of the unified spirit of the community. Democracy differs as to its means. This universal, this law, this unity of purpose, this fulfilling of function in devotion to the interests of the social organism, is not to be put into a man from without. It must begin in the man himself, however much the good and the wise of society contribute. Personal responsibility, individual initiation, these are the notes of democracy. Aristocracy and democracy both imply that the actual state of society exists for the sake of realizing an end which is ethical, but aristocracy implies that this is to be done primarily by means of special institutions or organizations within society, while democracy holds that the ideal is already at work in every personality, and must be trusted to care for itself. There is an individualism in democracy which there is not in aristocracy; but it is an ethical, not a numerical individualism; it is an individualism of freedom, of responsibility, of initiative to and for the ethical ideal, not an individualism of lawlessness. In one word, democracy means that *personality* is the first and final reality. It admits that the full significance of personality can be learned by the individual only as it is already presented to him in objective form in society; it admits that the chief stimuli and encouragements to the realization of personality come from society; but it holds, none the less, to the fact that personality cannot be procured for any one, however degraded and feeble, by any one else, however wise and strong. It holds that the spirit of personality indwells in every individual and that the choice to develop it must proceed from that individual. From this central position of personality result the other notes of democracy, liberty, equality, fraternity,— words which are not mere words to catch the mob, but symbols of the highest ethical idea which humanity has yet reached—the idea that personality is the one thing of permanent and abiding worth, and that in every human individual there lies personality.

By way of illustration (and what is said in the remainder of this paper is only by way of illustration), let us take the notion of liberty. Plato gives a vivid illustration of what he means by democratic freedom. It is doing as one likes. It is ordering life as one pleases. It is thinking and acting as one has a mind to. Liberty in a democracy can have no limit. Its result is loss of reverence and of order. It is the denial of moderation, of the principle of limit. Democratic liberty is the following out of individual wills, of particular desires, to the utmost degree. It has no order or law (*Republic* viii. 557–563). In a word, it is the extreme assertion of individualism, resulting in anarchy. In this conception of liberty he has been followed by all of the anti-democratic school. But from the democratic standpoint, it must be remembered that the individual is something more than the individual, namely, a personality. His freedom is not mere self-assertion, nor unregulated desire. You cannot say that he knows no law; you must say that he knows no law but his own, the law of personality; no law, in other words, externally imposed, however splendid the authority, and undoubted the goodness of those that impose it. Law is the objective expression of personality. It is not a limitation upon individual freedom; it is correlative with it. Liberty is not a numerical notion of isolation; it is the ethical idea that personality is the supreme and only law, that every man is an absolute end in himself. The democratic ideal includes liberty, because democracy without initiation from within, without an ideal chosen from within and freely followed from within, is nothing.

Again, for illustration, take the notion of equality. If we heed the aristocratic school, we learn that equality means numerical equality, that one number one is just as good as any other number one. Conceiving it to refer to bald individuality, they think its inevitable outcome, logical if not historical, is an equal division of all things from virtue to wealth. Democracy is condemned because it regards as equal the worst and the best of men, the wisest and the most ignorant. It is condemned because it is said to aim at an equal distribution of wealth and of the happiness that grows from material possessions and surroundings. It is said that it is both foolish and wicked to attempt by the lie of equality to blind one's eyes to the differences of men in wisdom, virtue, and industry; that upon these differences, indeed, rests the whole structure of society with its necessary grades of subordination and service; and that the only society which is either stable or progressive is one in which the motives of inequality, both political and industrial, have fair play. As Maine says, the motives which have always impelled mankind to the production of increasing industrial resources are such as infallibly entail inequality in its distribution. It is the never-ending struggle for existence, the private war which makes one man strive to climb upon the shoulders of another and stay there, which have been the springs to action. Take them away, introduce equality, and you have no motive to progress.

What shall we say to this indictment? Simply that it is beside the mark. As relates to democracy, it corresponds to no reality. Equality is not an arithmetical, but an ethical conception. Personality is as universal as humanity; it is indifferent to all distinctions which divide men from men. Wherever you have a man, there you have personality, and there is no trace by which one personality may be distinguished from another so as to be set above or below. It means that in every individual there lives an infinite and universal possibility; that of being a king and priest. Aristocracy is blasphemy against personality. It is the doctrine of the elect few applied not to some life in the future, but to all relations of humanity. Hero-worship means man despised. The true meaning of equality is synonymous with the definition of democracy given by James Russell Lowell. It is the form of society in which every man has a chance and knows that he has it—and we may add, a chance to which no possible limits can be put, a chance which is truly infinite, the chance to become a person. Equality, in short, is the ideal of humanity; an ideal in the consciousness of which democracy lives and moves.

One aspect of the indictment remains to be touched—the nature of industrial equality, or the supposed tendency of democracy towards socialism, if not communism. And there is no need to beat about the bush in saying that democracy is not in reality what it is in name until it is industrial, as well as civil and political. Such a condition is indeed far enough away; on this point, democracy is an ideal of the future, not a starting point. In this respect, society is still a sound aristocrat. And the reflex influence of this upon our civil and political organization is such that they are only imperfectly democratic. For their sakes, therefore, as well as for that of industrial relations, a democracy of wealth is a necessity.

All that makes such assertions seem objectionable is that this democracy of wealth is represented, often by its adherents, always by its opponents, as if it meant the numerical division into equal portions of all wealth, and its numerical redistribution. But all that has been said in this paper has been said in vain, unless it be now recognized that democracy is anything but a numerical notion; and that the numerical application of it is as much out of place here as it is everywhere else. What is meant in detail by a democracy of wealth we shall not know until it is more of a reality than it is now. In general, however, it means and must mean that all industrial relations are to be regarded as subordinate to human relations, to the law of personality. Numerical identity is not required, it is not even allowed; but it is absolutely required that industrial organization shall be made a *social* function. And if this expression again seems objectionable, it is because it is interpreted to mean that in some way society, as a whole, to the abolition of all individual initiative and result, is to take charge of all those undertakings which we call economic. It seems to imply socialism in the sense in which that mode of life destroys that individual responsibility and activity which are at the very heart of modern life. But when we are told that the family is a social institution, and that life in the family is a social function, do we understand this to mean that it is a form of existence in which all individuality is renounced, and an artificial entity created which absorbs the rightful activities of the individual? I think not; we mean that the family is an ethical community, and that life in the family conforms to its idea only when the individual realizes oneness of interest and purpose with it.

And this, in kind, is precisely what is meant when we speak of industrial relations as being necessarily social; we mean that they are to become the material of an ethical realization; the form and substance of a community of good (though not necessarily of goods) wider than any now known: that as the family, largely in its best examples, the state somewhat, though in a less degree, mean unity of purpose and interest, so economic society must mean unity of interest and purpose. The truth is that in these matters we are still largely in the intellectual bounds which bound pre-Christian thought. We still think of life as having two parts, one animal, the other truly human and therefore truly ethical. The getting and distributing of the material benefits of life are regarded as indeed a *means* to the possibility of the higher life, the life of men in their distinctively human relations, but as in themselves wholly outside of that life. Both Plato and Aristotle, for example, always take it as a matter of course, that everything which is industrial, which concerns the getting or distributing of wealth, lies wholly outside, nay, is opposed to the life of the citizen, that is, of the member of an ethical community. Plato's attacks upon the Sophists for receiving money for teaching were on the ground that they thus degraded a personal (that is, a moral) relation, that of teacher and pupil, to an industrial; as if the two were necessarily hostile. Aristotle denies that an artisan can have virtue, i.e., the qualities pertaining to the fulfillment of social functions. Mechanics are, indeed, indispensable to the state, "but not all who are indispensable to the state are citizens." (And we must remember that the terms "citizen" and "state" have, in Aristotle, always an ethical bearing.) It was necessary that there should be some who should give themselves to that which is purely material, the industrial, in order that others might have the leisure to give themselves to the social and political, the ethical. We have, nominally, at least, given up the idea that a certain body of men are to be set aside for the doing of this necessary work; but we still think of this work, and of the relations pertaining to it, as if they were outside of the ethical realm and wholly in the natural. We admit, nay, at times we claim, that ethical rules are to be *applied* to this industrial sphere, but we think of it as an external application. That the economic and industrial life is *in itself* ethical, that it is to be made contributory to the realization of personality through the formation of a higher and more complete unity among men, this is what we do not recognize; but such is the meaning of the statement that democracy must become industrial. *Then pay salary to get education and job training*

I have used these illustrations simply for the sake of showing what I understand the conception of democracy to mean, and to show that the ordinary objections to democracy rest upon ideas which conceive of it after the type of an individualism of a numerical character; and have tried to suggest that democracy is an ethical idea, the idea of a personality, with truly infinite capacities, incorporate with every man. Democracy and the one, the ultimate, ethical ideal of humanity are to my mind synonyms. The idea of democracy, the ideas of liberty, equality, and fraternity, represent a society in which the distinction between the spiritual and the secular has ceased, and as in Greek theory, as in the Christian theory of the Kingdom of God, the church and the state, the divine and the human organization of society are one. But this, you will say, is idealism. In reply, I can but quote James Russell Lowell once more and say that "it is indeed idealism, but that I am one of those who believe that the real will never find an irremovable basis till it rests upon the ideal"; and add that the best test of any form of society is the ideal which it proposes for the forms of its life, and the degree in which it realizes this ideal.

As little down-to-earth as a cloud floating a mile up, lots of form with very little substance.

Theories of Knowledge

in *Democracy and Education* (1916)

I

Continuity *versus* Dualism

A NUMBER OF THEORIES of knowing have been criticized in the previous pages. In spite of their differences from one another, they all agree in one fundamental respect which contrasts with the theory which has been positively advanced. The latter assumes *continuity;* the former state or imply certain basic divisions, separations, or antitheses, technically called dualisms. The origin of these divisions we have found in the hard and fast walls which mark off social groups and classes within a group: like those between rich and poor, men and women, noble and baseborn, ruler and ruled. These barriers mean absence of fluent and free intercourse. This absence is equivalent to the setting up of different types of life-experience, each with isolated subject matter, aim, and standard of values. Every such social condition must be formulated in a dualistic philosophy, if philosophy is to be a sincere account of experience. When it gets beyond dualism—as many philosophies do in form—it can only be by appeal to something higher than anything found in experience, by a flight to some transcendental realm. And in denying duality in name such theories restore it in fact, for they end in a division between things of this world as mere appearances and an inaccessible essence of reality.

So far as these divisions persist and others are added to them, each leaves its mark upon the educational system, until the scheme of education, taken as a whole, is a deposit of various purposes and procedures. The outcome is that kind of check and balance of segregated factors and values which has been described. (See Chapter 18.[1]) The present discussion is simply a formulation, in the terminology of philosophy, of various antithetical conceptions involved in the theory of knowing.

In the first place, there is the opposition of empirical and higher rational knowing. The first is connected with everyday affairs, serves the purposes of the ordinary individual who has no specialized intellectual pursuit, and brings his wants into some kind of working connection with the immediate environment. Such knowing is depreciated, if not despised, as purely utilitarian, lacking in cultural significance. Rational knowledge is supposed to be something which touches reality in ultimate, intellectual fashion; to be pursued for its own sake and properly to terminate in purely theoretical insight, not debased by application in behavior. Socially, the distinction corresponds to that of the intelligence used by the working classes and that used by a learned class remote from concern with the means of living.

Philosophically, the difference turns about the distinction of the particular and universal. Experience is an aggregate of more or less isolated particulars, acquaintance with each of which must be separately made. Reason deals with universals, with general principles, with laws, which lie above the welter of concrete details. In the educational precipitate, the pupil is supposed to have to learn, on one hand, a lot of items of specific information, each standing by itself, and upon the other hand, to become familiar with a certain number of laws and general relationships. Geography, as often taught, illustrates the former; mathematics, beyond the rudiments of figuring, the latter. For all practical purposes, they represent two independent worlds.

Another antithesis is suggested by the two senses of the word "learning." On the one hand, learning is the sum total of what is known, as that is handed down by books and learned men. It is something external, an accumulation of cognitions, as one might store material commodities in a warehouse. Truth exists ready-made somewhere. Study is then the process by which an individual draws on what is in storage. On the other hand, learning means something which the individual *does* when he studies. It is an active, personally conducted affair. The dualism here is between knowledge as something external, or, as it is often called, objective, and knowing as something purely internal, subjective, psychical. There is, on one side, a body of truth, ready-made, and, on the other, a ready-made mind equipped with a faculty of knowing—if it only wills to exercise it, which it is often strangely loath to do. The separation, often touched upon, between subject matter and method is the educational equivalent of this dualism. Socially the distinction has to do with the part of life which is dependent upon authority and that where individuals are free to advance.

Another dualism is that of activity and passivity in knowing. Purely empirical and physical things are often supposed to be known by receiving impressions. Physical things somehow stamp themselves upon the mind or convey themselves into consciousness by means of the sense-organs. Rational knowledge and knowledge of spiritual things is supposed, on the contrary, to spring from activity initiated within the mind, an activity carried on better if it is kept remote from all sullying touch of the senses and external objects. The distinction between sense-training and object lessons and laboratory exercises, and pure ideas contained in books, and appropriated—so it is thought—by some miraculous output of mental energy, is a fair expression in education of this distinction. Socially, it reflects a division between those who are controlled by direct concern with things and those who are free to cultivate themselves.

Another current opposition is that said to exist between the intellect and the emotions. The emotions are conceived to be purely private and personal, having nothing to do with the work of pure intelligence in apprehending facts and truths,—except perhaps the single emotion of intellectual curiosity. The intellect is a pure light; the emotions are a disturbing heat. The mind turns outward to truth; the emotions turn inward to considerations of personal advantage and loss. Thus in education we have that systematic depreciation of interest which has been noted, plus the necessity in practice, with most pupils, of recourse to extraneous and irrelevant rewards and penalties in order to induce the person who has a mind (much as his clothes have a pocket) to apply that mind to the truths to be known. Thus we have the spectacle of professional educators decrying appeal to interest while they uphold with great dignity the need of reliance upon examinations, marks, promotions and demotions, prizes, and the time-honored paraphernalia of rewards and punishments. The effect of this situation in crippling the teacher's sense of humor has not received the attention which it deserves.

All of these separations culminate in one between knowing and doing, theory and practice, between mind as the end and spirit of action and the body as its organ and means. We shall not repeat what has been said about the source of this dualism in the division of society into a class laboring with their muscles for material sustenance and a class which, relieved from economic pressure, devotes itself to the arts of expression and social direction. Nor is it necessary to speak again of the educational evils which spring from the separation. We shall be content to summarize the forces which tend to make the untenability of this conception obvious and to replace it by the idea of continuity. *(i.)* The advance of physiology and the psychology associated with it have shown the connection of mental activity with that of the nervous system. Too often recognition of connection has stopped short at this point; the older dualism of soul and body has been replaced by that of the brain and the rest of the body. But in fact the nervous system is only a specialized mechanism for keeping all bodily activities working together. Instead of being isolated from them, as an organ of knowing from organs of motor response, it is the organ by which they interact responsively with one another. The brain is essentially an organ for effecting the reciprocal adjustment to each other of the stimuli received from the environment and responses directed upon it. Note that the adjusting is reciprocal; the brain not only enables organic activity to be brought to bear upon any object of the environment in response to a sensory stimulation, but this response also determines what the next stimulus will be. See what happens, for example, when a carpenter is at work upon a board, or an etcher upon his plate—or in any case of a consecutive activity. While each motor response is adjusted to the state of affairs indicated through the sense-organs, that motor response shapes the next sensory stimulus. Generalizing this illustration, the brain is the machinery for a constant reorganizing of activity so as to maintain its continuity; that is to say, to make such modifications in future action as are required because of what has already been done. The continuity of the work of the carpenter distinguishes it from a routine repetition of identically the same motion, and from a random activity where there is nothing cumulative. What makes it continuous, consecutive, or concentrated is that each earlier act prepares the way for later acts, while these take account of or reckon with the results already attained—the basis of all responsibility. No one who has realized the full force of the facts of the connection of knowing with the nervous system and of the nervous system with the readjusting of activity continuously to meet new conditions, will doubt that knowing has to do with reorganizing activity, instead of being something isolated from all activity, complete on its own account.

(ii.) The development of biology clinches this lesson, with its discovery of evolution. For the philosophic significance of the doctrine of evolution lies precisely in its emphasis upon continuity of simpler and more complex organic forms until we reach man. The development of organic forms begins with structures where the adjustment of environment and organism is obvious, and where anything which can be called mind is at a minimum. As activity becomes more complex, coordinating a greater number of

factors in space and time, intelligence plays a more and more marked role, for it has a larger span of the future to forecast and plan for. The effect upon the theory of knowing is to displace the notion that it is the activity of a mere onlooker or spectator of the world, the notion which goes with the idea of knowing as something complete in itself. For the doctrine of organic development means that the living creature is a part of the world, sharing its vicissitudes and fortunes, and making itself secure in its precarious dependence only as it intellectually identifies itself with the things about it, and, forecasting the future consequences of what is going on, shapes its own activities accordingly. If the living, experiencing being is an intimate participant in the activities of the world to which it belongs, then knowledge is a mode of participation, valuable in the degree in which it is effective. It cannot be the idle view of an unconcerned spectator.

(iii.) The development of the experimental method as the method of getting knowledge and of making sure it *is* knowledge, and not mere opinion—the method of both discovery and proof—is the remaining great force in bringing about a transformation in the theory of knowledge. The experimental method has two sides. *(i.)* On one hand, it means that we have no right to call anything knowledge except where our activity has actually produced certain physical changes in things, which agree with and confirm the conception entertained. Short of such specific changes, our beliefs are only hypotheses, theories, suggestions, guesses, and are to be entertained tentatively and to be utilized as indications of experiments to be tried. *(ii.)* On the other hand, the experimental method of thinking signifies that thinking is of avail; that it is of avail in just the degree in which the anticipation of future consequences is made on the basis of thorough observation of present conditions. Experimentation, in other words, is not equivalent to blind reacting. Such surplus activity—a surplus with reference to what has been observed and is now anticipated—is indeed an unescapable factor in all our behavior, but it is not experiment save as consequences are noted and are used to make predictions

and plans in similar situations in the future. The more the meaning of the experimental method is perceived, the more our trying out of a certain way of treating the material resources and obstacles which confront us embodies a prior use of intelligence. What we call magic was with respect to many things the experimental method of the savage; but for him to try was to try his luck, not his ideas. The scientific experimental method is, on the contrary, a trial of ideas; hence even when practically—or immediately—unsuccessful, it is intellectual, fruitful; for we learn from our failures when our endeavors are seriously thoughtful.

The experimental method is new as a scientific resource—as a systematized means of making knowledge, though as old as life as a practical device. Hence it is not surprising that men have not recognized its full scope. For the most part, its significance is regarded as belonging to certain technical and merely physical matters. It will doubtless take a long time to secure the perception that it holds equally as to the forming and testing of ideas in social and moral matters. Men still want the crutch of dogma, of beliefs fixed by authority, to relieve them of the trouble of thinking and the responsibility of directing their activity by thought. They tend to confine their own thinking to a consideration of which one among the rival systems of dogma they will accept. Hence the schools are better adapted, as John Stuart Mill said, to make disciples than inquirers. But every advance in the influence of the experimental method is sure to aid in outlawing the literary, dialectic, and authoritative methods of forming beliefs which have governed the schools of the past, and to transfer their prestige to methods which will procure an active concern with things and persons, directed by aims of increasing temporal reach and deploying greater range of things in space. In time the theory of knowing must be derived from the practice which is most successful in making knowledge; and then that theory will be employed to improve the methods which are less successful.

2

Schools of Method

There are various systems of philosophy with characteristically different conceptions of the method of knowing. Some of them are named scholasticism, sensationalism, rationalism, idealism, realism, empiricism, transcendentalism, pragmatism, etc. Many of them have been criticized in connection with the discussion of some educational problem. We are here concerned with them as involving deviations from that method which has proved most effective in achieving knowledge, for a consideration of the deviations may render clearer the true place of knowledge in experience. In brief, the function of knowledge is to make one experience freely available in other experiences. The word "freely" marks the difference between the principle of knowledge and that of habit. Habit means that an individual undergoes a modification through an experience, which modification forms a predisposition to easier and more effective action in a like direction in the future. Thus it also has the function of making one experience available in subsequent experiences. Within certain limits, it performs this function successfully. But habit, apart from knowledge, does not make allowance for change of conditions, for novelty. Prevision of change is not part of its scope, for habit assumes the essential likeness of the new situation with the old. Consequently it often leads astray, or comes between a person and the successful performance of his task, just as the skill, based on habit alone, of the mechanic will desert him when something unexpected occurs in the running of the machine. But a man who understands the machine is the man who knows what he is about. He knows the conditions under which a given habit works, and is in a position to introduce the changes which will readapt it to new conditions.

In other words, knowledge is a perception of those connections of an object which determine its applicability in a given situation. To take an extreme example; savages react to a flaming comet as they are accustomed to react to other events which threaten the security of their life. Since they try to frighten wild animals or their enemies by shrieks, beating of gongs, brandishing of weapons, etc., they use the same methods to scare away the comet. To us, the method is plainly absurd—so absurd that we fail to note that savages are simply falling back upon habit in a way which exhibits its limitations. The only reason we do not act in some analogous fashion is because we do not take the comet as an isolated, disconnected event, but apprehend it in its connections with other events. We place it, as we say, in the astronomical system. We respond to its *connections* and not simply to the immediate occurrence. Thus our attitude to it is much freer. We may approach it, so to speak, from any one of the angles provided by its connections. We can bring into play, as we deem wise, any one of the habits appropriate to any one of the connected objects. Thus we get at a new event indirectly instead of immediately—by invention, ingenuity, resourcefulness. An ideally perfect knowledge would represent such a network of interconnections that any past experience would offer a point of advantage from which to get at the problem presented in a new experience. In fine, while a habit apart from knowledge supplies us with a single fixed method of attack, knowledge means that selection may be made from a much wider range of habits.

Two aspects of this more general and freer availability of former experiences for subsequent ones may be distinguished. . . . *(i.)* One, the more tangible, is increased power of control. What cannot be managed directly may be handled indirectly; or we can interpose barriers between us and undesirable consequences; or we may evade them if we cannot overcome them. Genuine knowledge has all the practical value attaching to efficient habits in any case. *(ii.)* But it also increases the meaning, the experienced significance, attaching to an experience. A situation to which we respond capriciously or by routine has only a minimum of conscious significance; we get nothing mentally from it But wherever knowledge comes into play in determining a new experience there is mental reward; even if we fail practically in getting the needed control we have the satisfaction of experiencing a meaning instead of merely reacting physically.

While the content of knowledge is what *has* happened, what is taken as finished and hence settled and sure, the *reference* of knowledge is future or prospective. For knowledge furnishes the means of understanding or giving meaning to what is still going on and what is to be done. The knowledge of a physician is what he has found out by personal acquaintance and by study of what others have ascertained and recorded. But it is knowledge to him because it supplies the resources by which he interprets the unknown things which confront him, fills out the partial obvious facts with connected suggested phenomena, foresees their probable future, and makes plans accordingly. When knowledge is cut off from use in giving meaning to what is blind and baffling, it drops out of consciousness entirely or else becomes an object of aesthetic contemplation. There is much emotional satisfaction to be had from a survey of the symmetry and order of possessed knowledge, and the satisfaction is a legitimate one. But this contemplative attitude is aesthetic, not intellectual. It is the same sort of joy that comes from viewing a finished picture or a well-composed landscape. It would make no difference if the subject matter were totally different, provided it had the same harmonious organization. Indeed, it would make no difference if it were wholly invented, a play of fancy. Applicability to the world means not applicability to what is past and gone—that is out of the question by the nature of the case; it means applicability to what is still going on, what is still unsettled, in the moving scene in which we are implicated. The very fact that we so easily overlook this trait, and regard statements of what is past and out of reach as knowledge is because we assume the continuity of past and future. We cannot entertain the conception of a world in which knowledge of its past would not be helpful in forecasting and giving meaning to its future. We ignore the prospective reference just because it is so irretrievably implied.

Yet many of the philosophic schools of method which have been mentioned transform the ignoring into a virtual denial. They regard knowledge as something complete in itself irrespective of its availability in dealing with what is yet to be. And it is this omission which vitiates them and which makes them stand as sponsors for educational methods which an adequate conception of knowledge condemns. For one has only to call to mind what is sometimes treated in schools as acquisition of knowledge to realize how lacking it is in any fruitful connection with the ongoing experience of the students—how largely it seems to be believed that the mere appropriation of subject matter which happens to be stored in books constitutes knowledge. No matter how true what is learned to those who found it out and in whose experience it functioned, there is nothing which makes it knowledge to the pupils. It might as well be something about Mars or about some fanciful country unless it fructifies in the individual's own life.

At the time when scholastic method developed, it had relevancy to social conditions. It was a method for systematizing and lending rational sanction to material accepted on authority. This subject matter meant so much that it vitalized the defining and systematizing brought to bear upon it. Under present conditions the scholastic method, for most persons, means a form of knowing which has no especial connection with *any* particular subject matter. It includes making distinctions, definitions, divisions, and classifications for the mere sake of making them—with no objective in experience. The view of thought as a purely psychical activity having its own forms, which are applied to any material as a seal may be stamped on any plastic stuff, the view which underlies what is termed formal logic is essentially the scholastic method generalized. The doctrine of formal discipline in education is the natural counterpart of the scholastic method.

The contrasting theories of the method of knowledge which go by the name of sensationalism and rationalism correspond to an exclusive emphasis upon the particular and the general respectively—or upon bare facts on one side and bare relations on the other. In real knowledge, there is a particularizing and a generalizing function working together. So far as a situation is confused, it has to be cleared up; it has to be resolved into details, as sharply defined as possible. Specified facts and qualities constitute the elements of the problem to be dealt with, and it is through our sense-organs that they are specified. As setting forth the problem, they may well be termed particulars, for they are fragmentary. Since our task is to discover their connections and to recombine them, *for us at the time* they are partial. They are to be given meaning; hence, just as they stand, they lack it. Anything which is *to be* known, whose meaning has still to be made out, offers itself as particular. But what is already known, if it has been worked over with a view to making it applicable to intellectually mastering new particulars, is general in function. Its function of introducing connection into what is otherwise unconnected constitutes its generality. Any fact is general if we use it to give meaning to the elements of a new experience. "Reason" is just the ability to bring the subject matter of prior experience to bear to perceive the significance of the subject matter of a new experience. A person is reasonable in the degree in which he is habitually open to seeing an event which immediately strikes his senses not as an isolated thing but in its connection with the common experience of mankind.

Without the particulars as they are discriminated by the active responses of sense-organs, there is no material for knowing and no intellectual growth. Without placing these particulars in the context of the meanings wrought out in the larger experience of the past—without the use of reason or thought—particulars are mere excitations or irritations. The mistake alike of the sensational and the rationalistic schools is that each fails to see that the function of sensory stimulation and thought is relative to reorganizing experience in applying the old to the new, thereby maintaining the continuity or consistency of life.

The theory of the method of knowing which is advanced in these pages may be termed pragmatic. Its essential feature is to maintain the continuity of knowing with an activity which purposely modifies the environment. It holds that knowledge in its strict sense of something possessed consists of our intellectual resources—of all the habits that render our action intelligent. Only that which has been organized into our disposition so as to enable us to adapt the environment to our needs and to adapt our aims and desires to the situation in which we live is really knowledge. Knowledge is not just something which we are now conscious of, but consists of the dispositions we consciously use in understanding what now happens. Knowledge as an act is bringing some of our dispositions to consciousness with a view to straightening out a perplexity, by conceiving the connection between ourselves and the world in which we live.

Summary

Such social divisions as interfere with free and full intercourse react to make the intelligence and knowing of members of the separated classes one-sided. Those whose experience has to do with utilities cut off from the larger end they subserve are practical empiricists; those who enjoy the contemplation of a realm of meanings in whose active production they have had no share are practical rationalists. Those who come in direct contact with things and have to adapt their activities to them immediately are, in effect, realists; those who isolate the meanings of these things and put them in a religious or so-called spiritual world aloof from things are, in effect, idealists. Those concerned with progress, who are striving to change received beliefs, emphasize the individual factor in knowing; those whose chief business it is to withstand change and conserve received truth emphasize the universal and the fixed—and so on. Philosophic systems in their opposed theories of knowledge present an explicit formulation of the traits characteristic of these cut-off and one-sided segments of experience—one-sided because barriers to intercourse prevent the experience of one from being enriched and supplemented by that of others who are differently situated.

In an analogous way, since democracy stands in principle for free interchange, for social continuity, it must develop a theory of knowledge which sees in knowledge the method by which one experience is made available in giving direction and meaning to another. The recent advances in physiology, biology, and the logic of the experimental sciences supply the specific intellectual instrumentalities demanded to work out and formulate such a theory. Their educational equivalent is the connection of the acquisition of knowledge in the schools with activities, or occupations, carried on in a medium of associated life.

from **The Need for a Recovery
of Philosophy**

(1917)

INTELLECTUAL ADVANCE occurs in two ways. At times increase
of knowledge is organized about old conceptions, while these are
expanded, elaborated and refined, but not seriously revised, much
less abandoned. At other times, the increase of knowledge demands qualitative rather than quantitative change; alteration, not
addition. Men's minds grow cold to their former intellectual concerns; ideas that were burning fade; interests that were urgent
seem remote. Men face in another direction; their older perplexi-
ties are unreal; considerations passed over as negligible loom up.
Former problems may not have been solved, but they no longer
press for solution.

Philosophy is no exception to the rule. But it is unusually conservative—not, necessarily, in proffering solutions, but in clinging
to problems. It has been so allied with theology and theological
morals as representatives of men's chief interests, that radical alteration has been shocking. Men's activities took a decidedly new
turn, for example, in the seventeenth century, and it seemed as if
philosophy, under the lead of thinkers like Bacon and Descartes,
was to execute an about-face. But, in spite of the ferment, it
turned out that many of the older problems were but translated
from Latin into the vernacular or into the new terminology furnished by science.

The association of philosophy with academic teaching has reinforced this intrinsic conservatism. Scholastic philosophy persisted in
universities after men's thoughts outside of the walls of colleges had
moved in other directions. In the last hundred years intellectual
advances of science and politics have in like fashion been crystal-

lized into material of instruction and now resist further change. I would not say that the spirit of teaching is hostile to that of liberal inquiry, but a philosophy which exists largely as something to be taught rather than wholly as something to be reflected upon is conducive to discussion of views held by others rather than to immediate response. Philosophy when taught inevitably magnifies the history of past thought, and leads professional philosophers to approach their subject-matter through its formulation in received systems. It tends, also, to emphasize points upon which men have divided into schools, for these lend themselves to retrospective definition and elaboration. Consequently, philosophical discussion is likely to be a dressing out of antithetical traditions, where criticism of one view is thought to afford proof of the truth of its opposite (as if formulation of views guaranteed logical exclusives). Direct preoccupation with contemporary difficulties is left to literature and politics.

If changing conduct and expanding knowledge ever required a willingness to surrender not merely old solutions but old problems it is now. I do not mean that we can turn abruptly away from all traditional issues. This is impossible; it would be the undoing of the one who attempted it. Irrespective of the professionalizing of philosophy, the ideas philosophers discuss are still those in which Western civilization has been bred. They are in the backs of the heads of educated people. But what serious-minded men not engaged in the professional business of philosophy most want to know is what modifications and abandonments of intellectual inheritance are required by the newer industrial, political, and scientific movements. They want to know what these newer movements mean when translated into general ideas. Unless professional philosophy can mobilize itself sufficiently to assist in this clarification and redirection of men's thoughts, it is likely to get more and more sidetracked from the main currents of contemporary life. . . .

Philosophy claims to be one form or mode of knowing. If, then, the conclusion is reached that knowing is a way of employing empirical occurrences with respect to increasing power to direct the consequences which flow from things, the application of the conclusion must be made to philosophy itself. It, too, becomes not a contemplative survey of existence nor an analysis of what is past and done with, but an outlook upon future possibilities with reference to attaining the better and averting the worse. Philosophy must take, with good grace, its own medicine.

It is easier to state the negative results of the changed idea of philosophy than the positive ones. The point that occurs to mind most readily is that philosophy will have to surrender all pretension to be peculiarly concerned with ultimate reality, or with reality as a complete (i.e., completed) whole: with *the* real object. The surrender is not easy of achievement. The philosophic tradition that comes to us from classic Greek thought and that was reinforced by Christian philosophy in the Middle Ages discriminates philosophical knowing from other modes of knowing by means of an alleged peculiarly intimate concern with supreme, ultimate, true reality. To deny this trait to philosophy seems to many to be the suicide of philosophy; to be a systematic adoption of skepticism or agnostic positivism.

The pervasiveness of the tradition is shown in the fact that so vitally a contemporary thinker as Bergson,[1] who finds a philosophic revolution involved in abandonment of the traditional identification of the truly real with the fixed (an identification inherited from Greek thought), does not find it in his heart to abandon the counterpart identification of philosophy with search for the truly Real; and hence finds it necessary to substitute an ultimate and absolute flux for an ultimate and absolute permanence. Thus his great empirical services in calling attention to the fundamental importance of considerations of time for problems of life and mind get compromised with a mystic, non-empirical "Intuition"; and we find him preoccupied with solving, by means of his new idea of ultimate reality, the traditional problems of realities-in-themselves and phenomena, matter and mind, free-will and determinism, God and the world. Is not that another evidence of the influence of the classic idea about philosophy?

Even the new realists are not content to take their realism as a plea for approaching subject-matter directly instead of through the intervention of epistemological apparatus; they find it necessary first to determine the status of *the* real object. Thus they too become entangled in the problem of the possibility of error, dreams, hallucinations, etc., in short, the problem of evil. For I take it that an uncorrupted realism would accept such things as real events, and find in them no other problems than those attending the consideration of any real occurrence—namely, problems of structure, origin, and operation.

It is often said that pragmatism, unless it is content to be a contribution to mere methodology, must develop a theory of Reality. But the chief characteristic trait of the pragmatic notion of reality is precisely that no theory of Reality in general, *uberhaupt,* is possible or needed. It occupies the position of an emancipated empiricism or a thoroughgoing naïve realism. It finds that "reality" is a *denotative* term, a word used to designate indifferently everything that happens. Lies, dreams, insanities, deceptions, myths, theories are all of them just the events which they specifically are. Pragmatism is content to take its stand with science; for science finds all such events to be subject-matter of description and inquiry—just like stars and fossils, mosquitoes and malaria, circulation and vision. It also takes its stand with daily life, which finds that such things really have to be reckoned with as they occur interwoven in the texture of events.

The only way in which the term reality can ever become more than a blanket denotative term is through recourse to specific events in all their diversity and thatness. Speaking summarily, I find that the retention by philosophy of the notion of a Reality feudally superior to the events of everyday occurrence is the chief source of the increasing isolation of philosophy from common sense and science. For the latter do not operate in any such region. As with them of old, philosophy in dealing with real difficulties finds itself still hampered by reference to realities more real, more ultimate, than those which directly happen.

I have said that identifying the cause of philosophy with the notion of superior reality is the cause of an *increasing* isolation from science and practical life. The phrase reminds us that there was a time when the enterprise of science and the moral interests of men both moved in a universe invidiously distinguished from that of ordinary occurrence. While all that happens is equally real— since it really happens—happenings are not of equal worth. Their respective consequences, their import, varies tremendously. Counterfeit money, although real (or rather *because* real), is really different from valid circulatory medium, just as disease is really different from health; different in specific structure and so different in consequences. In occidental thought, the Greeks were the first to draw the distinction between the genuine and the spurious in a generalized fashion and to formulate and enforce its tremendous significance for the conduct of life. But since they had at command no technique of experimental analysis and no adequate technique of mathematical analysis, they were compelled to treat the difference of the true and the false, the dependable and the deceptive, as signifying two kinds of existence, the truly real and the apparently real.

Two points can hardly be asserted with too much emphasis. The Greeks were wholly right in the feeling that questions of good and ill, as far as they fall within human control, are bound up with discrimination of the genuine from the spurious, of "being" from what only pretends to be. But because they lacked adequate instrumentalities for coping with this difference in specific situations, they were forced to treat the difference as a wholesale and rigid one. Science was concerned with vision of ultimate and true reality; opinion was concerned with getting along with apparent realities. Each had its appropriate region permanently marked off. Matters of opinion could never become matters of science; their intrinsic nature forbade. When the practice of science went on under such conditions, science and philosophy were one and the same thing. Both had to do with ultimate reality in its rigid and insuperable difference from ordinary occurrences.

We have only to refer to the way in which medieval life wrought the philosophy of an ultimate and supreme reality into the context of practical life to realize that for centuries political and moral interests were bound up with the distinction between the absolutely real and the relatively real. The difference was no matter of a remote technical philosophy, but one which controlled life from the cradle to the grave, from the grave to the endless life after death. By means of a vast institution, which in effect was state as well as church, the claims of ultimate reality were enforced; means of access to it were provided. Acknowledgment of The Reality brought security in this world and salvation in the next. It is not necessary to report the story of the change which has since taken place. It is enough for our purposes to note that none of the modern philosophies of a superior reality, or *the* real object, idealistic or realistic, holds that its insight makes a difference like that between sin and holiness, eternal condemnation and eternal bliss. While in its own context the philosophy of ultimate reality entered into the vital concerns of men, it now tends to be an ingenious dialectic exercised in professorial corners by a few who have retained ancient premises while rejecting their application to the conduct of life.

The increased isolation from science of any philosophy identified with the problem of *the* real is equally marked. For the growth of science has consisted precisely in the invention of an equipment, a technique of appliances and procedures, which, accepting all occurrences as homogeneously real, proceeds to distinguish the authenticated from the spurious, the true from the false, by specific modes of treatment in specific situations. The procedures of the trained engineer, of the competent physician, of the laboratory expert, have turned out to be the only ways of discriminating the counterfeit from the valid. And they have revealed that the difference is not one of antecedent fixity of existence, but one of mode of treatment and of the consequences thereon attendant. After mankind has learned to put its trust in specific procedures in order to make its discriminations between the false and the true, philosophy arrogates to itself the enforcement of the distinction at its own cost.

More than once, this essay has intimated that the counterpart of the idea of invidiously real reality is the spectator notion of knowledge. If the knower, however defined, is set over against the world to be known, knowing consists in possessing a transcript, more or less accurate but otiose, of real things. Whether this transcript is presentative in character (as realists say) or whether it is by means of states of consciousness which represent things (as subjectivists say), is a matter of great importance in its own context. But, in another regard, this difference is negligible in comparison with the point in which both agree. Knowing is viewing from outside. But if it be true that the self or subject of experience is part and parcel of the course of events, it follows that the self *becomes* a knower. It becomes a mind in virtue of a distinctive way of partaking in the course of events. The significant distinction is no longer between the knower *and* the world; it is between different ways of being in and of the movement of things; between a brute physical way and a purposive, intelligent way.

There is no call to repeat in detail the statements which have been advanced. Their net purport is that the directive presence of future possibilities in dealing with existent conditions is what is meant by knowing; that the self becomes a knower or mind when anticipation of future consequences operates as its stimulus. What we are now concerned with is the effect of this conception upon the nature of philosophic knowing.

As far as I can judge, popular response to pragmatic philosophy was moved by two quite different considerations. By some it was thought to provide a new species of sanctions, a new mode of apologetics, for certain religious ideas whose standing had been threatened. By others, it was welcomed because it was taken as a sign that philosophy was about to surrender its otiose and speculative remoteness; that philosophers were beginning to recognize that philosophy is of account only if, like everyday knowing and like science, it affords guidance to action and thereby makes a difference in the event. It was welcomed as a sign that philosophers were willing to have the worth of their philosophizing measured by responsible tests.

I have not seen this point of view emphasized, or hardly recognized, by professional critics. The difference of attitude can probably be easily explained. The epistemological universe of discourse is so highly technical that only those who have been trained in the history of thought think in terms of it. It did not occur, accordingly, to non-technical readers to interpret the doctrine that the meaning and validity of thought are fixed by differences made in consequences and in satisfactoriness to mean consequences in personal feelings. Those who were professionally trained, however, took the statement to mean that consciousness or mind in the mere act of looking at things modifies them. It understood the doctrine of test of validity by consequences to mean that apprehensions and conceptions are true if the modifications effected by them were of an emotionally desirable tone.

Prior discussion should have made it reasonably clear that the source of this misunderstanding lies in the neglect of temporal considerations. The change made in things by the self in knowing is not immediate and, so to say, cross-sectional. It is longitudinal—in the redirection given to changes already going on. Its analogue is found in the changes which take place in the development of, say, iron ore into a watch-spring, not in those of the miracle of transubstantiation. For the static, cross-sectional, non-temporal relation of subject and object, the pragmatic hypothesis substitutes apprehension of a thing in terms of the results in other things which it is tending to effect. For the unique epistemological relation, it substitutes a practical relation of a familiar type:—responsive behavior which changes in time the subject-matter to which it applies. The unique thing about the responsive behavior which

It shouldn't be called truth but a relevancy. The investigation shouldn't stop at matching.

constitutes knowing is the specific difference which marks it off from other modes of response, namely, the part played in it by anticipation and prediction. Knowing is the act, stimulated by this foresight, of securing and averting consequences. The success of the achievement measures the standing of the foresight by which response is directed. The popular impression that pragmatic philosophy means that philosophy shall develop ideas relevant to the actual crises of life, ideas influential in dealing with them and tested by the assistance they afford, is correct.

Reference to practical response suggests, however, another misapprehension. Many critics have jumped at the obvious association of the word pragmatic with practical. They have assumed that the intent is to limit all knowledge, philosophic included, to promoting "action," understanding by action either just any bodily movement, or those bodily movements which conduce to the preservation and grosser well-being of the body. James's statement that general conceptions must "cash in"[2] has been taken (especially by European critics) to mean that the end and measure of intelligence lies in the narrow and coarse utilities which it produces. Even an acute American thinker, after first criticizing pragmatism as a kind of idealistic epistemology, goes on to treat it as a doctrine which regards intelligence as a lubricating oil facilitating the workings of the body.[3]

One source of the misunderstanding is suggested by the fact that "cashing in" to James meant that a general idea must always be capable of verification in specific existential cases. The notion of "cashing in" says nothing about the breadth or depth of the specific consequences. As an empirical doctrine, it could not say anything about them in general; the specific cases must speak for themselves. If one conception is verified in terms of eating beefsteak, and another in terms of a favorable credit balance in the bank, that is not because of anything in the theory, but because of the specific nature of the conceptions in question, and because there exist particular events like hunger and trade. If there are also existences in which the most liberal esthetic ideas and the most generous moral conceptions can be verified by specific embodiment, assuredly so much the better. The fact that a strictly empirical philosophy was taken by so many critics to imply an *a priori* dogma about the kind of consequences capable of existence is evidence, I think, of the inability of many philosophers to think in concretely empirical terms. Since the critics were themselves accustomed to get results by manipulating the concepts of "consequences" and of "practice," they assumed that even a would-be empiricist must be doing the same sort of thing. It will, I suppose, remain for a long time incredible to some that a philosopher should really intend to go to specific experiences to determine of what scope and depth practice admits, and what sort of consequences the world permits to come into being. Concepts are so clear; it takes so little time to develop their implications; experiences are so confused, and it requires so much time and energy to lay hold of them. And yet these same critics charge pragmatism with adopting subjective and emotional standards!

As a matter of fact, the pragmatic theory of intelligence means that the function of mind is to project new and more complex ends—to free experience from routine and from caprice. Not the use of thought to accomplish purposes already given either in the mechanism of the body or in that of the existent state of society, but the use of intelligence to liberate and liberalize action, is the pragmatic lesson. Action restricted to given and fixed ends may attain great technical efficiency; but efficiency is the only quality to which it can lay claim. Such action is mechanical (or becomes so), no matter what the scope of the pre-formed end, be it the Will of God or *Kultur*. But the doctrine that intelligence develops within the sphere of action for the sake of possibilities not yet given is the opposite of a doctrine of mechanical efficiency. Intelligence *as* intelligence is inherently forward-looking; only by ignoring its primary function does it become a mere means for an end already given. The latter *is* servile, even when the end is labeled moral, religious, or esthetic. But action directed to ends to which the agent has not previously been attached inevitably carries with it a quickened and enlarged spirit. A pragmatic intelligence is a creative intelligence, not a routine mechanic.

All this may read like a defense of pragmatism by one concerned to make out for it the best case possible. Such is not, however, the intention. The purpose is to indicate the extent to which intelligence frees action from a mechanically instrumental character. Intelligence is, indeed, instrumental *through* action to the determination of the qualities of future experience. But the very fact that the concern of intelligence is with the future, with the as-yet-unrealized (and with the given and the established only as conditions of the realization of possibilities), makes the action in which it takes effect generous and liberal; free of spirit. Just that action which extends and approves intelligence has an intrinsic value of its own in being instrumental:—the intrinsic value of being informed with intelligence in behalf of the enrichment of life. By the same stroke, intelligence becomes truly liberal: knowing is a human undertaking, not an esthetic appreciation carried on by a refined class or a capitalistic possession of a few learned specialists, whether men of science or of philosophy.

More emphasis has been put upon what philosophy is not than upon what it may become. But it is not necessary, it is not even desirable, to set forth philosophy as a scheduled program. There are human difficulties of an urgent, deep-seated kind which may be clarified by trained reflection, and whose solution may be forwarded by the careful development of hypotheses. When it is understood that philosophic thinking is caught up in the actual course of events, having the office of guiding them towards a prosperous issue, problems will abundantly present themselves. Philosophy will not solve these problems; philosophy is vision, imagination, reflection—and these functions, apart from action, modify nothing and hence resolve nothing. But in a complicated and perverse world, action which is not informed with vision, imagination, and reflection, is more likely to increase confusion and conflict than to straighten things out. It is not easy for generous and sustained reflection to become a guiding and illuminating method in action. Until it frees itself from identification with problems which are supposed to depend upon Reality as such, or its distinction from a world of Appearance, or its relation to a Knower as such, the hands of philosophy are tied. Having no chance to link its fortunes with a responsible career by suggesting things to be tried, it cannot identify itself with questions which actually arise in the vicissitudes of life. Philosophy recovers itself when it ceases to be a device for dealing with the problems of philosophers and becomes a method, cultivated by philosophers, for dealing with the problems of men.

Emphasis must vary with the stress and special impact of the troubles which perplex men. Each age knows its own ills, and seeks its own remedies. One does not have to forecast a particular program to note that the central need of any program at the present day is an adequate conception of the nature of intelligence and its place in action. Philosophy cannot disavow responsibility for many misconceptions of the nature of intelligence which now hamper its efficacious operation. It has at least a negative task imposed upon it. It must take away the burdens which it has laid upon the intelligence of the common man in struggling with his difficulties. It must deny and eject that intelligence which is naught but a distant eye, registering in a remote and alien medium the spectacle of nature and life. To enforce the fact that the emergence of imagination and thought is relative to the connexion of the sufferings of men with their doings is of itself to illuminate those sufferings and to instruct those doings. To catch mind in its connexion with the entrance of the novel into the course of the world is to be on the road to see that intelligence is itself the most promising of all novelties, the revelation of the meaning of that transformation of past into future which is the reality of every present. To reveal intelligence as the organ for the guidance of this transformation, the sole director of its quality, is to make a declaration of present untold significance for action. To elaborate these

convictions of the connexion of intelligence with what men undergo because of their doings and with the emergence and direction of the creative, the novel, in the world is of itself a program
which will keep philosophers busy until something more worth
while is forced upon them. For the elaboration has to be made
through application to all the disciplines which have an intimate
connexion with human conduct:—to logic, ethics, esthetics, economics, and the procedure of the sciences formal and natural.

I also believe that there is a genuine sense in which the enforcement of the pivotal position of intelligence in the world and
thereby in control of human fortunes (so far as they are manage-
able) is the peculiar problem in the problems of life which come
home most closely to ourselves—to ourselves living not merely in
the early twentieth century but in the United States. It is easy to
be foolish about the connexion of thought with national life. But
I do not see how any one can question the distinctively national
color of English, or French, or German philosophies. And if of
late the history of thought has come under the domination of the
German dogma of an inner evolution of ideas, it requires but a little inquiry to convince oneself that that dogma itself testifies to a
particularly nationalistic need and origin. I believe that philosophy
in America will be lost between chewing a historic cud long since
reduced to woody fibre, or an apologetics for lost causes (lost to
natural science), or a scholastic, schematic formalism, unless it can
somehow bring to consciousness America's own needs and its own
implicit principle of successful action.

This need and principle, I am convinced, is the necessity of a
deliberate control of policies by the method of intelligence, an intelligence which is not the faculty of intellect honored in text-
books and neglected elsewhere, but which is the sum-total of
impulses, habits, emotions, records, and discoveries which forecast
what is desirable and undesirable in future possibilities, and which
contrive ingeniously in behalf of imagined good. Our life has no
background of sanctified categories upon which we may fall back;
we rely upon precedent as authority only to our own undoing—

for with us there is such a continuously novel situation that final reliance upon precedent entails some class interest guiding us by the nose whither it will. British empiricism, with its appeal to what has been in the past, is, after all, only a kind of *a priorism*. For it lays down a fixed rule for future intelligence to follow; and only the immersion of philosophy in technical learning prevents our seeing that this is the essence of *a priorism*.

We pride ourselves upon being realistic, desiring a hard-headed cognizance of facts, and devoted to mastering the means of life. We pride ourselves upon a practical idealism, a lively and easily moved faith in possibilities as yet unrealized, in willingness to make sacrifice for their realization. Idealism easily becomes a sanction of waste and carelessness, and realism a sanction of legal formalism in behalf of things as they are—the rights of the possessor. We thus tend to combine a loose and ineffective optimism with assent to the doctrine of take who take can: a deification of power. All peoples at all times have been narrowly realistic in practice and have then employed idealization to cover up in sentiment and theory their brutalities But never, perhaps, has the tendency been so dangerous and so tempting as with ourselves. Faith in the power of intelligence to imagine a future which is the projection of the desirable in the present, and to invent the instrumentalities of its realization, is our salvation. And it is a faith which must be nurtured and made articulate: surely a sufficiently large task for our philosophy.

Experience, Nature and Art

in *Experience and Nature* (1925)

EXPERIENCE, with the Greeks, signified a store of practical wisdom, a fund of insights useful in conducting the affairs of life. Sensation and perception were its occasion and supplied it with pertinent materials, but did not of themselves constitute it. They generated experience when retention was added and when a common factor in the multitude of felt and perceived cases detached itself so as to become available in judgment and exertion. Thus understood, experience is exemplified in the discrimination and skill of the good carpenter, pilot, physician, captain-at-arms; experience is equivalent to art. Modern theory has quite properly extended the application of the term to cover many things that the Greeks would hardly have called "experience," the bare having of aches and pains, or a play of colors before the eyes. But even those who hold this larger signification would admit, I suppose, that such "experiences" count only when they result in insight, or in an enjoyed perception, and that only thus do they define experience in its honorific sense.

Greek thinkers nevertheless disparaged experience in comparison with something called reason and science. The ground for depreciation was not that usually assigned in modern philosophy; it was not that experience is "subjective." On the contrary, experience was considered to be a genuine expression of cosmic forces, not an exclusive attribute or possession of animal or of human nature. It was taken to be a realization of inferior portions of nature, those infected with chance and change, the less *Being* part of the cosmos. Thus while experience meant art, art reflected the contingencies and partialities of nature, while science—theory—

exhibited its necessities and universalities. Art was born of need, lack, deprivation, incompleteness, while science—theory—manifested fullness and totality of Being. Thus the depreciatory view of experience was identical with a conception that placed practical activity below theoretical activity, finding the former dependent, impelled from outside, marked by deficiency of real being, while the latter was independent and free because complete and self-sufficing: that is, perfect.

In contrast with this self-consistent position we find a curious mixture in modern thinking. The latter feels under no obligation to present a theory of natural existence that links art with nature; on the contrary, it usually holds that science or knowledge is the only *authentic* expression of nature, in which case art must be an arbitrary addition to nature. But modern thought also combines exaltation of science with eulogistic appreciation of art, especially of fine or creative art. At the same time it retains the substance of the classic disparagement of the practical in contrast with the theoretical, although formulating it in somewhat different language: to the effect that knowledge deals with objective reality as it is in itself, while in what is "practical," objective reality is altered and cognitively distorted by subjective factors of want, emotion and striving. And yet in its encomium of art, it fails to note the commonplace of Greek observation—that the fine arts as well as the industrial technologies are affairs of practice.

This confused plight is partly cause and partly effect of an almost universal confusion of the artistic and the esthetic. On one hand, there is action that deals with materials and energies outside the body, assembling, refining, combining, manipulating them until their new state yields a satisfaction not afforded by their crude condition—a formula that applies to fine and useful art alike. On the other hand, there is the delight that attends vision and hearing, an enhancement of the receptive appreciation and assimilation of objects irrespective of participation in the operations of production. Provided the difference of the two things is recognized, it is no matter whether the words "esthetic" and "artistic" or other terms be used to designate the distinction, for the difference is not one of words but of objects. But in some form the difference must be acknowledged.

The community in which Greek art was produced was small; numerous and complicated intermediaries between production and consumption were lacking; producers had a virtually servile status. Because of the close connection between production and enjoyable fruition, the Greeks in their perceptive uses and enjoyments were never wholly unconscious of the artisan and his work, not even when they personally were exclusively concerned with delightful contemplation. But since the artist was an artisan (the term artist having none of the eulogistic connotations of present usage), and since the artisan occupied an inferior position, the enjoyment of works of any art did not stand upon the same level as enjoyment of those objects for the realization of which manual activity was not needed. Objects of rational thought, of contemplative insight were the only things that met the specification of freedom from need, labor, and matter. They alone were self-sufficient, self-existent, and self-explanatory, and hence enjoyment of *them* was on a higher plane than enjoyment of works of art.

These conceptions were consistent with one another and with the conditions of social life at the time. Nowadays we have a messy conjunction of notions that are consistent neither with one another nor with the tenor of our actual life. Knowledge is still regarded by most thinkers as direct grasp of ultimate reality, although the practice of knowing has been assimilated to the procedure of the useful arts;—involving, that is to say, doing that manipulates and arranges natural energies. Again while science is said to lay hold of reality, yet "art" instead of being assigned a lower rank is equally esteemed and honored. And when within art a distinction is drawn between production and appreciation, the chief honor usually goes to the former on the ground that it is "creative," while taste is relatively possessive and passive, dependent for its material upon the activities of the creative artist.

If Greek philosophy was correct in thinking of knowledge as

Workers produce, parasites enjoy.

contemplation rather than as a productive art, and if modern philosophy accepts this conclusion, then the only logical course is relative disparagement of all forms of production, since they are modes of practice which is by conception inferior to contemplation. The artistic is then secondary to the esthetic: "creation," to "taste," and the scientific *worker*—as we significantly say—is subordinate in rank and worth to the dilettante who enjoys the results of his labors. But if modern tendencies are justified in putting art and creation first, then the implications of this position should be avowed and carried through. It would then be seen that science is an art, that art is practice, and that the only distinction worth drawing is not between practice and theory, but between those modes of practice that are not intelligent, not inherently and immediately enjoyable, and those which are full of enjoyed meanings. When this perception dawns, it will be a commonplace that art—the mode of activity that is charged with meanings capable of immediately enjoyed possession—is the complete culmination of nature, and that "science" is properly a handmaiden that conducts natural events to this happy issue. Thus would disappear the separations that trouble present thinking: division of everything into nature *and* experience, of experience into practice *and* theory, art *and* science, of art into useful *and* fine, menial *and* free.

Thus the issue involved in experience as art in its pregnant sense and in art as processes and materials of nature continued by direction into achieved and enjoyed meanings, sums up in itself all the issues which have been previously considered. Thought, intelligence, science is the intentional direction of natural events to meanings capable of immediate possession and enjoyment; this direction—which is operative art—is itself a natural event in which nature otherwise partial and incomplete comes fully to itself; so that objects of conscious experience when reflectively chosen, form the "end" of nature. The doings and sufferings that form experience are, in the degree in which experience is intelligent or charged with meanings, a union of the precarious, novel, irregular with the settled, assured and uniform—a union which also de fines the artistic and the esthetic. For wherever there is art the contingent and ongoing no longer work at cross purposes with the formal and recurrent but commingle in harmony. And the distinguishing feature of conscious experience, of what for short is often called "consciousness," is that in it the instrumental and the final, meanings that are signs and clews and meanings that are immediately possessed, suffered and enjoyed, come together in one. And all of these things are preeminently true of art.

First, then, art is solvent union of the generic, recurrent, ordered, established phase of nature with its phase that is incomplete, going on, and hence still uncertain, contingent, novel, particular; or as certain systems of esthetic theory have truly declared, though without empirical basis and import in their words, a union of necessity and freedom, a harmony of the many and one, a reconciliation of sensuous and ideal. Of any artistic act and product it may be said both that it is inevitable in its rightness, that nothing in it can be altered without altering all, and that its occurrence is spontaneous, unexpected, fresh, unpredictable. The presence in art, whether as an act or a product, of proportion, economy, order, symmetry, composition, is such a commonplace that it does not need to be dwelt upon. But equally necessary is unexpected combination, and the consequent revelation of possibilities hitherto unrealized. "Repose in stimulation" characterizes art. Order and proportion when they are the whole story are soon exhausted; economy in itself is a tiresome and restrictive taskmaster. It is artistic when it releases.

The more extensive and repeated are the basic uniformities of nature that give form to art, the "greater" is the art, provided— and it is this proviso that distinguishes art—they are indistinguishably fused with the wonder of the new and the grace of the gratuitous. "Creation" may be asserted vaguely and mystically; but it denotes something genuine and indispensable in art. The merely finished is not fine but ended, done with, and the merely "fresh" is that bumptious impertinence indicated by the slang use of the word. The "magic" of poetry—and pregnant experience has poetical quality—is precisely the revelation of meaning in the old effected by its presentation through the new. It radiates the light that never was on land and sea but that is henceforth an abiding illumination of objects. Music in its immediate occurrence is the most varied and ethereal of the arts, but is in its conditions and structure the most mechanical. These things are commonplaces; but until they are commonly employed in their evidential significance for a theory of nature's nature, there is no cause to apologize for their citation.

The limiting terms that define art are routine at one extreme and capricious impulse at the other. It is hardly worth while to oppose science and art sharply to one another, when the deficiencies and troubles of life are so evidently due to separation between art and blind routine and blind impulse. Routine exemplifies the uniformities and recurrences of nature, caprice expresses its inchoate initiations and deviations. Each in isolation is unnatural as well as inartistic, for nature is an intersection of spontaneity and necessity, the regular and the novel, the finished and the beginning. It is right to object to much of current practice on the ground that it is routine, just as it is right to object to much of our current enjoyments on the ground that they are spasms of excited escape from the thraldom of enforced work. But to transform a just objection against the quality of much of our practical life into a description and definition of practice is on the same plane as to convert legitimate objection to trivial distraction, senseless amusement, and sensual absorption, into a Puritanical aversion to happiness. The idea that work, productive activity, signifies action carried on for merely extraneous ends, and the idea that happiness signifies surrender of mind to the thrills and excitations of the body are one and the same idea. The first notion marks the separation of activity from meaning, and the second marks the separation of receptivity from meaning. Both separations are inevitable as far as experience fails to be art:—when the regular, repetitious, and the novel, contingent in nature fail to sustain and inform each other in a productive activity possessed of immanent and directly enjoyed meaning.

Thus the theme has insensibly passed over into that of the relation of means and consequence, process and product, the instrumental and consummatory. Any activity that is simultaneously both, rather than in alternation and displacement, is art. Disunion of production and consumption is a common enough occurrence. But emphasis upon this separation in order to exalt the consummatory does not define or interpret either art or experience. It obscures their meaning, resulting in a division of art into useful and fine, adjectives which, when they are prefixed to "art," corrupt and destroy its intrinsic significance. For arts that are merely useful are not arts but routines; and arts that are merely final are not arts but passive amusements and distractions, different from other indulgent dissipations only in dependence upon a certain acquired refinement or "cultivation."

The existence of activities that have no immediate enjoyed intrinsic meaning is undeniable. They include much of our labors in home, factory, laboratory, and study. By no stretch of language can they be termed either artistic or esthetic. Yet they exist, and are so coercive that they require some attentive recognition. So we optimistically call them "useful" and let it go at that, thinking that by calling them useful we have somehow justified and explained their occurrence. If we were to ask useful for what? we should be obliged to examine their actual consequences, and when we once honestly and fully faced these consequences we should probably find ground for calling such activities detrimental rather than useful.

We call them useful because we arbitrarily cut short our consideration of consequences. We bring into view simply their efficacy in bringing into existence certain commodities; we do not ask for their effect upon the quality of human life and experience. They are useful to make shoes, houses, motor cars, money, and other things which *may* then be put to use; here inquiry and imagination stop. What they also *make* by way of narrowed, embittered, and crippled life, of congested, hurried, confused, and extravagant life, is left in oblivion. But to be useful is to fulfill need. The characteristic human need is for possession and appreciation of the meaning of things, and this need is ignored and unsatisfied in the traditional notion of the useful. We identify utility with the external relationship that some events and acts bear to other things that are their products, and thus leave out the only thing that is essential to the idea of utility, inherent place and bearing in experience. Our classificatory use of the conception of some arts as merely instrumental so as to dispose of a larger part of human activity is no solving definition; it rather conveys an immense and urgent problem.

The same statement applies to the conception of merely fine or final arts and works of art. In point of fact, the things designated by the phrase fall under three captions. There are activities and receptivities to which the name of "self-expression" is often applied as a eulogistic qualification, in which one indulges himself by giving free outward exhibition to his own states without reference to the conditions upon which intelligible communication depends—an act also sometimes known as "expression of emotion," which is then set up for definition of all fine art. It is easy to dispose of this art by calling it a product of egotism due to balked activity in other occupations. But this treatment misses a more significant point. For all art is a process of making the world a different place in which to live, and involves a phase of protest and of compensatory response. Such art as there is in these manifestations lies in this factor. It is owing to frustration in communication of meanings that the protest becomes arbitrary and the compensatory response wilfully eccentric.

In addition to this type—and frequently mingled with it—there is experimentation in new modes of craftsmanship, cases where the seemingly bizarre and over-individualistic character of the products is due to discontent with existing technique, and is associated with an attempt to find new modes of language. It is aside from the point either to greet these manifestations as if they con-stituted art for the first time in human history, or to condemn them as not art because of their violent departures from received canons and methods. Some movement in this direction has always been a condition of growth of new forms, a condition of salvation from that moral arrest and decay called academic art. Not this time

Then there is that which in quantity bulks most largely as fine art: the production of buildings in the name of the art of archi-tecture; of pictures in the name of the art of painting; of novels, dramas, etc., in the name of literary art; a production which in reality is largely a form of commercialized industry in production of a class of commodities that find their sale among well-to-do persons desirous of maintaining a conventionally approved status. As the first two modes carry to disproportionate excess that factor of particularity, contingency and difference which is indispensable in all art, deliberately flaunting avoidance of the repetitions and order of nature; so this mode celebrates the regular and finished. It is reminiscent rather than commemorative of the meanings of ex-perienced things. Its products remind their owner of things pleas-ant in memory though hard in direct-undergoing, and remind others that their owner has achieved an economic standard which makes possible cultivation and decoration of leisure.

Obviously no one of these classes of activity and product or all of them put together, mark off anything that can be called dis-tinctively fine art. They share their qualities and defects with many other acts and objects. But, fortunately, there may be mixed with any one of them, and, still more fortunately, there may occur without mixture, process and product that are characteristically excellent. This occurs when activity is productive of an object that affords continuously renewed delight. This condition requires that the object be, with its successive consequences, indefinitely in-strumental to *new* satisfying events. For otherwise the object is quickly exhausted and satiety sets in. Anyone who reflects upon the commonplace that a measure of artistic products is their ca-pacity to attract and retain observation with satisfaction under whatever conditions they are approached, while things of less quality soon lose capacity to hold attention becoming indifferent or repellent upon subsequent approach, has a sure demonstration that a genuinely esthetic object is not exclusively consummatory but is causally productive as well. A consummatory object that is not also instrumental turns in time to the dust and ashes of boredom. The "eternal" quality of great art is its renewed instrumentality for further consummatory experiences.

When this fact is noted, it is also seen that limitation of fineness of art to paintings, statues, poems, songs and symphonies is conventional, or even verbal. Any activity that is productive of objects whose perception is an immediate good, and whose operation is a continual source of enjoyable perception of other events exhibits fineness of art. There are acts of all kinds that directly refresh and enlarge the spirit and that are instrumental to the production of new objects and dispositions which are in turn productive of further refinements and replenishments. Frequently moralists make the acts *they* find excellent or virtuous wholly final, and treat art and affection as mere means. Estheticians reverse the performance, and see in good *acts* means to an ulterior external happiness, while esthetic appreciation is called a good in itself, or that strange thing an end in itself. But on both sides it is true that in being preeminently fructifying the things designated means are immediate satisfactions. They are their own excuses for being just because they are charged with an office in quickening apprehension, enlarging the horizon of vision, refining discrimination, creating standards of appreciation which are confirmed and deepened by further experiences. It would almost seem when their non-instrumental character is insisted upon as if what was meant were an indefinitely expansive and radiating instrumental efficacy.

The source of the error lies in the habit of calling by the name of means things that are not means at all; things that are only external and accidental antecedents of the happening of something else. Similarly things are called ends that are not ends save accidentally, since they are not fulfillments, consummatory, of means, but

merely last terms closing a process. Thus it is often said that a la-
borer's toil is the means of his livelihood, although except in the
most tenuous and arbitrary way it bears no relationship to his real
living. Even his wage is hardly an end or consequence of his labor.
He might—and frequently does—equally well or ill—perform
any one of a hundred other tasks as a condition of receiving payment. The prevailing conception of instrumentality is profoundly
vitiated by the habit of applying it to cases like the above, where,
instead of an operation of means, there is an enforced necessity of
doing one thing as a coerced antecedent of the occurrence of another thing which is wanted.

Means are always at least causal conditions; but causal conditions are means only when they possess an added qualification;
that, namely, of being freely used, because of perceived connection with chosen consequences. To entertain, choose and accomplish anything as an end or consequence is to be committed to a
like love and care for whatever events and acts are its means. Similarly, consequences, ends, are at least effects; but effects are not
ends unless thought has perceived and freely chosen the conditions
and processes that are their conditions. The notion that means are
menial, instrumentalities servile, is more than a degradation of
means to the rank of coercive and external necessities. It renders
all things upon which the name of end is bestowed accompani-
ments of privilege, while the name of utility becomes an apologetic justification for things that are not portions of a good and
reasonable life. Livelihood is at present not so much the consequence of a wage-earner's labor as it is the effect of other causes
forming the economic régime, labor being merely an accidental
appendage of these other causes.

Paints and skill in manipulative arrangement are means of a picture as end, because the picture is *their* assemblage and organization. Tones and susceptibility of the ear when properly interacting
are the means of music, because they constitute, make, are, music.
A disposition of virtue is a means to a certain quality of happiness
because it is a constituent of that good, while such happiness is

means in turn to virtue, as the sustaining of good in being. Flour, water, yeast are means of bread because they are ingredients of bread; while bread is a factor *in* life, not just *to* it. A good political constitution, honest police-system, and competent judiciary, are means of the prosperous life of the community because they are integrated portions of that life. Science is an instrumentality of and for art because it is the intelligent factor *in* art. The trite saying that a hand is not a hand except as an organ of the living body—except as a working coordinated part of a balanced system of activities—applies untritely to all things that are means. The connection of means-consequences is never one of bare succession in time, such that the element that is means is past and gone when the end is instituted. An active process is strung out temporally, but there is a deposit at each stage and point entering cumulatively and constitutively into the outcome. A genuine instrumentality *for* is always an organ *of* an end. It confers continued efficacy upon the object in which it is embodied.

The traditional separation between some things as mere means and others as mere ends is a reflection of the insulated existence of working and leisure classes, of production that is not also consummatory, and consummation that is not productive. This division is not a *merely* social phenomenon. It embodies a perpetuation upon the human plane of a division between need and satisfaction belonging to brute life. And this separation expresses in turn the mechanically external relationship that exists in nature between situations of disturbed equilibrium, of stress, and strain, and achieved equilibrium. For in nature, outside of man, except when events eventuate in "development" or "evolution" (in which a cumulative carrying forward of consequences of past histories in new efficiencies occurs) antecedent events are external transitive conditions of the occurrence of an event having immediate and static qualities. To animals to whom acts have no meaning, the change in the environment required to satisfy needs has no significance on its own account; such change is a mere incident of ego-centric satisfactions. This physically external relationship of antecedents and consequents is perpetuated; it continues to hold true of human industry wherever labor and its materials and products are externally enforced necessities for securing a living. Because Greek industry was so largely upon this plane of servile labor, all industrial activity was regarded by Greek thought as a *mere* means, an extraneous necessity. Hence satisfactions due to it were conceived to be the ends or goods of purely animal nature in isolation. With respect to a truly human and rational life, they were not ends or goods at all, but merely "means," that is to say, external conditions that were antecedently enforced requisites of the life conducted and enjoyed by free men, especially by those devoted to the acme of freedom, pure thinking. As Aristotle asserted, drawing a just conclusion from the assumed premises, there are classes of men who are necessary materials of society but who are not integral parts of it. And he summed up the whole theory of the external and coerced relationship of means and ends when he said in this very connection that: "When there is one thing that is means and another thing that is end, there is *nothing common* between them, except in so far as the one, the means, produces, and the other, the end, receives the product."[1]

It would thus seem almost self-evident that the distinction between the instrumental and the final adopted in philosophic tradition as a solving word presents in truth a problem, a problem so deep-seated and far-reaching that it may be said to be *the* problem of experience. For all the intelligent activities of men, no matter whether expressed in science, fine arts, or social relationships, have for their task the conversion of causal bonds, relations of succession, into a connection of means–consequence, into meanings. When the task is achieved the result is art: and in art everything is common between means and ends. Whenever so-called means remain external and servile, and so-called ends are enjoyed objects whose further causative status is unperceived, ignored, or denied, the situation is proof positive of limitations of art. Such a situation consists of affairs in which the problem has *not* been solved; namely that of converting physical and brute relationships into connections of meanings characteristic of the possibilities of nature.

It goes without saying that man begins as a part of physical and animal nature. In as far as he reacts to physical things on a strictly physical level, he is pulled and pushed about, overwhelmed, broken to pieces, lifted on the crest of the wave of things, like anything else. His contacts, his sufferings and doings, are matters of direct interaction only. He is in a "state of nature." As an animal, even upon the brute level, he manages to subordinate some physical things to his needs, converting them into materials sustaining life and growth. But in so far things that serve as material of satisfaction and the acts that procure and utilize them are not objects, or things-with-meanings. That appetite as such is blind, is notorious; it may push us into a comfortable result instead of into disaster; but we are pushed just the same. When appetite is perceived in its meanings, in the consequences it induces, and these consequences are experimented with in reflective imagination, some being seen to be consistent with one another, and hence capable of coexistence and of serially ordered achievement, others being incompatible, forbidding conjunction at one time, and getting in one another's way serially—when this estate is attained, we live on the human plane, responding to things in their meanings. A relationship of cause-effect has been transformed into one of means-consequence. Then consequences belong *integrally* to the conditions which may produce them, and the latter possess character and distinction. The meaning of causal conditions is carried over also into the consequence, so that the latter is no longer a mere end, a last and closing term of arrest. It is marked out in perception, distinguished by the efficacy of the conditions which have entered into it. Its value as fulfilling and consummatory is measurable by subsequent fulfillments and frustrations to which it is contributory in virtue of the causal means which compose it.

Thus to be conscious of meanings or to have an idea, marks a fruition, an enjoyed or suffered arrest of the flux of events. But there are all kinds of ways of perceiving meanings, all kinds of ideas. Meaning may be determined in terms of consequences hastily snatched at and torn loose from their connections; then is prevented the formation of wider and more enduring ideas. Or, we may be aware of meanings, may achieve ideas, that unite wide and enduring scope with richness of distinctions. The latter sort of consciousness is more than a passing and superficial consummation or end: it takes up into itself meanings covering stretches of existence wrought into consistency. It marks the conclusion of long continued endeavor; of patient and indefatigable search and test. The idea is, in short, art and a work of art. As a work of art, it directly liberates subsequent action and makes it more fruitful in a creation of more meanings and more perceptions.

It is the part of wisdom to recognize how sparse and insecure are such accomplishments in comparison with experience in which physical and animal nature largely have their way. Our liberal and rich ideas, our adequate appreciations, due to productive art are hemmed in by an unconquered domain in which we are everywhere exposed to the incidence of unknown forces and hurried fatally to unforeseen consequences. Here indeed we live servilely, menially, mechanically; and we so live as much when forces blindly lead us to ends that are liked as when we are caught in conditions and ends against which we blindly rebel. To call satisfactions which happen in this blind way "ends" in a eulogistic sense, as did classic thought, is to proclaim in effect our servile submission to accident. We may indeed enjoy the goods the gods of fortune send us, but we should recognize them for what they are, not asserting them to be good and righteous *altogether*. For, since they have not been achieved by any art involving deliberate selection and arrangement of forces, we do not know with what they are charged. It is an old true tale that the god of fortune is capricious, and delights to destroy his darlings after having made them drunk with prosperity. The goods of art are not the less good in their goodness than the gifts of nature; while in addition they are such as to bring with themselves open-eyed confidence. They are fruits of means consciously employed; fulfillments whose further consequences are secured by conscious control of the causal conditions which enter into them. Art is the sole alternative to luck; and divorce from each other of the meaning and value of instrumentalities and ends is the essence of luck. The esoteric character of culture and the supernatural quality of religion are both expressions of the divorce.

The modern mind has formally abjured belief in natural teleology because it found Greek and medieval teleology juvenile and superstitious. Yet facts have a way of compelling recognition of themselves. There is little scientific writing which does not introduce at some point or other the idea of tendency. The idea of tendency unites in itself exclusion of prior design and inclusion of movement in a particular direction, a direction that may be either furthered or counteracted and frustrated, but which is intrinsic. Direction involves a limiting position, a point or goal of culminating stoppage, as well as an initial starting point. To assert a tendency and to be fore-conscious of a possible terminus of movement are two names of the same fact. Such a consciousness may be fatalistic; a sense of inevitable march toward impending doom. But it may also contain a perception of meanings such as flexibly directs a forward movement. The end is then an end-in-view and is in constant and cumulative reenactment at each stage of forward movement. It is no longer a terminal point, external to the conditions that have led up to it; it is the continually developing meaning of present tendencies—the very things which as directed we call "means." The process is art and its product, no matter at what stage it be taken, is a work of art.

To a person building a house, the end-in-view is not just a remote and final goal to be hit upon after a sufficiently great number of coerced motions have been duly performed. The end-in-view is a plan which is *contemporaneously* operative in selecting and arranging materials. The latter, brick, stone, wood and mortar, are means only as the end-in-view is actually incarnate in them, in forming them. Literally, they *are* the end in its present stage of realization.

The end-in-view is present at each stage of the process; it is present as the *meaning* of the materials used and acts done; without its informing presence, the latter are in no sense "means"; they are merely extrinsic causal conditions. The statement is generic; it applies equally at every stage. The house itself, when building is complete, is "end" in no exclusive sense. It marks the conclusion of the organization of certain materials and events into effective means; but these materials and events still exist in causal interaction with other things. New consequences are foreseen; new purposes, ends-in-view, are entertained; they are embodied in the coordination of the thing built, now reduced to material, although significant material, along with other materials, and thus transmuted into means. The case is still clearer, when instead of considering a process subject to as many rigid external conditions as is the building of a house, we take for illustration a flexibly and freely moving process, such as painting a picture or thinking out a scientific process, when these operations are carried on artistically. Every process of free art proves that the difference between means and end is analytic, formal, not material and chronologic.

What has been said enables us to re-define the distinction drawn between the artistic, as objectively productive, and the esthetic. Both involve a perception of meanings in which the instrumental and the consummatory peculiarly intersect. In esthetic perceptions an object interpenetrated with meanings is given; it may be taken for granted; it invites and awaits the act of appropriative enjoyment. In the esthetic object tendencies are sensed as brought to fruition; in it is embodied a means-consequence relationship, as the past work of his hands was surveyed by the Lord and pronounced good. This good differs from those gratifications to which the name sensual rather than sensuous is given, since the former are pleasing endings that occur in ways not informed with the meaning of materials and acts integrated into them. In appreciative possession, perception goes out to tendencies which *have* been brought to happy fruition in such a way as to release and arouse.

Artistic sense on the other hand grasps tendencies as possibilities; the invitation of these possibilities to perception is more urgent and compelling than that of the given already achieved. While the means-consequence relationship is directly sensed, felt, in both appreciation and artistic production, in the former the scale descends upon the side of the attained; in the latter there predominates the invitation of an existent consummation to bring into existence further perceptions. Art in being, the active productive process, may thus be defined as an esthetic perception together with an *operative* perception of the efficiencies of the esthetic object. In many persons with respect to most kinds of enjoyed perceptions, the sense of possibilities, the arousal or excitation attendant upon appreciation of poetry, music, painting, architecture or landscape remains diffuse and inchoate; it takes effect only in direct and undefined channels. The enjoyed perception of a visual scene is in any case a function of that scene in its total connections, but it does not link up adequately. In some happily constituted persons, this effect is adequately coordinated with other endowments and habits; it becomes an integral part of craft, taking effect in the creation of a new object of appreciation. The integration is, however, progressive and experimental, not momentarily accomplished. Thus every creative effort is temporal, subject to risk and deflection. In that sense the difference between the diffuse and postponed change of action due in an ordinary person to release of energies by an esthetic object, and the special and axial direction of subsequent action in a gifted person is, after all, a matter of degree.

Without a sense of moving tendencies which are operative in conjunction with a state of fruition, there is appetitive gratification, but nothing that may be termed appreciation. Sense of moving tendencies supplies thrill, stimulation, excitation; sense of completion, consummation, affords composure, form, measure, composition. Emphasize the latter, and appreciation is of the classic type. This type fits conditions where production is professionalized among technical craftsmen, as among the Greeks; it is adapted to a contemplative enjoyment of the achievements of past ages or remote places, where conditions forbid urge to emulation or productive activity of a similar kind. Any work of art that persistently retains its power to generate enjoyed perception or appreciation becomes in time classic.

In so-called romantic art, the sense of tendencies operative beyond the limits of consummation is in excess; a lively sense of unrealized potentialities attaches to the object; but it is employed to enhance immediate appreciation, not to promote further productive achievement. Whatever is peculiarly romantic excites a feeling that the possibilities suggested go beyond not merely actual present realization, but are beyond effective attainment in any experience. In so far intentionally romantic art is wilful, and in so far not art. Excited and uneasy perceptual enjoyment is made ultimate, and the work of art is accommodated to production of these feelings. The sense of unachieved possibilities is employed as a compensatory equivalent for endeavor in achievement. Thus when the romantic spirit invades philosophy the possibilities present in imaginative sentiment are declared to be the real, although "transcendental," substance of Being itself. In complete art, appreciation follows the object and moves with it to its completion; romanticism reverses the process and degrades the object to an occasion for arousing a predetermined type of appreciation. In classicism, objective achievement is primary, and appreciation not only conforms to the object, but the object is employed to compose sentiment and give it distinction. Its vice, as an "ism," is that it turns the mind to what is given; the given is taken as if it were eternal and wholly separate from generation and movement. Art free from subjection to any "ism" has movement, creation, as well as order, finality.

To institute a difference of *kind* between useful and fine arts is, therefore, absurd, since art involves a peculiar interpenetration of means and ends. Many things are termed useful for reasons of social status, implying deprecation and contempt. Things are sometimes said to belong to the menial arts merely because they are cheap and used familiarly by common people. These things of daily use for ordinary ends may survive in later periods, or be transported to another culture, as from Japan and China to America, and being rare and sought by connoisseurs, rank forthwith as works of fine art. Other things may be called fine because their manner of use is decorative or socially ostentatious. It is tempting to make a distinction of degree and say that a thing belongs to the sphere of use when perception of its meaning is incidental to something else; and that a thing belongs to fine art when its other uses are subordinate to its use in perception. The distinction has a rough practical value, but cannot be pressed too far. For in production of a painting or a poem, as well as in making a vase or a temple, a perception is also employed as means for something beyond itself. Moreover, the perception of urns, pots and pans as commodities may be intrinsically enjoyable, although these things are primarily perceived with reference to some use to which they are put. The only *basic* distinction is that between bad art and good art, and this distinction, between things that meet the requirements of art and those that do not, applies equally to things of use and of beauty. Capacity to offer to perception meaning in which fruition and efficacy interpenetrate is met by different products in various degrees of fullness; it may be missed altogether by pans and poems alike. The difference between the ugliness of a mechanically conceived and executed utensil and of a meretricious and pretentious painting is one only of content or material; in form, both are articles, and bad articles.

Thinking is preeminently an art; knowledge and propositions which are the products of thinking, are works of art, as much so as statuary and symphonies. Every successive stage of thinking is a conclusion in which the meaning of what has produced it is condensed; and it is no sooner stated than it is a light radiating to other things—unless it be a fog which obscures them. The antecedents of a conclusion are as causal and existential as those of a building. They are not logical or dialectical, or an affair of ideas. While a conclusion follows from antecedents, it does not follow from "premises," in the strict, formal sense. Premises are the analysis of a conclusion into its logically justifying grounds; there are no premises till there is a conclusion. Conclusion and premise are reached by a procedure comparable to the use of boards and nails in making a box; or of paint and canvas in making a picture. If defective materials are employed or if they are put together carelessly and awkwardly, the result is defective. In some cases the result is called unworthy, in others, ugly; in others, inept; in others, wasteful, inefficient, and in still others untrue, false. But in each case, the condemnatory adjective refers to the resulting work judged in the light of its method of production. Scientific method or the art of constructing true perceptions is ascertained in the course of experience to occupy a privileged position in undertaking other arts. But this unique position only places it the more securely as an art; it does not set its product, knowledge, apart from other works of art.

The existential origin of valid cognitive perceptions is sometimes recognized in form and denied in substance; the name "psychological" is given to the events which generate valid beliefs. Then a sharp distinction is made between genesis as psychological and validity as logical. Of course lexicographic names are of no special moment; if any one wishes to call the efficient causes of knowledge and truth psychological, he is entitled to do so—provided the actual traits of these causative events are recognized. Such a recognition will note however that psychological does not mean psychic, or refer to events going on exclusively within the head or "subcutaneously." To become aware of an object cognitively as distinct from esthetically, involves external physical movements and external physical appliances physically manipulated. Some of these active changes result in unsound and defective perceptions; some have been ascertained to result usually in valid perceptions. The difference is precisely that which takes place when the art of architecture or sculpture is skilfully conducted or is carried on carelessly, and without adequate appliances. Sometimes the operations productive of tested beliefs are called "inductive"; with an implication in the naming, of discrediting them, as compared with deductive functions, which are assigned a superior exclusive status. Of deduction, when thus defined, the following assertions may be made. First, it has nothing to do with truth about any matter of existence. Secondly, it is not even concerned with consistency or correctness, save in a formal sense whose opposite (as has been previously pointed out) is not inconsistency but nonsense. Thirdly, the meanings which figure in it are the conclusions of prior inquiries which are "inductive," that is, are products of an experimental art of changing external things by appropriate external movements and appliances.

Deduction as it actually occurs in science is *not* deduction as deduction should be according to a common definition. Deduction deals directly with meanings in their relations to one another, rather than with meanings directly referred to existence. But these meanings are what they are in themselves and are related to one another by means of acts of taking and manipulating—an art of discourse. They possess intellectual import and enter fruitfully into scientific method only because they are selected, employed, separated and combined by acts extraneous to them, acts which are as existential and causative as those concerned in the experimental use of apparatus and other physical things. The *act* of knowing, whether solicitous about inference or about demonstration, is always inductive. There is only one mode of thinking, the inductive, when thinking denotes anything that actually happens. The notion that there is another kind called deduction is another evidence of the prevalent tendency in philosophy to treat functions as antecedent operations, and to take essential meanings *of* existence as if they were a kind of Being. As a concrete operation, deduction is generative, not sterile; but as a concrete operation, it contains an extraneous act of taking and using which is selective, experimental, and checked constantly by consequences.

Knowledge or science, as a work of art, like any other work of art, confers upon things traits and potentialities which did not *previously* belong to them. Objection from the side of alleged realism to this statement springs from a confusion of tenses. Knowledge is not a distortion or perversion which confers upon *its* subject-matter traits which *do* not belong to it, but is an act which confers upon non-cognitive material traits which *did* not belong to it. It marks a change by which physical events exhibiting properties of mechanical energy, connected by relations of push and pull, hitting, rebounding, splitting, and consolidating, realize characters, meanings, and relations of meanings *hitherto* not possessed by them. Architecture does not add to stone and wood something which does not belong to them, but it does add to them properties and efficacies which they did not possess in their earlier state. It adds them by means of engaging them in new modes of interaction, having a new order of consequences. Neither engineering nor fine art limits itself to imitative reproduction or copying of antecedent conditions. Their products may nevertheless be more effectively natural, more "life like" than were antecedent states of natural existence. So it is with the art of knowing and its works.

The failure to recognize that knowledge is a product of art accounts for an otherwise inexplicable fact: that science lies today like an incubus upon such a wide area of beliefs and aspirations. To remove the deadweight, however, recognition that it is an art will have to be more than a theoretical avowal that science is made by man for man, although such recognition is probably an initial preliminary step. But the real source of the difficulty is that the art of knowing is limited to such a narrow area. Like everything precious and scarce, it has been artificially protected; and through this very protection it has been dehumanized and appropriated by a class. As costly jewels of jade and pearl belong only to a few, so with the jewels of science. The philosophic theories which have set science on an altar in a temple remote from the arts of life, to be approached only with peculiar rites, are a part of the technique of retaining a secluded monopoly of belief and intellectual authority. Till the art of achieving adequate and liberal perceptions of the meanings of events is incarnate in education, morals and industry, science will remain a special luxury for a few; for the mass, it will consist of a remote and abstruse body of curious propositions having little to do with life, except where it lays the heavy hand of law upon spontaneity, and invokes necessity and mechanism to witness against generous and free aspiration.

Every error is attended with a contrary and compensatory error, for otherwise it would soon be self-revealing. The conception that causes are metaphysically superior to effects is compensated for by the conception that ends are superior esthetically and morally to means. The two beliefs can be maintained together only by removing "ends" out of the region of the causal and efficacious. This is accomplished nowadays by first calling ends intrinsic values, and then by making a gulf between value and existence. The consequence is that science, dealing as it must, with existence, becomes brutal and mechanical, while criticism of values, whether moral or esthetic, becomes pedantic or effeminate, expressing either personal likes and dislikes, or building up a cumbrous array of rules and authorities. The thing that is needful, discriminating judgment by methods whose consequences improve the art, easily slips through such coarse meshes, and by far the greater part of life goes on in a darkness unillumined by thoughtful inquiry. As long as such a state of things persists, the argument of this chapter that science is art—like many other propositions of this book—is largely prophetic, or more or less dialectical. When an art of thinking as appropriate to human and social affairs has grown up as that used in dealing with distant stars, it will not be necessary to argue that science is one among the arts and among the works of art. It will be enough to point to observable situations. The separation of science from art, and the division of arts into those concerned with mere means and those concerned with ends in themselves, is a mask for lack of conjunction between power and the goods of life. It will lose plausibility in the degree in which foresight of good informs the display of power.

Evidence of the interpenetration of the efficacious with the final in art is found in the slow emancipation of art from magical rite and cult, and the emergence of science from superstition. For

magic and superstition could never have dominated human culture, nor poetry have been treated as insight into natural causes, if
means and ends were empirically marked off from each other. The
intimacy of their union in one and the same object is that which
makes it easy to impute to whatever is consummatory a kind of efficacy which it does not possess. Whatever is final is important; to
say this is to enunciate a truism. Lack of instrumentalities and of
skill by which to analyze and follow the particular efficacies of the
immediately enjoyed object lead to imputation to it of wholesale
efficacy in the degree of its importance. To the short-cut pragmatism congenial to natural man, importance measures "reality" and
reality in turn defines efficacious power. Loyalties evoked in the
passionate citizen by sight of the flag or in the devout Christian by
the cross are attributed directly to the intrinsic nature of these objects. Their share in a consummatory experience is translated into
a mysterious inner sacred power, an indwelling efficacy. Thus a
souvenir of the beloved one, arousing in the lover enjoyment similar to that awakened by the precious one to whom it belonged,
possesses delightful, exciting, and consoling efficacies. No matter
what things are directly implicated in a consummatory situation,
they gain potencies for weal or woe similar to the good or evil
which directly marks the situation. Obviously error here resides in
the gross and undiscriminating way in which power is attributed;
inquiry to reveal the specified elements which form the sequential
order is lacking.

It is a commonplace of anthropologists that for the most part
clothing originated in situations of unusual awe or prestigious display, rather than as a utility or protection. It was part of a consummatory object, rather than a means to specified consequences.
Like the robes of priests, clothes were vestments, and investiture
was believed to convey directly to the one ceremonially garbed
dread potency or fascinating charm. Clothes were worn to confer
authority; a man did not lend his significance to them. Similarly, a
victorious hunter and warrior celebrated a triumphant return to
camp by affixing to his person in conspicuous fashion claws and

teeth of the wild beast or enemy that his prowess had subjugated. These signal proofs of power were integral portions of the object of admiration, loyalty and reverence. Thus the trophy became an emblem, and the emblem was endowed with mystic force. From a sign of glory it became a cause of glorification, and even when worn by another aroused the acclaim due to a hero. In time such trophies became the documented seal of prestigious authority. They had an intrinsic causal potency of their own. Legal history is full of like instances. Acts originally performed in connection with, say, the exchange of property, performed as part of the dramatic ceremony of taking possession of land, were not treated as mere evidences of title, but as having a mystic power to confer title.

Later, when such things lose their original power and become "mere matters of form," they may still be essential to the legal force of a transaction, as seals have had to be affixed to a contract to give it force, even though there was no longer sense or reason in their use. Things which have an efficacy imputed to them simply because they have shared in some eminent consummatory experience are symbols. They are called symbols, however, only afterwards and from without. To the devout in politics and religion they are other than symbols; they are articles possessed of occult potency. To one man, two crossed lines are an indication of an arithmetical operation to be performed; to another, they are evidence of the existence of Christianity as a historic fact, as a crescent is a reminder of the existence of Islam. But to another, a cross is more than a poignant reminder of a tragically significant death; it has intrinsic sacred power to protect and to bless. Since a flag stirs passionate loyalty to sudden and pervasive ebullition, the flag must have properties and potencies not possessed by other and differently configured pieces of cloth; it must be handled with reverence; it is the natural object of ceremonial adoration.

Phenomena like these when manifested in primitive culture are often interpreted as if they were attempts at a causal explanation of natural occurrences; magic is said to be science gone wrong. In employed; or else, if by emotion is meant the same sort of thing that is called emotion in daily life, the statement is demonstrably false. For emotion in its ordinary sense is something called out *by* objects, physical and personal; it is response *to* an objective situation. It is not something existing somewhere by itself which then employs material through which to express itself. Emotion is an indication of intimate participation, in a more or less excited way in some scene of nature or life; it is, so to speak, an attitude or disposition which is a function of objective things. It is intelligible that art should select and assemble objective things in such ways as to evoke emotional response of a refined, sensitive and enduring kind; it is intelligible that the artist himself is one capable of sustaining these emotions, under whose temper and spirit he performs his compositions of objective materials. This procedure may indeed be carried to a point such that the use of objective materials is economized to the minimum, and the evocation of the emotional response carried to its relative maximum. But it still remains true that the origin of the art-process lay in emotional responses spontaneously called out by a situation occurring without any reference to art, and without "esthetic" quality save in the sense in which all immediate enjoyment and suffering is esthetic. Economy in use of objective subject-matter may with experienced and trained minds go so far that what is ordinarily called "representation" is much reduced. But what happens is a highly funded and generalized representation of the formal sources of ordinary emotional experience.

The same sort of remark is to be made concerning "significant form"[3] as a definition of an esthetic object. Unless the meaning of the term is so isolated as to be wholly occult, it denotes a selection, for sake of emphasis, purity, subtlety, of those forms which give consummatory significance to every-day subject-matters of experience. "Forms" are not the peculiar property or creation of the esthetic and artistic; they are characters in virtue of which anything meets the requirements of an enjoyable perception. "Art" does not create the forms; it is their selection and organization in

reality, they are facts of direct emotional and practical response; beliefs, ideas, interpretations, only come later when responses not being direct and inevitably appropriate seem to demand explanation. As immediate responses they exemplify the fact that anything involved, no matter how incidentally, in a consummatory situation has the power of arousing the awe, excitement, relief, admiration belonging to the situation as a whole. Industry displaces magic, and science reduces myth, when the elements that enter into the constitution of the consummatory whole are discriminated, and each one has its own particular place in sequential order assigned it. Thus materials and efficacies characteristic of different kinds of arts are distinguished. But because the ceremonial, literary and poetic arts have quite other ways of working and other consequences than industrial and scientific arts, it is far from following, as current theories assume, that they have no instrumental power at all, or that a sense of their instrumental agency is not involved in their appreciative perception. The pervasive operation of symbolism in human culture is all the proof that is needed to show that an intimate and direct sense of place and connection in a prolonged history enters into the enjoyed and suffered constituents of the history, and especially into the final or terminal members.

Further confirmation of this proposition is found in classic philosophy itself, in its theory that essential forms "make" things *what* they are, even though not causing them to occur. "Essence," as it figures in Greek theory, represents the mysterious potency of earlier "symbols" emancipated from their superstitious context and envisaged in a dialectic and reflective context. The essences of Greek-medieval science were in short poetic objects, treated as objects of demonstrative science, used to explain and understand the inner and ultimate constitution of things. While Greek thought was sufficiently emancipated from magic to deny "efficient" causality to formal and final essences, yet the latter were conceived of as making particular things to be *what* they are, members of natural kinds.[2] Moreover, by a reversal of causal residence, intrinsic seeking for such forms was imputed to changing events. Thus the ground was prepared for the later frank return of patristic and scholastic thought to a frank animistic supernaturalism. The philosophic theory erred, as did magic and myth, regarding the nature of the efficacy involved in ends; and the error was due to the same causes, namely, failure of analysis into elements. It could not have occurred, were there that sharp division between means and ends, fruitions and instrumentalities, assumed by current thought.

In short, the history of human experience is a history of the development of arts. The history of science in its distinct emergence from religious, ceremonial and poetic arts is the record of a differentiation of arts, not a record of separation from art. The chief significance of the account just given, lies, for our present purpose, in its bearing upon the theory of experience and nature. It is not, however, without import for a theory of criticism. The present confusion, deemed chaos by some, in the fine arts and esthetic criticism seems to be an inevitable consequence of the underlying, even if unavowed, separation of the instrumental and the consummatory. The further men go in the concrete the more they are forced to recognize the logical consequence of their controlling assumptions. We owe it to theories of art prevalent to-day in one school of critics that certain implications, long obscured, of the traditional theory of art and nature have been brought to light. Gratitude for this debt should not be stinted because the adherents of the traditional theory regard the newer views as capricious heresies, wild aberrations. For these critics, in proclaiming that esthetic qualities in works of fine art are unique, in asserting their separation from not only every thing that is existential in nature but also from all other forms of good, in proclaiming that such arts as music, poetry, painting have characters unshared with any natural things whatsoever:—in asserting such things the critics carry to its conclusion the isolation of fine art from the useful, of the final from efficacious. They thus prove that the separation of the consummatory from the instrumental makes art wholly esoteric.

There are substantially but two alternatives. Either art is a con-

tinuation, by means of intelligent selection and arrangement, of natural tendencies of natural events; or art is a peculiar addition to nature springing from something dwelling exclusively within the breast of man, whatever name be given the latter. In the former case, delightfully enhanced perception or esthetic appreciation is of the same nature as enjoyment of any object that is consummatory. It is the outcome of a skilled and intelligent art of dealing with natural things for the sake of intensifying, purifying, prolonging and deepening the satisfactions which they spontaneously afford. That, in this process, new meanings develop, and that these afford uniquely new traits and modes of enjoyment is but what happens everywhere in emergent growths.

But if fine art has nothing to do with other activities and products, then of course it has nothing inherently to do with the objects, physical and social, experienced in other situations. It has an occult source and an esoteric character. It makes little difference what the source and the character be called. By strict logic it makes literally no difference. For if the quality of the esthetic experience is by conception unique, then the words employed to describe it have no significance derived from or comparable to the qualities of other experiences; their signification is hidden and specialized to a degree. Consider some of the terms which are in more or less current use among the critics who carry the isolation of art and the esthetic to its limit. It is sometimes said that art is the expression of the emotions; with the implication that, because of this fact, subject-matter is of no significance except as material through which emotion is expressed. Hence art becomes unique. For in works of science, utility and morals the character of the objects forming this subject-matter is all-important. But by this definition, subject-matter is stripped of all its own inherent characters in art in the degree in which it is genuine art; since a truly artistic work is manifest in the reduction of subject-matter to a mere medium of expression of emotion.

In such a statement emotion either has no significance at all, and it is mere accident that this particular combination of letters is

such ways as to enhance, prolong and purify the perceptual experience. It is not by accident that some objects and situations afford marked perceptual satisfactions; they do so because of their structural properties and relations. An artist may work with a minimum of analytic recognition of these structures or "forms"; he may select them chiefly by a kind of sympathetic vibration. But they may also be discriminatively ascertained; and an artist may utilize his deliberate awareness of them to create works of art that are more formal and abstract than those to which the public is accustomed. Tendency to composition in terms of the formal characters marks much contemporary art, in poetry, painting, music, even sculpture and architecture. At their worst, these products are "scientific" rather than artistic; technical exercises, sterile and of a new kind of pedantry. At their best, they assist in ushering in new modes of art and by education of the organs of perception in new modes of consummatory objects; they enlarge and enrich the world of human vision.

Thus, by only a slight forcing of the argument, we reach a conclusion regarding the relations of instrumental and fine art which is precisely the opposite of that intended by seclusive estheticians; namely, that fine art *consciously* undertaken as such is peculiarly instrumental in quality. It is a device in experimentation carried on for the sake of education. It exists for the sake of a specialized use, use being a new training of modes of perception. The creators of such works of art are entitled, when successful, to the gratitude that we give to inventors of microscopes and microphones; in the end, they open new objects to be observed and enjoyed. This is a genuine service; but only an age of combined confusion and conceit will arrogate to works that perform this special utility the exclusive name of fine art.

Experience in the form of art, when reflected upon, we conclude by saying, solves more problems which have troubled philosophers and resolves more hard and fast dualisms than any other theme of thought. As the previous discussion has indicated, it demonstrates the intersection in nature of individual and generic;

of chance and law, transforming one into opportunity and the other into liberation; of instrumental and final. More evidently still, it demonstrates the gratuitous falsity of notions that divide overt and executive activity from thought and feeling and thus separate mind and matter. In creative production, the external and physical world is more than a mere means or external condition of perceptions, ideas and emotions; it is subject-matter and sustainer of conscious activity; and thereby exhibits, so that he who runs may read, the fact that consciousness is not a separate realm of being, but is the manifest quality of existence when nature is most free and most active.

I Believe

(1939)

MY CONTRIBUTION to the first series of essays in *Living Philosophies* put forward the idea of faith in the possibilities of experience as the heart of my own philosophy. In the course of that contribution I said, "Individuals will always be the centre and the consummation of experience, but what the individual actually *is* in his life-experience depends upon the nature and movement of associated life."[1] I have not changed my faith in experience nor my belief that individuality is its centre and consummation. But there has been a change in emphasis. I should now wish to emphasize more than I formerly did that individuals are the finally decisive factors of the nature and movement of associated life.

The cause of this shift of emphasis is the events of the intervening years. The rise of dictatorships and totalitarian states and the decline of democracy have been accompanied with loud proclamation of the idea that only the state, the political organization of society, can give security to individuals. In return for the security thus obtained, it is asserted even more loudly (and with much greater practical effect) that individuals owe everything to the state.

This fundamental challenge compels all who believe in liberty and democracy to rethink the whole question of the relation of individual choice, belief, and action to institutions, to reflect on the kind of social changes that will make individuals in actuality the centres and the possessors of worth-while experience. In rethinking this issue in the light of the rise of totalitarian states, I am led to emphasize the idea that only the voluntary initiative and voluntary cooperation of individuals can produce social institutions that will protect the liberties necessary for achieving development of genuine individuality.

This change of emphasis does not in any way minimize the belief that the ability of individuals to develop genuine individuality is intimately connected with the social conditions under which they associate with one another. But it attaches fundamental importance to the activities of individuals in determining the social conditions under which they live. It has been shown in the last few years that democratic *institutions* are no guarantee for the existence of democratic individuals. The alternative is that individuals who prize their own liberties and who prize the liberties of other individuals, individuals who are democratic in thought and action, are the sole final warrant for the existence and endurance of democratic institutions.

The belief that the voluntary activities of individuals in voluntary association with one another is the only basis of democratic institutions does not mean a return to the older philosophy of individualism. That philosophy thought of the individual after the analogy of older physical science. He was taken to be a centre without a field. His relations to other individuals were as mechanical and external as those of Newtonian atoms to one another. Liberty was supposed to be automatically acquired by abolition of restraints and constraints; all the individual needed was to be let alone.

The negative and empty character of this individualism had consequences which produced a reaction toward an equally arbitrary and one-sided collectivism. This reaction is identical with the rise of the new form of political despotism. The decline of democracy and the rise of authoritarian states which claim they can do for individuals what the latter cannot by any possibility do for themselves are the two sides of one and the same indivisible picture.

Political collectivism is now marked in all highly industrialized countries, even when it does not reach the extreme of the totalitarian state. It is the social consequence of the development of private capitalistic collectivism in industry and finance. For this reason those who look backward to restoration of the latter system are doomed to fight a losing battle. For the tendency toward state socialism and state capitalism is the product of the economic collectivism of concentrated capital and labor that was produced by mass production and mass distribution. The inherent identity of the two forms of collectivism is disguised by the present angry and clamorous controversy waged between representatives of private and public collectivism, both claiming to speak, moreover, in the interest of the individual, one for his initiative, the other for his security.

The strict reciprocity that exists between the two collectivisms is also covered from view because they are promoted in the respective interests of different social groups. Roughly speaking, the "haves" stand for private collectivism and the "have nots" for state collectivism. The bitter struggle waged between them in the political arena conceals from recognition the fact that both favor some sort of collectivism and represent complementary aspects of the same total picture.

Between the struggles of the two parties, both purporting to serve the cause of ultimate individual freedom, the individual has in fact little show and little opportunity. Bewildered and temporarily lost anyway, the din of the contending parties increases his bewilderment. Everything is so big that he wants to ally himself with bigness, and he is told that he must make his choice between big industry and finance and the big national political state. For a long time, what political agencies did and did not do in legislation and in the courts favored the growth of private capitalistic collectivism. By way of equalizing conditions, I do not doubt that for some time to come political activity will move in the direction of support of underprivileged groups who have been oppressed and made insecure by the growth of concentrated industry and finance. The imminent danger, as events of recent years demonstrate, is that political activity will attempt to retrieve the balance by moving in the direction of state socialism.

Indeed, many persons will ask how it is possible for political action to restore the balance except by direct control over and even ownership of big industrial and financial enterprises. The answer in general is that political activity can, first and foremost, engage in aggressive maintenance of the civil liberties of free speech, free publication and intercommunication, and free assemblage. In the second place, the government can do much to encourage and promote in a positive way the growth of a great variety of voluntary cooperative undertakings.

This promotion involves abolition or drastic modification of a good many institutions that now have political support, since they stand in the way of effective voluntary association for social ends. There are tariffs and other monopoly-furthering devices that keep back individual initiative and voluntary cooperation. There is our system of land tenure and taxation that puts a premium on the holding of land—including all natural resources—for the sake of private profit in a way that effectively prevents individuals from access to the instruments of individual freedom. There is the political protection given to return on long-term capital investments which are not now accompanied by any productive work, and which are, therefore, a direct tax levied on the productive work of others: an almost incalculable restriction, in its total effect, upon individual freedom. *Abolish inheritance!*

The intrinsic likeness of political and private collectivism is shown in the fact that the government has had recourse to promotion of a regime of scarcity instead of increased productivity. It is evident on its face that enforced restriction of productivity, whether enforced in the name of private profit or of public relief, can have only a disastrous effect, directly and indirectly, upon individual freedom. But given existing conditions, it is the sole alternative to governmental activity that would abolish such limitations upon voluntary action as have been mentioned, a list that would easily be made more specific and more extensive.

Moreover, the principle of confining political action to policies that provide the conditions for promoting the voluntary associa-

tion of free individuals does not limit governmental action to negative measures. There are, for example, such political activities as
are now represented by provision of public highways, public
schools, protection from fire, etc., etc., supported by taxation. This
type of activity can doubtless be extended in a way which will release individual liberties instead of restricting them. The principle
laid down does not deter political activity from engaging in constructive measures. But it does lay down a criterion by which
every political proposal shall be judged: Does it tend definitely in
the direction of increase of voluntary, free choice and activity on
the part of individuals?

The danger at present, as I have already said, is that in order to
get away from the evils of private economic collectivism we shall
plunge into political economic collectivism. The danger is so great
that the course that has been suggested will be regarded as an unrealistic voice crying in the wilderness. It would be unrealistic to
make light of the present drive in the direction of state socialism.
But it is even more unrealistic to overlook the dangers involved in
taking the latter course. For the events of recent years have
demonstrated that state capitalism leads toward the totalitarian
state whether of the Russian or the Fascist variety.

We now have demonstrations of the consequences of two social
movements. Earlier events proved that private economic collectivism produced social anarchy, mitigated by the control exercised
by an oligarchic group. Recent events have shown that state socialism or public collectivism leads to suppression of everything
that individuality stands for. It is not too late for us in this country
to learn the lessons taught by these two great historic movements.
The way is open for a movement which will provide the fullest
opportunity for cooperative voluntary endeavor. In this movement
political activity will have a part, but a subordinate one. It will be
confined to providing the conditions, both negative and positive,
that favor the voluntary activity of individuals.

There is, however, a socialism which is not state socialism. It
may be called functional socialism. Its nature may be illustrated by

the movement for socialization of medicine. I think this socialization is bound to come anyway. But it may come about in two very different ways. It may come into existence as a state measure, under political control; or it may come about as the result of the efforts of the medical profession made aware of its social function and its responsibilities. I cannot develop the significance of the illustration. But as an illustration, its significance applies to all occupational groups; that is, to all groups that are engaged in any form of socially useful, productive, activity.

The technocrats of recent memory had a glimpse of the potentialities inherent in self-directed activities of autonomous groups performing necessary social functions. But they ruined their vision when they fell into the pit dug by Wells and Shaw,[2] that of rule from above by an elite of experts—although according to technocracy, engineers were to be the samurai. The N.I.R.A.[3] had a glimpse of self-governing industrial groups. But, quite apart from its conflict with the existing legal system, the plan loaded the dice in favor of the existing system of control of industry—with a few sops thrown in to "labor." At best it could not have worked out in the direction of freely functioning occupational groups. The Marxists professed the idea, but they held it as an ultimate goal to be realized through seizure of political power by a single class, the proletariat. The withering away of the state which was supposed to take place is not in evidence. On the contrary, seizure of political power as the means to the ultimate end of free individuals organized in functional occupational groups has led to the production of one more autocratic political state.

The dialectic that was supposed to work in solving the contradiction between increase of political power and its abolition is conspicuous by its absence—and inherently so. The Fascists also proclaim the idea of a corporate state. But again there is reliance upon uncontrolled and irresponsible political power. Instead of a corporate society of functional groups there is complete suppression of every formal voluntary association of individuals.

Before concluding that in America adoption of the method of

voluntary effort in voluntary associations of individuals with one another is hopeless, one should observe the course of history. For if history teaches anything it is that judgments regarding the future have been predicated upon the basis of the tendencies that are most conspicuous at the time, while in fact the great social changes which have produced new social institutions have been the cumulative effect of flank movements that were not obvious at the time of their origin.

During the height of expanding competitive industrialism, for example, it was freely predicted that its effect would be a future society of free individuals and of free nations so interdependent that lasting peace would be achieved—*vide* Herbert Spencer.[4] Now that the actual result has been the opposite, it is prophesied on the basis of the tendencies that are now most prominent that increased control of industrial activity by the state will usher in an era of abundance and security. Nevertheless those who can escape the hypnotic influence exercised by the immediate contemporary scene are aware that movements going on in the interstices of the existing order are those which will in fact shape the future. As a friend of mine puts it, the last thing the lord of the feudal castle would have imagined was that the future of society was with the forces that were represented by the humble trader who set up his post under the walls of his castle.

I am not optimistic enough to believe that voluntary associations of individuals, which are even now building up within the cracks of a crumbling social order, will speedily reverse the tendency toward political collectivism. But I am confident that the ultimate way out of the present social dead end lies with the movement these associations are initiating. Individuals who have not lost faith in themselves and in other individuals will increasingly ally themselves with these groups. Sooner or later they will construct the way out of present confusion and conflict. The sooner it is done the shorter will be the time of chaos and catastrophe.

Jane Addams

Addams was born in Cedarville, Illinois, in 1860. She attended the Rockford Seminary and, in 1881–82, the Woman's Medical College in Philadelphia, but had to withdraw because of chronic ill health. In 1889 she opened Hull House, one of the first social settlement houses in the United States, which served as an educational and community service center for immigrant, minority, and poor inhabitants of Chicago. She was closely associated with John Dewey, who taught at the University of Chicago from 1894 until 1904. She was active in the women's suffrage movement and, after the entry of the United States into the First World War, the peace movement. She received the Nobel Peace Prize in 1931, and died in 1935. Among her many writings are *Democracy and Social Ethics* (1902), *Twenty Years at Hull-House* (1910), *Peace and Bread in Time of War* (1922), and *The Second Twenty Years at Hull-House* (1930).

from **A Function of the Social Settlement**

(1899)

THE WORD "SETTLEMENT," which we have borrowed from London, is apt to grate a little upon American ears. It is not, after all, so long ago that Americans who settled were those who had adventured into a new country, where they were pioneers in the midst of difficult surroundings. The word still implies migrating from one condition of life to another totally unlike it, and against this implication the resident of an American settlement takes alarm.

We do not like to acknowledge that Americans are divided into "two nations," as her prime minister once admitted of England.[1] We are not willing, openly and professedly, to assume that American citizens are broken up into classes, even if we make that assumption the preface to a plea that the superior class has duties to the inferior. Our democracy is still our most precious possession, and we do well to resent any inroads upon it, even although they may be made in the name of philanthropy.

And yet because of this very democracy, superior privileges carry with them a certain sense of embarrassment, founded on the suspicion that intellectual and moral superiority too often rest upon economic props which are, after all, matters of accident, and that for an increasing number of young people the only possible way to be comfortable in the possession of those privileges, which result from educational advantages, is in an effort to make common that which was special and aristocratic. Added to this altruistic compunction one may easily discover a selfish suspicion that advantages thus held apart slowly crumble in their napkins, and are not worth having.

The American settlement, perhaps, has represented not so much a sense of duty of the privileged toward the unprivileged, of the "haves" to the "have nots," to borrow Canon Barnett's[2] phrase, as a desire to equalize through social effort those results which superior opportunity may have given the possessor.

The settlement, however, certainly represents more than compunctions. Otherwise it would be but "the monastery of the nineteenth century," as it is indeed sometimes called, substituting the anodyne of work for that of contemplation, but still the old attempt to seek individual escape from the common misery through the solace of healing.

If this were the basis of the settlement, there would no longer be need of it when society had become reconstructed to the point of affording equal opportunity for all, and it would still be at the bottom a philanthropy, although expressed in social and democratic terms. There is, however, a sterner and more enduring aspect of the settlement which this paper would attempt to present.

It is frequently stated that the most pressing problem of modern life is that of a reconstruction and a reorganization of the knowledge which we possess; that we are at last struggling to realize in terms of life all that has been discovered and absorbed, to make it over into healthy and direct expression of free living. Dr. John Dewey, of the University of Chicago, has written: "Knowledge is no longer its own justification, the interest in it has at last transferred itself from accumulation and verification to its application to life." And he adds: "When a theory of knowledge forgets that its value rests in solving the problem out of which it has arisen, that of securing a method of action, knowledge begins to cumber the ground. It is a luxury, and becomes a social nuisance and disturber."[3]

We may quote further from Professor James, of Harvard University, who recently said in an address before the Philosophical Union of the University of California: "Beliefs, in short, are really rules of action, and the whole function of thinking is but one step in the production of habits of action," or "the ultimate test for us of what a truth means is indeed the conduct it dictates or inspires."[4]

Having thus the support of two philosophers, let us assume that the dominating interest in knowledge has become its use, the conditions under which, and ways in which it may be most effectively employed in human conduct; and that at last certain people have consciously formed themselves into groups for the express purpose of effective application. These groups which are called settlements have naturally sought the spots where the dearth of this applied knowledge was most obvious, the depressed quarters of great cities. They gravitate to these spots, not with the object of finding clinical material, not to found "sociological laboratories," not, indeed, with the analytical motive at all, but rather in a reaction from that motive, with a desire to use synthetically and directly whatever knowledge they, as a group, may possess, to test its validity and to discover the conditions under which this knowledge may be employed.

That, just as groups of men, for hundreds of years, have organized themselves into colleges, for the purpose of handing on and disseminating knowledge already accumulated, and as other groups have been organized into seminars and universities, for the purpose of research and the extension of the bounds of knowledge, so at last groups have been consciously formed for the purpose of the application of knowledge to life. This third attempt also would claim for itself the enthusiasm and advantage of collective living. It has become to be a group of people who share their methods, and who mean to make experience continuous beyond the individual. It may be urged that this function of application has always been undertaken by individuals and unconscious groups. This is doubtless true, just as much classic learning has always been disseminated outside the colleges, and just as some of the most notable discoveries of pure science have been made outside of the universities. Still both these institutions do in the main accomplish the bulk of the disseminating, and the discovering; and it is upon the same basis that the third group may establish its value.

The ideal and developed settlement would attempt to test the value of human knowledge by action, and realization, quite as the complete and ideal university would concern itself with the discovery of knowledge in all branches. The settlement stands for application as opposed to research; for emotion as opposed to abstraction, for universal interest as opposed to specialization. This certainly claims too much, absurdly too much, for a settlement, in the light of its achievements, but perhaps not in the light of its possibilities.

This, then, will be my definition of the settlement: that it is an attempt to express the meaning of life in terms of life itself, in forms of activity. There is no doubt that the deed often reveals when the idea does not, just as art makes us understand and feel what might be incomprehensible and inexpressible in the form of an argument. And as the artist tests the success of his art when the recipient feels that he knew the thing before, but had not been able to express it, so the settlement, when it attempts to reveal and apply knowledge, deems its results practicable, when it has made knowledge available which before was abstract, when through use, it has made common that knowledge which was partial before, because it could only be apprehended by the intellect.

The chief characteristic of art lies in freeing the individual from a sense of separation and isolation in his emotional experience, and has usually been accomplished through painting, writing and singing; but this does not make it in the least impossible that it is now being tried, self-consciously and most bunglingly we will all admit, in terms of life itself.

A settlement brings to its aid all possible methods to reveal and make common its conception of life. All those arts and devices which express kindly relation from man to man, from charitable effort to the most specialized social intercourse, are constantly tried. There is the historic statement, the literary presentation, the fellowship which comes when great questions are studied with the hope of modifying actual conditions, the putting forward of the essential that the trivial may appear unimportant, as it is, the attempt to select the more typical and enduring forms of social life, and to eliminate, as far as possible, the irrelevant things which crowd into actual living. There are so-called art exhibits, concerts, dramatic representations, every possible device to make operative on the life around it, the conception of life which the settlement group holds. The demonstration is made not by reason, but by life itself. There must, of course, be a certain talent for conduct and unremitting care lest there grow to be a divergence between theory and living, for however embarrassing this divergence may prove in other situations, in a settlement the artist throws away his tools as soon as this thing happens. He is constantly transmitting by means of his human activity, his notion of life to others. He hopes to produce a sense of infection which may ultimately result in identity of interest. . . .

. . . The phrase "applied knowledge" or science has so long been used in connection with polytechnic schools that it may be well to explain that I am using it in a broader sense. These schools have applied science primarily for professional ends. They are not so commercial, but they may easily become quite as specialized in their departments as the chemical laboratories attached to certain large manufacturing concerns. In the early days of Johns Hopkins University, one of the men in the biological department invented a contrivance which produced a very great improvement in the oyster raft at that time in use in the Chesapeake Bay. For months afterward, in all the commencement orations and other occasions when "prominent citizens" were invited to speak, this oyster raft was held up as the great contribution of the University to the commercial interest of the city, and as a justification of the University's existence, much to the mortification of the poor inventor. This . . . is an excellent example of what I do not mean.

The application which I have in mind is one which cannot be measured by its money-making value. I have in mind an applica-

Touchy-feely

tion to a given neighborhood of the solace of literature, of the up-
lift of the imagination, and of the historic consciousness which
gives its possessor a sense of connection with the men of the past
who have thought and acted, an application of the stern mandates
of science, not only to the conditions of sewers and the care of al-
leys, but to the methods of life and thought; the application of the
metaphysic not only to the speculations of the philosopher, but to
the events of the passing moment; the application of the moral
code to the material life, the transforming of the economic relation into an ethical relation until the sense that religion itself embraces all relations, including the ungodly industrial relation, has
become common property.

An ideal settlement would have no more regard for the "commercial" than would the most scientific of German seminars. The
word application must be taken quite aside from its commercial or
professional sense. Leave money-making to the rich.

In this business of application, however, a settlement finds itself
tending not only to make common those good things which before were partial and remote, but it finds itself challenging and
testing by standards of moral democracy those things which it before regarded as good, if they could but be universal, and it sometimes finds that the so-called good things will not endure this test
of being universalized. This may be illustrated by various good
things. We may take first the so-called fine arts.

Let us consider the experience of a resident of a settlement who
cares a great deal for that aspect and history of life, which has been
portrayed in the fine arts. For years she has had classes studying
through photographs and lectures the marbles of Greece, the
paintings, the renaissance of Italy and the Gothic architecture of
mediaeval Europe. She has brought into the lives of scores of people a quality of enjoyment, a revelation of experience which they
never knew before. Some of them buy photographs to hang in
their own houses, a public school art society is started, schoolroom
walls are tinted and hung with copies of the best masters; so that
in the end hundreds of people have grown familiar with the names

of artists, and with conceptions of life which were hidden from them before. Some of these young women were they students of a fresh-water college could successfully pass an examination in the "History of Art." The studio of Hull House is well filled with young men and women who successfully copy casts and paint accurately what they see around them, and several of them have been admitted to the Chicago Art Institute upon competitive scholarships. Now, the first of these achievements would certainly satisfy the average college teacher whose business it is faithfully to transmit the accumulations of knowledge upon a given subject, and, of course, if possible, to add to the sum total of that knowledge in the matter of arrangement or discovery. The second achievement would certainly satisfy the ordinary philanthropic intent, which is to give to others the good which it possesses. But a settlement would have little vitality if it were satisfied with either of these achievements, and would at once limit its scope to that of the school on the one hand, or that of philanthropy on the other. And a settlement is neither a school nor a philanthropy, nor yet a philanthropic school or a scholarly philanthropy.

A settlement looks about among its neighbors and finds a complete absence of art. It sees people working laboriously without that natural solace of labor which art gives; they have no opportunity of expressing their own thoughts to their fellows by means of that labor. It finds the ambitious members of the neighborhood over-anxious and hurried. Wrapping up bars of soap in pieces of paper might at least give the pleasure of accuracy and repetition if it could be done at leisure but, when paid for by the piece, speed is the sole requirement, and the last suggestion of human interest has been taken away. The settlement soon discovers how impossible it is to put a fringe of art on the end of a day thus spent. It is not only bad pedagogics, but is an impossible undertaking, to appeal to a sense of beauty and order which has been crushed by years of ugly and disorderly work. May I relate an experience of a friend of Hull House, who took a party of visitors to the Art Institute of Chicago? In a prominent place upon that excellent

building there have been carved in good stone, and with some degree of skill, several fine, large skulls of oxen. The bulk of the settlement party had no armor of erudition with which to protect
themselves against such hideousness, and the leader of the party
carefully explained that in Greece, after a sacrifice was made, skulls
of the animals were hung upon the temples. But when he came to
tell why they were upon the Art Institute of Chicago, he found his
discourse going lame. That they were once religious symbols
charged with meaning, was hardly a sufficient defence. They
struck no response, certainly gave no delight nor sense of infection
to the bewildered group who stood in front of them. It may be
well to say in passing that this group were too unsophisticated to
take great pride in the mere fact that they knew what this meant,
as a club in search of culture would certainly have done. In his
chagrin the Hull House friend found himself reflecting that the
sacrifices, after all, did represent brotherhood and he made an attempt to compare them with the present symbols of brotherhood
which are found upon the engraved charters hanging upon those
walls which shelter the meetings of labor organizations. These
charters make a sincere attempt to express the conviction of
brotherhood, yet they have but the crudest symbolic representation, two hands clasping each other. It is not only that the print is
cheap, but the hands are badly drawn and badly modeled; they express no tenderness nor firmness, and are done without any interpretive skill. The hands upon the old-fashioned tombstones which
indicated a ghostly farewell might be interchanged with this pair of
hands which indicate vital standing together, and no one would
detect the difference. It occurred to this Hull House friend, with
a sense of shame and chagrin, that the artists of Chicago had been
recreant to their trust, that they had been so caught by a spirit of
imitation that they slavishly represented the symbols of animal sacrifice which no longer existed, and kept away from a great human
movement, which in America at least, has not yet found artistic
expression. If the skulls had been merely an obsolete symbol of
the brotherhood which had survived and developed its own artis-

tic symbols, they might easily have been made intelligible and full of meaning. The experience of the resident who teaches the history of art, of the good friend who is ashamed of the lack of democracy and interpretive power among modern artists, added to many other bits of experience and emotion has resulted in the establishment of a Chicago Arts and Crafts Society, which was founded at Hull House more than a year ago. This society has developed an amazing vitality of its own. And perhaps a quotation from its constitution will show its trend:

"To consider the present state of the factories and the workmen therein, and to devise lines of development which shall retain the machine in so far as it relieves the workmen from drudgery, and tends to perfect his product but which shall insist that the machine be no longer allowed to dominate the workman and reduce his production into a mechanical distortion."

The Chicago Arts and Crafts Society has challenged the present condition and motive of art. Its protest is certainly feeble and may be ineffective, but it is at least genuine and vital. Under the direction of several of its enthusiastic members a shop has been opened at Hull House where articles are designed and made. It is not merely a school where people are taught and then sent forth to use their teaching in art according to their individual initiative and opportunity, but where those who have been carefully trained and taught may remain, to express the best they may in wood or metal. A settlement would avoid the always getting ready for life which seems to dog the school, and would begin with however small a group to really accomplish and to live.

This may indeed bring us quite naturally to the attitude of the settlement toward the organized education with which it is brought in contact, the two forms of organization being naturally the public school and university extension lectures.

The resident finds the use of the public school constantly limited because it occupies such an isolated place in the community. The school board and the teachers have insensibly assumed that they have to do exclusively with children, or a few adult evening classes, only in certain settled directions. The newly arrived South Italian peasants who come to the night schools are thoroughly ill-adjusted to all their surroundings. To change suddenly from picking olives to sewer extension is certainly a bewildering experience. They have not yet obtained control of their powers for the performance of even the humblest social service, and have no chance to realize within themselves the social relation of that service which they are performing. Feeling this vaguely perhaps, but very strongly as only a dull peasant mind can feel, they go to the night schools in search of education. They are taught to read and write concerning small natural objects, on the assumption that the undeveloped intellect works best with insects and tiny animals, and they patiently accept this uninteresting information because they expect "education" to be dull and hard. Never for an instant are their own problems of living in the midst of unfamiliar surroundings even touched upon. There seems to be a belief among educators that it is not possible for the mass of mankind to have experiences which are of themselves worth anything, and that accordingly, if a neighborhood is to receive valuable ideas at all, they must be brought in from the outside, and almost exclusively in the form of books. Such scepticism regarding the possibilities of human nature as has often been pointed out results in equipping even the youngest children with the tools of reading and writing, but gives them no real participation in the industrial and social life with which they come in contact.

The residents in a settlement know that for most of their small neighbors life will be spent in handling material things either in manufacturing or commercial processes, and yet little is done to unfold the fascinating history of industrial evolution or to illuminate for them the materials among which they will live. The settlement sees boys constantly leave school to enter the factory at fourteen or fifteen without either of the requirements involved in a social life, on the one hand "without a sense of the resources already accumulated," and on the other "without the individual ability to respond to those resources."

If it is one function of a settlement to hold a clue as to what to select and what to eliminate in the business of living, it would bring the same charge of overwrought detail against the university extension lectures. A course of lectures in astronomy, illustrated by "stereopticon slides," will attract a large audience the first week who hope to hear of the wonders of the heavens, and the relation of our earth thereto, but instead of that they are treated to spectrum analyses of star dust, or the latest theories concerning the milky way. The habit of research and the desire to say the latest word upon any subject overcoming any sympathetic understanding of his audience which the lecturer might otherwise develop.

The teachers in the night schools near Hull House struggle with Greeks and Armenians, with Bohemians and Italians, and many another nationality. I once suggested to a professor of anthropology in a neighboring university that he deliver a lecture to these bewildered teachers upon simple race characteristics and, if possible, give them some interest in their pupils, and some other attitude than that all persons who do not speak English are ignorant. The professor kindly consented to do this, but when the time came frankly acknowledged that he could not do it—that he had no information available for such a talk. I was disappointed, of course, and a little chagrined when, during the winter, three of his pupils came to me at different times, anxiously inquiring if I could not put them on the track of people who had six toes, or whose relatives had been possessed of six toes. It was inevitable that the old charge should occur to me, that the best trained scientists are inclined to give themselves over to an idle thirst for knowledge which lacks any relation to human life, and leave to the charlatans the task of teaching those things which deeply concern the welfare of mankind. *Not the brightest any more than couch-potato sports fans are athletic*

Tolstoy points out that the mass of men get their intellectual food from the abortive outcasts of science, who provide millions of books, pictures and shows, not to instruct and guide, but for the sake of their own profit and gain, while the real student too often stays in a laboratory, occupied in a mysterious activity called

science. He does not even know what is required by the working-
men. He has quite forgotten their mode of life, their views of
things and their language. Tolstoy claims that the student has lost
sight of the fact that it is his duty, not to study and depict, but to
serve. This is asking a great deal from one man, or even from one
institution. It may be necessary that the university be supplemented by the settlement, or something answering thereto; but let
the settlement people recognize the value of their own calling,
and see to it that the university does not swallow the settlement,
and turn it into one more laboratory: another place in which to
analyze and depict, to observe and record. A settlement which
performs but this function is merely an imitative and unendowed
university, as a settlement which gives all its energies to classes and
lectures and athletics is merely an imitative college. We ourselves
may have given over attending classes and may be bored by lectures, but to still insist that working people shall have them is to
take the priggish attitude we sometimes allow ourselves toward
children, when we hold up rigid moral standards to them, although permitting ourselves a greater latitude. If without really
testing the value of mental pabulum, we may assume it is nutritious and good for working people, because some one once
assumed that it was good for us, we throw away the prerogative
of a settlement, and fall into the rigidity of the conventional
teacher. . . .

A settlement might bring the same charge against university extension as against the public schools, that it is bookish and remote.
Simple people want the large and vital—they are still in the tribal
stage of knowledge, so to speak. It is not that simple people like to
hear about little things; they want to hear about great things, simply told. We remember that the early nomads did not study the
blades of grass at their feet, but the stars above their heads—
although commercially considered, the study of grass would have
been much more profitable. . . .

So far as my experience goes a settlement finds itself curiously more companionable with the state and national bureaus in their efforts in collecting information and analyzing the situation, than it does with university efforts. This may possibly be traced to the fact that the data is accumulated by the bureaus on the assumption that it will finally become the basis for legislation, and is thus in the line of applicability. The settlements from the first have done more or less work under the direction of the bureaus. The head of a federal department quite recently begged a settlement to transform into readable matter a certain mass of material which had been carefully collected into tables and statistics. He hoped to make a connection between the information concerning diet and sanitary conditions, and the tenement house people who sadly needed this information. The head of the bureau said quite simply that he hoped that the settlements could accomplish this, not realizing that to put information into readable form is not nearly enough. It is to confuse a simple statement of knowledge with its application.

Permit me to illustrate from a group of Italian women who bring their underdeveloped children several times a week to Hull House for sanitary treatment, under the direction of a physician. It has been possible to teach some of these women to feed their children oatmeal instead of tea-soaked bread, but it has been done, not by statement at all but by a series of gay little Sunday morning breakfasts given to a group of them in the Hull House nursery. A nutritious diet was thus substituted for an inferior one by a social method. At the same time it was found that certain of the women hung bags of salt about their children's necks, to keep off the evil eye, which was supposed to give the children crooked legs at first, and in the end to cause them to waste away. The salt bags gradually disappeared under the influence of baths and cod liver oil. In short, rachitis was skillfully arrested, and without mention that disease was caused not by evil eye but by lack of cleanliness and nutrition, and without passing through the intermediate belief that disease was sent by Providence, the women form a little centre for the intelligent care of children, which is making itself felt in the Italian colony. Knowledge was applied in both cases, but scarcely as the statistician would have applied it.

We recall that the first colleges of the Anglo-Saxon race were established to educate religious teachers. For a long time it was considered the mission of the educated to prepare the mass of the people for the life beyond the grave. Knowledge dealt largely in theology, but it was ultimately to be applied, and the test of the successful graduate, after all, was not his learning, but his power to save souls. As the college changed from teaching theology to teaching secular knowledge the test of its success should have shifted from the power to save men's souls to the power to adjust them in healthful relations to nature and their fellow men. But the college failed to do this, and made the test of its success the mere collecting and disseminating of knowledge, elevating the means into an end and falling in love with its own achievement. The application of secular knowledge need be no more commercial and so-called practical than was the minister's when he applied his theology to the delicate problems of the human soul. This attempt at application on the part of the settlements may be, in fact, an apprehension of the situation.

It would be a curious result if this word "applied science," which the scholar has always been afraid of, lest it lead him into commercial influences, should have in it the salt of saving power, to rescue scholarship from the function of accumulating and transmitting to the higher and freer one of directing human life.

Recognizing the full risk of making an absurd, and as yet totally unsubstantiated claim, I would still express the belief that the settlement has made a genuine contribution in this direction by its effort to apply knowledge to life, to express life itself in terms of life.

George Herbert Mead

Mead was born in South Hadley, Massachusetts, in 1863. He attended Oberlin College and did graduate work in philosophy and psychology at Harvard University, where William James was teaching. In 1891 he joined the faculty at the University of Michigan, where he began his friendship with John Dewey. Along with Dewey, he left Michigan in 1894 for the University of Chicago, where he became a major figure in the "Chicago School" of philosophy and psychology and where he taught until his death, in 1931. His principal books are all posthumous collections: *The Philosophy of the Present* (1932), *Mind, Self, and Society* (1934), *Movements of Thought in the Nineteenth Century* (1936), and *The Philosophy of the Act* (1938).

The Mechanism of Social Consciousness

(1912)

THE ORGANIZATION of consciousness may be regarded from the standpoint of its objects and the relation of these objects to conduct. I have in mind to present somewhat schematically the relation of social objects or selves to the form of social conduct, and to introduce this by a statement of the relation of the physical object to the conduct within which it appears.

A physical object or percept is a construct in which the sensuous stimulation is merged with imagery which comes from past experience. This imagery on the cognitive side is that which the immediate sensuous quality stands for, and insofar satisfies the mind. The reason for this satisfaction is found in the fact that this imagery arises from past experience of the result of an act which this stimulus has set going. Thus the wall as a visual stimulus tends to set free the impulse to move toward it and push against it. The perception of the wall as distant and hard and rough is related to the visual experience as response to stimulation. A peculiar stimulus value stands for a certain response value. A percept is a collapsed act in which the result of the act to which the stimulus incites is represented by imagery of the experience of past acts of a like nature.

Insofar as our physical conduct involves movements toward or away from distant objects and their being handled when we come into contact with them, we perceive all things in terms of distance sensation—color, sound, odor—which stand for hard or soft, big or little, objects of varying forms, which actual contact will reveal.

Our conduct in movement and manipulation, with its stimulations and responses, gives the framework within which objects of perception arise—and this conduct is in so far responsible for the organization of our physical world. Percepts—physical objects—are compounds of the experience of immediate stimulation and the imagery of the response to which this stimulation will lead. The object can be properly stated in terms of conduct.

I have referred to percepts as objects which arise in physical experience because it is a certain phase of conduct which, with its appropriate stimuli and responses, gives rise to such products, i.e., movement under the influence of distant stimuli leading to contact experiences of manipulation.

Given a different type of conduct with distinguishable stimulations and responses, and different objects would arise—such a different field is that of social conduct. By social conduct I refer simply to that which is mediated by the stimulations of other animals belonging to the same group of living forms, which lead to responses which again affect these other forms—thus fighting, reproduction, parental care, much of animal play, hunting, etc., are the results of primitive instincts or impulses which are set going by the stimulation of one form by another, and these stimulations again lead to responses which affect other forms.

It is of course true that a man is a physical object to the perception of another man, and as real as is a tree or a stone. But a man is more than a physical object, and it is this more which constitutes him a social object or self, and it is this self which is related to that peculiar conduct which may be termed social conduct.

Most social stimulation is found in the beginnings or early stages of social acts which serve as stimuli to other forms whom these acts would affect. This is the field of gestures, which reveal the motor attitude of a form in its relation to others; an attitude which psychologists have conceived of as predominantly emotional, though it is emotional only insofar as an ongoing act is inhibited. That certain of these early indications of an incipient act have persisted, while the rest of the act has been largely suppressed or has lost its original value, e.g., the baring of the teeth or the lifting of the nostrils, is true, and the explanation can most readily be found in the social value which such indications have acquired. It is an error, however, to overlook the relation which these truncated acts have assumed toward other forms of reactions which complete them as really as the original acts, or to forget that they occupy but a small part of the whole field of gesture by means of which we are apprised of the reactions of others toward ourselves. The expressions of the face and attitudes of body have the same functional value for us that the beginnings of hostility have for two dogs, who are maneuvering for an opening to attack.

This field of gesture does not simply relate the individual to other individuals as physical objects, but puts him *en rapport* with their actions, which are as yet only indicated, and arouses instinctive reactions appropriate to these social activities. The social response of one individual, furthermore, introduces a further complication. The attitude assumed in response to the attitude of another becomes a stimulus to him to change his attitude, thus leading to that conversation of attitudes which is so vividly illustrated in the early stages of a dog fight. We see the same process in courting and mating, and in the fondling of young forms by the mother, and finally in much of the play of young animals.

It has been recognized for some time that speech belongs in its beginnings, at least, to this same field of gesture, so-called vocal gesture. Originally indicating the preparation for violent action, which arises from a sudden change of breathing and circulation rhythms, the articulate sounds have come to elaborate and immensely complicate this conversation of attitudes by which social forms so adjust themselves to each other's anticipated action that they may act appropriately with reference to each other.

Articulate sounds have still another most important result. While one feels but imperfectly the value of his own facial expression or bodily attitude for another, his ear reveals to him his own vocal gesture in the same form that it assumes to his neighbor. One shakes his fist primarily only at another, while he talks to himself as really as he talks to his vis-à-vis. The genetic import of this has long been recognized. The young child talks to himself, i.e., uses the elements of articulate speech in response to the sounds he hears himself make, more continuously and persistently than he does in response to the sounds he hears from those about him, and displays greater interest in the sounds he himself makes than in those of others. We know also that this fascination of one's own vocal gestures continues even after the child has learned to talk with others, and that the child will converse for hours with himself, even constructing imaginary companions, who function in the child's growing self-consciousness as the processes of inner speech—of thought and imagination—function in the consciousness of the adult.

To return to the formula given above for the formation of an object in consciousness, we may define the social object in terms of social conduct as we defined the physical object in terms of our reactions to physical objects. The object was found to consist of the sensuous experience of the stimulation to an act plus the imagery from past experience of the final result of the act. The social object will then be the gestures, i.e., the early indications of an ongoing social act in another plus the imagery of our own response to that stimulation. To the young child the frowns and smiles of those about him, the attitude of body, the outstretched arms, are at first simply stimulations that call out instinctive responses of his own appropriate to these gestures. He cries or laughs, he moves toward his mother, or stretches out his arms. When these gestures in others bring back the images of his own responses and their results, the child has the material out of which he builds up the social objects that form the most important part of his environment. We are familiar with this phase of a baby's development, being confident that he recognizes the different members of the group about him. He acts then with confidence toward them since their gestures have come to have meaning for him. His own response to their stimulations and its consequences are there to interpret the facial expressions and attitudes of body and tones of voice. The awakening social intelligence of the child is evidenced not so much through his ready responses to the gestures of others, for these have been in evidence much earlier. It is the inner assurance of his own readiness to adjust himself to the attitudes of others that looks out of his eyes and appears in his own bodily attitudes.

If we assume that an object arises in consciousness through the merging of the imagery of experience of the response with that of the sensuous experience of the stimulation, it is evident that the child must merge the imagery of his past responses into the sensuous stimulation of what comes to him through distance senses. His contact and kinesthetic experiences must be lodged in the sensuous experiences that call them out if they are to achieve objective character in his consciousness.

It will be some time before he can successfully unite the different parts of his own body, such as his hands and feet, which he sees and feels, into a single object. Such a step must be later than the formation of the physical objects of his environment. The form of the object is given in the experience of things, which are not his physical self. When he has synthesized his various bodily parts with the organic sensations and affective experiences, it will be upon the model of objects about him. The mere presence of experiences of pleasure and pain, together with organic sensations, will not form an object unless this material can fall into the scheme of an object—that of sensuous stimulation plus the imagery of the response.

In the organization of the baby's physical experience the appearance of his body as a unitary thing, as an object, will be relatively late, and must follow upon the structure of the objects of his environment. This is as true of the object that appears in social conduct, the self. The form of the social object must be found first of all in the experience of other selves. The earliest achievement of social consciousness will be the merging of the imagery of the baby's first responses and their results with the stimulations of the gestures of others. The child will not succeed in forming an object of himself—of putting the so-called subjective material of consciousness within such a self—until he has recognized about him social objects who have arisen in his experience through this process of filling out stimulations with past experiences of response. And this is indeed our uniform experience with children. The child's early social percepts are of others. After these arise incomplete and partial selves—or "me's"—which are quite analogous to the child's percepts of his hands and feet, which precede his perception of himself as a whole. The mere presence of affective experience, of imagery, or organic sensations, does not carry with it consciousness of a self to which these experiences belong. Nor does the unitary character of the response which tends to synthesize our objects of perception convey that same unitary character to the inner experience until the child is able to experience himself as he experiences other selves.

It is highly probable that lower animals never reach any such objective reference of what we term subjective experiences to selves, and the question presents itself—what is there in human social conduct that gives rise to a "me," a self which is an object? Why does the human animal transfer the form of a social object from his environment to an inner experience?

The answer to the question is already indicated in the statement of vocal gesture. Certainly the fact that the human animal can stimulate himself as he stimulates others and can respond to his stimulations as he responds to the stimulations of others, places in his conduct the form of a social object out of which may arise a "me" to which can be referred so-called subjective experiences.

Of course the mere capacity to talk to oneself is not the whole of self-consciousness, otherwise the talking birds would have souls or at least selves. What is lacking to the parrot are the social objects which can exist for the human baby. Part of the mechanism for transferring the social objects into an inner experience the parrot possesses, but he has nothing to import into such an inner world. Furthermore, the vocal gesture is not the only form which can serve for the building-up of a "me," as is abundantly evident from the building-up gestures of the deaf mutes. Any gesture by which the individual can himself be affected as others are affected, and which therefore tends to call out in him a response as it would call it out in another, will serve as a mechanism for the construction of a self. That, however, a consciousness of a self as an object would ever have arisen in man if he had not had the mechanism of talking to himself, I think there is every reason to doubt.

If this statement is correct the objective self of human consciousness is the merging of one's responses with the social stimulation by which he affects himself. The "me" is a man's reply to his own talk. Such a "me" is not then an early formation, which is then projected and ejected into the bodies of other people to give them the breadth of human life. It is rather an importation from the field of social objects into an amorphous, unorganized field of what we call inner experience. Through the organization of this object, the self, this material is itself organized and brought under the control of the individual in the form of so-called self-consciousness.

It is a commonplace of psychology that it is only the "me"— the empirical self—that can be brought into the focus of attention—that can be perceived. The "I" lies beyond the range of immediate experience. In terms of social conduct this is tantamount to saying that we can perceive our responses only as they appear as images from past experience, merging with the sensuous stimulation. We cannot present the response while we are responding. We cannot use our responses to others as the materials for construction of the self—this imagery goes to make up other selves. We must socially stimulate ourselves to place at our own disposal the material out of which our own selves as well as those of others must be made.

The "I" therefore never can exist as an object in consciousness, but the very conversational character of our inner experience, the very process of replying to one's own talk, implies an "I" behind the scenes who answers to the gestures, the symbols, that arise in consciousness. The "I" is the transcendental self of Kant, the soul that James conceived behind the scene holding on to the skirts of an idea to give it an added increment of emphasis.[1]

The self-conscious, actual self in social intercourse is the objective "me" or "me's" with the process of response continually going on and implying a fictitious "I" always out of sight of himself.

Inner consciousness is socially organized by the importation of the social organization of the outer world.

A Contrast of Individualistic
and Social Theories of the Self

(ca. 1927)

THE DIFFERENCES between the type of social psychology which derives the selves of individuals from the social process in which they are implicated and in which they empirically interact with one another, and the type of social psychology which instead derives that process from the selves of the individuals involved in it, are clear. The first type assumes a social process or social order as the logical and biological precondition of the appearance of the selves of the individual organisms involved in that process or belonging to that order. The other type, on the contrary, assumes individual selves as the presuppositions, logically and biologically, of the social process or order within which they interact.

The difference between the social and the individual theories of the development of mind, self, and the social process of experience or behavior is analogous to the difference between the evolutionary and the contract theories of the state as held in the past by both rationalists and empiricists.[1] The latter theory takes individuals and their individual experiencing—individual minds and selves—as logically prior to the social process in which they are involved, and explains the existence of that social process in terms of them; whereas the former takes the social process of experience or behavior as logically prior to the individuals and their individual experiencing which are involved in it, and explains their existence in terms of that social process. But the latter type of theory cannot explain that which is taken as logically prior at all, cannot explain the existence of minds and selves; whereas the former type of theory can explain that which it takes as logically prior, namely, the existence of the social process of behavior, in terms of such fundamental biological or physiological relations and interactions as reproduction, or the co-operation of individuals for mutual protection or for the securing of food.

Our contention is that mind can never find expression, and could never have come into existence at all, except in terms of a social environment; that an organized set or pattern of social relations and interactions (especially those of communication by means of gestures functioning as significant symbols and thus creating a universe of discourse) is necessarily presupposed by it and involved in its nature. And this entirely social theory or interpretation of mind[2]—this contention that mind develops and has its being only in and by virtue of the social process of experience and activity, which it hence presupposes, and that in no other way can it develop and have its being—must be clearly distinguished from the partially (but only partially) social view of mind. On this view, though mind can get expression only within or in terms of the environment of an organized social group, yet it is nevertheless in some sense a native endowment—a congenital or hereditary biological attribute—of the individual organism, and could not otherwise exist or manifest itself in the social process at all; so that it is not itself essentially a social phenomenon, but rather is biological both in its nature and in its origin, and is social only in its characteristic manifestations or expressions. According to this latter view, moreover, the social process presupposes, and in a sense is a product of, mind; in direct contrast is our opposite view that mind presupposes, and is a product of, the social process. The advantage of our view is that it enables us to give a detailed account and actually to explain the genesis and development of mind; whereas the view that mind is a congenital biological endowment of the individual organism does not really enable us to explain its nature and origin at all: neither what sort of biological endowment it is, nor how organisms at a certain level of evolutionary progress come to possess it. Furthermore, the supposition that the social process presupposes, and is in some sense a product of, mind seems to be contradicted by the existence of the social communities of certain of the lower animals, especially the highly complex social organizations of bees and ants, which apparently operate on a purely instinctive or reflex basis, and do not in the least involve the existence of mind or consciousness in the individual organisms which form or constitute them. And even if this contradiction is avoided by the admission that only at its higher levels—only at the levels represented by the social relations and interactions of human beings—does the social process of experience and behavior pre-suppose the existence of mind or become necessarily a product of mind, still it is hardly plausible to suppose that this already ongoing and developing process should suddenly, at a particular stage in its evolution, become dependent for its further continuance upon an entirely extraneous factor, introduced into it, so to speak, from without.

The individual enters as such into his own experience only as an object, not as a subject; and he can enter as an object only on the basis of social relations and interactions, only by means of his experiential transactions with other individuals in an organized social environment. It is true that certain contents of experience (particularly kinaesthetic) are accessible only to the given individual organism and not to any others; and that these private or "subjective," as opposed to public or "objective," contents of experience are usually regarded as being peculiarly and intimately connected with the individual's self, or as being in a special sense self-experiences. But this accessibility solely to the given individual organism of certain contents of its experience does not affect, nor in any way conflict with, the theory as to the social nature and origin of the self that we are presenting; the existence of private or "subjective" contents of experience does not alter the fact that self-consciousness involves the individual's becoming an object to himself by taking the attitudes of other individuals toward himself within an organized setting of social relationships, and that unless the individual had thus become an object to himself he would not be self-conscious or have a self at all. Apart from his social interactions with other individuals, he would not relate the private or "subjective" contents of his experience to himself, and he could not become aware of himself as such, that is, as an individual, a person, merely by means or in terms of these contents of his experience; for in order to become aware of himself as such he must, to repeat, become an object to himself, or enter his own experience as an object, and only by social means—only by taking the attitudes of others toward himself—is he able to become an object to himself.[3]

It is true, of course, that once mind has arisen in the social process it makes possible the development of that process into much more complex forms of social interaction among the component individuals than was possible before it had arisen. But there is nothing odd about a product of a given process contributing to, or becoming an essential factor in, the further development of that process. The social process, then, does not depend for its origin or initial existence upon the existence and interactions of selves; though it does depend upon the latter for the higher stages of complexity and organization which it reaches after selves have arisen within it.

In decadent, exclusive eras dominated by mediocrities ($42K = 4lK$), the individual mind can only be misled and crippled by interaction with the ruling confusion. It is time to turn inward for fulfilment. There is no obligation to a parasitic society except not to interfere with its necessary and well-deserved self-destruction. Mead's fallacy is to assume that all societies have some healthy effect on individual self-development. His failure to distinguish between these is compounded by including insects as role models.

Contemporary Pragmatism

Richard Rorty

Rorty is University Professor of the Humanities at the University of Virginia, where he has taught since 1982. His books include *Philosophy and the Mirror of Nature* (1979), *Consequences of Pragmatism (Essays: 1972–1980)* (1982), *Contingency, Irony, and Solidarity* (1989), and two volumes of *Philosophical Papers: Objectivity, Relativism, and Truth* and *Essays on Heidegger and Others* (1991).

Philosophy as a Kind of Writing: An Essay on Derrida

(1978–79)

I

HERE IS ONE WAY to look at physics: there are some invisible things which are parts of everything else and whose behavior determines the way everything else works. Physics is the search for an accurate description of those invisible things, and it proceeds by finding better and better explanations of the visible. Eventually, by way of microbiological accounts of the mental, and through causal accounts of the mechanisms of language, we shall be able to see the physicists' accumulation of truths about the world as itself a transaction between these invisible things.

Here is another way of looking at physics: the physicists are men looking for new interpretations of the Book of Nature. After each pedestrian period of normal science, they dream up a new model, a new picture, a new vocabulary, and then they announce that the true meaning of the Book has been discovered. But, of course, it never is, any more than is the true meaning of *Coriolanus* or the *Dunciad* or the *Phenomenology of Spirit* or the *Philosophical Investigations*. What makes them physicists is that their writings are commentaries on the writings of earlier interpreters of Nature, not that they all are somehow "talking about the same thing," the *invisibilia Dei sive naturae*[1] toward which their inquiries steadily converge.

Here is a way of thinking about right and wrong: the common moral consciousness contains certain intuitions concerning equality, fairness, human dignity, and the like, which need to be made explicit through the formulation of principles—principles of the sort which can be used to write legislation. By thinking about puzzle-cases, and by abstracting from differences between our (European) culture and others, we can formulate better and better principles, principles corresponding ever more closely to the moral law itself.

Here is another way of thinking about right and wrong: the longer men or cultures live, the more φρόνησις[2] they may, with luck, acquire—the more sensitivity to others, the more delicate a typology for describing their fellows and themselves. Mingling with others helps; Socratic discussion helps; but since the Romantics, we have been helped most of all by the poets, the novelists, and the ideologues. Since the *Phenomenology of Spirit* taught us to see not only the history of philosophy, but that of Europe, as portions of a *Bildungsroman,* we have not striven for moral knowledge as a kind of ἐπιστήμη.[3] Rather, we have seen Europe's self-descriptions, and our own self-descriptions, not as ordered to subject matter, but as designs in a tapestry which they will still be weaving after we, and Europe, die.

Here is a way of looking at philosophy: from the beginning, philosophy has worried about the relation between thought and its object, representation and represented. The old problem about reference to the inexistent, for example, has been handled in various unsatisfactory ways because of a failure to distinguish properly philosophical questions about meaning and reference from extraneous questions motivated by scientific, ethical, and religious concerns. Once these questions *are* properly isolated, however, we can see philosophy as a field which has its center in a series of questions about the relations between words and the world. The recent purifying move from talk of ideas to talk of meanings has dissipated the epistemological skepticism which motivated much of past philosophy. This has left philosophy a more limited, but more self-conscious, rigorous, and coherent area of inquiry.

Here is another way of looking at philosophy: philosophy started off as a confused combination of the love of wisdom and the love of argument. It began with Plato's notion that the rigor of mathematical argumentation exposed, and could be used to correct, the pretensions of the politicians and the poets. As philosophical thought changed and grew, inseminated by this ambivalent ἔρως,[4] it produced shoots which took root on their own. Both wisdom and argumentation became far more various than Plato dreamed. Given such nineteenth-century complications as the *Bildungsroman,* non-Euclidean geometries, ideological historiography, the literary dandy, and the political anarchist, there is no way in which one can isolate philosophy as occupying a distinctive place in culture or concerned with a distinctive subject or proceeding by some distinctive method. One cannot even seek an essence for philosophy as an academic *Fach*[5] (because one would first have to choose the country in whose universities' catalogs one was to look). The philosophers' own scholastic little definitions of "philosophy" are merely polemical devices—intended to exclude from the field of honor those whose pedigrees are unfamiliar. We can pick out "the philosophers" in the contemporary intellectual world only by noting who is commenting on a certain sequence of historical figures. All that "philosophy" as a name for a sector of culture means is "talk about Plato, Augustine, Descartes, Kant, Hegel, Frege, Russell . . . and that lot." Philosophy is best seen as a kind of writing. It is delimited, as is any literary genre, not by form or matter, but by tradition—a family romance involving, e.g., Father Parmenides, honest old Uncle Kant, and bad brother Derrida.

There, then, are two ways of thinking about various things. I have drawn them up as reminders of the differences between a philosophical tradition which began, more or less, with Kant, and one which began, more or less, with Hegel's *Phenomenology*. The first tradition thinks of truth as a vertical relationship between representations and what is represented. The second tradition thinks of truth horizontally—as the culminating reinterpretation of our predecessors' reinterpretation of their predecessors' reinterpretation. . . .[6] This tradition does not ask how representations are related to nonrepresentations, but how representations can be seen as hanging together. The difference is not one between "correspondence" and "coherence" theories of truth—though these so-called theories are partial expressions of this contrast. Rather, it is the difference between regarding truth, goodness, and beauty as eternal objects which we try to locate and reveal, and regarding them as artifacts whose fundamental design we often have to alter. The first tradition takes scientific truth as the center of philosophical concern (and scorns the notion of incommensurable scientific world-pictures). It asks how well other fields of inquiry conform to the model of science. The second tradition takes science as one (not especially privileged nor interesting) sector of culture, a sector which, like all the other sectors, only makes sense when viewed historically. The first likes to present itself as a straightforward, down to earth, scientific attempt to get things right. The second needs to present itself obliquely, with the help of as many foreign words and as much allusiveness and name-dropping as possible. Neo-Kantian philosophers like Putnam, Strawson, and Rawls[7] have arguments and theses which are connected to Kant's by a fairly straightforward series of "purifying" transformations, transformations which are thought to give clearer and clearer views of the persistent problems. For the non-Kantian philosophers, there are no persistent problems—save perhaps the existence of the Kantians. Non-Kantian philosophers like Heidegger and Derrida are emblematic figures who not only do not solve problems, they do not *have* arguments or theses. They are connected with their predecessors not by common subjects or methods but in the "family resemblance" way in which latecomers in a sequence of commentators on commentators are connected with older members of the same sequence. *Anything goes.*

To understand Derrida, one must see his work as the latest development in this non-Kantian, dialectical tradition—the latest attempt of the dialecticians to shatter the Kantians' ingenuous image of themselves as accurately representing how things really are. Derrida talks a lot about language, and it is tempting to view him as a "philosopher of language" whose work one might usefully compare with other inquiries concerning the relations between words and the world. But it would be less misleading to say that his writing about language is an attempt to show why there should be no philosophy of language.[8] On his view, language is the last refuge of the Kantian tradition, of the notion that there is something eternally present to man's gaze (the structure of the universe, the moral law, the nature of language) which philosophy can let us see more clearly. The reason why the notion of "philosophy of language" is an illusion is the same reason why philosophy—*Kantian* philosophy, philosophy as more than a kind of writing—is an illusion. The twentieth-century attempt to purify Kant's general theory about the relation between representations and their objects by turning it into philosophy of language is, for Derrida, to be countered by making philosophy even more impure—more unprofessional, funnier, more allusive, sexier, and above all, more "written." Thus, insofar as he has an attitude towards, for example, the mini-tradition which stretches from Frege to Davidson, it is the same as his attitude towards Husserl's discussion of language.[9] The attitude, roughly, is that most twentieth-century concern with language is Kantian philosophy in extremis, a last desperate attempt to do on a pathetically small scale what Kant (and before him Plato) attempted to do on a large scale—show how the atemporally true can be contained in a spatio-temporal vehicle, regularize the relation between man and what man seeks by exhibiting its "structure," freezing the historical process of successive reinterpretations by exhibiting the structure of all possible interpretation.

Derrida, then, has little to tell us about language, but a great deal to tell us about philosophy. To get a handle on his work, one might take him as answering the question, "Given that philosophy *is* a kind of writing, why does this suggestion meet with such resistance?" This becomes, in his work, the slightly more particular question, "What must philosophers who object to this characterization think *writing* is, that they should find the notion that that is what they are doing so offensive?" Whereas Heidegger, Derrida's great father-figure, was the first to "place" (or if you prefer, "transcend" or "castrate") Hegel by giving a historical characterization of Hegel's historicism, Derrida wishes to "place" (or whatever) Heidegger by explaining Heidegger's distrust of writing. Heidegger, it is true, wrote a lot, but always (after the "turn") in the interests of urging us to be still and listen to the single line of verse, the individual Greek word. Derrida is suspicious of Heidegger's preference for the simplicity and splendor of the word spoken on the hill, and also of his contempt for the footnote scribbled in the ergastulum down in the valley. The preference, he thinks, betrays a fatal taint of Kantianism, of the Platonic "metaphysics of presence." For it is characteristic of the Kantian tradition that, no matter how much writing it does, it does not think that philosophy *should* be "written," any more than science should be. Writing is an unfortunate necessity; what is really wanted is to show, to demonstrate, to point out, to exhibit, to make one's interlocutor stand at gaze before the world. The copy theory of ideas, the spectator theory of knowledge, the notion that "understanding representation" is the heart of philosophy, are expressions of this need to substitute an epiphany for a text, to "see through" representation. In a mature science, the words in which the investigator "writes up" his results should be as few and as transparent as possible. Heidegger, though struggling manfully against this cluster of notions, and especially against the notion of the "research project" as model for philosophical thinking, in the end succumbed to the same nostalgia for the innocence and brevity of the spoken word. His substitution of auditory for visual metaphors—of listening to the voice of Being for being a spectator of time and eternity—was, Derrida thinks, only a dodge. The Kantian urge to bring philosophy to an end by solving all its problems, having everything fall into place, and the Heideggerian urge towards *Gelassenheit* and *Unverborgenheit*,[10] are the same urge. Philosophical writing, for Heidegger as for the Kantians, is really aimed at putting an end to writing. For Derrida, writing always leads to more writing, and more, and still more—just as history does not lead to Absolute Knowledge or the Final Struggle, but to more history, and more, and still more. The *Phenomenology*'s vision of truth as what you get by reinterpreting all the previous reinterpretations of reinterpretations still embodies the Platonic ideal of the Last Reinterpretation, the *right* interpretation at last. Derrida wants to keep the horizontal character of Hegel's notion of philosophy without its teleology, its sense of direction, its seriousness.

II

So far in this paper I have merely been trying to locate Derrida in philosophical space. Now I want to focus on a few of his remarks about writing, with an eye to seeing more clearly how he answers the question, "What must philosophers think writing is that they resent so much the suggestion that this is what they do?" His answer is, roughly, that they think that writing is a means of representing facts, and that the more "written" writing is—the less transparent to what it represents and the more concerned with its relation to others' writings—the worse it must be. The way he spells out his answer, I think, can help us see why he thinks writing about writing will help to "deconstruct" the Kantian way of looking at things. Consider, to begin with, the following passage:

> There is therefore good and bad writing: the good and natural is the divine inscription in the heart and the soul; the perverse and artful is technique, exiled in the exteriority of the body. A modification well within the Platonic diagram: writing of the soul and of the body, writing of the interior and of the exterior, writing of conscience and of the passions, as there is a voice of the soul and a voice of the body. . . .
>
> The good writing has therefore always been comprehended. Comprehended as that which had to be comprehended: within a nature or a natural law, created or not, but first thought within an eternal presence. Comprehended, therefore, within a totality, and enveloped in a volume or a book. The idea of the book is the idea

of a totality, finite or infinite, of the signifier; this totality of the
signifier cannot be a totality, unless a totality constituted by the signified preexists it, supervises its inscriptions and its signs, and is independent of it in its ideality. The idea of the book, which always
refers to a natural totality, is profoundly alien to the sense of writing. . . . If I distinguish the text from the book, I shall say that the
destruction of the book as it is now under way in all domains, de-
nudes the surface of the text.[11]

Consider Derrida as trying, in such passages as this, to create a
new thing for writing to be about—not the world, but texts.
Books tell the truth about things. Texts comment on other texts,
and we should stop trying to test texts for accuracy of representation: "reading . . . cannot legitimately transgress the text toward
something other than it, toward the referent (a reality that is metaphysical, historical, psychobiographical, etc.) or toward a signifier
outside the text whose content could take place, could have taken
place outside of language, that is to say, in the sense that we give
here to that word, outside of writing in general. . . . There is
nothing outside of the text."[12] Derrida regards the need to overcome "the book"—the notion of a piece of writing as aimed at
accurate treatment of a subject, conveying a message which (in
more fortunate circumstances) might have been conveyed by ostensive definition or by injecting knowledge straight into the
brain—as justifying his use of any text to interpret any other text.
The most shocking thing about his work—even more shocking
than, though not so funny as, his sexual interpretations of the history of philosophy—is his use of multilingual puns, joke ety-
mologies, allusions from anywhere to anywhere, and phonic and
typographical gimmicks. It is as if he really thought that the fact
that, for example, the French pronunciation of "Hegel" sounds
like the French word for "eagle" was supposed to be relevant for
comprehending Hegel. But Derrida does not want to comprehend Hegel's books; he wants to play with Hegel. He doesn't want

to write a book about the nature of language; he wants to play with the texts which other people have thought they were writing about language.

At this point one can imagine serious-minded philosophers on both sides of the Channel murmuring about "idealism." There is a deep terror among Kantian philosophers of a certain job-related health hazard: the philosopher, after overstrenuous inquiry into our relation to the world, may lose his nerve, his reason, and the world simultaneously. He does this by withdrawing into a dream world of ideas, of representations—even, God help us, of texts. To guard against this temptation, Kantian philosophers tell us, we must remember that only the transcendental idealist can be an empirical realist. Only the man who comprehends the relation between representation and represented, in that arduous but rigorously scientific way characteristic of the epistemologist in the last century and the philosopher of language in this, can be transcendental in the required sense. For only he can represent *representing itself* accurately. Only such an accurate transcendental account of the relationship of representation will keep the Knowing Subject in touch with the Object, word with world, scientist with particle, moral philosopher with the Law, philosophy itself with reality itself. So whenever dialecticians start developing their coherentist and historicist views, Kantians explain that it is another sad case of Berkeley's Disease, and that there is no cure save a still better, more luminously convincing, more transparent philosophical account of representation.

When dialectical philosophers are accused of idealism, they usually reply as Berkeley replied to his critics—by explaining that they are only protesting against the errors of a certain philosophical school and that they are really not saying anything at which the plain man would demur. As Austin said in this connection, "There's the bit where you say it and the bit where you take it back."[13] The nice thing about Derrida is that he doesn't take it back. He has no interest in bringing "his philosophy" into accord with common sense. He is not writing a philosophy. He is not giving an account of anything; he is not offering a comprehensive view of anything. He is not protesting against the *errors* of a philosophical school. He is, however, protesting against the notion that the philosophy of language, pursued "realistically" as the study of how language hooks on to the world, is something more than one more quaint little genre, that it is first philosophy. But the protest is not because he has a different candidate for the position of "first philosophy," it is against the notion of "first philosophy." He could, if he liked, say that he, too, can pass judgments within this genre—that he recognizes better and worse "realistic" philosophy of language, that he agrees with all up-to-date philosophers of language that Strawson and Searle[14] were terribly wrong about the referents of proper names, and so on. But what he really wants to do is to say, "You used to think that it was terribly important to get meaning and reference, and all that, right. But it isn't. You only thought that because . . ." He might be compared with the secularist who says not "There is no God" but rather "All this talk about our relation to God is getting in our way." James, when he said that "the true is what is good in the way of belief"[15] was simply trying to debunk epistemology; he was not offering a "theory of truth." So Derrida, when he says "il n'y a pas de hors-texte,"[16] is not putting forward an ontological view; he is trying to debunk Kantian philosophy generally.

Well then, one might reply, he *does* take it back. For he admits that all this stuff about there not being any such thing as accuracy of representation is *metaphorical,* just a way of speaking. But why doesn't he say what he means? Why doesn't he come right out and tell his views about language and about reality? To this one can only reiterate that Derrida is in the same situation in regard to language that many of us secularists are in regard to God. It isn't that we believe in God, or don't believe in God, or have suspended judgment about God, or consider that the God of theism is an inadequate symbol of our ultimate concern; it is just that we wish we didn't have to have a view about God. It isn't that we know that "God" is a cognitively meaningless expression, or that it has its

role in a language-game other than the fact-stating, or whatever.
We just regret the fact that the word is used so much. So it is for
Derrida with the vocabulary of Kantian philosophy. His attitude
towards centuries of worry about the relation between subject and
object, representations and the real, is like the Enlightenment attitude toward centuries of worry about the relation between God
and man, faith and reason. Indeed, for Derrida as for Heidegger,
these worries are all the same worry: the worry that we may lose
touch with certain exigencies, conformity with which is the
whole duty of man. For Derrida as for Freud, these are all forms
of the worry about what our fathers require of us. For Derrida as
for Sartre, these are all forms of the attempt to know oneself by
transforming oneself into a knowable object—an *être-en-soi* which
obeys the laws of its kind.

So, to sum up the gloss I want to put upon the texts I have
quoted from Derrida, Derrida is trying to do for our highbrow
culture what secularist intellectuals in the nineteenth century tried
to do for theirs. *He is suggesting how things might look if we did not
have Kantian philosophy built into the fabric of our intellectual life, as his
predecessors suggested how things might look if we did not have religion
built into the fabric of our moral life.* The secularists I speak of were
continually assailed by the question, "What argument do you have
for not believing in God?" Derrida is continually assailed by the
question, "What argument do you have for saying that we should
not refer the text to something which is not a text?" Neither has
any interesting arguments, because both are not working by the
same rules as their opponents. They are trying to make up some
new rules. Lack of seriousness, in the sense in which I just attributed it to Derrida, is simply this refusal to take the standard rules
seriously, conjoined with the refusal to give a clear answer to the
question, "Is it the old game played differently, or rather a new
game?"

There is another sense, however, in which Derrida is very serious indeed—as serious as the prophets of secularization. He is serious about the need to change ourselves, serious about what he

There is a good attack on Derrida in Updike's Memories of the Ford Administration. The fact that he gave meaning to a trivialized calls "deconstruction." Thus he warns us against taking "gramma- *subject is* tology" as the name of a new research program, as an attempt at *vice* doing something constructive and progressive, when he speaks of *versa* "the systematic crossing-out of the ἀρχή[17] and the transformation *to* of general semiology into a grammatology, the latter performing a *D.* critical work upon everything within semiology—right down to its matrical concept of signs—that retains any metaphysical pre-suppositions incompatible with the theme of differance."[18] One can easily conclude from such passages as this that Derrida con-ceives of his work as purely negative—deconstructing the meta-physics of presence in order to leave the texts bare, unburdened by the need to represent. Such a view is also suggested by his excus-ing his high-handed treatment of Saussure[19] in this way: "My jus-tification would be as follows: This [a text of Saussure's] and some other indices (in a general way the treatment of the concept of writing) already give us the assured means of broaching the de construction of *the greatest totality*—the concept of the episteme and logocentric metaphysics—from which are produced, without ever posing the radical question of writing, all the Western meth-ods of analysis, explication, reading, or interpretation."[20] This pas-sage conforms to the picture of Derrida I have offered so far—one in which he wants to do better than Heidegger the job of "over-coming the tradition of Western metaphysics" which Heidegger attempted. This picture may, however, be too charitable. For there is a side of Derrida which looks unfortunately constructive, a side which makes it look as if he in the end succumbs to nostalgia, to the lure of philosophical system-building, and specifically that of constructing yet another transcendental idealism. I turn now, therefore, to a discussion of the luminous, constructive, bad side of Derrida's work, as opposed to the shadowy, deconstructive, good side which I have been discussing so far. *Derrida's non-sequitur: calling something useless, but then glori-fying uselessness. Also in Nietzsche, where he writes that Oedipus was totally innocent, but then masochistically (like some Nazi cannon fodder) glorifies the purity of his submission to total injustice.*

III

To explain where and why Derrida seems to get constructive, I need to go back to the point I was making earlier about his attitude towards "the philosophy of language." One can see Derrida's attempt to "deconstruct the greatest totality" as an attempt to get rid of the notion that language is an attempt to represent something nonlinguistic. He is taking the Wittgensteinian doctrine which Sellars calls "psychological nominalism"—the doctrine that "all awareness is a linguistic affair"—to its extreme.[21] But he sees the recent attention to language (as a general subject matter of inquiry, comparable in scope to God, nature, history, or man) as a kind of pseudonominalism.[22] It is as if the Kantians had been forced, by attacks on the notions of "thought" and "the mind," to see that there is no way to cut beneath language to the thought which language expresses, no way, as Wittgenstein said, to "get between language and its object." But instead of concluding that we should stop viewing language as representing something, the Kantian response has been to say something like, "Now that we see that language is not the expression of thought, but since we know that language *does* represent the world, we can now be properly serious about language, can pay language the attention it deserves, by exploring *direct* word-world connections." What looks to modern philosophers of language like a new-found respect for language is, for Derrida, simply a disguised attempt to put language in its place, to insist that language has responsibilities to something outside itself, that it must be "adequate" to do its representative job. Derrida thinks that the proper moral to draw is that language is *not* a tool, but that in which we live and move. So to ask "how does language manage to do its job?" betrays psychological nominalism. If all awareness is a linguistic affair, then we are never going to be aware of a word on the one hand and a thing-denuded-of-words on the other and see that the first is adequate to the second. But the very notions of "sign" and "representation" and "language" convey the notion that we *can* do something like that. The notion of philosophy of language as the successor-subject to epistemology suggests that we have now found out how to study representation *properly,* and thus to do properly the job which Kant saw needed to be done.

Given this situation, Derrida looks about for a way to say something about language which will *not* convey the idea of "sign" or "representation" or "supplement." His solution consists in such notions as *trace,* which have, recently, become something very much like a new "subject matter" for his followers. But in developing this alternative, Derrida comes perilously close to giving us a philosophy of language, and thereby perilously close to slipping back into what he and Heidegger call "the tradition of onto-theology." That tradition is kept going by the following dialectical movement: first one notices that something all-encompassing and unconditioned is being treated as if it were just one more limited and conditioned thing. Then one explains that this thing is so distinctive that it requires an entirely different vocabulary for its description, and proceeds to create one. Finally, one's disciples become so bemused by one's new vocabulary that they think one has invented a new field of inquiry, and the whole sequence starts up once again. This happened to "God" when the Platonism of the Church Fathers lifted the divine out of space and time and insisted on His consequent ineffability. God thus became a pigeon for Doctors of the Church who had read Aristotle; they explained how the ineffable *could* be effed after all, but only *analogically*. It happened to "Mind" when Kant explained (in the "Paralogisms") that the subject was not a substance, thus permitting Fichte and the nineteenth century to explain that really there was a lot to say about the Subject, but only *transcendentally*. In both cases, somebody (Augustine, Kant) warns us against trying to describe the unconditioned, and somebody else (Aquinas, Fichte) dreams up a special technique designed especially for the purpose. If I am right in my suspicions about Derrida, we are in some danger of seeing

To defy imperial warnings is the right attitude.

this same pattern repeated by Heidegger and Derrida. We may find ourselves thinking that what Heidegger thought could not be effed really can be, if only *grammatologically*.

Heidegger spent his life explaining that all his predecessors had ignored the "ontological difference" between beings and Being, and finally wound up suggesting that one should only write the word *Being* X-ed out.[23] Heidegger kept trying to fend off disciples who said, "Now that we have the ontological difference clearly in mind, tell us something about Being." Finally he said that the attempt to say that the tradition of metaphysics, of onto-theology, had confused beings with Being was itself a misleadingly metaphysical attempt. He ends his "Time and Being" by saying:

> To think Being without beings means: to think Being without regard to metaphysics. Yet a regard for metaphysics still prevails even in the intention to overcome metaphysics. Therefore, our task is to cease all overcoming, and leave metaphysics to itself.
>
> If overcoming remains necessary, it concerns that thinking that explicitly enters Appropriation in order to say It in terms of It about It.
>
> Our task is unceasingly to overcome the obstacles that tend to render such saying inadequate.
>
> The saying of Appropriation in the form of a lecture remains itself an obstacle of this kind. The lecture has spoken merely in propositional statements.[24] *An old trick from Dialectic: to create a mental vacuum that will suck on nonsense.*

But, of course, Appropriation (*Ereignis*) looks like one more name for the goal of our inquiries. This movement of Heidegger's thought back from one ineffable to another (e.g., from "Being" to "Appropriation"), just as soon as people begin to eff the first ineffable, can be viewed as an attempt to find *something* which cannot be the subject of a commentary, something which cannot be the subject of an inquiry into, for example, "Heidegger's doctrine of *Ereignis*." Derrida thinks, or at least thought when he began *De la Grammatologie,* that the only way to solve Heidegger's problem was to get away from terminology borrowed from the visual and aural imagery of earlier authors and invent a new way which had to do *only* with writing. One can see this impulse in the following passages:

> The reassuring evidence within which Western tradition had to organize itself and must continue to live would therefore be as follows: the order of the signified is never contemporary, is at best the subtly discrepant inverse or parallel—discrepant by the time of a breath—from the order of the signifier. And the sign must be the unity of a heterogeneity, since the signified (sense or thing, noeme or reality) is not in itself a signifier, a *trace*: in any case is not constituted in its sense by its relationship with a possible trace. The formal essence of the signified is *presence*, and the privilege of its proximity to the logos as *phonè* is the privilege of presence. This is the inevitable response as soon as one asks: "what is the sign?," this is to say, when one submits the sign to the question of essence, to the "ti esti." The "formal essence" of the sign can only be determined in terms of presence. One cannot get around that response, except by challenging the very form of the question and beginning to think that the sign is that ill-named ~~thing~~, the only one, that escapes the instituting question of philosophy: "what is . . . ?"[25]

What should give one pause in this passage is the phrase "the only one." It is as if Derrida thought he had done the one thing Heiddegger failed to do—find the one word which cannot be the subject of a commentary, a Ph.D. thesis on "Derrida's doctrine of the sign," the one expression of the unconditioned which nobody will ever be able to treat as if it were the name of one more conditioned. In the following passage also one can see such a notion: "The movement of the effacement of the trace has been, from Plato to Rousseau to Hegel, imposed upon writing in the narrow sense; the necessity of such a displacement may now be apparent. Writing is one of the representatives of the trace in general, it is not the trace itself. *The trace itself does not exist.* (To exist is to be, to be an entity, a being-present, *to on*.)"[26] One can comment cynically on this passage that, if you want to know what notion takes the place of God for a writer in the onto-theological tradition, always look for the one which he says does not exist. That will be the name of the Ineffable, of what can be shown but not said, believed but not known, presupposed but not mentioned, that in which we live and move and have our being. It is the need to express the unconditioned while realizing that it is inexpressible which brings us to the point described by Wittgenstein: "Sometimes, in doing philosophy, one just wants to utter an inarticulate sound."[27] But that will not prevent somebody from writing a thesis on whatever sound one makes.

Fortunately, however, Derrida was the first to warn us against the temptation I have just described—the temptation to divinize the *trace,* and to treat writing as "one of the representatives of the trace in general, but not the trace itself" (a passage which seems to make *trace* one of the *invisibilia Dei,* which *per ea quae facta sunt cognoscuntur*[28]). In "Differance," published just after *On Grammatology,* he identifies the difference he hoped to find between "the sign" as the only thing that escapes the instituting question of philosophy and all the other failed candidates for this role with Heidegger's "ontological difference." He turns himself, in this essay, from something dangerously like a philosopher of language, into a philosopher of philosophy, where philosophy is just the self-consciousness of the play of a certain kind of writing. *Différance,*[29] unlike *trace,* has no more to do with signs than it does with things or gods or minds or any of the other things for which Kantian philosophy has sought the unconditioned conditions. *Différance* is a name of the situation which the dialectical philosopher starts from—the wish to revolt against the eternalization and cosmologization of the present vocabulary by creating a new vocabulary which will not permit the old questions to be asked. In "Differance," Derrida has a passage which forms a splendid rebuke both to Heidegger and to his previous self: When incompetents fail, they claim it can't be done.

For us, differance remains a metaphysical name: and all the names that it receives from our language are still, so far as they are names, metaphysical. . . .

"Older" than Being itself, our language has no name for such a differance. But we "already know" that if it is unnamable, this is not simply provisional; it is not because our language has still not found or received this *name,* or because we would have to look for it in another language, outside the finite system of our language. It is because there is no *name* for this—not even essence or Being—not even the name "differance," which is not a name, which is not a pure nominal unity, and continually breaks up in a chain of different substitutions. . . .

There will be no unique name, not even the name of Being. It must be conceived without *nostalgia;* that is, it must be conceived outside the myth of the purely maternal or paternal language belonging to the lost fatherland of thought. On the contrary we must *affirm* it—in the sense that Nietzsche brings affirmation into play— with a certain laughter and with a certain dance.[30]

Monkey see, monkey do.

IV

Hollow men howling.

Let me now turn to what may seem the chief question raised by what I've said so far: granted that Derrida is the latest and largest flower on the dialectical kudzu vine of which the *Phenomenology of Spirit* was the first tendril, does that not merely show the need to uproot this creeping menace? Can we not now see all the better the need to strip the suckers of this parasitic climber from the still unfinished walls and roofs of the great Kantian edifice which it covers and conceals? Granted that if all this nonsense about language not being a system of representations were true, Derrida would have drawn some interesting consequences from it, cannot we now return to sanity and say that it is false, and that philosophy would do well to return to the slow and patient work of understanding how representation is accomplished?

The dialetical response to this should, I think, be twofold. First, one can reply that the question of whether language is a system of representations is not the sort of question *anybody* (Kantian or non-Kantian) knows how to answer, and so whatever is at issue, that cannot be it. The question is not whether "language is a system of representations" is a correct representation of how things are. Second, one can reply that *of course* language can usefully, for many purposes, be viewed as a system of representations, just as physical theory can usefully be seen as an approximation to what we would see if we could get down there among the quanta, moral philosophy as an approximation to the Moral Law, and philosophy as a quest for a purer and better way to answer traditional questions. All that one has to do to make *any* of these approaches useful and productive is to take the vocabulary of the present historical period (or class or society or academy) for granted and to work within it. Once one is safely ensconced within this language-game, questions about what correctly represents what, how we know that it does, and how it manages to do so will make admirable sense and will get useful answers. There is nothing done within the Kantian tradition which the dialectical tradition cannot treat as the description of the practices of a certain historical moment—the sort of description one gets when one blinkers one's historical consciousness temporarily for the sake of getting a clear view of what is currently going on. The traditions come into real conflict *only* when the Kantian tradition cosmologizes and eternalizes its current view of physics, or right and wrong, or philosophy, or language. Thus, for example, if we freeze physics at a period of what Kuhn calls "normal science,"[31] we can describe the practice of justifying theories in terms of a determinate observation-language, a list of meaning-rules, and some canons of theory-choice. If we try to bring this heuristic apparatus to bear on all the things that might count as explaining nature in various periods and cultures, however, we either become viciously anachronistic or fall into pointless puzzlement about, e.g., "criteria for change of reference of theoretical terms." Analogously, if we take as data a range of assertions running the gamut from "the cat is on the mat" to "the particle went through the left-hand slit," we may be able to construct an account of the contribution of the parts of the expressions to the wholes, and of the conditions under which a language-user would be justified in employing them. We go wrong only when we invoke this account to be condescending about, or be baffled by, such assertions as "caloric fluid is just a lot of moving molecules," "language speaks man," or "God's essence is His existence." If we then try to be systematically invidious or reductive by talking about "literal vs. metaphorical" or "non-statement-making uses of declarative sentences," or the like, philosophy of language will begin to seem relevant to epistemology, controversial, and essential to our self-understanding. It will also seem to come into conflict with the sort of thing that Heidegger and Derrida are telling us. Worse yet, the sort of thing Heidegger and Derrida are saying may seem to be in competition with what, e.g., Frege and Carnap[32] and Putnam say.

No such competition exists. There is no topic—and in particular not that of the relation between sign and signified, language and the world—on which Derrida holds a different view than that of any of the philosophers of language I have mentioned. Nor does he have any insights which complement theirs. He is not, to repeat, a philosopher of language. The closest Derrida comes to the philosophy of language is his interest in the historical question of why a view about the relation between sign and signified, the nature of representation, could ever have been thought to have been essential to our self-understanding, the starting point of the love of wisdom, first philosophy. He is interested in the connection between the "Kantian" view of philosophy and the "Kantian" view of language—in why the latest Kantian effort to cosmologize or eternalize the present should have centered on language. Here he *does* have something to say—but it is something about philosophy, not about language.

Kantian philosophy, on Derrida's view, is a kind of writing which would like not to be a kind of writing. It is a genre which

would like to be a gesture, a clap of thunder, an epiphany. *That* is
where God and man, thought and its object, words and the world
meet, we want speechlessly to say; let no further words come between the happy pair. Kantian philosophers would like not to
write, but just to *show*. They would like the words they use to be
so simple as to be presuppositionless. Some of them like to think
that physics, too, is not a kind of writing. So they cherish the
thought that, at least in some countries, philosophy has no literary
pretensions because it has attained the secure path of a science. Just
as, on the Kantian view of physics, physics has no need of a historical self-understanding to enable it to point straight to the heart
of matter, so, on the Kantian view of philosophy, philosophers
need not be concerned with their own Kantian motives in order
to point straight to the heart of spirit—the relation of representation itself. Derrida's reply is that anybody can get along without
literary pretensions—without writing—if he is content simply to
demonstrate how something falls into place in a previously established context. In normal physics, normal philosophy, normal
moralizing or preaching, one hopes for the normal thrill of just
the right piece fitting into just the right slot, with a shuddering
resonance which makes verbal commentary superfluous and inappropriate. Writing, as Derrida says in commenting on Rousseau,
is to this kind of simple "getting it right" as masturbation is to
standard, solid, reassuring sex. This is why writers are thought effete in comparison with scientists—the "men of action" of our
latter days. The important thing to notice is that the difference between the two forms of activity is not subject matter—not, for instance, a matter of the difference between the flinty particles of
the hard sciences and the flexible behavior of the soft ones—*but
rather is determined by normality or abnormality*. Normality, in this
sense, is accepting without question the stage-setting in the language which gives demonstration (scientific or ostensive) its legitimacy. Revolutionary scientists need to write, as normal scientists
do not. Revolutionary politicians need to write, as parliamentary

politicians do not. Dialectical philosophers like Derrida need to write, as Kantian philosophers do not.

The Freudian distinction between the normal and the abnormal, drawn with the concreteness which is given by Derrida's exhibition of the sexual overtones of most metaphilosophical debate, seems to me just what is needed to be properly playful about the difference between the Kantians and the dialecticians. If one thinks of this difference as that between the partisans of Eternity and of Time, or those of Theory and of Practice, Nature and History, Permanence and Change, Intellect and Intuition, the Sciences and the Arts, it all looks too momentous, too much as if there were a serious and debatable issue around. The issue between Kantian and non-Kantian philosophy is, I think, about as serious as the issue between normal and deviant sexual practices.

It is, to be sure, an issue upon which men may well feel their identity and their integrity depend. ("Men," rather than "people," since taking how and what one does in bed as definitive of one's being seems a specifically masculine trait.) So it is not unserious in the sense of unimportant. But it is *not* a serious issue in the sense of a debatable one, on which there is much to be said on both sides. It is not an issue which we ought all to pitch in and try to resolve (in some more discursive way than massacring the opposition). Indeed, we had better not. For if the issue *were* ever resolved, there might not be any more philosophy. (Or any more interesting writing at all. Philosophy is, after all, *dominatrix disciplinarum* if no longer *regina scientiarum,*[33] nobody does any really "written" writing without timidly hoping that what he writes may have "philosophical implications.") Similarly, if the difference between normal and deviant sex ever got settled—not by massacre, but by rational demonstration of the moral superiority of one side or the other, or of their being morally equivalent—then it is not clear that sex would matter nearly as much as it does now. When Freud told us that we had sexual repression to thank for the hang-ups of the neurotics who created European culture, he meant exactly what he said. If Derrida is on the right track in his post-*Grammatology* treatment of philosophical texts, we can be a bit more specific about just how this culture was fed by sublimated sexuality. The Kantian versus non-Kantian contrast now appears as that between the man who wants to take (and see) things as they are, and thus make sure that the right pieces go in the right holes, and the man who wants to change the vocabulary presently used for isolating pieces and holes. This helps us see why the dialectic of the conditioned and the unconditioned, the effable and the ineffable, has the peculiar thrill that it does. Unspeakable possibilities, unmentionable acts are those which are spoken and mentioned in the new, revolutionary, Hegelian, abnormal vocabulary. Sartre's account of the attempt of the philosopher to become God by recreating himself as a *pour-soi-en-soi* joins up with Freud's to suggest that the Kantian tradition plays the role in recent European culture of the normal man, the man whose respect for the law is such that he would wish the natural and the moral law to be as one.

This Freudian twist also helps us see why, even given the compatibility of, e.g., everything which Derrida says and everything Quine[34] says, we cannot relax and split the difference. We cannot just let Kantians have their (self-eliminating) kind of writing and the Hegelians their (self-extending, kudzu-like) alternative kind. Being conciliatory in this way would obscure the fact that these traditions live each other's death, die each other's life—the same relation which holds between normal and abnormal sex. The dialectician will always win if he waits long enough, for the Kantian norm will in time become tedious, full of anomie and anomaly. The Kantian, on the other hand, escapes triviality, and achieves self-identity and self-conscious pride, only by the contrast between his mighty deeds and the mere words of the dialectician. *He* is no effete parasite, but one who does his share in the mighty time-binding work of building the edifice of human knowledge, human society, the City of Real Men. The non-Kantian knows that the edifice will itself one day be deconstructed, and the great deeds reinterpreted, and reinterpreted again, and again. But of course the non-Kantian *is* a parasite—flowers could not sprout from the dialectical vine unless there were an edifice into whose chinks it could insert its tendrils. No constructors, no deconstructors. No norms, no perversions. Derrida (like Heidegger) would have no writing to do unless there were a "metaphysics of presence" to overcome. Without the fun of stamping out parasites, on the other hand, no Kantian would bother to continue building. Normal philosophers need to think, for example, that in forging the powerful tools of modern analytic philosophy, they are developing weapons to ensure victory in the coming final struggle with the decadent dialecticians. Everybody needs everybody else.

Kantian and non-Kantian metaphilosophers, when this point in the development of their self-consciousness is reached, like to explain that their opponents really want to do what they themselves are doing. The Kantian thinks of the non-Kantian as somebody who would like to have a proper, disciplined, philosophical view about, e.g., words and the world, but can't quite manage to get it together into a coherent, rigorous form. The Hegelian likes to think that there is not really a contrast between the vine and the edifice it covers—rather, the so-called edifice is just accumulated dead wood, parts of the Great Vine itself, which once were fresh and flower-laden but now have come to lie in positions which suggest the outlines of a building. So the normal man sees the abnormal as not quite up to it—more to be pitied than censured. The abnormal sees the normal as someone who never had the courage to come out, and so died inside while his body lived on— more to be helped than despised. *Between the weak and the wrong*

This kind of crosstalk can continue indefinitely. Derrida's point, I take it, is that that crosstalk is all that we are going to get, and that no gimmick like "the new science of grammatology" is going to end or *aufheben*[35] it. Once one thinks of philosophy as a kind of writing, one should not be surprised at this result. For to think this is to stop trying to have a philosophy of language which is "first philosophy," a view of all possible views, an ἐπιστήμη ἐπιστήμης,[36] a bootstrap self-elevation to a point from which all past and future writing can be seen as contained within a permanent framework. Only one who *had* levitated to such a point would have the right to look down on writing, to view it as a second-best (like Plato) or as an abnormal activity to which sin has condemned him (like Rousseau), or as something which a discipline can dispense with on reaching the secure path of a science. Derrida's polemic against the notion that speech is prior to writing should be seen as a polemic against what Sartre calls "bad faith"—the attempt to divinize oneself by seeing in advance the terms in which all possible problems are to be set, and the criteria for their resolution. If the "logocentric," Platonic notion of speech as prior to writing were right, there might be a last Word. Derrida's point is that no one can make sense of the notion of a last commentary, a last discussion note, a good piece of writing which is more than the occasion for a better piece.

Integrate Hegel and ignore this dust from the 20th Century implosion.

Postmodernist Bourgeois Liberalism

(1983)

COMPLAINTS about the social irresponsibility of the intellectuals typically concern the intellectual's tendency to marginalize herself, to move out from one community by interior identification of herself with some other community—for example, another country or historical period, an invisible college, or some alienated subgroup within the larger community. Such marginalization is, however, common to intellectuals and to miners. In the early days of the United Mine Workers its members rightly put no faith in the surrounding legal and political institutions and were loyal only to each other. In this respect they resembled the literary and artistic avant-garde between the wars.

It is not clear that those who thus marginalize themselves can be criticized for social irresponsibility. One cannot be irresponsible toward a community of which one does not think of oneself as a member. Otherwise runaway slaves and tunnelers under the Berlin Wall would be irresponsible. If such criticism were to make sense there would have to be a supercommunity one *had* to identify with—humanity as such. Then one could appeal to the needs of that community when breaking with one's family or tribe or nation, and such groups could appeal to the same thing when criticizing the irresponsibility of those who break away. Some people believe that there is such a community. These are the people who think there are such things as intrinsic human dignity, intrinsic human rights, and an ahistorical distinction between the demands of morality and those of prudence. Call these people "Kantians." They are opposed by people who say that "humanity" is a biological rather than a moral notion, that there is no human dignity that is not derivative from the dignity of some specific community, and no appeal beyond the relative merits of various actual or proposed communities to impartial criteria which will help us weigh those merits. Call these people "Hegelians." Much of contemporary social philosophy in the English-speaking world is a three-cornered debate between Kantians (like Ronald Dworkin) who want to keep an ahistorical morality-prudence distinction as a buttress for the institutions and practices of the surviving democracies, those (like the post-Marxist philosophical left in Europe, Roberto Unger, and Alasdair MacIntyre) who want to abandon these institutions both because they presuppose a discredited philosophy and for other, more concrete, reasons, and those (like Michael Oakeshott and John Dewey) who want to preserve the institutions while abandoning their traditional Kantian backup.[1] These last two positions take over Hegel's criticism of Kant's conception of moral agency, while either naturalizing or junking the rest of Hegel.

If the Hegelians are right, then there are no ahistorical criteria for deciding when it is or is not a responsible act to desert a community, any more than for deciding when to change lovers or professions. The Hegelians see nothing to be responsible to except persons and actual or possible historical communities; so they view the Kantians' use of "social responsibility" as misleading. For that use suggests not the genuine contrast between, for example, Antigone's loyalties to Thebes and to her brother, or Alcibiades' loyalties to Athens and to Persia, but an illusory contrast between loyalty to a person or a historical community and to something "higher" than either. It suggests that there is a point of view that abstracts from any historical community and adjudicates the rights of communities vis-à-vis those of individuals.

Kantians tend to accuse of social irresponsibility those who doubt that there is such a point of view. So when Michael Walzer says that "A given society is just if its substantive life is lived in . . . a way faithful to the shared understandings of the members,"[2] Dworkin calls this view "relativism." "Justice," Dworkin retorts, "cannot be left to convention and anecdote."[3] Such Kantian complaints can be defended using the Hegelians' own tactics, by noting that the very American society which Walzer wishes to commend and to reform is one whose self-image is bound up with the Kantian vocabulary of "inalienable rights" and "the dignity of man." Hegelian defenders of liberal institutions are in the position of defending, on the basis of solidarity alone, a society which has traditionally asked to be based on something more than mere solidarity. Kantian criticism of the tradition that runs from Hegel through Marx and Nietzsche, a tradition which insists on thinking of morality as the interest of a historically conditioned community rather than "the common interest of humanity," often insists that such a philosophical outlook is—if one values liberal practices and institutions—irresponsible. Such criticism rests on a prediction that such practices and institutions will not survive the removal of the traditional Kantian buttresses, buttresses which include an account of "rationality" and "morality" as transcultural and ahistorical.

I shall call the Hegelian attempt to defend the institutions and practices of the rich North Atlantic democracies without using such buttresses "postmodernist bourgeois liberalism." I call it "bourgeois" to emphasize that most of the people I am talking about would have no quarrel with the Marxist claim that a lot of those institutions and practices are possible and justifiable only in certain historical, and especially economic, conditions. I want to contrast bourgeois liberalism, the attempt to fulfill the hopes of the North Atlantic bourgeoisie, with philosophical liberalism, a collection of Kantian principles thought to justify us in having those hopes. Hegelians think that these principles are useful for *summarizing* these hopes, but not for justifying them. I use "postmodernist" in a sense given to this term by Jean-François Lyotard, who says that the postmodern attitude is that of "distrust of metanarratives,"[4] narratives which describe or predict the activities of such entities as the noumenal self or the Absolute Spirit or the Proletariat. These metanarratives are stories which purport to justify loyalty to, or breaks with, certain contemporary communities, but which are neither historical narratives about what these or other communities have done in the past nor scenarios about what they might do in the future.

"Postmodernist bourgeois liberalism" sounds oxymoronic. This is partly because, for local and perhaps transitory reasons, the majority of those who think of themselves as beyond metaphysics and metanarratives also think of themselves as having opted out of the bourgeoisie. But partly it is because it is hard to disentangle bourgeois liberal institutions from the vocabulary that these institutions inherited from the Enlightenment—e.g., the eighteenth-century vocabulary of rights, which judges, and constitutional lawyers such as Dworkin, must use *ex officiis*. This vocabulary is built around a distinction between morality and prudence. In what follows I want to show how this vocabulary, and in particular this distinction, might be reinterpreted to suit the needs of us postmodernist bourgeois liberals. I hope thereby to suggest how such liberals might convince our society that loyalty to itself is morality enough, and that such loyalty no longer needs an ahistorical backup. I think they should try to clear themselves of charges of irresponsibility by convincing our society that it need be responsible only to its own traditions, and not to the moral law as well.

The crucial move in this reinterpretation is to think of the moral self, the embodiment of rationality, not as one of Rawls's original choosers,[5] somebody who can distinguish her *self* from her talents and interests and views about the good, but as a network of beliefs, desires, and emotions with nothing behind it—no substrate behind the attributes. For purposes of moral and political deliberation and conversation, a person just *is* that network, as for purposes of ballistics she is a point-mass, or for purposes of chemistry a linkage of molecules. She is a network that is constantly reweaving itself in the usual Quinean manner[6]—that is to say, not by reference to general criteria (e.g., "rules of meaning" or "moral principles") but in the hit-or-miss way in which cells readjust themselves to meet the pressures of the environment. On a Quinean view, rational behavior is just adaptive behavior of a sort which roughly parallels the behavior, in similar circumstances, of the other members of some relevant community. Irrationality, in both physics and ethics, is a matter of behavior that leads one to abandon, or be stripped of, membership in some such community. For some purposes this adaptive behavior is aptly described as "learning" or "computing" or "redistribution of electrical charges in neural tissue," and for others as "deliberation" or "choice." None of these vocabularies is privileged over against another.

What plays the role of "human dignity" on this view of the self? The answer is well expressed by Michael Sandel, who says that we cannot regard ourselves as Kantian subjects "capable of constituting meaning on our own," as Rawlsian choosers,

> . . . without great cost to those loyalties and convictions whose moral force consists partly in the fact that living by them is insepa-rable from understanding ourselves as the particular people we are—as members of this family or community or nation or people, as bearers of this history, as sons and daughters of that revolution, as citizens of this republic.[7] *The Preppy Republic*
>
> *The living dead living off the past.*

I would argue that the moral force of such loyalties and convic-tions consists *wholly* in this fact, and that nothing else has *any* moral force. There is no "ground" for such loyalties and convictions save the fact that the beliefs and desires and emotion which buttress them overlap those of lots of other members of the group with which we identify for purposes of moral or political deliberations, and the further fact that these are *distinctive* features of that group, features which it uses to construct its self-image through contrasts with other groups. This means that the naturalized Hegelian ana-logue of "intrinsic human dignity" is the comparative dignity of a group with which a person identifies herself. Nations or churches or movements are, on this view, shining historical examples not because they reflect rays emanating from a higher source, but be-cause of contrast-effects—comparisons with other, worse com-munities. Persons have dignity not as an interior luminescence, but

The Enron Generation, libs and cons both.

because they share in such contrast-effects. It is a corollary of this view that the moral justification of the institutions and practices of one's group—e.g., of the contemporary bourgeoisie—is mostly a matter of historical narratives (including scenarios about what is likely to happen in certain future contingencies), rather than of philosophical metanarratives. The principal backup for historiography is not philosophy but the arts, which serve to develop and modify a group's self-image by, for example, apotheosizing its heroes, diabolizing its enemies, mounting dialogues among its members, and refocusing its attention.

A further corollary is that the morality/prudence distinction now appears as a distinction between appeals to two parts of the network that is the self—parts separated by blurry and constantly shifting boundaries. One part consists of those beliefs and desires and emotions which overlap with those of most other members of some community with which, for purposes of deliberation, she identifies herself, and which contrast with those of most members of other communities with which hers contrasts itself. A person appeals to morality rather than prudence when she appeals to this overlapping, shared part of herself, those beliefs and desires and emotions which permit her to say "WE do not do this sort of thing." Morality is, as Wilfrid Sellars has said, a matter of "we-intentions."[8] Most moral dilemmas are thus reflections of the fact that most of us identify with a number of different communities and are equally reluctant to marginalize ourselves in relation to any of them. This diversity of identifications increases with education, just as the number of communities with which a person may identify increases with civilization.

Intra-societal tensions, of the sort which Dworkin rightly says mark our pluralistic society, are rarely resolved by appeals to general principles of the sort Dworkin thinks necessary. More frequently they are resolved by appeals to what he calls "convention and anecdote." The political discourse of the democracies, at its best, is the exchange of what Wittgenstein called "reminders for a particular purpose"—anecdotes about the past effects of various practices and predictions of what will happen if, or unless, some of these are altered. The moral deliberations of the postmodernist bourgeois liberal consists largely in this same sort of discourse, avoiding the formulation of general principles except where the situation may require this particular tactic—as when one writes a constitution, or rules for young children to memorize. It is useful to remember that this view of moral and political deliberation was a commonplace among American intellectuals in the days when Dewey—a postmodernist before his time—was the reigning American philosopher, days when "legal realism"[9] was thought of as desirable pragmatism rather than unprincipled subjectivism.

It is also useful to reflect on why this tolerance for anecdote was replaced by a reattachment to principles. Part of the explanation, I think, is that most American intellectuals in Dewey's day still thought their country was a shining historical example. They identified with it easily. The largest single reason for their loss of identification was the Vietnam War. The War caused some intellectuals to marginalize themselves entirely. Others attempted to rehabilitate Kantian notions in order to say, with Chomsky,[10] that the War not merely betrayed America's hopes and interests and self-image, but was *immoral,* one which we had had no *right* to engage in in the first place. *So was WWII. The tradition broken was what we didn't do about Napoleon*

Dewey would have thought such attempts at further self-castigation pointless. They may have served a useful cathartic purpose, but their long-run effect has been to separate the intellectuals from the moral consensus of the nation rather than to alter that consensus. Further, Dewey's naturalized Hegelianism has more overlap with the belief-systems of the communities we rich North American bourgeois need to talk with than does a naturalized Kantianism. So a reversion to the Deweyan outlook might leave us in a better position to carry on whatever conversation between nations may still be possible, as well as leaving American intellectuals in a better position to converse with their fellow citizens.

I shall end by taking up two objections to what I have been saying. The first objection is that on my view a child found

Interventionists would like us to believe that the majority has it made here.

Let her learn the lesson from her people's cowardice.

wandering in the woods, the remnant of a slaughtered nation whose temples have been razed and whose books have been burned, has no share in human dignity. This is indeed a consequence, but it does not follow that she may be treated like an animal. For it is part of the tradition of *our* community that the human stranger from whom all dignity has been stripped is to be taken in, to be reclothed with dignity. This Jewish and Christian element in our tradition is gratefully invoked by freeloading atheists like myself, who would like to let differences like that between the Kantian and the Hegelian remain "merely philosophical." The existence of human rights, in the sense in which it is at issue in this meta-ethical debate, has as much or as little relevance to our treatment of such a child as the question of the existence of God. I think both have equally little relevance.

The second objection is that what I have been calling "postmodernism" is better named "relativism," and that relativism is self-refuting. Relativism certainly is self-refuting, but there is a difference between saying that every community is as good as every other and saying that we have to work out from the networks we are, from the communities with which we presently identify. Postmodernism is no more relativistic than Hilary Putnam's suggestion that we stop trying for a "God's-eye view" and realize that "We can only hope to produce a more rational conception of rationality or a better conception of morality if we operate from within our tradition."[11] The view that every tradition is as rational or as moral as every other could be held only by a god, someone who had no need to use (but only to mention) the terms "rational" or "moral," because she had no need to inquire or deliberate. Such a being would have escaped from history and conversation into contemplation and metanarrative. To accuse postmodernism of relativism is to try to put a metanarrative in the postmodernist's mouth. One will do this if one identifies "holding a philosophical position" with having a metanarrative available. If we insist on such a definition of "philosophy," then postmodernism is postphilosophical. But it would be better to change the definition.[12]

Like a pathetic gang member, Rorty only wants to belong.

Hilary Putnam

Putnam is Pearson Professor of Mathematical Logic in the Department of Philosophy at Harvard University. His books include *Meaning and the Moral Sciences* (1978), *Reason, Truth and History* (1981), *The Many Faces of Realism* (1987), *Representation and Reality* (1988), *Realism with a Human Face* (1990), *Renewing Philosophy* (1992), *Words and Life* (1994), *Pragmatism: An Open Question* (1995), and three volumes of *Philosophical Papers: Mathematics, Matter and Method* (1975), *Mind, Language and Reality* (1975), and *Realism and Reason* (1983).

Fact and Value

in *Reason, Truth and History* (1981)

UNDERSTOOD in a sufficiently wide sense, the topic of fact and value is a topic which is of concern to everyone. In this respect, it differs sharply from many philosophical questions. Most educated men and women do not feel it obligatory to have an opinion on the question whether there really is a real world or only appears to be one, for example. Questions in philosophy of language, epistemology, and even in metaphysics may appear to be questions which, however interesting, are somewhat optional from the point of view of most people's lives. But the question of fact and value is a forced choice question. Any reflective person *has* to have a real opinion upon it (which may or may not be the same as their notional opinion). If the question of fact and value is a forced choice question for reflective people, one particular answer to that question, the answer that fact and value are totally disjoint realms, that the dichotomy "statement of fact *or* value judgment" is an absolute one, has assumed the status of a cultural institution.

By calling the dichotomy a cultural institution, I mean to suggest that it is an unfortunate fact that the received answer will go on being the received answer for quite some time regardless of what philosophers may say about it, and regardless of whether or not the received answer is *right*. Even if I could convince you that the fact–value dichotomy is without rational basis, that it is a rationally indefensible dichotomy, or even if some better philosopher than I could show this by an absolutely conclusive argument (of course there are no such in philosophy), still the next time you went out into the street, or to a cocktail party, or had a discussion at some deliberative body of which you happen to be a member, you would find someone saying to you, "Is that supposed to be a statement of fact or a value judgment?" The view that there is no fact of the matter as to whether or not things are good or bad or better or worse, etc. has, in a sense, become *institutionalized*.

The strategy of my argument is not going to be a new one. I'm going to rehabilitate a somewhat discredited move in the debate about fact and value, namely the move that consists in arguing that the distinction is at the very least hopelessly fuzzy because factual statements themselves, and the practices of scientific inquiry upon which we rely to decide what is and what is not a fact, presuppose values.

The reason this is a somewhat discredited move is that there is an obvious rejoinder to it. The rejoinder to the view that science presupposes values is a protective concession. The defenders of the fact–value dichotomy concede that science does presuppose some values, for example, science presupposes that we want *truth,* but argue that these values are not *ethical* values. I shall imagine a somewhat strawman opponent who takes the view that science presupposes *one* value, namely the value of truth itself.

As we have seen, truth is not a simple notion. The idea that truth is a passive copy of what is "really" (mind-independently, discourse-independently) "there" has collapsed under the critiques of Kant, Wittgenstein, and other philosophers even if it continues to have a deep hold on our thinking.

Some philosophers have appealed to the *equivalence principle,* that is the principle that *to say of a statement that it is true is equivalent to asserting the statement,* to argue that there are no real philosophical problems about truth. Others appeal to the work of Alfred Tarski, the logician who showed how, given a formalized language (a formal notation for expressing certain statements, employing symbolic logic), one can define "true" *for that language* in a stronger language (a so-called "metalanguage").[1]

Tarski's work was itself based on the equivalence principle: in fact his criterion for a successful definition of "true" was that it should yield all sentences of the form *"P" is true if and only if P,* e.g.

(*T*) "Snow is white" is true if and only if snow is white

as theorems of the meta-language (where *P* is a sentence of the formal notation in question).

But the equivalence principle is philosophically neutral, and so is Tarski's work. On *any* theory of truth, "Snow is white" is equivalent to " 'Snow is white' is true."

Positivist philosophers would reply that if you know (*T*) above, you *know* what " 'Snow is white' is true" means: it means *snow is white*. And if you don't understand "snow" and "white," they would add, you are in trouble indeed! But the problem is not that we don't understand "Snow is white"; the problem is that we don't understand *what it is to understand* "Snow is white." *This* is the philosophical problem. About this (*T*) says nothing.

And indeed does this not accord with our intuitions about these matters? If someone approaches us with a gleam in his eye and says, "Don't you want to know the 'Truth'?", our reaction is generally to be pretty leery of this person. And the reason that we are leery (apart from the gleam in the eye) is precisely because someone's telling us that they want us to know the truth tells us really *nothing* as long as we have no idea what standards of rational acceptability the person adheres to: what they consider a rational way to pursue an inquiry, what their standards of objectivity are, when they consider it rational to terminate an inquiry, what grounds they will regard as providing good reason for accepting one verdict or another on whatever sort of question they may be interested in. Applied to the case of science, I would say that to tell us that science "seeks to discover the truth" is really a purely formal statement. It is to say no more than that scientists don't want to assert that snow is white if snow is not white, that they don't want to assert that there are electrons flowing through a wire if electrons are not flowing through the wire, and so on. But these purely formal statements are quite empty as long as we don't have some idea what the system of criteria of rational acceptability is which distinguishes scientific ways of attempting to determine whether snow is white from other ways of attempting to determine whether snow is white, scientific ways of attempting to determine whether electrons are flowing through a wire from other ways of attempting to determine whether there are electrons flowing through a wire, and so on.

If the notion of comparing our system of beliefs with unconceptualized reality to see if they match makes no sense, then the claim that science seeks to discover the truth can mean no more than that science seeks to construct a world picture which, in the ideal limit, satisfies certain criteria of rational acceptability. That science seeks to construct a world picture which is *true* is itself a true statement, an almost empty and formal true statement; the aims of science are given material content only by the criteria of rational acceptability implicit in science. In short I am saying that the answer to the "strawman" position I considered, that the only aim of science is to discover truth (besides pointing out that science has additional aims, which is of course true), is that *truth is not the bottom line*: truth itself gets its life from our criteria of rational acceptability, and these are what we must look at if we wish to discover the values which are really implicit in science.

For the purpose of an example let me now imagine an extreme case of disagreement. The disagreement I'm going to imagine is not an ordinary scientific disagreement, although I hope our response to it will enable us to discover something about the nature of scientific values.

The hypothesis that the disagreement is going to be about, in the case I am about to describe, is just the hypothesis we discussed in Chapter 1, the hypothesis that we are all Brains in a Vat.[2] We have argued that this hypothesis cannot possibly be true; but we shall suppose that our arguments have failed to convince one side of this disagreement (which is not improbable, since philosophical arguments never convince everyone). In short, the hypothesis is that everything is a collective hallucination in the way we described before.

Of course, if it were all one collective hallucination in this way, there are many people to whom this need not make any differ-ence. It would make little or no difference to lovers, for example.[3] And I imagine it would make no difference at all to economists. (Why should an economist care if all the money in the world isn't physically real? Most of it isn't physically real on any theory!)

I want the reader to imagine that this crazy (and, I would claim, incoherent) theory, the theory that we are all brains in a vat, is held not by an isolated lunatic, but by virtually all the people in some large country, say, Australia. Imagine that in Australia only a small minority of the people believe what we do and the great majority believe that we are Brains in a Vat. Perhaps the Australians believe this because they are all disciples of a Guru, the Guru of Sydney, perhaps. Perhaps when we talk to them they say, "Oh if you could talk to the Guru of Sydney and look into his eyes and see what a good, kind, wise man he is, you too would be convinced." And if we ask, "But how does the Guru of Sydney know that we are brains in a vat, if the illusion is as perfect as you say?," they might reply, "Oh, the Guru of Sydney *just knows.*"

As I said before, this is not a scientific disagreement in the ordi-nary sense. We can imagine that the Australians are just as good as we are at anticipating experiences, at building bridges that stay up (or seem to stay up), etc. They may even be willing to accept our latest scientific discoveries, not as true, but as correct descriptions of what seems to go on in the image. We may or may not imagine that they disagree with us about some predictions concerning the very distant future (for example, they might expect that some day the automatic machinery will break down and then people will begin to have collective hallucinations of a kind which will give evidence that their view is right),[4] but whether they do make such predictions, or whether they commit themselves to no predictions different from the ones afforded by standard theory, will not affect my argument. The point is that here I've imagined a case where a vast number of people have a self-contained belief system which violently disagrees with ours. Moslems

There is no question of a disagreement in "ethical" values here; the Australians can have ethics just as similar to ours as you like. (Although an ancient Greek would have said that being *wise* is an *ethical* value; Judaism and Christianity have, in fact, narrowed the notion of the ethical because of a certain conception of Salvation.)

The first thing I want to observe about the hypothetical Australians is that their world view is *crazy*. Sometimes, to be sure, "*crazy*" is used almost as a term of approval; but I don't mean it in that sense here. I think we would regard a community of human beings who held so insane a world view with great sadness. The Australians would be regarded as crazy in the sense of having *sick* minds; and the characterization of their minds as sick is an ethical one, or verges on the ethical. But how, other than by calling them names, could one argue with the Australians? (Or try to argue with them, for I shall suppose that they are not to be convinced.)

One argument that one can immediately think of has to do with the *incoherence* of their view. I don't just mean the incoherence that we found in the view in Chapter 1. That is a *deep* incoherence, which requires a philosophical (and hence controversial) argument to expose. But the Australian's view is incoherent at a much more superficial level. One of the things that we aim at is that we should be able to give an account of how we know our statements to be true. In part we try to do this by developing a causal theory of perception, so that we can account for what we take to be the reliability of our perceptual knowledge, viewed from within our theory itself, by giving an account within the theory of how our perceptions result from the operation of transducing organs upon the external world. In part we try to do this by a theory of statistics and experimental design, so that we can show, within our theory itself, how the procedures that we take to exclude experimental error really do have a tendency in the majority of cases to exclude experimental error. In short, it is an important and extremely useful constraint on our theory itself that our developing theory of the world taken as a whole should include an account of the very activity and processes by which we are able to know that that theory is correct.

The Australians' system, however, does not have this property of coherence (at least as we judge it, and "coherence" is not something that we have an algorithm for, but something that we ultimately judge by "seat of the pants" feel). The Australians, remember, have themselves postulated an illusion so perfect that there is no rational way in which the Guru of Sydney can possibly *know* that the belief system which he has adopted and persuaded all the others to adopt is correct. Judged by our standards of coherence, *their* belief system is totally incoherent.

Other methodological virtues could be listed which their belief system lacks. Their belief system, as I described it, agrees with ours concerning what the laws of nature are *in the image;* but does it tell us whether or not the laws of nature that appear to hold in the image are the laws of nature that actually hold outside the vat? If it fails to, then it lacks a certain kind of comprehensiveness which we aim after, for it does not, even in its own terms, tell what the true and ultimate laws of nature are. Certainly it violates Ockham's razor. Again, Ockham's razor seems difficult or impossible to formalize as an algorithm, but the very fact that the Brain in a Vatist theory postulates all kinds of objects outside the vat which play no role in the explanation of our experiences, according to their theory itself, makes it clear that this is a case in which we can definitely say that the maxim . . .[5] "don't multiply entities without necessity" is violated. Let us call a theory which obeys Ockham's razor, in spirit as opposed to just in letter, *functionally simple.*

What I have been saying is that the procedures by which we decide on the acceptability of a scientific theory have to do with whether or not the scientific theory as a whole exhibits certain "virtues." I am assuming that the procedure of building up scientific theory cannot be correctly analyzed as a procedure of verifying scientific theories *sentence by sentence.* I am assuming that verification in science is a holistic matter, that it is whole theoretical systems that meet the test of experience "as a corporate body," and that the judgment of how well a whole system of sentences meets the test of experience is ultimately somewhat of an intuitive matter which could not be formalized short of formalizing total human psychology. But let us come back to our original question. What are the values implicit in science?

I've been arguing that if we take the values to which we appeal in our criticism of the Brain-in-a-Vatists, and add, of course, other values which are not at issue in this case, e.g. our desire for instrumental efficacy, which we presumably share with the Brain-in-a-Vatists, then we get a picture of science as presupposing a rich system of values. The fact is that, if we consider the ideal of rational acceptability which is revealed by looking at what theories scientists and ordinary people consider rational to accept, then we see that what we are trying to do in science is to construct a representation of the world which has the characteristics of being instrumentally efficacious, coherent, comprehensive, and functionally simple. But why?

I would answer that the reason we want this sort of representation, and not the "sick" sort of notional world possessed by the Australians, possessed by the Brain-in-a-Vatists, is that having this sort of representation system is *part of our idea of human cognitive flourishing,* and hence part of our idea of total human flourishing, of Eudaemonia.

Of course, if metaphysical realism[6] were right, and one could view the aim of science simply as trying to get our notional world to "match" the world in itself, then one could contend that we are interested in coherence, comprehensiveness, functional simplicity, and instrumental efficacy only because these are instruments to the end of bringing about this "match." But the notion of a transcendental match between our representation and the world in itself is nonsense. To deny that we want this kind of metaphysical match with a noumenal world is not to deny that we want the usual sort of empirical fit (as judged by our criteria of rational acceptability) with an *empirical* world. But the empirical world, as opposed to the

noumenal world, depends upon our criteria of rational acceptability (and, of course, vice versa). We use our criteria of rational
acceptability to build up a theoretical picture of the "empirical
world" and then as that picture develops we revise our very criteria of rational acceptability in the light of that picture and so on
and so on forever. The dependence of our methods on our picture
of the world is something I have stressed in my other books; what
I wish to stress here is the other side of the dependence, the dependence of the empirical world on our criteria of rational acceptability. What I am saying is that we must have criteria of
rational acceptability to even have an empirical world, that these
reveal part of our notion of an optimal speculative intelligence. In
short, I am saying that the "real world" depends upon our values
(and, again, vice versa).

At Least Some Values Must Be Objective

The fact that science is not "value neutral," as has been thought,
does not, to be sure, show that "ethical" values are objective, or
that ethics could be a science. In fact, there is no prospect of a
"science" of ethics, whether in the sense of a laboratory science
or of a deductive science. As Aristotle long ago remarked,[7]

> We must be content, then, in speaking of such subjects and with
> such premises to indicate the truth roughly and in outline, and in
> speaking about things which are only for the most part true, and
> with premises of the same kind, to reach conclusions which are no
> better. In the same spirit, therefore, should each kind of statement
> be received, for it is the mark of an educated man to look for pre-
> cision in each class of things just so far as the nature of the subject
> admits; it is evidently foolish to accept probable reasoning from a
> mathematician and to demand from a rhetorician scientific proofs.

But the fact that rational acceptability in the exact sciences (which
are certainly central examples of rational thinking) does depend

on such cognitive *virtues* as "coherence" and "functional simplicity" shows that at least some value terms stand for properties of the things they are applied to, and not just for feelings of the person who uses the terms.

If the terms "coherent" and "simple" do not stand for *properties* of theories, not even fuzzy or imperfectly defined ones, but only for "attitudes" that some people have towards theories, then such terms for rational acceptability as "justified," "well confirmed," "best of the available explanations" must also be entirely subjective: for rational acceptability cannot be more objective than the parameters upon which it depends. But . . . the view that rational acceptability itself is simply subjective is a self-refuting one. So we are compelled to conclude that at least *these* value-terms have some sort of objective application, some sort of objective justification conditions.

Of course, one might attempt to avoid conceding that there are objective values of any kind by choosing to deny that "coherent," "simple," "justified," and the like are *value* terms. One might hold that they stand for properties which we do value, but that there is no objective rightness about our doing so. But this line runs into difficulties at once. "Coherent" and "simple" have too many characteristics in common with the paradigmatic value words. Like "kind," "beautiful," and "good," "coherent" and "simple" are often used as terms of *praise*. Our conceptions of coherence, simplicity, and justification are just as historically conditioned as our conceptions of kindness, beauty, and goodness; these epistemic terms figure in the same sorts of perennial philosophical controversies as do the terms for ethical and aesthetic values. The conception of rationality of a John Cardinal Newman is obviously quite different from that of a Rudolf Carnap.[8] It is highly unlikely that either could have convinced the other, had they lived at the same time and been able to meet. The question: *which is the rational conception of rationality itself* is difficult in *exactly* the way that the justification of an ethical system is difficult. There is no *neutral* conception of rationality to which to appeal.

One might attempt various conventionalist moves here, e.g. saying that "justified$_{\text{Carnap}}$" is one "property" and "justified$_{\text{Newman}}$" is a different "property," and that a "subjective value judgment" is involved in the decision to mean "justified$_{\text{Carnap}}$" or "justified$_{\text{Newman}}$" by the word "justified" but that no value judgment is involved in stating the fact that a given statement S is justified$_{\text{Carnap}}$ or justified$_{\text{Newman}}$. But from whose standpoint is the word "*fact*" being used? If there is no conception of rationality one objectively *ought* to have, then the notion of a "fact" is empty. Without the cognitive values of coherence, simplicity, and instrumental efficacy we have no world and no "facts," not even facts about what is so *relative* to what, for those are in the same boat with all other facts. And these cognitive values are arbitrary considered as anything but a part of a holistic conception of human flourishing. Bereft of the old realist idea of truth as "correspondence" and of the positivist idea of justification as fixed by public "criteria," we are left with the necessity of seeing our search for better conceptions of rationality as an intentional human activity, which, like every activity that rises above habit and the mere following of inclination or obsession, is guided by our idea of the good.

Rationality in Other Areas

If the values implicit in science, especially in the exact sciences, reveal a part of our idea of the good, I think that the rest of our idea of the good can be read off from our standards of rational acceptability in yet other areas of knowledge. At this point, however, it is necessary to broaden the notion of *standards of rational acceptability*.

So far, we have only considered standards of rational acceptability in the literal sense: standards which tell us when we should and when we should not *accept* statements. But standards of rationality in the wide sense have to do not only with how we judge the truth or falsity of systems of statements, but also with how we judge their *adequacy* and *perspicuousness*. There are ways—purely cogni-

What about a self-fulfilling fact?

tive ways—in which a system of statements can fall short of giving us a satisfactory description other than by being false.

Had I chosen I could have made this point even in connection with theoretical science. I could have pointed out that the concern of exact science is not just to discover statements which are true, or even statements which are true and universal in form ("laws"), but to find statements that are true and *relevant*. And the notion of *relevance* brings with it a wide set of interests and values. But this would have only been to argue that our *knowledge* of the world presupposes values, and not to make the more radical claim that what *counts* as the real world depends upon our values.

When we come to perceptual rationality, that is to the implicit standards and skills on the basis of which we decide whether someone is able to give a true, adequate, and perspicuous account of even the simplest *perceptual* facts, then we see a large number of factors at play. Recently psychologists have stressed just how much theory construction is involved in even the simplest cases of perception. Not only is this true at the neurophysiological level, but it is also true at the cultural level. Someone from a culture which had no furniture might be able to come into a room and give some kind of description of the room, but, if he did not know what a table or a chair or a desk was, his description would hardly convey the information that a member of this culture would wish to have about the room. His description might consist only of true statements but it would not be adequate.

What this simple example shows is that the requirement that a description be adequate is implicitly a requirement that the describer have available a certain set of *concepts;* we expect rational describers with respect to certain kinds of *descripta* to be capable of acquiring certain concepts and of seeing the need to use them; the fact that the describer did not employ a certain concept may be a ground for criticizing both him and his description.

What is true at the simple level of talk about tables and chairs in a room without people in it is also true at the level of description of interpersonal relations and situations. Consider the terms we use every day in describing what other people are like, e.g. *considerate* or *inconsiderate*. *Considerate* and *inconsiderate* may of course be used to praise or blame; and one of the many distinctions which have gotten confused together under the general heading "fact–value distinction" is the distinction between using a linguistic expression to describe and using that linguistic expression to praise or blame. But this distinction is not a distinction which can be drawn on the basis of vocabulary. The judgment that someone is inconsiderate may indeed be used to blame; but it may be used simply to describe, and it may also be used to explain or to predict.

For example I may say to you, "Don't let Jones hurt your feelings. You're likely to think that he's taken a dislike to you from the way he will talk, but that's a common misimpression. No matter what he feels about you he'll likely behave in such a way that your feelings will be hurt. He's just a rather inconsiderate man, but don't think that it has anything to do with you."

In this little imaginary speech someone is using the word "inconsiderate" not for the purpose of blaming Jones, but with the intention of predicting and explaining Jones' behavior to someone else. And both the prediction and the explanation may be perfectly *correct*. And similarly, "jealous" may be a term of blame and may be used without any intention of blaming at all. (Sometimes one has a perfect right to be jealous.) ~Jealous not used neutrally~

The use of the word "inconsiderate" seems to me a very fine example of the way in which the fact–value distinction is hopelessly fuzzy in the real world and in the real language. The importance of terms like "inconsiderate," "pert," "stubborn," "pesky," etc., in actual moral evaluation, has been emphasized by Iris Murdoch in *The Sovereignty of "Good."* [9] Even though each of the statements "John is a very inconsiderate man," "John thinks about nobody but himself," "John would do practically anything for money" may be simply a true description in the most positivistic sense (and notice "John would do practically anything for money" does not contain any value term), if one has asserted the conjunction of these three statements it is hardly necessary to add "John is not a very good person." When we think of facts and values as independent we typically think of "facts" as stated in some physicalistic or bureaucratic jargon, and the "values" as being stated in the most abstract value terms, e.g. "good," "bad." The independence of value from fact is harder to maintain when the facts themselves are of the order of "inconsiderate," "thinks only about himself," "would do anything for money."

Just as we criticize a describer who does not employ the concepts of *table* and *chair* when their use is called for, so also, someone who fails to remark that someone is *considerate* or *spontaneous* may open himself to the criticism that he is imperceptive or superficial; his description is not an adequate one.

The fact that something works is given a value enough to obscure the questions of cost, necessity, alternatives, and consequences.

The Super-Benthamites

Let me go back and modify my previous example of the "Brain-in-a-Vatists." This time let us imagine that the continent of Australia is peopled by a culture which agrees with us on history, geography, and exact science, but which disagrees with us in ethics. I don't want to take the usual case of super-Nazis or something of that kind, but I want to take rather the more interesting case of super-Benthamites. Let us imagine that the continent of Australia is peopled with people who have some elaborate scientific measure of what they take to be "hedonic tone," and who believe that one should always act so as to maximize hedonic tone (taking that to mean the greatest hedonic tone of the greatest number). I will assume that the super-Benthamites are extremely sophisticated, aware of all the difficulties of predicting the future and exactly estimating the consequences of actions and so forth. I will also assume that they are extremely ruthless, and that while they would not cause someone suffering for the sake of the greatest happiness of the greatest number if there were reasonable doubt that *in fact* the consequence of their action would *be* to bring about the greatest happiness of the greatest number, that in cases where one knows with certainty what the consequences of the actions would be, they would be willing to perform the most horrible actions—willing to torture small children or to condemn people for crimes which they did not commit—if the result of these actions would be to increase the general satisfaction level in the long run (after due allowance for the suffering of the innocent victim in each case) by any positive ϵ, however small.

I imagine that we would not feel very happy about this sort of super-Benthamite morality. Most of us would condemn the super-Benthamites as having a sick system of values, as being bureaucratic, as being ruthless, etc. They are the "new man" in his most horrible manifestation. And they would return our invective by saying that we are soft-headed, superstitious, prisoners of irrational tradition, etc.

The disagreement between us and the super-Benthamites is just the sort of disagreement that is ordinarily imagined in order to make the point that two groups of people might agree on all the facts and still disagree about the "values." But let us look at the case more closely. Every super-Benthamite is familiar with the fact that sometimes the greatest satisfaction of the greatest number (measured in "utils") requires one to tell a lie. And it is not counted as being "dishonest" in the pejorative sense to tell lies out of the motive of maximizing the general pleasure level. So after a while the use of the description "honest" among the super-Benthamites would be extremely different from the use of that same descriptive term among us. And the same will go for "considerate," "good citizen," etc. The vocabulary available to the super-Benthamites for the description of people-to-people situations will be quite different from the vocabulary available to us. Not only will they lack, or have altered beyond recognition, many of our descriptive resources, but they will very likely invent new jargon of their own (for example, exact terms for describing hedonic tones) that are unavailable to us. The texture of the human world will begin to change. In the course of time the super-Benthamites and we will end up living in different human worlds.

In short, it will not be the case that we and the super-Benthamites "agree on the facts and disagree about values." In the case of almost all interpersonal situations, the description we give of the facts will be quite different from the description they give of the facts. Even if none of the statements they make about the situation are *false,* their description will not be one that we will count as adequate and perspicuous; and the description we give will not be one that they could count as adequate and perspicuous. In short, even if we put aside our "disagreement about the values," we could not regard their total representation of the human world as fully rationally acceptable. And just as the Brain-in-a-Vatists' inability to get *the way the world is* right is a direct result of their sick standards of rationality—their sick standards of theoretical rationality—so the inability of the super-Benthamites to get the way the human world is right is a direct result of *their* sick conception of human flourishing.

Subjectivism About Goodness

It has often been claimed that the step from "John is considerate, truthful, kind, courageous, responsible, etc." to "John is morally good" involves at least one unproved (and unprovable) "premiss," namely, "Consideration is morally good." And it has been held that the need for moral "premisses" before one can draw moral conclusions from "factual" statements shows that ethical statements are not rationally justifiable.

This picture of ethics as a sort of inverted pyramid, with the tip (which is itself unsupported) consisting of "ethical axioms" which support our whole body of moral belief and thinking, is naive. No one has ever succeeded in imposing an axiomatic structure upon ethics (as Aristotle remarked in the passage I cited a few pages ago, such moral maxims as we are able to list are almost always true only "for the most part"). And the same trick, of picturing a body of thinking one wishes to cast into doubt as resting upon unsupportable "axioms" is one which sceptics have employed in every

Perfectionism leads to paralysis.

area. Sceptics who doubt the existence of material objects, for example, argue that the principle that "if our sensations occur as they would if there were a material world, then there probably is a material world" is a *rationally unsupportable premiss* which we tacitly invoke whenever we claim to "observe" a material object, or try otherwise to justify belief in their existence. In fact, ethics and mathematics and talk of material objects presuppose concepts not "axioms." Concepts are used in observation and generalization, and are themselves made legitimate by the success we have in using them to describe and generalize.

A more sophisticated attack on the idea of ethical objectivity concedes that our ethical beliefs rest on observations of specific cases, "intuitions," general maxims, etc., and not on some collection of arbitrary "ethical axioms," but makes the charge that ethical "observation" itself is infected with an incurable disease: *projection*.

According to this account, humans are naturally, if intermittently, compassionate. So when we see something terrible happening, as it might be, someone torturing a small child just for his own sadistic pleasure, we are (sometimes) horrified. But the psychological mechanism of "projection" leads us to experience the feeling quality as a quality of the deed itself: we say "the act was horrible" when we should really say "my reaction was to be horrified." Thus we build up a body of what we take to be "ethical observations," which are really just observations of our own subjective ethical *feelings*.

This story has more sophisticated forms (like any other). Hume postulated a human tendency he called "sympathy," which has gradually become wider under the influence of culture. Contemporary sociobiologists postulate an instinct they call "altruism," and speak of "altruistic genes." But the key idea remains the same: there are ethical *feelings*, but no objective value properties.

We have already seen that this is not right: there are at least *some* objective values, for example, *justification*. It could still be claimed that the *ethical* values are subjective while the *cognitive* values are objective; but the argument that there can't be any objective values at all has been refuted.

In order to show what is wrong with arguments for moral subjectivism, I must now recall the arguments that were used against metaphysical realism in Chapter 2. This may seem queer: isn't subjectivism the *opposite* of metaphysical realism? If one thinks so, then it will seem that any argument against metaphysical realism must *support* subjectivism; the strategy I am going to follow of using the *same* argument against both metaphysical realism and subjectivism will seem an impossible one.

But in fact, metaphysical realism and subjectivism are not simple "opposites." Today we tend to be too realistic about physics and too subjectivistic about ethics, and these are connected tendencies. It is *because* we are too realistic about physics, because we see physics (or some hypothetical future physics) as the One True Theory, and not simply as a rationally acceptable description suited for certain problems and purposes, that we tend to be subjectivistic about descriptions we cannot "reduce" to physics. Becoming less realistic about physics and becoming less subjectivistic about ethics are likewise connected.

The argument at the end of Chapter 2 was directed against the "physicalistic" or naturalistic version of metaphysical realism. To recall it, let us suppose that the standard interpretation I (Under which "cat" refers to cats, "cherry" to cherries, etc.) is either co-extensive with or identical with physicalistic relation R. So R holds between tokens of "cat" (or physical events of someone's using those tokens suitably) and cats, etc. The non-standard interpretation J we described will then also be co-extensive with a certain relation R', definable in terms of R and the possible worlds and permutations used in constructing J. . . . So R' holds between tokens of "cat" (or the physical events of someone's using those tokens in the standard way) and *cherries,* etc. R and R' are *both* "correspondences": The same sentences are "true" under both correspondences. The actions called for by the R'-truth of a sentence (i.e. the actions which will "succeed," from the agent's point of view) are the same as the actions called for when the sentence is R-true. If R is "identical with reference"; if R, R', and all the other relations which assign extensions to our words in ways which satisfy our operational and theoretical constraints are not equally correct; if R, R' and the others are not equally correct because one of them—R—just *is* reference; then that fact itself is an *inexplicable* fact from a physicalist perspective.

This argument is not just an argument against (the physicalist version of) metaphysical realism, but an argument against *reductionism*. If there is nothing in the physicalist world-picture that corresponds to the obvious fact that "cat" refers to cats and not to cherries, then that is a decisive reason for rejecting the demand that all the notions we use must be reduced to physical terms. For reference and truth are notions we cannot consistently give up. If I think "a cat is on a mat," then I am committed to believing that "cat" refers to something (though not to a metaphysical realist account of "reference") and to believing that "a cat is on a mat" is true (though not to a metaphysical realist account of truth).

Having reviewed the argument of Chapter 2, let us now see how it bears on the arguments for moral subjectivism. The "projection" theory gave one account of moral experience: moral experience is, so to speak, mislocated subjective feeling. Contrast the "projection" theory with the following account: "all humans have, to some extent, a sense of justice and some idea of the good. So we respond (intermittently) to such appeals as 'be kind to the stranger among you, *because you know what it was like to be a stranger in Egypt.*' Our sympathy becomes broader, partly because we are persuaded that it *ought* to be broader; we feel that an atrocity is wrong (sometimes) even when we don't easily or spontaneously find the victim a person we can sympathize with. We come to see similarities between injuries to others and injuries to ourselves, and between benefits to others and benefits to ourselves. We invent moral words for morally relevant features of situations, and we gradually begin to make explicit moral generalizations, which lead to still further refinement of our moral notions, and so on."

This account is, on the face of it, simpler and more sophisticated than the "projection" theory. (For one thing, it acknowledges the role of *argument* in shaping moral attitudes.) Nevertheless, many intelligent people feel that today we must reject talk of a "sense of justice" and talk of "having an idea of the good" (where this is not taken in a purely subjective sense), as "unscientific." So moral knowledge becomes problematical; perhaps downright impossible. *Slick, simplistic nitpicking is not intelligence*

But what does "unscientific" mean here? A belief that there is such a thing as justice is not a belief in *ghosts,* nor is a "sense of justice" a para-normal sense which enables us to perceive such ghosts. Justice is not something anyone proposes to *add to* the list of objects recognized by physics as eighteenth-century chemists proposed to add "phlogiston" to the list of objects recognized by chemical theory. Ethics does not *conflict with* physics, as the term "unscientific" suggests; it is simply that "just" and "good" and "sense of justice" are concepts in a discourse which is not *reducible to* physical discourse. As we have just seen, *other* kinds of essential discourse are not reducible to physical discourse and are not for that reason illegitimate. Talk of "justice," like talk of "reference," can be *non*-scientific without being *un*scientific.

As a way of seeing what is going on, let us consider any basic principle of logic or mathematics, say, the principle that the series of whole numbers can always be continued ("every number has a successor"), or the principle that a non-empty set of whole numbers must contain a smallest member. Suppose someone put forward the following view: "These principles are true for the numbers and sets of numbers we deal with in practice. So they come to seem necessary. By the mechanism called 'projection,' we attach this *feeling of necessity* to the principles themselves; we feel the *statements* have a mysterious 'necessity.' But in reality this has no justification. For all we know, these principles may not even be true."

Virtually no one would agree with this. Virtually every mathematician would say, instead, something like this: "Most humans have mathematical intuition to some extent. So we intuitively 'see,' or can be brought by examples (or by skillful questioning, like the slave-boy in Plato's dialogue) to 'see' that the principles are necessarily true."

Kurt Gödel[10] believed that "mathematical intuition" was analogous to *perception*: mathematical objects (which he called "concepts") are *out there,* and our intuition enables us to intellectually perceive these Platonic entities; but few mathematicians would commit themselves to such a Platonic metaphysics. Gödel's comparison of mathematical intuition to perception reveals an oversimple idea of perception. Vision does not really give us direct access to a ready made world, but gives us a description of objects which are partly structured and constituted by vision itself. If we take the physicist's rainbow to be the rainbow "in itself," then the rainbow "in itself" has no *bands* (a spectroscopic analysis yields a smooth distribution of frequencies); the red, orange, yellow, green, blue, and violet bands are a feature of the *perceptual* rainbow, not the physicist's rainbow. The perceptual rainbow depends on the nature of our perceptual apparatus itself, on our visual "world making" as Nelson Goodman has termed it.[11] (The physicist's "objects" also depend on our worldmaking, as is shown by the plethora of radically different versions physics constructs of the "same" objects.) Yet we do not consider vision as *defective* because it sees bands in the rainbow; someone who *couldn't* see them would have defective vision. Vision is certified as good by its ability to deliver a description which fits the objects *for us,* not metaphysical things-in-themselves. Vision is good when it enables us to see the world "as it is"—that is, the human, functional world which is partly created by vision itself.

A proposed new axiom of set theory, such as the "Axiom of choice," may be adopted partly because of its agreement with the "intuition" of expert mathematicians, and partly for its yield. If the axiom of choice did not deliver results which count as successful mathematics the fact that some people find it "intuitive" would have little interest. Mathematical intuition itself is demonstrated or tested by grasping mathematical principles and by following proofs. In short, mathematical intuition is good when it enables us to see mathematical facts "as they are"—that is, as they are in the mathematical world which is constructed by human mathematical practice (including the application of mathematics to other subject matters).

A physiological or psychological description of vision cannot tell us whether seeing bands in the rainbow counts as seeing "correctly" or not. Even less could a physiological or psychological description of the brain-process which goes on when one "grasps" the Principle of Mathematical Induction tell us whether that principle is *true* or not. Once one sees this, it should be no surprise that a description of the brain process which goes on when one "sees" that an action is unjust cannot tell us whether the action really *is* unjust.

Talk of moral "perception," like talk of mathematical intuition, or of reference and understanding, is not reducible to the language or the world-picture of physics. That does not mean physics is "incomplete." Physics can be "complete"—that is, complete for physical purposes. The completeness physics *lacks* is a completeness all particular theories, pictures, and discourses lack. For no theory or picture is complete for *all* purposes. If the irreducibility of ethics to physics shows that values are projections, then *colors* are also projections. So are the natural numbers. So, for that matter, is "the physical world." But being a projection in *this* sense is not the same thing as being *subjective*.[12]

Authoritarianism and Pluralism

I have been arguing that it is necessary to have standards of rational acceptability in order to have a world at all; either a world of "empirical facts" or a world of "value facts" (a world in which there is beauty and tragedy). It should go without saying that it is not possible both to have standards of rational acceptability and not to accept them, or to stand at arm's length from them. (The kind of scepticism which consists in refusing to have any standards of rational acceptability commits one to not having any concepts at all. As Sextus Empiricus recognized, that kind of empiricism ultimately is unexpressible in language.) We have just as much right to regard some "evaluational" casts of mind as sick (and we all do) as we do to regard some "cognitional" casts of mind as sick. But to say this is not to reject pluralism or to commit oneself to authoritarianism.

Even in science, holding that science is an objective enterprise (by a standard of "objectivity" which is admittedly anthropocentric, but, as David Wiggins once remarked, the only standard of objectivity available to us) is not to hold that every scientific question has a determinate answer. Some scientific questions may have *objectively indeterminate* answers, i.e. there may be no convergence with respect to an answer to them even in the ideal limit of scientific inquiry; and some scientific questions may have determinate but context-relative answers (e.g. "What was the cause of John's heart attack?" may have different correct answers depending on who asks the question and why). And, similarly, holding that ethical inquiry is objective in the sense that some "value judgments" are definitely true and some are definitely false, and more generally that some value positions (and some "ideologies") are definitely wrong, and some are definitely inferior to some others, is not the same thing as holding the silly position that there are no indeterminate cases at all. (One especially important kind of indeterminate case has been emphasized by Bernard Williams.[13] This is the case where all the alternatives are so horrible that there is no one of the alternatives that would clearly be chosen by an ideally rational and wise person.) And that there are context relativities in ethics goes without saying.

If today we differ with Aristotle it is in being much more pluralistic than Aristotle was. Aristotle recognized that different ideas of Eudaemonia, different conceptions of human flourishing, might be appropriate for different individuals on account of the difference in their constitution. But he seemed to think that ideally there was some sort of constitution that every one ought to have; that in an ideal world (overlooking the mundane question of who would grow the crops and who would bake the bread) everyone would be a philosopher. We agree with Aristotle that different ideas of human flourishing are appropriate for individuals with different constitutions, but we go further and believe that even in the ideal world there would be different constitutions, that diversity is part of the ideal. And we see some degree of tragic tension between ideals, that the fulfillment of some ideals always excludes the fulfillment of some others. But to emphasize the point again, belief in a pluralistic ideal is not the same thing as belief that every ideal of human flourishing is as good as every other. We reject ideals of human flourishing as wrong, as infantile, as sick, as one-sided.

Nor should commitment to ethical objectivity be confused with what is a very different matter, commitment to ethical or moral authoritarianism. It is perhaps this confusion that has led one outstanding philosopher[14] to espouse what he himself regards as a limited version of "non-cognitivism," and to say "Concerning what 'living most fully' is for each man, the final authority must be the man himself." (Notice the ambiguity in "the final authority": does he mean the final *political* authority? The final *epistemological* authority? Or does he mean that *there is no fact of the matter,* as his use of the term "non-cognitivism" suggests?) Respect for persons as autonomous moral agents requires that we accord them the right to choose a moral standpoint for themselves, however repulsive we may find their choice. According to the philosophy of political liberalism, it also requires that we also insist the government not preempt individual moral choices by setting up a state religion or a state morality. But diehard opposition to all forms of political and moral authoritarianism should not commit one to moral

relativism or moral scepticism. The reason that it is wrong for the
government to dictate a morality to the individual citizen is not
that there is no fact of the matter about what forms of life are fulfilling and what forms of life are not fulfilling, or morally wrong
in some other way. (If there were no such thing as moral wrong,
then it would not be *wrong* for the government to impose moral
choices.) The fact that many people fear that if they concede any
sort of moral objectivity out loud then they will find some government shoving *its* notion of moral objectivity down their throats
is without question one of the reasons why so many people subscribe to a moral subjectivism to which they give no real assent.

Steven Knapp
and Walter Benn Michaels

Knapp is Dean of the Humanities at Johns Hopkins University and the author of *Personification and the Sublime: Milton to Coleridge* (1985) and *Literary Interest: The Limits of Anti-Formalism* (1993). Michaels is Professor of English at Johns Hopkins University and the author of *The Gold Standard and the Logic of Naturalism* (1987) and *Our America* (1995). Both were members of the English Department at the University of California at Berkeley when "Against Theory" was first published.

from Against Theory

(1982)

BY "THEORY" we mean a special project in literary criticism: the attempt to govern interpretations of particular texts by appealing to an account of interpretation in general. The term is sometimes applied to literary subjects with no direct bearing on the interpretation of individual works, such as narratology, stylistics, and prosody. Despite their generality, however, these subjects seem to us essentially empirical, and our argument against theory will not apply to them.

Contemporary theory has taken two forms. Some theorists have sought to ground the reading of literary texts in methods designed to guarantee the objectivity and validity of interpretations. Others, impressed by the inability of such procedures to produce agreement among interpreters, have translated that failure into an alternative mode of theory that denies the possibility of correct interpretation. Our aim here is not to choose between these two alternatives but rather to show that both rest on a single mistake, a mistake that is central to the notion of theory per se. The object of our critique is not a particular way of doing theory but the idea of doing theory at all.

Theory attempts to solve—or to celebrate the impossibility of solving—a set of familiar problems: the function of authorial intention, the status of literary language, the role of interpretive assumptions, and so on. We will not attempt to solve these problems, nor will we be concerned with tracing their history or surveying the range of arguments they have stimulated. In our view, the mistake on which all critical theory rests has been to imagine that these problems are real. In fact, we will claim such problems only seem real—and theory itself only seems possible or relevant—when theorists fail to recognize the fundamental inseparability of the elements involved.

The clearest example of the tendency to generate theoretical problems by splitting apart terms that are in fact inseparable is the persistent debate over the relation between authorial intention and the meaning of texts. Some theorists have claimed that valid interpretations can only be obtained through an appeal to authorial intentions. This assumption is shared by theorists who, denying the possibility of recovering authorial intentions, also deny the possibility of valid interpretations. But once it is seen that the meaning of a text is simply identical to the author's intended meaning, the project of *grounding* meaning in intention becomes incoherent. Since the project itself is incoherent, it can neither succeed nor fail; hence both theoretical attitudes toward intention are irrelevant. The mistake made by theorists has been to imagine the possibility or desirability of moving from one term (the author's intended meaning) to a second term (the text's meaning), when actually the two terms are the same. One can neither succeed nor fail in deriving one term from the other, since to have one is already to have them both. *The text's intention*

In the following [section] we will try to show in detail how theoretical accounts of intention always go wrong. In the [final] section we will undertake a similar analysis of an influential account of the role interpretive assumptions or beliefs play in the practice of literary criticism. The issues of belief and intention are, we think, central to the theoretical enterprise; our discussion of them is thus directed not only against specific theoretical arguments but against theory in general. Our examples are meant to represent the central mechanism of all theoretical arguments, and our treatment of them is meant to indicate that all such arguments will fail and fail in the same way. If we are right, then the whole enterprise of critical theory is misguided and should be abandoned.

The fact that what a text means is what its author intends is clearly stated by E. D. Hirsch when he writes that the meaning of a text "is, and can be, nothing other than the author's meaning" and "is determined once and for all by the character of the speaker's intention."[1] Having defined meaning as the author's intended meaning, Hirsch goes on to argue that all literary interpretation "must stress a reconstruction of the author's aims and attitudes in order to evolve guides and norms for construing the meaning of his text." Although these guides and norms cannot guarantee the correctness of any particular reading—nothing can—they nevertheless constitute, he claims, a "fundamentally sound" and "objective" method of interpretation (pp. 224, 240).

What seems odd about Hirsch's formulation is the transition from definition to method. He begins by defining textual meaning as the author's intended meaning and then suggests that the best way to find textual meaning is to look for authorial intention. But if meaning and intended meaning are already the same, it's hard to see how looking for one provides an objective method— or any sort of method—for looking for the other; looking for one just *is* looking for the other. The recognition that what a text means and what its author intends it to mean are identical should entail the further recognition that any appeal from one to the other is useless. And yet, as we have already begun to see, Hirsch thinks the opposite; he believes that identifying meaning with the expression of intention has the supreme theoretical usefulness of providing an objective method of choosing among alternative interpretations.

Hirsch, however, has failed to understand the force of his own formulation. In one moment he identifies meaning and intended meaning; in the next moment he splits them apart. This mistake is clearly visible in his polemic against formalist critics who deny the importance of intention altogether. His argument against these critics ends up invoking their account of meaning at the expense of his own. Formalists, in Hirsch's summary, conceive the text as a "'piece of language,'" a "public object whose character is defined by public norms." The problem with this account, according to Hirsch, is that "no mere sequence of words can represent an actual verbal meaning with reference to public norms alone. Referred to these alone, the text's meaning remains indeterminate." Hirsch's example, "My car ran out of gas," is, as he notes, susceptible to an indeterminate range of interpretations. There are no public norms which will help us decide whether the sentence means that my automobile lacks fuel or "my Pullman dash[ed] from a cloud of Argon." Only by assigning a particular intention to the words "My car ran out of gas" does one arrive at a determinate interpretation. Or, as Hirsch himself puts it, "The array of possibilities only begins to become a more selective system of *probabilities* when, instead of confronting merely a word sequence, we also posit a speaker who very likely means something" (p. 225).[2]

This argument seems consistent with Hirsch's equation of meaning and intended meaning, until one realizes that Hirsch is imagining a moment of interpretation before intention is present. This is the moment at which the text's meaning "remains indeterminate," before such indeterminacy is cleared up by the *addition* of authorial intention. But if meaning and intention really are inseparable, then it makes no sense to think of intention as an ingredient that needs to be added; it must be present from the start. The issue of determinacy or indeterminacy is irrelevant. Hirsch thinks it's relevant because he thinks, correctly, that the movement from indeterminacy to determinacy involves the addition of information, but he also thinks, incorrectly, that adding information amounts to adding intention. Since intention is already present, the only thing added, in the movement from indeterminacy to determinacy, is information *about* the intention, not the intention itself. For a sentence like "My car ran out of gas" even to be recognizable as a sentence, we must already have posited a speaker and hence an intention. Pinning down an interpretation of the sentence will not involve adding a speaker but deciding among a range of possible speakers. Knowing that the speaker inhabits a planet with an atmosphere of inert gases and on which the primary means of transportation is railroad will give one interpretation; knowing that the speaker is an earthling who owns a Ford will give another. But even if we have none of this information, as soon as we attempt to interpret at all we are already committed to a characterization of the speaker as a speaker of language. We know, in other words, that the speaker intends to speak; otherwise we wouldn't be interpreting. In this latter case, we have less information about the speaker than in the other two (where we at least knew the speaker's planetary origin), but the relative lack of information has nothing to do with the presence or absence of intention.

This mistake no doubt accounts for Hirsch's peculiar habit of calling the proper object of interpretation the "author's meaning" and, in later writings, distinguishing between it and the "reader's meaning."[3] The choice between these two kinds of meaning becomes, for Hirsch, an ethical imperative as well as an "operational" necessity. But if all meaning is always the author's meaning, then the alternative is an empty one and there is no choice, ethical or operational, to be made. Since theory is designed to help us make such choices, all theoretical arguments on the issue of authorial intention must at some point accept the premises of anti-intentionalist accounts of meaning. In debates about intention, the moment of imagining intentionless meaning constitutes the theoretical moment itself. From the standpoint of an argument against critical theory, then, the only important question about intention is whether there can in fact be intentionless meanings. If our argument against theory is to succeed, the answer to this question must be no.

The claim that all meanings are intentional is not, of course, an unfamiliar one in contemporary philosophy of language. John Searle, for example, asserts that "there is no getting away from intentionality," and he and others have advanced arguments to support this claim.[4] Our purpose here is not to add another such argument but to show how radically counterintuitive the alternative would be. We can begin to get a sense of this simply by noticing how difficult it is to imagine a case of intentionless meaning. Suppose that you're walking along a beach and you come upon a curious sequence of squiggles in the sand. You step back a few paces and notice that they spell out the following words:

> A slumber did my spirit seal;
> I had no human fears:
> She seemed a thing that could not feel
> The touch of earthly years.[5]

This would seem to be a good case of intentionless meaning: you recognize the writing as writing, you understand what the words mean, you may even identify them as constituting a rhymed poetic stanza—and all this without knowing anything about the author and indeed without needing to connect the words to any notion of an author at all. You can do all these things without thinking of anyone's intention. But now suppose that, as you stand gazing at this pattern in the sand, a wave washes up and recedes, leaving in its wake (written below what you now realize was only the first stanza) the following words:

> No motion has she now, no force;
> She neither hears nor sees;
> Rolled round in earth's diurnal course,
> With rocks, and stones, and trees.

One might ask whether the question of intention still seems as irrelevant as it did seconds before. You will now, we suspect, feel compelled to explain what you have just seen. Are these marks mere accidents, produced by the mechanical operation of the waves on the sand (through some subtle and unprecedented process of erosion, percolation, etc.)? Or is the sea alive and striving to express its pantheistic faith? Or has Wordsworth, since his death, become a sort of genius of the shore who inhabits the waves and periodically inscribes on the sand his elegiac sentiments? You might go on extending the list of explanations indefinitely, but you would find, we think, that all the explanations fall into two categories. You will either be ascribing these marks to some agent capable of intentions (the living sea, the haunting Wordsworth, etc.), or you will count them as nonintentional effects of mechanical processes (erosion, percolation, etc.). But in the second case—where the marks now seem to be accidents—will they still seem to be words?

Clearly not. They will merely seem to *resemble* words. You will be amazed, perhaps, that such an astonishing coincidence could occur. Of course, you would have been no less amazed had you decided that the sea or the ghost of Wordsworth was responsible. But it's essential to recognize that in the two cases your amazement would have two entirely different sources. In one case, you would be amazed by the identity of the author—who would have thought that the sea can write poetry? In the other case, however, in which you accept the hypothesis of natural accident, you're amazed to discover that what you thought was poetry turns out not to be poetry at all. It isn't poetry because it isn't language; that's what it means to call it an accident. As long as you thought the marks were poetry, you were assuming their intentional character. You had no idea who the author was, and this may have tricked you into thinking that positing an author was irrelevant to your ability to read the stanza. But in fact you had, without realizing it, already posited an author. It was only with the mysterious arrival of the second stanza that your tacit assumption (e.g., someone writing with a stick) was challenged and you realized that you had made one. Only now, when positing an author seems impossible, do you genuinely imagine the marks as authorless. But to deprive them of an author is to convert them into accidental likenesses of language. They are not, after all, an example of intentionless meaning; as soon as they become intentionless they become meaningless as well.

The arrival of the second stanza made clear that what had seemed to be an example of intentionless language was either not intentionless or not language. The question was whether the marks counted as language; what determined the answer was a de-

Against Theory   *Dark clouds mean rain. No*   371
intention, no author. What if an author is incom-
petent? Treat the text as you would a salesman's line.

cision as to whether or not they were the product of an intentional agent. If our example has seemed farfetched, it is only because there is seldom occasion in our culture to wonder whether the *sea* is an intentional agent. But there *are* cases where the question of intentional agency might be an important and difficult one. Can computers speak? Arguments over this question reproduce exactly the terms of our example. Since computers are machines, the issue of whether they can speak seems to hinge on the possibility of intentionless language. But our example shows that there is no such thing as intentionless language; the only real issue is whether computers are capable of intentions. However this issue may be decided—and our example offers no help in deciding it— the decision will not rest on a theory of meaning but on a judgment as to whether computers can be intentional agents. This is not to deny that a great deal—morally, legally, and politically— might depend on such judgments. But no degree of practical importance will give these judgments theoretical force.

The difference between theoretical principle and practical or empirical judgments can be clarified by one last glance at the case of the wave poem. Suppose, having seen the second stanza wash up on the beach, you have decided that the "poem" is really an accidental effect of erosion, percolation, and so on and therefore not language at all. What would it now take to change your mind? No theoretical argument will make a difference. But suppose you notice, rising out of the sea some distance from the shore, a small submarine, out of which clamber a half dozen figures in white lab coats. One of them trains his binoculars on the beach and shouts triumphantly, "It worked! It worked! Let's go down and try it again." Presumably, you will now once again change your mind, not because you have a new account of language, meaning, or intention but because you now have new evidence of an author. The question of authorship is and always was an empirical question; it has now received a new empirical answer. The theoretical temptation is to imagine that such empirical questions must, or should, have theoretical answers.

Even a philosopher as committed to the intentional status of language as Searle succumbs to this temptation to think that intention is a theoretical issue. After insisting, in the passage cited earlier, on the inescapability of intention, he goes on to say that "in serious literal speech the sentences are precisely the realizations of the intentions" and that "there need be no *gulf* at all between the illocutionary intention and its expression."[6] The point, however, is not that there *need* be no gulf between intention and the meaning of its expression but that there *can* be no gulf. Not only in serious literal speech but in *all* speech what is intended and what is meant are identical. In separating the two Searle imagines the possibility of expression without intention and so, like Hirsch, misses the point of his own claim that when it comes to language "there is no getting away from intentionality." Missing this point, and hence imagining the possibility of two different *kinds* of meaning, is more than a theoretical mistake; it is the sort of mistake that makes theory possible. It makes theory possible because it creates the illusion of a choice between alternative methods of interpreting.[7]

To be a theorist is only to think that there is such a choice. In this respect intentionalists and anti-intentionalists are the same. They are also the same in another respect: neither can really escape intention. But this doesn't mean the intentionalists win, since what intentionalists want is a guide to valid interpretation; what they get, however, is simply a description of what everyone always does. In practical terms, then, the stakes in the battle over intention are extremely low—in fact, they don't exist. Hence it doesn't matter who wins. In theoretical terms, however, the stakes are extremely high, and it still doesn't matter who wins. The stakes are high because they amount to the existence of theory itself; it doesn't matter who wins because as long as one thinks that a position on intention (either for or against) makes a difference in achieving valid interpretations, the ideal of theory itself is saved. Theory wins. But as soon as we recognize that there are no theoretical choices to be made, then the point of theory vanishes. Theory loses. . . .[8]

The wave poem, as encountered by a theorist, presents a choice between two kinds of meaning or, what comes to the same thing, two kinds of language. The issue in both cases is the presence or absence of intention; the positive theorist adds intention, the negative theorist subtracts it.[9] In our view, however, the relation between meaning and intention or, in slightly different terms, between language and speech acts is such that intention can neither be added nor subtracted. Intention cannot be added to or subtracted from meaning because meanings are always intentional; intention cannot be added to or subtracted from language because language consists of speech acts, which are also always intentional. Since language has intention already built into it, no recommendation about what to do with intention has any bearing on the question of how to interpret any utterance or text. For the non-theorist, the only question raised by the wave poem is not *how* to interpret but *whether* to interpret. Either the marks are a poem and hence a speech act, or they are not a poem and just happen to resemble a speech act. But once this empirical question is decided, no further judgments—and therefore no theoretical judgments—about the status of intention can be made.

Our argument so far has concerned what might be called the ontological side of theory—its peculiar claims about the nature of its object. We have suggested that those claims always take the form of generating a difference where none in fact exists, by imagining a mode of language devoid of intention—devoid, that is, of what makes it language and distinguishes it from accidental or mechanical noises and marks. But we have also tried to show that this strange ontological project is more than a spontaneous anomaly; it is always in the service of an epistemological goal. That goal is the goal of method, the governance of interpretive practice by some

larger and more principled account. Indeed, theoretical controversy in the Anglo-American tradition has more often taken the
form of arguments about the epistemological situation of the interpreter than about the ontological status of the text. If the ontological project of theory has been to imagine a condition of
language before intention, its epistemological project has been to
imagine a condition of knowledge before interpretation.

The aim of theory's epistemological project is to base interpretation on a direct encounter with its object, an encounter undis-
torted by the influence of the interpreter's particular beliefs.
Several writers have demonstrated the impossibility of escaping
beliefs at any stage of interpretation and have concluded that theory's epistemological goal is therefore unattainable. Some have
gone on to argue that the unattainability of an epistemologically
neutral stance not only undermines the claims of method but prevents us from ever getting any correct interpretations. For these
writers the attack on method thus has important practical consequences for literary criticism, albeit negative ones.[10]

But in discussing theory from the ontological side, we have
tried to suggest that the impossibility of method has no practical
consequences, positive or negative. And the same conclusion has
been reached from the epistemological side by the strongest critic
of theoretical attempts to escape belief, Stanley Fish. In his last essay in *Is There a Text in This Class?,* Fish confronts the "final question" raised by his critique of method, namely, "what implications
it has for the practice of literary criticism." His answer is, "none
whatsoever":

> That is, it does not follow from what I have been saying that you
> should go out and do literary criticism in a certain way or refrain
> from doing it in other ways. The reason for this is that the position
> I have been presenting is not one that you (or anyone else) could
> live by. Its thesis is that whatever seems to you to be obvious and in-
> escapable is only so within some institutional or conventional struc-
> ture, and that means that you can never operate outside some such

structure, even if you are persuaded by the thesis. As soon as you descend from theoretical reasoning about your assumptions, you will once again inhabit them and you will inhabit them without any reservations whatsoever; so that when you are called on to talk about Milton or Wordsworth or Yeats, you will do so from within whatever beliefs you hold about these authors.[11] *Blocks finding the truth: Gatsby's not a victim, he's just as shallow as Daisy.*

At the heart of this passage is the familiar distinction between "theoretical reasoning" and the "assumptions" or "beliefs" that inform the concrete "practice of literary criticism." Where most theorists affirm the practical importance of their theories, Fish's originality lies in his denial that his theory has any practical consequences whatsoever. But once theory gives up all claims to affect practice, what is there left for theory to do? Or, since Fish's point is that there is nothing left for theory to *do,* what is there left for theory to *be*? Understood in these terms, Fish's work displays the theoretical impulse in its purest form. Stripped of the methodological project either to ground or to undermine practice, theory continues to imagine a position outside it. While this retreat to a position outside practice looks like theory's last desperate attempt to save itself, it is really, as we hope to show, the founding gesture of all theoretical argument.

Fish's attack on method begins with an account of belief that is in our view correct. The account's two central features are, first, the recognition that beliefs cannot be grounded in some deeper condition of knowledge and, second, the further recognition that this impossibility does not in any way weaken their claims to be true. "If one believes what one believes," Fish writes, "then one believes that what one believes is *true,* and conversely, one believes that what one doesn't believe is not true" (p. 361). Since one can neither escape one's beliefs nor escape the sense that they are true, Fish rejects both the claims of method and the claims of skepticism. Methodologists and skeptics maintain that the validity of beliefs depends on their being grounded in a condition of knowledge prior to and independent of belief; they differ only about whether this is possible. The virtue of Fish's account is that it shows why an insistence on the inescapability of belief is in no way inimical to the ordinary notions of truth and falsehood implicit in our sense of what knowledge is. The character of belief is precisely what gives us those notions in the first place; having beliefs just *is* being committed to the truth of what one believes and the falsehood of what one doesn't believe. But to say all this is, as Fish asserts, to offer no practical help or hindrance to the task of acquiring true beliefs. We can no more get true beliefs by looking for knowledge than we can get an author's meaning by looking for his or her intention, and for the same reason: knowledge and true belief are the same.

So far, this argument seems to us flawless. But Fish, as it turns out, fails to recognize the force of his own discussion of belief, and this failure is what makes him a theorist. It commits him, ultimately, to the ideal of knowledge implicit in all epistemological versions of theory, and it leads him to affirm, after all, the methodological value of his theoretical stance. Fish's departure from his account of belief shows up most vividly in his response to charges that his arguments lead to historical relativism. The fear of relativism is a fear that the abandonment of method must make all inquiry pointless. But, Fish rightly says, inquiry never seems pointless; our present beliefs about an object always seem better than any previous beliefs about the same object: "In other words, the idea of progress is inevitable, not, however, because there *is* a progress in the sense of a clearer and clearer sight of an independent object but because the *feeling* of having progressed is an inevitable consequence of the firmness with which we hold our beliefs" (pp. 361–62).

As an account of the inevitable psychology of belief, this is irreproachable. But when he later turns from the general issue of intellectual progress to the particular case of progress in literary criticism, Fish makes clear that he thinks our psychological assurance is unfounded. Our present beliefs only *seem* better than earlier ones; they never really *are*. And, indeed, the discovery of this truth about our beliefs gives us, Fish thinks, a new understanding of the history of literary criticism and a new sense of how to go about studying it. According to what Fish calls the "old model" for making sense of the history of criticism, the work of critics "like Sidney, Dryden, Pope, Coleridge, Arnold" could only be seen as "the record of the rather dismal performances of men . . . who simply did not understand literature and literary values as well as we do." But Fish's new model enables us to "regard those performances not as unsuccessful attempts to approximate our own but as extensions of a literary culture whose assumptions were *not inferior but merely different*" (pp. 367–68; our emphasis).

To imagine that we can see the beliefs we hold as no better than but "merely different" from opposing beliefs held by others is to imagine a position from which we can see our beliefs without really believing them. To be in this position would be to see the truth about beliefs without actually having any—to know without believing. In the moment in which he imagines this condition of knowledge outside belief, Fish has forgotten the point of his own earlier identification of knowledge and true belief.

Once a theorist has reached this vision of knowledge, there are two epistemological ways to go: realism and idealism. A realist thinks that theory allows us to stand outside our beliefs in a neutral encounter with the objects of interpretation; an idealist thinks that theory allows us to stand outside our beliefs in a neutral encounter with our beliefs themselves. The issue in both cases is the relation between objects and beliefs. For the realist, the object exists independent of beliefs, and knowledge requires that we shed our beliefs in a disinterested quest for the object. For the idealist, who insists that we can never shed our beliefs, knowledge means recognizing the role beliefs play in *constituting* their objects. Fish, with his commitment to the primacy of beliefs, chooses idealism: "objects," he thinks, "are made and not found"; interpretation "is not the art of construing but the art of constructing" (pp. 331, 327). Once he arrives at epistemological idealism, Fish's methodological payoff immediately follows. Knowing that "interpreters

do not decode poems" but "make them," "we are free to consider
the various forms the literary institution has taken and to uncover
the interpretative strategies by which its canons have been produced and understood" (pp. 327, 368). By thinking of the critic as
an idealist instead of a realist, Fish is able to place literary criticism
at the very center of all literary practice:

> No longer is the critic the humble servant of texts whose glories
> exist independently of anything he might do; it is what he does,
> within the constraints embedded in the literary institution, that
> brings texts into being and makes them available for analysis and
> appreciation. The practice of literary criticism is not something one
> must apologize for; it is absolutely essential not only to the mainte-
> nance of, but to the very production of, the objects of its attention.
> (p. 368)

We began this section by noting that Fish, like us, thinks that no
general account of belief can have practical consequences. But, as
we have just seen, *his* account turns out to have consequences after all. Why, then, is Fish led both to assert that his argument has
no practical consequences and to proclaim its importance in providing a new model for critical practice? The answer is that, despite his explicit disclaimers, he thinks a true account of belief
must be a *theory* about belief, whereas we think a true account of
belief can only be a *belief* about belief.[12] The difference between
these two senses of what it means to have a true account of something is the difference between theory and the kind of pragmatist
argument we are presenting here. These two kinds of positions
conceive their inconsequentiality in two utterly different ways. A
belief about the nature of beliefs is inconsequential because it
merely tells you what beliefs are, not whether they are true or false
in particular or in general. From this point of view, knowing the
truth about belief will no more help you in acquiring true beliefs
than knowing that meaning is intentional will help you find correct meanings. This is not in the least to say that you can't have

true beliefs, only that you can't get them by having a good account of what beliefs are.

Fish's *theory* about beliefs, on the other hand, strives to achieve inconsequentiality by standing outside all the practical commitments that belief entails. It is perfectly true that one can achieve inconsequentiality by going outside beliefs but only because, as Fish himself insists, to be outside beliefs is to be nowhere at all. But of course Fish doesn't think that his theory about beliefs leaves him nowhere at all; he thinks instead that it gives him a way of arriving at truth, not by choosing some beliefs over others but by choosing beliefless knowledge over all beliefs. The truth of knowledge, according to Fish, is that no beliefs are, in the long run, truer than others; all beliefs, in the long run, are equal. But, as we have noted, it is only from the standpoint of a theory about belief which is not itself a belief that this truth can be seen. Hence the descent from "theoretical reasoning" about our beliefs to the actual practice of believing—from neutrality to commitment— demands that we forget the truth theory has told us. Unlike the ordinary methodologist, Fish wants to repudiate the attempt to derive practice from theory, insisting that the world of practice must be founded not on theoretical truth but on the repression of theoretical truth. But the sense that practice can only begin with the repression of theory already amounts to a methodological prescription: when confronted with beliefs, forget that they are not really true. This prescription gives Fish everything theory always wants: knowledge of the truth-value of beliefs and instructions on what to do with them.[13]

We can now see why Fish, in the first passage quoted, says that his position is "not one that you (or anyone else) could live by . . . even if you [were] persuaded" by it. Theory, he thinks, can have no practical consequences; it cannot be lived because theory and practice—the truth about belief and belief itself—can never in principle be united. In our view, however, the only relevant truth about belief is that you can't go outside it, and, far from being un-livable, this is a truth you can't help but live. It has no practical consequences not because it can never be *united* with practice but because it can never be *separated* from practice.

The theoretical impulse, as we have described it, always involves the attempt to separate things that should not be separated: on the ontological side, meaning from intention, language from speech acts; on the epistemological side, knowledge from true belief. Our point has been that the separated terms are in fact inseparable. It is tempting to end by saying that theory and practice too are inseparable. But this would be a mistake. Not because theory and practice (unlike the other terms) really are separate but because theory is nothing else but the attempt to escape practice. Meaning is just another name for expressed intention, knowledge just another name for true belief, but theory is not just another name for practice. It is the name for all the ways people have tried to stand outside practice in order to govern practice from without. Our thesis has been that no one can reach a position outside practice, that theorists should stop trying, and that the theoretical enterprise should therefore come to an end. *The blind leading the blind*

Richard J. Bernstein

Bernstein is Vera List Professor of Philosophy at the New School for Social Research. His books include *John Dewey* (1966), *The Restructuring of Social and Political Theory* (1976), *Beyond Objectivism and Relativism: Science, Hermeneutics, and Praxis* (1983), *Philosophical Profiles: Essays in a Pragmatic Mode* (1986), and *The New Constellation: The Ethical-Political Horizons of Modernity/Postmodernity* (1991).

Pragmatism, Pluralism, and the Healing of Wounds

(1988)

SEVERAL YEARS AGO, Hans-Georg Gadamer visited my college and gave an eloquent lecture on hermeneutics. After the lecture, several of us took him out to dinner to a local Chinese restaurant. We concluded the meal by reading the messages of our fortune cookies. The art of writing a good fortune message is to be sufficiently vague and ambiguous so when it is read it seems to have specific and unique relevance. But in this instance, Gadamer's fortune message was especially apt. For it summed up his lecture and epitomized his philosophy. When his turn came his "fortune" read: "Sometimes to understand the present, one needs to study the past." When I was preparing this address that message kept intruding itself. For I want to try to understand and gain a critical perspective on our present situation in philosophy. To do so one must study the past—the traditions that have shaped and still are shaping us. For I agree with Gadamer that we belong to traditions before they belong to, and are appropriated by, us: but as soon as one speaks in this manner, treacherous problems come pouring in. Not the least of which is, who is this "we"? Even if one limits oneself to philosophy in America, or more specifically, to philosophy in the United States, we are an extremely heterogeneous bunch, perhaps more so today than at any time in our past. And "we" have been shaped by conflicting rival traditions.

Alasdair MacIntyre has given one of the best succinct characterizations of a tradition when he tells us that a tradition "not only embodies the narrative of an argument, but is only recovered by an argumentative retelling of that narrative which will itself be in conflict with other argumentative retellings."[1] Today I want to sketch an argumentative retelling of the pragmatic tradition. Although it is only one of the traditions to which we belong, it is nevertheless one of the richest traditions that has shaped philosophy in America. I want to draw upon this tradition because it enables us to gain a critical perspective on our present situation in philosophy. It will become clear that I think this tradition is very much alive and that pragmatic themes weave through diverse contemporary orientations of many philosophers who do not think of themselves as belonging to this tradition. Indeed, the pragmatic thinkers were ahead of their times. Recently there has been a good deal of loose talk about our "postmodern condition." Yet if we pay close attention to the characteristic themes and challenges of the "postmodern" discourses, we will see how they were anticipated by the pragmatists. What is even more impressive and important is that the pragmatists were concerned with the question of how to *respond* to these challenges. The dialectic of many contemporary trends in philosophy leads us back to pragmatic insights.

It is that pragmatic *ēthos* that I hope to elicit by focusing on some of the dominant interrelated motifs characteristic of this style of thinking. I do not think of pragmatism as a set of doctrines or even as a method. Any close student of Peirce, James, Dewey, Mead, and Royce[2] in his late pragmatic writings is immediately struck by their clashing philosophic temperaments, and by the different problems that preoccupied them. We can best appreciate the vitality and diversity of this tradition when we approach it as an ongoing engaged conversation consisting of distinctive— sometimes competing—voices.

Before turning to highlighting themes running through this tradition that are relevant to our present situation, let me remind you of some of the striking features of the outburst and flourishing of philosophy in the latter part of the nineteenth century. We must not forget that the institution of the graduate school and the "professionalization" of academic philosophy as we know it today did

not exist in the post–Civil War period in the United States. Philosophically, Peirce and James were autodidacts. They were not
"formally" trained as philosophers. Peirce was a practicing experimental scientist and thought of himself as a logician. James was
trained as a medical doctor, and his philosophic speculations grew
out of his psychological investigations. Dewey was among the first
to receive a Ph.D. in philosophy at the newly founded graduate
school at Johns Hopkins. When they turned to philosophy, they
drew upon diverse sources and traditions. Peirce's early philosophic work began with reflections on the Kantian categories. He
even claimed to know the *Critique of Pure Reason* "almost by
heart." At a time when there was scarcely any knowledge or appreciation of the intricacies of scholastic philosophy, Peirce identified himself as a "Scotistic realist." James' deepest philosophic
affinities were with the tradition of British empiricism, although
he was also a sharp critic of what he took to be the artificial, thin,
emasculated conception of experience in this tradition. In his later
years, he recognized his affinities (and differences) with Bergson.
Dewey, as a graduate student, was profoundly influenced by
Hegelianism. Each drew upon diverse European philosophic traditions, reshaping and criticizing them in distinctive ways. The very
idea of an Anglo-American/Continental split in philosophy
would have made no sense during this creative formative stage of
the pragmatic *ēthos*.

We should also remember the fluidity of academic disciplines at
this time. There was no sense of sharp boundaries or that philosophy was a well-defined *Fach* or discipline to be rigorously demar-
cated from other types of inquiry. The pragmatic thinkers moved
freely over the range of different areas of inquiry and experience.
This fluidity and openness deeply marked their philosophic approach to problems. For the pragmatic thinkers were skeptical and
critical of the metaphysical and epistemological dichotomies that
had dominated so much of traditional and modern philosophy. Finally, we must remember that while they all resisted scientism—

the conviction that science and science alone is the standard for determining what counts as legitimate knowledge and for determining what is "real"—they were equally strong in their conviction that any responsible philosophic reflection must be responsive to scientific developments and practices. Collectively the classical pragmatic thinkers drew upon a variety of philosophic traditions, were deeply suspicious of hard and fixed boundaries, and grappled with new scientific developments, especially those brought into the foreground by the Darwinian revolution.

With an eye to the present, let me turn to five interrelated substantive themes that enable us to characterize the pragmatic *ēthos*:

1. "Anti-foundationalism" is not an expression that the pragmatists used. They certainly did not mean what is sometimes meant today when "anti-foundationalism" is polemically used to attack the very idea of philosophy. Yet I do not think there is an important argument in the anti-foundational arsenal that was not anticipated (and sometimes stated in a much more trenchant form) in the remarkable series of articles that Peirce published in 1868.[3] Peirce presents a battery of arguments directed against the idea that knowledge rests upon fixed foundations, and that we possess a special faculty of insight or intuition by which we can know these foundations. Peirce was exposing what has come to be called "the metaphysics of presence." Peirce realized that in criticizing foundationalism he was attacking many of the most cherished doctrines and dogmas that constituted modern philosophy. He makes this clear when he contrasts Cartesianism with the scholasticism that it displaced. He begins his article "Some Consequences of Four Incapacities" by declaring:

Descartes is the father of modern philosophy, and the spirit of Cartesianism—that which principally distinguishes it from the scholasticism which it displaced—may be compendiously stated as follows:

1. It teaches that philosophy must begin with universal doubt, whereas scholasticism had never questioned fundamentals.

2. It teaches that the ultimate test of certainty is to be found in individual consciousness; whereas scholasticism had rested on the testimony of sages and of the Catholic Church.

3. The multiform argumentation of the Middle Ages is replaced by a single thread of inference depending often on inconspicuous premises.

4. Scholasticism had its mysteries of faith, but undertook to explain all created things. But there are many facts which Cartesianism not only does not explain but renders absolutely inexplicable, unless to say "God makes them so" is regarded as an explanation.

In some, or all these respects, most modern philosophers have been, in effect, Cartesians. Now without wishing to return to scholasticism, it seems to me that modern science and modern logic require us to stand upon a very different platform from this.[4]

Peirce realized that his critique of Cartesianism, his elaboration of a different platform that is required by modern science and logic, required a rethinking of every major philosophic problem. For in one fell swoop he sought to demolish the idea that there are or can be any absolute beginnings or endings in philosophy. He sought to exorcise what Dewey later called "the quest for certainty" and the "spectator theory of knowledge." He called into question the privileged status of subjectivity and consciousness that had dominated so much of modern philosophy. He elaborated a theory of signs where interpretants are always and necessarily open to further interpretation, determination, and critical correction.

We find variations on these themes in all the pragmatic thinkers. We can see how subsequent philosophers have continued to refine the anti-foundational arguments adumbrated by Peirce. They are developed further in Quine's own distinctive version of pragmatism and in Wilfrid Sellars' work when he criticizes "the myth of the given" and declares that "empirical knowledge, like its sophis-

ticated extension science, is rational, not because it has a foundation, but because it is a self-correcting enterprise which can put
any claim in jeopardy, though not *all* at once."[5]

2. But if we abandon foundationalism and the craving for absolutes, then what is the alternative? There are many who have
thought that to give up foundationalism can lead only to some
version of skepticism or relativism. But this was not the response
of Peirce and the pragmatists. Their alternative to foundationalism
was to elaborate a thoroughgoing fallibilism where we realize that
although we must begin any inquiry with prejudgments and can
never call everything into question at once, nevertheless there is
no belief or thesis—no matter how fundamental—that is not open
to further interpretation and criticism. Peirce advocated that we
displace the "foundation" metaphor with the metaphor of a "cable." In philosophy, as in the sciences, we ought to "trust rather to
the multitude and variety of its arguments than to the conclusiveness of any one. Its reasoning should not form a chain which is no
stronger than its weakest link, but a cable whose fibers may be ever
so slender, provided they are sufficiently numerous and intimately
connected."[6] The pragmatists argued not only that fallibilism is
characteristic of the experimental habit of mind but that philosophy itself is intrinsically fallibilistic. Philosophy is interpretive, tentative, always subject to correction. *Only by results*

3. It is this fallibilism that brings me to the next theme that is
so vital for the pragmatists—the social character of the self and the
need to nurture a critical community of inquirers. If we are falli-
ble and always limited in our perspectives then "we individually
cannot reasonably hope to attain the ultimate philosophy which
we pursue; we can only seek it, therefore, for the *community* of
philosophers. Hence, if disciplined and candid minds carefully examine a theory and refuse to accept it, this ought to create doubts
in the mind of the author of the theory himself."[7] The theme of
the social character of the self and of community is played out in
many variations by the pragmatic thinkers. The very idea of an
individual consciousness that is independent of shared social

What if you live in a village of idiots?

practices is criticized. In this respect, the pragmatists sought to dismantle and deconstruct the philosophy of consciousness and the philosophy of subjectivity. What has come to be called the decentering of the subject is integral to the pragmatic project. Peirce appeals to the regulative ideal of a critical community of inquirers. Royce sought to extend this ideal to a universal community of interpreters. Dewey explored the social and political consequences of the idea of community for understanding the moral ideal of democracy. Mead was a pioneer in developing a theory of the social-psychological genesis of the social self—a theory of "practical intersubjectivity."[8]

Today there are many who have raised doubts about the Peircian conviction that—in the long run—there will be a convergence of inquiry. But doubts about an ideal convergence do not undermine the necessity of always appealing to a critical community. On the contrary, they heighten its importance. For it is only by submitting our hypothesis to public critical discussion that we become aware of what is valid in our claims and what fails to withstand critical scrutiny. It is only by the serious encounter with what is other, different, and alien that we can hope to determine what is idiosyncratic, limited, and partial. *They are.*

4. Anti-foundationalism, fallibilism, and the nurturing of critical communities leads to the fourth theme running through the pragmatic tradition—the awareness and sensitivity to radical contingency and chance that mark the universe, our inquiries, our lives. Contingency and chance have always been problematic for philosophy. In the concern with universality and necessity, there has been a deep desire to master, contain, and repress contingency—to assign it to its "proper" restricted place. For the pragmatists, contingency and chance are not merely signs of human ignorance, they are ineradicable and pervasive features of the universe. Long before the rise of quantum physics, Peirce developed a variety of arguments against the doctrine of mechanical necessity. He speculatively advanced a theory of cosmic evolution where there is a continuous interplay between evolving laws—

habits of nature—and chance. But the insistence on the inescapability of chance and contingency—on what Dewey called "the precariousness of existence" where the "world is a scene of risk" and is "uncannily unstable"[9]—conditioned their understanding of experience and philosophy itself. We can never hope to "master" unforeseen and unexpected contingencies. We live in an "open universe" which is always at once threatening and a source of tragedy and opportunity. This is why the pragmatists placed so much emphasis on how we are to respond to contingencies—on developing the complex of dispositions and critical habits that Dewey called "reflective intelligence."

5. I come finally to the theme of plurality. We can see how it pervades the other themes that I have sketched. There can be no escape from plurality—a plurality of traditions, perspectives, philosophic orientations. Later I will try to clarify what the pragmatists did and did not mean by pluralism and how it is relevant for understanding our present situation in philosophy. James described his own pluralistic orientation as follows:

> It is curious how little countenance radical pluralism has ever had from philosophers. Whether materialistically or spiritualistically minded, philosophers have always aimed at cleaning up the litter with which the world apparently is filled. They have substituted economical and orderly conceptions for the first sensible tangle; whether these were morally elevated or only intellectually neat, they were at any rate always aesthetically pure and definite, and aimed at ascribing to the world something clean and intellectual in the way of inner structure. As compared with all these rationalizing pictures, the pluralistic empiricism which I profess offers but a sorry appearance. It is a turbid, muddled, gothic sort of affair without a sweeping outline and with little pictorial nobility.[10]

I have sketched some of the interrelated themes of the pragmatic style of thinking—the pragmatic *ēthos*. These themes are intended to serve as reminders because the richness and diversity of this

The heirs were airheads.

tradition consists in the ways in which they have been explored and refined. But what has happened to this pragmatic legacy? I have already indicated that these themes keep resurfacing—even in the works of those who are not directly indebted to the pragmatists. But there has also been a forgetfulness of this tradition. By the mid-twentieth century, many philosophers in America thought of pragmatism as a movement that had exhausted itself. Other agendas had much greater appeal for our burgeoning profession. No one can underestimate the ways in which the émigré philosophers from Europe—Reichenbach, Carnap, Feigl, Tarski, Hempel (and many others)—were reshaping philosophy in America. There were, of course, transitional figures like C. I. Lewis and Ernest Nagel who had a grounding in the pragmatic tradition, but their interests in logic and the philosophy of science helped to foster an ambience for the receptivity of logical positivism and logical empiricism. Logical positivism in the militant form of the Vienna Circle or in its polemical form advocated by A. J. Ayer did not take deep root in America.[11] But a positivistic temper, and the legacy of logical empiricism, did flourish. During the period following the Second World War, when there was an enormous growth of academic philosophy, there was virtually a scurrying to refashion graduate schools so that they would become respectable analytic departments. This was a time of great confidence among professional philosophers. It was felt by the growing analytic community that "we" philosophers had "finally" discovered the conceptual tools and techniques to make progress in solving or dissolving philosophic problems. This was also the time when the Anglo-American/Continental split became an almost unbridgeable chasm. What was going on in European "philosophy" was taken to be pretentious, obscure, woolly, and muddled. By the new standards of what constituted "doing philosophy," Continental philosophy no longer counted as "serious" philosophy. Of course, there were pockets of resistance to the new analytic styles of "doing philosophy." There were those who defended and practiced speculative metaphysics in the manner of Whitehead;[12] there were those who saw greater promise in phenomenology and existentialism, there were those who sought to keep the pragmatic tradition alive; there were those who still believed that a careful study of the history of philosophy was relevant for contemporary philosophizing. But philosophers who had not taken the analytic "linguistic turn" were clearly on the defensive. Richard Rorty captures the mood of this time when he writes:

> In 1951, a graduate student who (like myself) was in the process of learning about, or being converted to, analytic philosophy could still believe that there were a finite number of distinct specifiable problems to be resolved—problems which any serious analytic philosopher would agree to be *the* outstanding problems. For example, there was the problem of the counterfactual conditional, the problem of whether an "emotive" analysis of ethical terms was satisfactory, Quine's problem about the nature of analyticity, and a few more. These were problems which fitted nicely into the vocabulary of the positivists. They could be seen as the final, proper formulation of problems which had been seen, as in a glass darkly, by Leibniz, Hume, and Kant. Further, there was agreement on what a solution to a philosophic problem looked like—e.g. Russell on definite descriptions, Frege on meaning and reference, Tarski on truth. In those days, when my generation was young, all of the conditions for a Kuhnian "normal" problem-solving discipline were fulfilled.[13]

There were other influences shaping the character of analytic philosophy. In the post–Second World War period, there was also a receptivity to the type of "ordinary language philosophy" or "conceptual analysis" that was so fashionable at Oxford. Ryle, Austin, and the later Wittgenstein[14] (as filtered and domesticated through Anglo-American spectacles) rivaled the more formalistic methods favored by logical empiricists. But whether one's allegiances were to the more formal or informal methods of analysis, there was a growing conviction that philosophers could now make genuine progress in solving well-formulated problems. Soon a new generation of philosophers were trained in America who not only mastered analytic techniques, but whose contributions surpassed the work of their teachers. Quine was a new hero, for he represented a figure who had assimilated what was taken to be most enduring in the pragmatic tradition but whose style of argumentation and logical finesse owed more to Carnap and Tarski than to Peirce, James, or Dewey. With the increased sophistication of analytic philosophy, there was also a growing internal complexity. Whereas with an earlier generation of logical positivists and empiricists, the consequences of their claims for other fields of inquiry could be clearly discerned—even if they were provocative and controversial—it was difficult for many outsiders (or even insiders to philosophy who were not tuned in to the latest debates in the professional journals) to figure out the significance of the problems that analytic philosophers took to be so central. It looked as if philosophers were perfecting a jargon that was barely intelligible to others. But for insiders this is what was to be properly expected as philosophy became more rigorous and sophisticated. Looking back at the development of analytic philosophy a generation after its initial triumph, Rorty continues his sketch:

What Arthur Andersen did to accounting.

> To recite this list of problems and paradigms is to evoke memories of a simple, brighter, vanished world. In the interlocking "central" areas of analytic philosophy—epistemology, philosophy of language, and metaphysics—there are now as many paradigms as there are major philosophy departments. . . . Any problem that enjoys a simultaneous vogue in ten of the hundred or so "analytic" philosophy departments in America is doing exceptionally well. The field these days is a jungle of competing research programs, programs which seem to have a shorter and shorter half-life as the years go by. . . . The best hope for an American philosopher is Andy Warhol's promise that we shall *all* be superstars, for approximately fifteen minutes apiece.[15]

Rorty's portrait may seem to be a caricature, but it is nevertheless a revealing one. It does not do justice to what has been achieved by analytic styles of philosophizing, nor does it mention what has always been characteristic of philosophy in America—its sheer heterogeneity and plurality. For even when the analytic *ēthos* had its greatest influence, it never completely dominated the American scene. It is important to distinguish the many impressive achievements of analytic work from the arrogant ideology that surrounded it during the first wave of its flourishing in America. For it is this ideology—the frequently unspoken belief that it was the *only* serious and proper way of doing philosophy—that is now breaking up. I do not think we should be naive, for there are still many analytic philosophers who believe in their hearts that there is no serious alternative, and are hostile and disdainful of other philosophic orientations. But such an ideology, which is still a source of intellectual violence and wounds in our profession, is becoming increasingly archaic and quaint.

Suppose we ask how this breakup of ideology has come about—and what its consequences are. Here we need to focus on both external and internal factors, although they have been intertwined. By external factors, I mean what has been happening in the world outside of academic philosophy. For at the very time when analytic philosophy seemed to be consolidating during the decades of the 1950s and 1960s, many philosophers resisted the constraints imposed by analytic philosophy on what counted as serious philosophizing. Both James and Dewey had warned us about the dangers of a growing professionalism and specialization of the "problems of philosophy." Dewey spoke of the need to address the "problems of men"[16]—the problems of human beings. In the turmoil taking place in the outside world, many philosophers in America turned their attention to other philosophic orientations—to phenomenology, hermeneutics, critical theory, the varieties of structuralism and poststructuralism which they believed provided more powerfully illuminating ways of philosophizing. There was also a rebellion against the ahistorical and anti-historical biases of the analytic ideology. In the past few decades there has been a flourishing of historical studies with a systematic intent. This growing interest in the history of philosophy is itself an expression of the impulse to enlarge the scope of philosophic reflection. New voices also demanded to be heard—as evidenced by feminist and minority concerns. And as the philosophy curriculum in many prestigious analytic graduate departments began to shrink—excluding or marginalizing philosophers who were no longer to be taken "seriously"—our colleagues in departments of religion and literature began teaching Hegel, Nietzsche, Kierkegaard, and Heidegger.

"We" philosophers have all sorts of defense mechanisms and techniques for deflating or ignoring the criticisms of "outsiders." But "we" are much more sensitive to the criticisms of "insiders." During the past two decades, it is the criticisms of insiders that have shaken us up and stirred so much controversy and resentment. Consider the controversies generated by the writings of three former presidents of our division, Richard Rorty, Alasdair MacIntyre, and Hilary Putnam. No one could fault them for being ignorant of analytic styles of philosophizing. Each had made major contributions to the ongoing debates that have been at the cutting edge of analytic philosophy. But in different ways each has severely criticized the exclusionary biases of the analytic ideology. Each has helped to open up and expand what Rorty calls the conversation of philosophy. Each has questioned the boundary-fixing tendency of the ideological phase of analytic philosophy. Indeed, we are beginning to see how silly and unfruitful it is to think in terms of an Anglo-American/Continental split. If we "look and see," we find elaborate crisscrossings taking place, and discover how similar issues crop up in what were once taken to be radically different philosophic vocabularies. Kuhn comes to recognize the affinities of his work with hermeneutics. The French discover Austin and Wittgenstein. Habermas appropriates speech act theory in his theory of communicative action. Apel's transcendental pragmatics builds on the pioneering work of Peirce.[17]

But something else has been happening—especially among younger members of our profession—which is perhaps even more important. For what James wrote in 1904 seems especially relevant in our situation:

> It is difficult not to notice a curious unrest in the philosophic atmosphere of the time, a loosening of old landmarks, a softening of oppositions, a mutual borrowing from one another on the part of systems anciently closed, and an interest in new suggestions, however vague, as if the one thing sure was the inadequacy of the extant school-solutions. The dissatisfaction with these seems due for the most part to a feeling that they are too abstract and academic. Life is confused and superabundant, and what the younger generation appears to crave is more of the temperament of life in its philosophy, even though it were at some cost of logical rigor and formal purity.[18]

One of the most hopeful signs for philosophy in America today is this "unrest in the philosophic atmosphere," this "loosening of old landmarks." The ideological battles of my generation are beginning to seem remote and irrelevant. Scars from the wounds of these battles still remain, but there are encouraging signs of the emergence of a new *ēthos*—one which bears strong affinities with the *ēthos* characteristic of the formative stages of the pragmatic movement. There are all sorts of crisscrossings and interweavings. One may discover the ways in which deconstruction shows affinities with pragmatism or with the investigations of the later Wittgenstein. One may realize that Hegel's distinction between *Moralität* and *Sichlichkeit* is relevant for understanding contemporary moral and ethical theory.[19] One may realize that Popper and Foucault are relevant for untangling the complexities of historicism.[20] These interweavings extend to the interplay of disciplines which not so long ago were taken to be quite distinct—philosophy and law, philosophy and literature, philosophy and the social disciplines, philosophy and medicine, and so forth.

Indeed, there is another emerging phenomenon that exhibits a new intellectual mood of fluidity and breaking down of boundaries. Throughout the country in our universities and colleges there has been an explosion of study and discussion groups that cluster about new constellations of texts and themes that cut across disciplines. What distinguishes these groups from older models of "interdisciplinary" discussions is that there is no longer the presumption of a distinctive disciplinary approach to a given problem—as if there were a unique philosophic, literary, or anthropological point of view. The intermingling and overlapping is much more radical where pursuing issues in one's own field necessitates drawing upon the ways in which issues are explored in other fields of inquiry. It is almost as if there is a "counter-disciplinary" movement developing which no longer finds the disciplinary matrices that have shaped our academic departments helpful in dealing with intellectual problems. Some of us are beginning to discover that we share more intellectually with colleagues trained in different disciplines than with our own departmental philosophic colleagues.

What then is our situation in philosophy today? Perhaps the simplest and most direct answer is Babel, a confusion of tongues. But Babel itself is not so simple. We cannot escape the fact that there has been a decentering of philosophy itself. There has been a radical pluralization of different vocabularies, research programs, voices demanding to be heard. I sometimes think that a primary reason why there has been so much concern with problems of incommensurability and relativism is because this is the condition that we find ourselves in as philosophers, where we speak such radically different tongues that we are unable to understand what even our closest neighbors are saying—as if we were becoming like windowless monads. There are dangers and challenges in this situation.

Here I want to return to the theme of pluralism, or rather to the question of how one is to respond to this extreme pluralization. For pluralism itself is open to many interpretations and we need to make some important distinctions. For there is a danger of a *fragmenting* pluralism where the centrifugal forces become so strong that we are only able to communicate with the small group that already shares our own biases, and no longer even experience the need to talk with others outside of this circle. There is a *flabby* pluralism where our borrowings from different orientations are little more than glib superficial poaching. There is *polemical* pluralism where the appeal to pluralism doesn't signify a genuine willingness to listen and learn from others, but becomes rather an ideological weapon to advance one's own orientation. There is *defensive* pluralism, a form of tokenism, where we pay lip service to others "doing their own thing" but are already convinced that there is nothing important to be learned from them.

The type of pluralism that represents what is best in our pragmatic tradition is an *engaged fallibilistic pluralism*. Such a pluralistic *ēthos* places new responsibilities upon each of us. For it means taking our own fallibility seriously—resolving that however much we are committed to our own styles of thinking, we are willing to listen to others without denying or suppressing the otherness of the other. It means being vigilant against the dual temptations of simply dismissing what others are saying by falling back on one of those standard defensive ploys where we condemn it as obscure, woolly, or trivial, or thinking we can always easily translate what is alien into our own entrenched vocabularies. Sometimes understanding rival traditions requires what Alasdair MacIntyre characterizes as learning a second first language where we come to recognize the ways in which rival traditions are and are not translatable.[21] What makes this task so difficult and unstable is the growing realization that there are no uncontested rules or procedures "which will tell us how rational agreement can be reached on what would settle the issue on every point where statements seem to conflict."[22] But this doesn't mean that we have to fall back to some version of what Popper called the "myth of the framework" where we are prisoners caught in the framework of our theories—our expectations, our past experiences, our language—

Appeasing the Terminators

"and that we are so imprisoned into these frameworks that we cannot even communicate with those imprisoned in radically different frameworks."[23] Or rather, to the extent that this does happen, it is, I believe, primarily an *ethical* failure rather than a cognitive or linguistic one. Ultimately the appeal to the regulative ideal of a community of inquirers or interpreters is—as the pragmatists emphasized—an ethical or normative ideal.

Whether one draws upon Davidsonian[24] or Habermasian[25] arguments, we can question the very idea of conceptual schemes that are so self-enclosed that there is no possibility of reciprocal translation, understanding, and argumentation. But because there are no uncontested decision procedures for adjudicating the claims of rival philosophic orientations, it is always a *task* to seek out commonalities and points of difference and conflict. The *achievement* of a "we"—where "we" are locked in argument with others—is a fragile and temporary achievement that can always be ruptured by unexpected contingencies. Conflict and disagreement are unavoidable in our pluralistic situation. There is little reason to believe that "we" philosophers will ever achieve any substantive permanent consensus, and there are many good reasons for questioning the desirability of such a consensus. What matters, however, is how we respond to conflict. The response that the pragmatists call for is a dialogical response where we genuinely seek to achieve a mutual reciprocal understanding—an understanding that does not preclude disagreement.

One of the consequences of the analytic movement has been to encourage the "adversarial" or "confrontational" style of argumentation. According to this style, when one is confronted with a claim or thesis that one takes to be mistaken one relentlessly "goes after it." The other is viewed as an opponent, and the aim is to locate specifically what is wrong in the opponent's position, to expose its weaknesses. The practice of this style of argumentation requires attention to details, working through specific claims and arguments in order to show up their falsity and sometimes to expose their triviality. There are great advantages to this style of ar-

gumentation. It is never satisfied with vague claims, it helps to pin-
point issues in dispute, and it can expose difficulties that need to
be confronted. But there are also dangers in this style of argumentation when carried to extremes. For in being primarily concerned with exposing weaknesses, with showing the absurdities in
what is taken to be mistaken, we can be blind to what the other is
saying and to the truth that the other is contributing to the discussion. *White flag*

The adversarial confrontational style can be contrasted with a
model of dialogical encounter. Here one begins with the assumption that the other has something to say to us and to contribute to
our understanding. The initial task is to grasp the other's position
in the *strongest* possible light. One must always attempt to be responsive to what the other is saying and showing. This requires
imagination, sensitivity, and perfecting hermeneutical skills. There
is a play, a to-and-fro movement in dialogical encounters, a seeking for a common ground in which we can understand our differences. The other is not an adversary or an opponent, but a
conversational partner. Conflict is just as important in dialogical
encounters, because understanding does not entail agreement. On
the contrary, it is the way to clarify our disagreements. Gadamer
states the point succinctly when he writes: "One does not seek to
score a point by exploiting the other's weaknesses; rather, one
seeks to strengthen the other's argument as much as possible so as
to render it plausible. Such an effort seems to me to be constitu-
tive for any communication."[26] An engaged fallibilistic pluralism
that is true to what is best in the pragmatic tradition requires a delicate balance between these different styles of argumentation and
encounter. Unfortunately, during the past few decades, "we"
philosophers have not only perfected our adversarial skills but have
carried them to excess. In this respect, our practices reflect what is
occurring throughout society. "We" need to counterbalance these
practices with cultivating dialogical encounters. Such encounters
require what Rorty calls the Socratic virtues, "the willingness to
talk, to listen to other people, to weigh the consequences of our

actions upon other people."[27] Perhaps "we" philosophers might even play a modest role in encouraging the type of civility that is becoming so rare in our social practices. A time to kill.

I began by seeking to elicit the pragmatic *ēthos* by adumbrating the themes of anti-foundationalism, fallibilism, the social character of the self, and the regulative ideal of a critical community, contingency, and pluralism. I did this in order to gain a critical perspective on our present situation in philosophy. But in speaking about the present I have slipped into making an *appeal*—with a future reference. An appeal presupposes a sense of disparity between what presently exists and what one hopes will prevail. Because "we" philosophers are human-all-too-human, it is perhaps utopian to think that we will ever completely escape from ideological contentiousness. Nevertheless, we can aspire to displace ideological labeling with reasonable philosophic engagement.

The time has come to realize that there has been an ideological cultural lag in our profession—to realize that the ideological battles characteristic of the first wave of the reception of analytic philosophy in America no longer make much sense. The time has come to heal the wounds of these ideological battles. The time has come to realize how unilluminating and unfruitful it is to think in terms of an Anglo-American/Continental split. The philosophic interminglings that are now taking place defy any such simplistic dichotomy. Philosophy has been decentered. There is no single paradigm, research program, or orientation that dominates philosophy. The fact is that our situation is pluralistic. But the question becomes how we are to *respond* to this pluralism. There are powerful centrifugal tendencies toward fragmentation. But there are also counter-tendencies—not toward convergence, consensus, and harmony—but toward breaking down of boundaries, "a loosening of old landmarks," and dialogical encounters where we reasonably explore our differences and conflicts. In this situation, the pragmatic legacy is especially relevant, in particular the call to nurture the type of community and solidarity where there is an engaged fallibilistic pluralism—one that is based upon mutual

A time for round-the-clock bombings

respect, where we are willing to risk our own prejudgments, are open to listening and learning from others, and we respond to others with responsiveness and responsibility.

I conclude with a citation from John Courtney Murray, who eloquently expressed the *ēthos* of an engaged fallibilistic pluralism.

> Barbarism . . . threatens when men cease to talk together according to reasonable laws. There are laws of argument, the observance of which is imperative if discourse is to be civilized. Argument ceases to be civil when it is dominated by passion and prejudice; when its vocabulary becomes solipsist, premised on the theory that my insight is mine alone and cannot be shared; when dialogue gives way to a series of monologues; when the parties to the conversation cease to listen to one another, or hear only what they want to hear, or see the other's argument only through the screen of their own categories. . . . When things like this happen, men cannot be locked together in argument. Conversation becomes merely quarrelsome or querulous. Civility dies with the death of dialogue.[28]

We have not been here before. This is a counter-revolution against the Renaissance, not growing pains but a death rattle.

Cornel West

West is Professor of African-American Studies and the philosophy of religion and Du Bois Fellow at Harvard University, where he has taught since 1994. His books include *Prophetic Fragments* (1988), *The American Evasion of Philosophy* (1989), *Keeping Faith: Philosophy and Race in America* (1993), and *Race Matters* (1993). He is the editor, with John Rajchman, of *Post-Analytic Philosophy* (1985).

from **Prophetic Pragmatism**

in *The American Evasion of Philosophy* (1989)

A MAJOR SHORTCOMING of Emersonian pragmatism is its optimistic theodicy. The point here is not so much that Emerson himself had no sense of the tragic but rather that the way he formulated the relation of human powers and fate, human agency and circumstances, human will and constraints made it difficult for him and for subsequent pragmatists to maintain a delicate balance between excessive optimism and exorbitant pessimism regarding human capacities. The early Emerson stands at one pole and the later Trilling at another pole. For prophetic pragmatism only the early Hook and Niebuhr—their work in the early thirties—maintain the desirable balance.[1]

This issue of balance raises a fundamental and long-ignored issue for the progressive tradition: the issue of the complex relations between tragedy and revolution, tradition and progress. Prophetic pragmatism refuses to sidestep this issue. The brutalities and atrocities in human history, the genocidal attempts in this century, and the present-day barbarities require that those who accept the progressive and prophetic designations put forth some conception of the tragic. To pose the issue in this way is, in a sense, question begging since the very term "tragic" presupposes a variety of religious and secular background notions. Yet prophetic pragmatism is a child of Protestant Christianity wedded to left romanticism. So this question begging is warranted in that prophetic pragmatism stands in a tradition in which the notion of the "tragic" requires attention.

It is crucial to acknowledge from the start that the "tragic" is a polyvalent notion; it has different meanings depending on its context. For example, the context of Greek tragedy—in which the action of ruling families generates pity and terror in the audience—is a society that shares a collective experience of common metaphysical and social meanings. The context of modern tragedy, on the other hand—in which ordinary individuals struggle against meaninglessness and nothingness—is a fragmented society with collapsing metaphysical meanings. More pointedly, the notion of the "tragic" is bound to the idea of human agency, be the agent a person of rank or a retainer, a prince or a pauper.

> The real key, to the modern separation of tragedy from "mere suffering," is the separation of ethical control and, more critically, human agency, from our understanding of social and political life.
> . . . The events which are not seen as tragic are deep in the pattern of our own culture: war, famine, work, traffic, politics. To see no ethical content or human agency in such events, or to say that we cannot connect them with general meanings, and especially with permanent and universal meanings, is to admit a strange and particular bankruptcy, which no rhetoric of tragedy can finally hide.[2]

It is no accident that James, Hook, Niebuhr, and Trilling focused on the content and character of heroism when they initially grappled with theodicy and the "tragic." Although they had little or no interest in revolution, their preoccupation with human agency, will, and power resembles that of the Promethean romantics, e.g., Blake, Byron, Shelley. Yet the ideological sources of their conceptions of the "tragic" loom large in their deployment of the term.

James's focus on the individual and his distrust of big institutions and groups led him to envision a moral heroism in which each ameliorative step forward is a kind of victory, each minute battle won a sign that the war is not over, hence still winnable. Hook's early Marxism provided him with a historical sense in which the "tragic" requires a choice between a proven evil, i.e., capitalism, and a possible good, i.e., socialism. As the possible good proved to be more and more evil, the old "proven evil" appeared more and more good. The notion of the "tragic" in Hook underwent a metamorphosis such that all utopian quests were trashed in the name of limits, constraints, and circumstances. The later Trilling is even more extreme, for the mere exertion of will was often seen as symptomatic of the self's utopian quest for the unconditioned.

Niebuhr held the most complex view of the "tragic" in the pragmatist tradition. Even more than the middle Trilling's intriguing ruminations on Keatsian theodicy, Niebuhr's struggle with liberal Protestantism—especially with Richard Rorty's grandfather, Walter Rauschenbusch—forced him to remain on the tightrope between Promethean romanticism and Augustinian pessimism. In fact, Niebuhr never succumbs to either, nor does he ever cease to promote incessant human agency and will against limits and circumstances. In his leftist years, mindful of the novel forms of evil in the new envisioned social order yet fed up with those in the present, he supported the insurgency of exploited workers. In his liberal years, obsessed with the evil structures in the communist world and more and more (though never fully) forgetful of the institutional evil in American society, Niebuhr encourages state actions against the Soviet Union and piecemeal reformist practice within America.

Prophetic pragmatism affirms the Niebuhrian strenuous mood, never giving up on new possibilities for human agency—both individual and collective—in the present, yet situating them in light of Du Bois' social structural analyses that focus on working-class, black, and female insurgency. Following the pioneering work of Hans-Georg Gadamer and Edward Shils, prophetic pragmatism acknowledges the inescapable and inexpungible character of tradition, the burden and buoyancy of that which is transmitted from the past to the present.[3] This process of transmittance is one of socialization and appropriation, of acculturation and construction. Tradition, in this sense, can be both a smothering and a liberating affair, depending on which traditions are being invoked, internalized, and invented.

In this way, the relation of tragedy to revolution (or resistance) is intertwined with that of tradition to progress (or betterment). Prophetic pragmatism, as form of third-wave left romanticism, tempers its utopian impulse with a profound sense of the tragic character of life and history. This sense of the tragic highlights the irreducible predicament of unique individuals who undergo dread, despair, disillusionment, disease, and death *and* the institutional forms of oppression that dehumanize people. Tragic thought is not confined solely to the plight of the individual; it also applies to social experiences of resistance, revolution, and societal reconstruction. Prophetic pragmatism is a form of tragic thought in that it confronts candidly individual and collective experiences of evil in individuals and institutions—with little expectation of ridding the world of *all* evil. Yet it is a kind of romanticism in that it holds many experiences of evil to be neither inevitable nor necessary but rather the results of human agency, i.e., choices and actions.

This interplay between tragic thought and romantic impulse, inescapable evils and transformable evils makes prophetic pragmatism seem schizophrenic. On the one hand, it appears to affirm a Sisyphean outlook in which human resistance to evil makes no progress. On the other hand, it looks as if it approves a utopian quest for paradise. In fact, prophetic pragmatism denies Sisyphean pessimism and utopian perfectionism. Rather, it promotes the possibility of human progress and the human impossibility of paradise. This progress results from principled and protracted Promethean efforts, yet even such efforts are no guarantee. And all human struggles—including successful ones—against specific forms of evil produce new, though possibly lesser, forms of evil. Human struggle sits at the center of prophetic pragmatism, a struggle guided by a democratic and libertarian vision, sustained by moral courage and existential integrity, and tempered by the recognition of human finitude and frailty. It calls for utopian ener-

gies and tragic actions, energies and actions that yield permanent
and perennial revolutionary, rebellious, and reformist strategies
that oppose the status quos of our day. These strategies are never
to become ends-in-themselves, but rather to remain means
through which are channeled moral outrage and human desperation in the face of prevailing forms of evil in human societies and
in human lives. Such outrage must never cease, and such desperation will never disappear, yet without revolutionary, rebellious,
and reformist strategies, credible and effective opposition wanes.
Prophetic pragmatism attempts to keep alive the sense of alternative ways of life and of struggle based on the best of the past. In
this sense, the praxis of prophetic pragmatism is tragic action with
revolutionary intent, usually reformist consequences, and always
visionary outlook. It concurs with Raymond Williams' tragic revolutionary perspective:

> The tragic action, in its deepest sense, is not the confirmation of
> disorder, but its experience, its comprehension and its resolution. In
> our own time, this action is general, and its common name is rev-
> olution. We have to see the evil and the suffering, in the factual dis-
> order that makes revolution necessary, and in the disordered
> struggle against the disorder. We have to recognize this suffering in
> a close and immediate experience, and not cover it with names. But
> we follow the whole action: not only the evil, but the men who
> have fought against evil; not only the crisis, but the energy released
> by it, the spirit learned in it. We make the connections, because that
> is the action of tragedy, and what we learn in suffering is again rev-
> olution, because we acknowledge others as men and any such ac-
> knowledgment is the beginning of struggle, as the continuing
> reality of our lives. Then to see revolution in this tragic perspective
> is the only way to maintain it.[4]

This oppositional consciousness draws its sustenance principally
from a tradition of resistance. To keep alive a sense of alternative
ways of life and of struggle requires memory of those who prefig-

ured such life and struggle in the past. In this sense, tradition is to be associated not solely with ignorance and intolerance, prejudice and parochialism, dogmatism and docility. Rather, tradition is also to be identified with insight and intelligence, rationality and resistance, critique and contestation. Tradition per se is never a problem, but rather those traditions that have been and are hegemonic over other traditions. All that human beings basically have are traditions—those institutions and practices, values and sensibilities, stories and symbols, ideas and metaphors that shape human identities, attitudes, outlooks, and dispositions. These traditions are dynamic, malleable, and revisable, yet all changes in a tradition are done in light of some old or newly emerging tradition. Innovation presupposes some tradition and inaugurates another tradition. The profound historical consciousness of prophetic pragmatism shuns the Emersonian devaluing of the past. Yet it also highlights those elements of old and new traditions that promote innovation and resistance for the aims of enhancing individuality and expanding democracy. This enhancement and expansion constitute human progress. And all such progress takes place within the contours of clashing traditions. In this way, just as tragic action constitutes resistance to prevailing status quos, the critical treatment and nurturing of a tradition yield human progress. Tragedy can be an impetus rather than an impediment to oppositional activity; tradition may serve as a stimulus rather than a stumbling block to human progress.

Prophetic pragmatism understands the Emersonian swerve from epistemology—and the American evasion of philosophy—not as a wholesale rejection of philosophy but rather as a reconception of philosophy as a form of cultural criticism that attempts to transform linguistic, social, cultural, and political traditions for the purposes of increasing the scope of individual development and democratic operations. Prophetic pragmatism conceives of philosophy as a historically circumscribed quest for wisdom that puts forward new interpretations of the world based on past traditions in order to promote existential sustenance and political relevance.

Like Emerson and earlier pragmatists, it views truth as a species of the good, as that which enhances the flourishing of human progress. This does not mean that philosophy ignores the ugly facts and unpleasant realities of life and history. Rather, it highlights these facts and realities precisely because they provoke doubt, curiosity, outrage, or desperation that motivates efforts to overcome them. These efforts take the forms of critique and praxis, forms that attempt to change what is into a better what can be.

Prophetic pragmatism closely resembles and, in some ways, converges with the metaphilosophical perspectives of Antonio Gramsci. Both conceive of philosophical activity as "a cultural battle to transform the popular 'mentality.'"[5] It is not surprising that Gramsci writes:

> What the pragmatists wrote about this question merits re-examination . . . they felt real needs and "described" them with an exactness that was not far off the mark, even if they did not succeed in posing the problems fully or in providing a solution.[6]

Prophetic pragmatism is inspired by the example of Antonio Gramsci principally because he is the major twentieth-century philosopher of praxis, power, and provocation without devaluing theory, adopting unidimensional conceptions of power, or reducing provocation to Clausewitzian calculations of warfare. Gramsci's work is historically specific, theoretically engaging, and politically activistic in an exemplary manner. His concrete and detailed investigations are grounded in and reflections upon local struggles, yet theoretically sensitive to structural dynamics and international phenomena. He is attuned to the complex linkage of socially constructed identities to human agency while still convinced of the crucial role of the ever-changing forms in class-ridden economic modes of production. Despite his fluid Leninist conception of political organization and mobilization (which downplays the democratic and libertarian values of prophetic pragmatists) and his unswerving allegiance to sophisticated Marxist social theory (which is an indispensable yet ultimately inadequate weapon for prophetic pragmatists), Gramsci exemplifies the critical spirit and oppositional sentiments of prophetic pragmatism.

This is seen most clearly in Gramsci's view of the relation of philosophy to "common sense." For him, the aim of philosophy is not only to become worldly by imposing its elite intellectual views upon people, but to become part of a social movement by nourishing and being nourished by the philosophical views of oppressed people themselves for the aims of social change and personal meaning. Gramsci viewed this mutually critical process in world-historical terms.

> From the disintegration of Hegelianism derives the beginning of a new cultural process, different in character from its predecessors, a process in which practical movement and theoretical thought are united (or are trying to unite through a struggle that is both theoretical and practical).
>
> It is not important that this movement had its origins in mediocre philosophical works or, at best, in works that were not philosophical masterpieces. What matters is that a new way of conceiving the world and man is born and that this conception is no longer reserved to the great intellectuals, to professional philosophers, but tends rather to become a popular, mass phenomenon, with a concretely world-wide character, capable of modifying (even if the result includes hybrid combinations) popular thought and mummified popular culture.
>
> One should not be surprised if this beginning arises from the convergence of various elements, apparently heterogeneous. . . . Indeed, it is worth noting that such an overthrow could not but have connections with religion.[7]

Gramsci's bold suggestion here relates elite philosophical activity to the cultures of the oppressed in the name of a common effort for social change. Prophetic pragmatist sensibilities permit (or even encourage) this rejection of the arrogant scientistic self-privileging or haughty secular self-images of many modern philosophers and intellectuals. The point here is not that serious contemporary thinkers should surrender their critical intelligence, but rather that they should not demand that all peoples mimic their version of critical intelligence, especially if common efforts for social change can be strengthened. On this point, even the nuanced secularism of Edward Said—the most significant and salient Gramscian critic on the American intellectual scene today—can be questioned.[8] For Gramsci, ideologies of secularism or religions are less sets of beliefs and values, attitudes and sensibilities and more ways of life and ways of struggle manufactured and mobilized by certain sectors of the population in order to legitimate and preserve their social, political, and intellectual powers. Hence, the universities and churches, schools and synagogues, mass media and mosques become crucial terrain for ideological and political contestation. And philosophers are in no way exempt from this fierce battle—even within the "serene" walls and halls of the academy. Similar to the American pragmatist tradition, Gramsci simply suggests that philosophers more consciously posit these battles themselves as objects of investigation and thereby intervene in these battles with intellectual integrity and ideological honesty.

Prophetic pragmatism purports to be not only an oppositional cultural criticism but also a material force for individuality and democracy. By "material force" I simply mean a practice that has some potency and effect or makes a difference in the world. There is—and should be—no such thing as a prophetic pragmatist movement. The translation of philosophic outlook into social motion is not that simple. In fact, it is possible to be a prophetic pragmatist and belong to different political movements, e.g., feminist, Chicano, black, socialist, left-liberal ones. It also is possible to subscribe to prophetic pragmatism and belong to different religious and/or secular traditions. This is so because a prophetic pragmatist commitment to individuality and democracy, historical consciousness and systematic social analyses, and tragic action in an evil-ridden world can take place in—though usually on the margin of—a variety of traditions. The distinctive hallmarks of a prophetic pragmatist are a universal consciousness that promotes an all-embracing democratic and libertarian moral vision, a historical consciousness that acknowledges human finitude and conditionedness, and a critical consciousness which encourages relentless critique and self-criticism for the aims of social change and personal humility.

My own version of prophetic pragmatism is situated within the Christian tradition. Unlike Gramsci, I am religious not simply for political aims but also by personal commitment. To put it crudely, I find existential sustenance in many of the narratives in the biblical scriptures as interpreted by streams in the Christian heritage; and I see political relevance in the biblical focus on the plight of the wretched of the earth. Needless to say, without the addition of modern interpretations of racial and gender equality, tolerance, and democracy, much of the tradition warrants rejection. Yet the Christian epic, stripped of static dogmas and decrepit doctrines, remains a rich source of existential empowerment and political engagement when viewed through modern lenses (indeed the only ones we moderns have!).

Like James, Niebuhr, and to some extent Du Bois, I hold a religious conception of pragmatism. I have dubbed it "prophetic" in that it harks back to the Jewish and Christian tradition of prophets who brought urgent and compassionate critique to bear on the evils of their day. The mark of the prophet is to speak the truth in love with courage—come what may. Prophetic pragmatism proceeds from this impulse. It neither requires a religious foundation nor entails a religious perspective, yet prophetic pragmatism is compatible with certain religious outlooks.

My kind of prophetic pragmatism is located in the Christian tradition for two basic reasons. First, on the existential level, the self-understanding and self-identity that flow from this tradition's insights into the crises and traumas of life are indispensable *for me* to remain sane. It holds at bay the sheer absurdity so evident in life, without erasing or eliding the tragedy of life. Like Kierkegaard, whose reflections on Christian faith were so profound yet often so frustrating, I do not think it possible to put forward rational defenses of one's faith that verify its veracity or even persuade one's critics. Yet it is possible to convey to others the sense of deep emptiness and pervasive meaninglessness one feels if one is not critically aligned with an enabling tradition. One risks not logical inconsistency but actual insanity; the issue is not reason or irrationality but life or death. Of course, the fundamental philosophical question remains whether the Christian gospel is ultimately true.[9] And, as a Christian prophetic pragmatist whose focus is on coping with transient and provisional penultimate matters yet whose hope goes beyond them, I reply in the affirmative, bank my all on it, yet am willing to entertain the possibility in low moments that I may be deluded.

Second, on the political level, the culture of the wretched of the earth is deeply religious. To be in solidarity with them requires not only an acknowledgment of what they are up against but also an appreciation of how they cope with their situation. This appreciation does not require that one be religious; but if one is religious, one has wider access into their life-worlds. This appreciation also does not entail an uncritical acceptance of religious narratives, their interpretations, or, most important, their often oppressive consequences. Yet to be religious permits one to devote one's life to accenting the prophetic and progressive potential within those traditions that shape the everyday practices and deeply held perspectives of most oppressed peoples. What a wonderful privilege and vocation this is!

The prophetic religious person, much like C. Wright Mills's activist intellectual, puts a premium on educating and being educated by struggling peoples, organizing and being organized by resisting groups. This political dimension of prophetic pragmatism as practiced within the Christian tradition impels one to be an organic intellectual, that is, one who revels in the life of the mind yet relates ideas to collective praxis. An organic intellectual, in contrast to traditional intellectuals who often remain comfortably nested in the academy, attempts to be entrenched in and affiliated with organizations, associations, and, possibly, movements of grass-roots folk. Of course, he or she need be neither religious nor linked to religious institutions. Trade unions, community groups, and political formations also suffice. Yet, since the Enlightenment in eighteenth-century Europe, most of the progressive energies among the intelligentsia have shunned religious channels. And in these days of global religious revivals, progressive forces are reaping the whirlwind. Those of us who remain in these religious channels see clearly just how myopic such an antireligious strategy is. The severing of ties to churches, synagogues, temples, and mosques by the left intelligentsia is tantamount to political suicide; it turns the pessimism of many self-deprecating and self-pitying secular progressive intellectuals into a self-fulfilling prophecy. This point was never grasped by C. Wright Mills, though W. E. B. Du Bois understood it well.

Like Gramsci, Du Bois remained intimately linked with oppositional forces in an oppressed community. And in his case, these forces were (and are) often led by prophetic figures of the black Christian tradition. To be a part of the black freedom movement is to rub elbows with some prophetic black preachers and parishioners. And to be a part of the forces of progress in America is to rub up against some of these black freedom fighters.

If prophetic pragmatism is ever to become more than a conversational subject matter for cultural critics in and out of the academy, it must inspire progressive and prophetic social motion. One precondition of this kind of social movement is the emergence of potent prophetic religious practices in churches, synagogues, temples, and mosques. And given the historical weight of such practices in the American past, the probable catalyst for social motion will be the prophetic wing of the black church. Need we remind ourselves that the most significant and successful organic intellectual in twentieth-century America—maybe in American history—was a product of and leader in the prophetic wing of the black church? Rarely has a figure in modern history outside of elected public office linked the life of the mind to social change with such moral persuasiveness and political effectiveness.

The social movement led by Martin Luther King, Jr., represents the best of what the political dimension of prophetic pragmatism is all about. Like Sojourner Truth, Walter Rauschenbusch, Elizabeth Cady Stanton, and Dorothy Day, King was not a prophetic pragmatist. Yet like them he was a prophet, in which role he contributed mightily to the political project of prophetic pragmatism. His all-embracing moral vision facilitated alliances and coalitions across racial, gender, class, and religious lines. His Gandhian method of nonviolent resistance highlighted forms of love, courage, and discipline worthy of a compassionate prophet. And his appropriation and interpretation of American civil religion extended the tradition of American jeremiads, a tradition of public exhortation that joins social criticisms of America to moral renewal and admonishes the country to be true to its founding ideals of freedom, equality, and democracy. King accented the antiracist and anti-imperialist consequences of taking seriously these ideals, thereby linking the struggle for freedom in America to those movements in South Africa, Poland, South Korea, Ethiopia, Chile, and the Soviet Union.

Prophetic pragmatism worships at no ideological altars. It condemns oppression anywhere and everywhere, be it the brutal butchery of third-world dictators, the regimentation and repression of peoples in the Soviet Union and Soviet-bloc countries, or the racism, patriarchy, homophobia, and economic injustice in the first-world capitalist nations. In this way, the precious ideals of individuality and democracy of prophetic pragmatism oppose all those power structures that lack public accountability, be they headed by military generals, bureaucratic party bosses, or corporate tycoons. Nor is prophetic pragmatism confined to any preordained historical agent, such as the working class, black people, or women. Rather, it invites all people of goodwill both here and abroad to fight for an Emersonian culture of creative democracy in which the plight of the wretched of the earth is alleviated.

Richard A. Posner

Posner is Chief Judge, U.S. Court of Appeals for the Seventh Circuit, on which he has sat since 1981, and a senior lecturer at the University of Chicago Law School. His books include *Economic Analysis of Law* (4th ed., 1992), *The Economics of Justice* (1981), *Law and Literature: A Misunderstood Relation* (1988), *The Problems of Jurisprudence* (1990), *Cardozo: A Study in Reputation* (1990), *Sex and Reason* (1992), *Aging and Old Age* (1995), and *Overcoming Law* (1995). He is the editor of *The Essential Holmes: Selections from the Letters, Speeches, Judicial Opinions, and Other Writings of Oliver Wendell Holmes, Jr.* (1992).

A Pragmatist Manifesto

in *The Problems of Jurisprudence* (1990)

I HAVE ENDEAVORED to use the methods of analytic philosophy to guide a critical appraisal of modern American law. My focus has been on the twin preoccupations of the legal establishment in its rationalizing moods. One is a preoccupation with the autonomy of legal reasoning as a methodology of decision making. The other is a preoccupation with objectivity—here used in the strong sense that persons with different political or ideological commitments can nevertheless be brought to agree on the answer to even the most testing, the most politically charged, legal question—as a goal of the legal enterprise. I have emphasized the precarious position of the judge, forced to make unpopular decisions—every judicial decision is unpopular with one of the parties and with those in the same position as that party—without the intrinsic authority of the more "organic" (popular, authentically sovereign) branches of government from which the judiciary has studiously and even ostentatiously separated itself in an effort to secure political independence. The creation of an independent judiciary involves a substitution of professionalism, of expertise, for political legitimacy and sets up the eternal tension between the law and politics in the discharge of the judicial function, a tension mirrored on the jurisprudential plane in the age-old dispute between Legalists and Skeptics.

What I have just said is familiar enough. Any novelty is in the bill of particulars that I have drawn up against the defenders of law's autonomy and objectivity—the formalists, as one might call them, because the essence of formalism is to conceive of law as a system of relations among ideas rather than as a social practice. I do

Emperor hermits. Termites on the top floor

not reject formalism *tout court;* not only are there immensely worthwhile formal systems such as logic, mathematics, and art, but logic has an important role to play in legal decision making. I reject the exaggerated legal formalism that considers relations among legal ideas to be the essence of law and legal thought. Formalism in this sense is sometimes thought a discredited position in law. This is far from true. Many of the most powerful minds in the profession are formalists, whether or not they use the label; and at this writing the formalist style is resurgent in the Supreme Court and in the lower federal courts as well. Formalism is the official jurisprudence of lawyers and laypeople alike, and of both positivists and natural lawyers, although not of all individuals in either camp.

Let me review very briefly the main points of the analysis. I began with the epistemological and ontological dimensions of adjudication and searched for keys that might enable cogent answers, offered from within the conventions of legal argument and evidence, to be given to difficult questions, both legal and factual. No keys were found. The constructive as distinct from the critical role of logic in law (the critical role being to expose inconsistencies), though important, is limited. For while rules have a logical structure, *legal* rules are often vague, open-ended, tenuously grounded, highly contestable, and not only alterable but frequently altered. From the judge's standpoint they are more like guides or practices than like orders. The role of scientific inquiry in law is also limited, partly because of attitude and tradition but partly too because of essential characteristics of the legal enterprise, in particular the value rightly placed on the stability, certainty, and predictability of legal obligations.

Unable to base decisions in the difficult cases on either logic or science, judges are compelled to fall back on the grab bag of informal methods of reasoning that I call "practical reason" (using the term in a slightly unorthodox sense). These methods often succeed but sometimes fail; in any event they owe less than one might think to legal training and experience. In particular, reasoning by analogy has been oversold as a method of reasoning at once

cogent and distinctively legal. It is neither. The power of an analogy is a stimulus to thinking. The law seeks a logic of justification
rather than merely or primarily a logic of discovery. As a method
of justification, reasoning by analogy is really either enthymematic
(that is, deductive) or weakly inductive, rather than being its own
kind of thing; and whatever it is, there is nothing distinctively legal about it. Precedents that are squarely on the point do have authority in a court of law, but their authority is political—that is,
rooted ultimately in force—rather than epistemic in character.
Judges follow the previous decisions of their court when they
agree with them or when they deem legal stability more important
in their circumstances than getting the law right.[1] But a precedent's *analogical* significance means simply that the precedent contains information relevant to the decision of the present case.

Many changes of legal doctrine owe nothing either to analogies
(except insofar as they operate as similes or metaphors—powerful
though alogical modes of persuasion) or to logically or empirically
powerful arguments or evidence. Instead they are the result of
gestalt switches or religious-type conversions. Indeed, of such limited power are the tools of inquiry available to courts that the
highest realistic aspiration of a judge faced with a difficult case is
to make a "reasonable" (practical, sensible) decision, as distinct
from a demonstrably correct one—the latter will usually be out of
the question. The ingredients of reasonableness include, but are
not exhausted in, conventional legal materials such as precedents
and the principles of using precedents. Often the judge will have
no choice but to reason to the outcome by nonlegal methods from
nonlegal materials, and sometimes he will have to set inarticulable
intuition against legal arguments.

I have emphasized the difficulties, in the forensic setting, of factual as well as of legal analysis and noted that often the legal system settles for "formal" rather than "substantive" accuracy—that
is, settles for procedural rules (such as rules on burden of proof)
that force determinacy on outcomes notwithstanding irresolvable
factual uncertainties. Uncertainty about matters of fact pervades

efforts not only to determine what happened in the dispute that gave rise to the litigation but also to measure the consequences of legal doctrines, and as a result the factual substrate of those doctrines often is tenuous. And, partly for evidentiary reasons, partly for deeper philosophical ones, the law's ostensible commitment to a rich mentalist ontology of free will, intent, and the like turns out to be superficial. As Holmes said, the law deals with externals.[2] The operative model of human action in such fields as criminal law is a behaviorist (determinist) one; even the concept of a "voluntary" confession is seen to be determinist in character.

Law itself is best approached in behaviorist terms. It cannot accurately or usefully be described as a set of concepts, whether of positive law or of natural law. It is better, though not fully, described as the activity of the licensed professionals we call judges, the scope of their license being limited only by the diffuse outer bounds of professional propriety and moral consensus. Holmes was on the right track in proposing the prediction theory of law,[3] which is an activity theory; his critics have been too quick to dismiss it. Redescribing law in activity terms tends to erase the distinction between natural law and positive law, and the distinction has indeed outlived its usefulness. Judges make rather than find law, and they use as inputs both the rules laid down by legislatures and previous courts ("positive law") and their own ethical and policy preferences. These preferences are all that remains of "natural law," now that so many of us have lost confidence that nature constitutes a normative order.

If epistemology and ontology will not save the law's objectivity and autonomy, neither will hermeneutics. Neither interpretive theory in the large nor the rich literature on legal interpretation (a real embarrassment of riches)[4] will underwrite objective interpretations of common law, statutes, or the Constitution. Of course one can go too far with interpretive skepticism. Communication works—verifiably so—and statutes and constitutional provisions are efforts at communication. But often in dealing with statutes and the Constitution the channels of communication are obstructed, and when that happens the concept of interpretation is altogether too loose and vague to discipline legal inquiry. We see this when we ask what the *goal* of legal interpretation is and discover that there is no agreed-upon answer to the question and no rational means of compelling agreement, that it all depends on the interpreter's political theory. We might do best to discard the term "interpretation" and focus directly on the consequences of proposed applications of statutory and constitutional provisions to specific disputes.

The situation for the defenders of law's autonomy and objectivity is not improved when the searchlight is trained on overarching principles that might organize and discipline legal inquiry. Natural law as the name for ethical and policy considerations that bear on the exercise of judicial discretion—considerations such as those encapsulated in the equity maxims (for example, no man shall profit from his wrongdoing and *pacta sunt servanda*[5])—is in fine shape. But natural law as a system of thought that generates definite answers to difficult moral and legal questions is hopeless in a society that is morally heterogeneous, as ours is. Distributive justice cannot replace natural law, for it too is riven by unbridgeable political disagreements. Although corrective justice, which is rooted in our deep-seated retributive emotions, and wealth maximization—especially, I think, the latter—have significant domains of application, particularly to common law, neither can provide a complete framework that will enable adjudication to be made determinate. Nor can the literary, feminist, and communitarian perspectives that are receiving increasing attention or the nostalgia-soaked movement to return to traditional legalism via philosophy that I call neotraditionalism provide comprehensive frameworks for adjudication. The cat is out of the bag. Efforts in this scientific and pluralistic age to regain a confident sense in the law's autonomy and objectivity seem futile. Yet the radical skepticism and vague communitarian yearnings of critical legal studies[6] are a dead end too.

The underlying problem can be stated simply. Law uses a crude methodology to deal with extremely difficult questions. The crudeness is concealed when no other inquirers have a powerful methodology, and now they do, thanks to advances in natural and social science. The difficulty is concealed when the legal establishment is homogeneous, for then its priors and prejudices fix the necessary premises for confident decision. As a result of social and political changes, America no longer has a homogeneous legal establishment. The more diverse the judiciary, the more robust are the decisions that command strong support within it—but the less likely is a given decision to command such support and the more exposed, therefore, is the contingency of legal doctrine. Some lawyers and judges believe that a diverse judiciary is bad, because it makes law uncertain, unpredictable. They have a point. But from the standpoint not of order but of knowledge, they are wrong. A diverse judiciary exposes—yet at the same time reduces—the intellectual poverty of law, viewed as a method not just of settling disputes authoritatively but also of generating cogent answers to social questions.

A diverse judiciary must be distinguished from a judiciary selected on the basis of racial and sexual politics. Of course persons of a different race or sex from that of most judges may have relevant life experiences that contribute to the moral and intellectual diversity of the bench, but this is also true of individuals of different religious and professional background, different temperament, different health, and even different hobbies. A machinery of judicial selection that merely seeks a balance among clamoring, politically effective interest groups will not generate an optimally diverse judiciary.

The concept of law that has emerged here can be summarized in the following theses. First, there is no such thing as "legal reasoning." Lawyers and judges answer legal questions through the use of simple logic and the various methods of practical reasoning that everyday thinkers use. In part because of the law's (salutary) emphasis on stability, the scientific attitude and the methodology of science are not at home in law.

Second, partly for the reason just given, partly because many methods of practical reason are inarticulate (for example, tacit knowledge), partly because "prejudgment" in the sense of resistance to rational arguments that contradict strong priors often is itself rational, partly because there is little feedback in the legal process (that is, the consequences of judicial decisions are largely unknown), the *justification* (akin to scientific verification) of legal decisions—the demonstration that a decision is correct—often is impossible.

Third, a closely related point is that *difficult* legal cases can rarely be decided objectively if objectivity is taken to mean more than reasonableness. The more uniform the judiciary is, however, the more agreement there will be on the premises for decision, and therefore the fewer difficult cases there will be. I have stressed both the costs of this uniformity and the degree of disuniformity in the contemporary American judiciary. But it should be borne in mind that even within a judiciary as diverse as ours, there will be many shared intuitions (of course, it could be more diverse, and then there would be fewer), which will provide premises for objective decision making. Moral and legal nihilism is as untenable as moral realism or legal formalism.

Fourth, large changes in law often come about as a result of a nonrational process akin to conversion. Rhetoric in the sense of persuasion not necessarily addressed to the rational intellect (the sense famously criticized by Plato in *Gorgias*) may change the law as much as hard reality does.

Fifth, law is an activity rather than a concept or a group of concepts. No bounds can be fixed a priori on what shall be allowed to count as an argument in law. The modern significance of natural law is not as a body of objective norms that underwrite positive law but as a source of the ethical and political arguments that judges use to challenge, change, or elaborate positive law—in other words to produce new positive law. There are no moral "reals" (at least none available to decide difficult legal cases), but neither is there a body of positive law that somehow preexists the judicial decisions applying, and in the process confirming, modifying, extending, and rejecting, the "sovereign's" commands. The line between positive law and natural law is no longer interesting or important and the concepts themselves are jejune.

Sixth, there is no longer a useful sense in which law is interpretive. This is true of statutory and constitutional law as well as common law. Interpretation butters no parsnips; it is at best a reminder that there is a text in the picture (and there is not even that in common law fields). The essence of interpretive decision making is considering the consequences of alternative decisions. There are no "logically" correct interpretations; interpretation is not a logical process.

Seventh, there are no overarching concepts of justice that our legal system can seize upon to give direction to the enterprise. (This point is related to the earlier one about the absence of moral "reals.") Corrective justice and wealth maximization have important but limited domains of applicability, the former reflecting the residue of vengeance thinking in law and society, the latter the persistent utilitarian, instrumentalist, pragmatic spirit of American society. Distributive justice seems quite hopeless, however, and it has yet to be shown that the literary, feminist, or communitarian perspectives have much to contribute to the legal enterprise that is both new and useful. The prudentialism of a Burke[7] has cautionary value in law, but that may be all.

And eighth, law is functional, not expressive or symbolic either in aspiration or—so far as yet appears—in effect. Hence in areas where the social function is the efficient allocation of resources, law appropriately takes its cue from economics. The law is not interested in the soul or even the mind. It has adopted a severely behaviorist concept of human activity as sufficient to its ends and tractable to its means. It has yet to be shown that law changes the people's attitudes toward compliance with social norms, as distinct from altering their incentives.

All this is not to deny the indispensability of law or the importance of its contributions to civilized society. But it amounts to a less than thrilling vision of law. It is remote from "law day" rhetoric and even from most academic views of law.

Yet a pragmatist might ask what all this nay-saying, this carping, this harping on dubiety, this heaping on of wet blankets, is *good* for. I am not claiming that the condition of law spells a crisis for capitalism or the liberal state. I have not presented dramatic proposals for improvement. Although I can imagine radical changes in the legal system that would imbue legal institutions with greater respect for scientific methodology, I am not sure they would be justified, given the competing social functions that law serves. Have I, therefore, ended at dead center, violating Voltaire's dictum (improving on Socrates) to be moderate in everything, including moderation?

My colleagues in the legal profession will not consider the picture of law that I have painted merely a dull monochrome; some of them will even say that I have announced "the death of law." And the approach has practical as well as conceptual or atmospheric implications, only a few of which I have tried to draw out in this book. A moment ago I remarked the pros and cons of a diverse judiciary, and the remark bears on the perennial proposal for an Intercircuit Tribunal that would on reference from the Supreme Court resolve conflicts among the federal courts of appeal that the Supreme Court lacks the time to resolve.[8] At first glance it might seem that the resolution of conflicts that generate legal uncertainty would be an unequivocal good, so that the only question about the proposal would be its cost (principally delay), the difficulties of staffing such a tribunal, and so forth. But from a pragmatic perspective the main concern is with the danger of premature closure of legal debate. Intercircuit conflict provides a method of unforced inquiry in the nation's most important judicial system. Of course debate continues after the judges have ruled, and sometimes their decision is overruled. But once a national precedent is laid down and begins to accrete reliance and interest-group support, it may be difficult to overrule, however powerful the criticisms of it. So intercircuit conflict has epistemic value that must be traded off against the undoubted loss in legal certainty from the absence of a method for prompt resolution of all intercircuit conflicts. My analysis also suggests a more hospitable attitude toward judicial dissents than is found in some circles. They are not only, as they so often seem to be, a nuisance (my frequent reaction as a judge). They compromise the authoritarian character of law, but in doing so they exemplify unforced inquiry, of which American law could perhaps use more. To quote William Blake, "without contraries is no progression."

I would stress the implications of my analysis for research—in the suggestions, for example, . . . that a careful study would show that specialized courts are less rather than more attentive to precedent than generalist courts,   that we ought to study the effects of an inefficient state legal system on the state's welfare and the feedback effect on the legal system, and . . . that conviction of the innocent is less rather than, as one might think, more common in a society in which the crime rate is high. There are implications, too, for teaching (it is a scandal that law students are not instructed in the fundamentals of statistical inference), for practice (legal advocates should place much greater emphasis on facts and on policy than they do), and for judging (judges should at long last abandon the rhetoric, and the reality, of formalist adjudication). I have proposed a new explanation of the pattern of the coerced-confession cases—that under the rubric of "involuntariness" some voluntary confessions are excluded from evidence in criminal trials because they are unreliable and some reliable confessions are excluded because they are involuntary on a determinist account of "free will"—and a new approach to statutory interpretation. And I have embraced (or rejected, which comes to the same thing) both legal positivism and natural law.

But the most important implications have to do with attitudes. The traditional—and neotraditional, and liberal, and radical—pieties of jurisprudence should be discarded, and the legal enterprise reconceived in pragmatic terms. Once this is done the dichotomy between legal positivism and natural law collapses, with no loss. But I do not suggest that it is easy to change attitudes.

The attack on foundations, on certitudes, on tradition, on Grand Theories owes much, as I have emphasized throughout, to the pragmatist tradition. It is a pity that it is so hard to define the tradition, both generally and in relation to law. Conventional histories of pragmatism begin with Charles Sanders Peirce, although he himself gave credit for the basic idea to a lawyer friend, Nicholas St. John Green. From Peirce the baton was handed to William James, then to John Dewey, George Mead, and the British pragmatist, F. C. S. Schiller. The pragmatic movement gave legal realism much of its intellectual shape and content. But with the coming of World War II, both philosophical pragmatism and legal realism seemed to expire, the first superseded by logical positivism and other "hard" analytic philosophy, the second absorbed into the legal mainstream and particularly into the "legal process" school that was to reach its apogee in the 1950s. Then, beginning in the 1960s with the waning of logical positivism, pragmatism came charging back in the person of Richard Rorty, followed in the 1970s by critical legal studies—the radical child of legal realism—and in the 1980s by a school of legal neopragmatists, including some feminists. In this account pragmatism, whether of the paleo- or the neovariety, stands for a progressively more emphatic rejection of Enlightenment dualisms such as subject and object, mind and body, perception and reality, form and substance, these dualisms being regarded as the props of a conservative social, political, and legal order. *Not pluralistic to exclude them.*

This picture is too simple by far. The triumphs of science, and particularly of Newtonian physics, in the seventeenth and eighteenth centuries persuaded most thinking people that the physical universe had a uniform structure accessible to human reason; and it began to seem that human nature and human social systems might have a similarly mechanical structure. This emerging worldview cast humankind in an observing mold. Through perception, measurement, and mathematics the human mind would uncover the secrets of nature—including the mind as a part of nature and the laws of social interactions: laws that decreed balanced government, economic behavior in accordance with the principles of supply and demand, and moral and legal principles based on immutable principles of psychology and human behavior. The mind was a camera, recording activities both natural and social and alike determined by natural laws.

This view, broadly scientific but flavored with a Platonic sense of a world of order behind the chaos of sense impressions, was challenged by the Romantic poets (such as Blake and Wordsworth) and Romantic philosophers. They emphasized the plasticity of the world, and especially the esemplastic power of the human imagination. Institutional constraints they despised along with all other limits on human aspiration, as merely contingent; science they found dreary; they celebrated the sense of community—of oneness with humankind and with nature—the sense of unlimited potential, that an infant feels. They were Prometheans. The principal American representative of this school was Emerson, and he left traces of his thought on Peirce and Holmes alike. Emerson's European counterpart (and admirer) was Nietzsche. It is not that Peirce, or Holmes, or even Nietzsche was a "Romantic" in a precise sense (if there is a precise sense). It is that they wished to shift attention from a passive, contemplative relation between an observing subject and an objective reality, whether natural or social, to an active, creative relation between striving human beings and the problems that beset them and that they seek to overcome. They believed that thought was an exertion of will instrumental to some human desire (and we see here the link between pragmatism and utilitarianism), and that social institutions—whether science, law, or religion—were the product of shifting human desires rather than the reflection of a reality external to those desires.

This account should help us see why "truth" is a problematic concept for a pragmatist. Its essential meaning, after all, is observer independence, which is just what the pragmatist is inclined to deny. It is no surprise, therefore, that the pragmatists' stabs at defining truth—truth is what is fated to be believed in the long run (Peirce), truth is what is good to believe (James), or truth is what survives in the competition among ideas (Holmes)[9]—are riven by paradox. The pragmatist's real interest is not in truth at all but in belief justified by social need.

This need not make the pragmatist unfriendly to science—far from it—but it shifts the emphasis in the philosophy of science from the discovery of nature's laws by observation to the formulation of theories about nature (including man and society) on the basis of man's desire to predict and control his environment, both social and natural. The implication, later to become explicit in the writings of Thomas Kuhn,[10] is that scientific theories are a function of human need and desire rather than of the way things are in nature, so that the succession of theories on a given topic need not produce a linear growth in scientific knowledge. Science in the pragmatic view is a social enterprise.

The spirit of pragmatism is not limited to the handful of philosophers who have called themselves pragmatists (and a tiny handful it is—Peirce himself, the founder, having renounced the term because he disagreed with William James's definition of it). Rival of pragmatism though it is thought to be, logical positivism, with its emphasis on verifiability and its consequent hostility to metaphysics, is pragmatic in demanding that theory make a difference in the world of fact, the empirical world. Popper's falsificationist philosophy of science[11] is close to Peirce's view of science, for in both philosophies doubt is the engine of progress and truth an ever-receding goal rather than an attainment. Wittgenstein's emphasis on the "sociality" of knowledge[12] marks him as pragmatist, while Habermas has acknowledged the influence of the pragmatists on his own theory of "conversational" rationality.[13] Plainly we are dealing with an immensely diverse tradition rather than with a single, coherent school of thought.

Latterly pragmatism has come to be thought a left-wing ideology, a celebration of the plasticity of social institutions. The discussion in Chapter 12 of a recent article by Richard Rorty[14] shows why, and Rorty is not even on the left of the neopragmatist movement. But the connection between pragmatism and socialism is adventitious. Rorty is a Romanticist, and this is only one of the flavors that pragmatism comes in. Pragmatism in the sense that I find congenial means looking at problems concretely, experimentally, without illusions, with full awareness of the limitations of human reason, with a sense of the "localness" of human knowledge, the difficulty of translations between cultures, the unattainability of "truth," the consequent importance of keeping diverse paths of inquiry open, the dependence of inquiry on culture and social institutions, and above all the insistence that social thought and action be evaluated as instruments to valued human goals rather than as ends in themselves. These dispositions, which are more characteristic of scientists than of lawyers (and in an important sense pragmatism is the ethics of scientific inquiry), have no political valence. They can, I believe, point the way to a clearer understanding of law. Law as currently conceived in the academy and the judiciary has too theocratic a cast. There is too much emphasis on authority, certitude, rhetoric, and tradition, too little on consequences and on social-scientific techniques for measuring consequences. There is too much confidence, too little curiosity, and insufficient regard for the contributions of other disciplines. Jurisprudence itself is much too solemn and self-important. Its votaries write too marmoreal, hieratic, and censorious a prose. Law and religion were long intertwined, and many parallels and overlaps remain.[15] Law, too, has its high priests, its sacred texts and sacred cows, its hermeneutic mysteries, its robes and temples, rituals and ceremonies.

Admittedly, much that I am complaining about is surface rather than substance, for on the whole the law *has* been shaped by practical needs (the same may be true of religion). Influential judicial decisions as diverse as *Farwell* (the fellow-servant case) and *Barnette* (the second flag-salute case)[16]—one conservative, the other liberal, as these terms are used today; one common law, the other constitutional law; one decided in 1842, the other in 1943—are quintessentially pragmatic. Still, law needs more of the scientific spirit than it has—the spirit of inquiry, challenge, fallibilism, open-mindedness, respect for fact, and acceptance of change. I use "spirit" advisedly. I am not referring to the particulars of scientific discourse, although economics and other social sciences have a large role to play in any modern system of law.[17]

I find pragmatism bracing; others may find it paralyzing. Pragmatist skepticism about "truth" might, for example, be thought to undermine the nation's commitment to free speech. If there is no truth "out there," how can free speech be defended by reference to its efficacy in bringing us nearer to the truth?[18] Actually that is not such a difficult question. If there is no truth out there, this should make us particularly wary of people who claim to have found the truth and who argue that further inquiry would be futile or subversive and therefore should be forbidden. If there is no objective truth, moreover, this makes it all the more important to maintain the conditions necessary for the unforced inquiry required to challenge and defeat all those false claims to have found the truth at last. There is knowledge if not ultimate truth,[19] and a fallibilist theory of knowledge emphasizes, as preconditions to the growth of scientific and other forms of knowledge, the continual testing and retesting of accepted "truths," the constant kicking over of sacred cows—in short, a commitment to robust and free-wheeling inquiry with no intellectual quarter asked or given.

Such a theory is wary of proposals to give less protection to scientific than to political freedom of expression on the ground that scientific truth is objectively determinable and therefore need not be left to the hurly-burly of the marketplace of ideas, or to limit protection of artistic expression on the superficially inconsistent ground that fiction is parasitic on and therefore less important than fact.[20] If, consistent with the skepticism of the pragmatist, we reject essentialist ideas of art and moral-realist ideas of offensiveness, we deny the competence of courts to condemn expressive works on the ground that their offensiveness outweighs their artistic

If any thing goes, they all go down.

value.[21] The emphasis in this book on the importance of meta-phor and other forms of "warm" argument for legal change supplies a further argument against sharply distinguishing rational from emotive expression and can even be thought to argue for defining speech more broadly than courts have as yet done, so that it would encompass the burning of draft cards and other expressive activity now classified as "action" rather than as "speech."[22] The danger of warm rhetoric is that it will become hot—by which I refer not to burning one's draft card but to attacking one's opponents physically. Violence is a way of getting people to alter their perspectives, and despite all its emphasis on unforced inquiry pragmatism has difficulty drawing and defending the line between peaceable and forcible means of changing the way people think. But the pragmatist will not be insensitive to the costs of free speech, including the costs of providing police protection at public expense to speakers who desire to provoke violence.

Although American lawyers have made significant contributions to the theory of free speech, their attitude toward law itself is pious and reverential rather than inquiring and challenging. Law is not a sacred text, however, but a usually humdrum social practice vaguely bounded by ethical and political convictions. The soundness of legal interpretations and other legal propositions is best gauged, therefore, by an examination of their consequences in the world of fact. That is a central contention of this book. In making it I do not mean to deny that the legal tradition includes insights and sensitivities of great social value. The rule of law is a genuine, indeed an invaluable, public good, and one to which formalists like Coke have made great contributions. The refusal to acknowledge these contributions is one of the flaws of critical legal studies. But there is a tendency in law to look backward rather than forward—to search for essences rather than to embrace the experiential flux. The consequences of law are what are least well known about law. The profession's indifference to studies that cast doubt on the lawyer's faith in the expressive, symbolic, and norm-reinforcing consequences of law is appalling.

The situation is unlikely to be changed (to continue the religious metaphor) by preaching. It is deeply rooted in the nature of legal education, which in turn reflects the age-old practices and traditions of the profession. Judges and lawyers do not have the leisure or the training to conduct systematic investigations of the causes and consequences of law. That is work for the academy. But the law schools conceive their function to be the training of legal professionals rather than legal scientists. (There are good economic reasons for this.) The emphasis is on imparting the skills, knowledge, and folkways most essential to the effective practice of law, and that means the skills of doctrinal analysis and legal argumentation, knowledge of legal doctrines, and the folkways of the judge and practicing lawyer.

I mentioned in the Introduction that the study of law is begun *in medias res,* and here I add that this procedure forestalls the emergence of a critical, an external, perspective. It presents law as something not to be questioned, as something that has always existed and in approximately its contemporary form. Within a few months of entering law school the law student has lost the external perspective. There is very little postgraduate legal education in this country other than for foreigners, and little effort is made to equip the law student who may one day become a law professor with the skills, knowledge, and attitudes requisite for studying the causes of law, the direct and indirect consequences of law on behavior, the experience of other nations with law, and the scientific laws of the legal system. Skills of mathematical modeling, statistical analysis, survey research, and experimentation; knowledge of legal institutions here and abroad and of the pertinent parts of the disciplines (economics, political science, statistics, philosophy, psychology) that bear on law; the scientific ethic—all these are for the most part ignored. This neglect is the obverse of the law schools' preoccupation with imparting skills of immediate use in the practice of law. It is no surprise that so much legal scholarship and judicial analysis is unoriginal, unempirical, conventional, and unworldly, overwhelmingly verbal and argumentative (indeed, verbose and polemical), narrowly focused on doctrinal questions, mesmerized by the latest Supreme Court decisions, and preoccupied with minute and ephemeral distinctions—rather than bold, scientific, and descriptive. The academy does not generate the knowledge that judges, lawyers, and legislators need in order to operate a legal system, yet there is no other institution capable of generating it. Unless these grave deficiencies of academic law are overcome, ambitious programs for improving law are unlikely to succeed.

Let us begin to recognize the problems by noting that a carapace of falsity and pretense surrounds law and is obscuring the enterprise. It is time we got rid of it. I end as I began with a quotation from William Butler Yeats—this one, from "A Coat," made apt by the importance of the robe as a judicial symbol: "there's more enterprise / In walking naked."

Richard Poirier

Poirier is Distinguished Professor of English at Rutgers University, where he has taught since 1963. He is the editor of *Raritan: A Quarterly Review* and the chairman of the Library of America. His books include *A World Elsewhere* (1966), *The Performing Self* (1971), *Robert Frost: The Work of Knowing* (1977), *The Renewal of Literature: Emersonian Reflections* (1987), and *Poetry and Pragmatism* (1992).

Reading Pragmatically

in *Poetry and Pragmatism* (1992)

AS BOOKS PROLIFERATE on the history of contemporary theory, so does the likelihood that most will eventually be consigned to the history of public relations. Their common theme is that every half-decade or so, since about 1960, new theories have been rushed into the perilous deadly breach of literary studies to rout older ones, by then ready for early retirement, or ideologically discredited, or just plain boring. Inexorably, according to a narrative now in vogue, we have moved from New Criticism to structuralism to post-structuralism, all thanks to "moves" among competing schools and masters. Literary departments of academia have never been able to plot achievements in their fields with the assurance vouchsafed departments of science, however illusory the assurance is, and they are easily persuaded by almost any scenario of alleged progress. These scenarios create reality rather than describe it, however, and do it by dint of conspicuous omissions. They are likely to ignore, for example, critical works of stunning individuality, like those of Empson or Blackmur, works written before the story of theory is now said to have begun, and predictive of many of its recent conclusions.[1] And insofar as these histories touch upon the thorny subject of reading, they shy away also from evidence that some of the close linguistic analyses conducted in classrooms for several decades past were able to unearth the theories of language already deployed *within* literary works themselves, notably the canonical ones. Indeed, works tend to remain canonical, as Frank Kermode has argued, not because of their alleged dalliance with political or social stabilities, but because of their own linguistic instability, their tendency to slip their moorings and thus to encourage alternative interpretations, continually over time.[2]

While theory should not, of course, be confused with the fabrications of its annalists, and while the benefits of the one outweigh the distortions of the other, the balance between them is only perilously maintained. A theory, as apologists argue, comes into existence by asserting its capacity to make quite specific historical differences. Its laudable function is to create vantage points outside daily practice—particularly when practice presupposes, as it notoriously does in the United States, that it is innocent of politics—from which it can then show that such practice is itself necessarily governed by theories, however much it tries to shun them. In order to be politically or culturally efficacious, that is, theory, like the histories of it, must insistently point to and mark its progressive steps. Only by so doing can it inculcate that degree of self-consciousness and that redirection of effort which might redeem it from the frequent charge of professional opportunism.

But such balances as do exist between theory and the history of theory need to be asserted so as to avoid the sort of neglectful historicizing that slips into a review by Terry Eagleton in the *Times Literary Supplement* (November 24, 1989), where he remarks that "post-structuralist concern with the devious stratagems of language, not least with its ineradicably metaphorical nature, is cognate with the literary objects such criticism examines." It is unfortunate that Eagleton's guarded hospitality to canonical works of the past for their contribution to contemporary theory doesn't prompt a corresponding recognition about works of criticism written in the past. Instead, it seems to suggest that only with a French benchmark called "post-structuralism" was Anglo-American criticism alerted to a "concern with the devious stratagems of language." The term "post-structuralism" looks for its beginnings only to the year 1967, the publication date of Derrida's *De la grammatologie,*[3] but all the term itself announces to me is some late conversions to a kind of linguistic skepticism, allied to pronounced theological and cultural skepticisms, already familiar to a number of readers and critics in England and the United States. As I have argued, a strong, particularly energizing mode of linguistic skepticism was already available to those who had learned to appreciate the distrusts of language implicit in the anti-foundationalism of Charles Peirce or William James or John Dewey, or who, even without exposure to these philosophers or to Santayana or Cavell,[4] had otherwise come to appreciate the movements of language in Stein, Stevens, or Frost.

Without necessarily depending on any of these writers, however, certain kinds of intense close reading were being pedagogically advanced, well before the post–World War II period, which without defining themselves theoretically—at the time that would have been thought inappropriate in undergraduate classrooms—or calling themselves skeptical, managed to inculcate in more than a few teachers and students a habit of enjoying the way words undo and redo themselves to the benefit of social as well as literary practice. This latter development was fairly frequent in the more enterprising small colleges, where intimate and intense workshop teaching most frequently occurs. On this occasion I have in mind my own experiences as an undergraduate after World War II at Amherst College and in an undergraduate course I later helped teach at Harvard called "Humanities 6: The Interpretation of Literature." Others have doubtless had comparable experiences; I am here speaking only of what I know best.

In telling the story of Hum 6 I want in part to help disrupt the calendar of theory and to loosen its intimidating hold. Along the way I hope also to show that the influences that passed through the course were American and English rather than European in origin, and that this had important consequences for its tone and character. Specifically, the influences included Emerson, Peirce, William James and John Dewey, Wittgenstein, Kenneth Burke, and F. R. Leavis, most of whom have been afforded little or no place in the history of contemporary theory. And I chose to print the piece in *Raritan Quarterly* because two of its editors who have had the most to do with setting the magazine's direction, Thomas

Edwards and I, remain greatly affected by our roughly similar educational experiences as Amherst undergraduates and, later, as
teachers in Hum 6. I am acutely aware in all my references to
Amherst that the credit I give to Hum 6 at Harvard, and to its
founder Reuben Brower, could be differently distributed so as to
allow more prominence to some teachers at Amherst who were
Brower's colleagues when he taught there, who initiated with him
the parent courses of Hum 6, and who helped fashion many of
the assignments used in the course after Brower started it at Harvard. Before long I hope someone will tell that fuller story, along
with the story of Amherst English in general.

This piece began as a talk at a session of the Modern Language
Association in December 1988, at which J. Hillis Miller and I were
asked to discuss some problems of reading and their relation to
criticism and pedagogy. I understood the topic to include the responsibilities to words which reading entails, an obligation to all
the barely audible cultural inheritances carried within them.
Reading can be a civilizing process, not because the meanings it
gathers may be good for us—they may in fact sometimes be quite
pernicious—but because that most demanding form of writing
and reading called literature often asks us to acknowledge, in the
twists and turns of its language, the presence of ancestral kin who
cared deeply about what words were doing to them and what they
might do in return. Traces of these earlier efforts make us aware,
as few other things can, of the opportunities and limits of culture
itself. Good reading and good writing are, first and last, lots of
work. It was fitting, in that regard, that the papers the students
were asked to write in Hum 6, in response to printed handouts of
carefully phrased and detailed questions, were called "exercises."
These exercises made reading an acutely meditative process without ever inviting anything so mechanical as the mere tracking of
images.

One eventually gets beyond "exercises" of this kind, acquiring
an easy and natural familiarity with the disciplines they instill, and
yet any athlete or dancer or musician—or reader—must have

learned *how* to exercise and when to get back to exercise in order always to know the rigors by which any degree of mastery is attained. Reading is an acquired talent with words, which is all that reading ever can be directly engaged with, and it involves the measured recognition that words can do unexpected and disturbing things to you. People who vocalize their reading, who let it register on the ear and not simply on the eye, are apt to be more than ordinarily sensitive to the fantastic and baffling variability of sounds in any sentence or phrase, and of how this precludes their arriving at any sure sense of meaning. The meaning of a piece of writing for them is in the perceived difficulty of securing one. If, as Wordsworth said in "Essay, Supplementary to the Preface" of 1815, the poet is "in the condition of Hannibal among the Alps . . . called upon to clear and often to shape his own road," then it cannot be supposed, he later goes on to say, that "the reader can make progress of this kind, like an Indian prince or general—stretched on his palanquin, and borne by his slaves." Reading must be actively synchronized with the generative energies of writing itself. It is not enough to understand what is being said, since this is always less than what is being expressed.

Obviously, reading/writing of this kind cannot occur in space; it occurs in time, word by word, sentence by sentence, responsive to opportunities as they open up, to resistances as they are encountered, to entrapments which must be dodged, all of these latent in the words just previously laid down and in the forms, both large and small, that reading and writing often fall into. Reading, even more than writing, needs to be alert to these possibilities, if only because most writers cannot usually afford the degree of skepticism which is the privilege—some would say the obligation—of a reader. In that sense Shakespeare is the greatest writer of all time because he was also the greatest reader of his own words, never oblivious to their implications no matter how apparently at odds with his characterizations, never cheating on them even in the pursuit of theatrical spectacle or shapeliness, continuously renewing his words out of possibilities salvaged from the

very decomposition into which he allows them just as continuously to slide.

The three people from whom I learned most about reading, and
who seem to me exemplary in showing how reading asks for some
of the same energies that go into writing, were not themselves
writers of theory, and, so far as could be discerned, knew very little about Emerson, and still less about William James. They are
G. Armour Craig, from whose teaching at Amherst I profited
most as an undergraduate and who did nearly all of his critical
work for and in his classes; F. R. Leavis, who was my tutor after
that at Downing College, Cambridge, a famous classroom teacher
who refused René Wellek's much publicized invitation to translate
his practices into theoretical justifications; and Reuben Brower,
from whom I never took a class but for whom I worked at Harvard from 1953 to 1961 in Hum 6.

I want to call attention to the importance of Brower's course
and give it a lineage. Out of several possibilities, the one I think
most important belongs to a tradition of linguistic criticism that I
have tried, ever since leaving the course, to locate in a line that
runs from Emerson through William James, Kenneth Burke, Frost,
Stein, and Stevens. As has been apparent, I read all these as poets
and read their poetry as a species of linguistic criticism, no less
than are their lectures, letters, and essays. Together with the others
in this line, they are at once grateful to the cultural inheritance of
language and suspicious of it, congenitally uncertain as to the
meaning of words and correspondingly attentive to nuance. Theirs
is a criticism persuaded always of the instability of any formation
of language.

Brower's course taught me, as did Emerson's linguistic skepticism, much that has since been theoretically formulated, though
neither Brower, who boned up on Emerson for his Frost book,
nor those in the course who subsequently were most responsive to
European theory, ever knew enough about Emerson to acknowledge his influence on Hum 6. Surely Paul de Man did not, when,
in the *TLS* of December 10, 1982, he wrote appreciatively that

"my own awareness of the critical, even subversive, power of literary instruction does not stem from philosophical allegiances but
from a very specific teaching experience." And then he identifies
it: "In the 1950's . . . Reuben Brower . . . taught an undergraduate
course [at Harvard] in General Education entitled 'The Interpretation of Literature' (better known on the Harvard campus and in
the profession at large as Hum 6)."

Over nearly the same number of years, de Man and I were
among the half-dozen or so section leaders in the course. Not all
of them would find the word "subversive" appropriate to the
kinds of activity with language that went on in class and that was
asked for in the writing assignments out of class. It was my impression that only some of the teachers and still fewer of the students in the course were aware that their activity could prove to be
subversive. Many thought of Hum 6 as a more subtle and ideologically neutral version of New Criticism, a mode of criticism
which in my view, and for reasons I will get to presently, was in
fact subservient to quite specific social and even religious forms of
authority. It is therefore disappointing to discover that on other
occasions de Man casually, or possibly for professionalist reasons,
makes equations among New Criticism, close reading, Derrida,
and himself, to the point where he gives the unintended and erroneous impression that any kind of critical-linguistic study which
focuses on texts is by nature subversive. The spirit of Hum 6 and
of its American derivations does seem to me "subversive," but
only in quite limited ways.

It is in the very nature of Hum 6 that it has never blown its own
horn. There was nothing of the theorist in Brower, and it could be
argued, as did Robert Elliott in a commemoratory talk at the
Modern Language Association meeting of 1976, that Brower in
his writing might now and then have profitably been more of a
theorist, especially when it came to the key term in his *Alexander
Pope: The Poetry of Allusion*. Even more than his friend Leavis, he
was disinclined to summarize what he was doing, and he avoided
critical controversy as assiduously as Leavis sought it out. (The

fourteen essays by people who had taught the course, edited by
Brower and me and published in 1962 under the title *In Defense of
Reading*,[5] is filled with good moments, but not one of the essays is
polemical even to the point of contrasting the sort of thing we did
in class with what went on in most other humanities and literature
classes.) Given the degree to which the course anticipated and indeed moved beyond many later theoretical propositions about language, it is not surprising that those who taught it have not
subsequently waxed theoretical about things they long ago took
for granted. Of those who have since become known for their
work in the academy, some, like Paul Bertram, Thomas Edwards,
Neil Rudenstine, and William Pritchard, are indifferent when
not opposed to out-and-out theorizing; others, like Paul Alpers,
David Kalstone, Anne Ferry, and Margery Sabin, have been hospitable to theoretical formulations of what they would be doing
anyway; and those who have become known as theorists, like Neil
Hertz, Peter Brooks, and de Man, readily admit some prior obligation to Hum 6.

In trying to understand where a course like Hum 6 came from,
it is essential to remember that while the course itself flourished at
Harvard in the mid-fifties and early sixties, which is when de Man
got to know about its "subversiveness," a precursor had existed in
a course which Armour Craig, Theodore Baird, and Brower had
created at Amherst College in the preceding decade. The Amherst
course was for sophomores, most of whom would have taken in
their first year another course, specifically in writing, that was
fashioned by Baird on lines that, despite his disclaimers, have been
identified as Wittgensteinian. This freshman course was an even
more radical immersion in the waywardness of language, too off-
beat and subtle to be summarized here. English 19–20, as the
sophomore course was called, appeared to be less daring than the
Baird course, English 1–2, perhaps because it emphasized, as did
courses then being given at other places, the close reading of texts
or, in Brower's better phrase, "reading in slow motion."[6] For him
reading ideally remained *in* motion, not choosing to encapsulate

itself, as New Critical readings nearly always ultimately aspire to do. It was different from Brooks and Warren, with their *Understanding Poetry*[7]—importantly so.

The Harvard undergraduates in Hum 6 numbered just over two hundred; they met together once a week for a lecture and then met again with section teachers in groups of about twenty-five. The sections were devoted to demonstrations, taking off from the lectures, and to discussions of the three-to-five page papers written outside class every couple of weeks. These would be returned to the students heavily marked up, usually with complaints that something had not been shown sufficiently to derive from the language of the work in question. The introductory lectures at the beginning of each term—in the first term on reading a poem or story, in the second on reading a work within the context of other writings—were almost always given by Brower. Once past the first year of the course, which began in 1954, he now and again turned some of the lectures over to me, and after they joined the staff in 1956–57, to Ferry or de Man. The three of us ran the course whenever Brower was on leave, except on one such occasion when it was supervised by Craig, on a year's visit from Amherst. Ferry, de Man, and I were a bit older than the others on the staff; we had all taught elsewhere and had a fairly clear idea of what we wanted to do as critics. But we all shared with the rest of the group both a temperamental commitment to the course and an affectionate admiration for Brower as our leader and example. The teachers in Hum 6 were thought to have a special bond that set them off from other graduate students or junior faculty in literature at Harvard; many in the English department resented the course. Understandably so, since we taught students to respond to those inflections of language which most teachers of literature, even as they dig away at metaphoric patterns, often cannot hear or which they ignore in the interest of a variously motivated eloquence.

By describing our allegiance as "temperamental," I mean that we were willing, indeed anxious to deny ourselves the embarrassing Big Talk promised by the titles of the other Humanities courses, like "Ideas of Good and Evil" or "The Individual and Society." I think one reason why certain students became deeply attached to Hum 6 and have remained so for life is that it offered them a way to avoid such resounding terms. They discovered that *not* to become grand is often the best way to stay in a particularly vital relation to what you are reading. To Brower's recurrent question, "What is it like to read this?" they came upon an Emersonian answer without knowing Emerson—"An imaginative book," he says in "The Poet," "renders us much more service, at first, by stimulating us through its tropes, than afterward, when we arrive at the precise sense of the author." Emerson himself at other points makes the few exceptions to this proposal that need to be made. If the stimulation is "first," why should it not also be last? Why, in that case, should anyone want ever to arrive at a "precise sense"? Much better to practice the art of *not* arriving. We shared with Brower a wariness of the rhetorical power of the very things we taught—it could often be found to undo itself anyway—and we tried not to let it empower any rhetorical displays of our own. Like Craig, Brower seldom italicized anything he said when he addressed a work in class; he gave almost no indication that he was especially moved by a passage. Students, many of them not yet emotionally and certainly not intellectually formed, were grateful to discover that they were not to be emotionally or intellectually overawed by us or by the reading. They had simply to work on it, "concentrating," as de Man describes it, "on the way the meaning is conveyed rather than on meaning itself."

Deprived of illusions about "meaning," there was little chance that the students would become disillusioned about literature, as so many now claim to be, because it failed to measure up to a priori political or ideological purposes, including the ideologies of selfhood. Speaking with almost no heightening of voice, patiently inquiring, as the students were themselves asked to do, into the many possible and competing voices to be heard in writing, with all its waverings and fractures, Brower induced a feeling, without ever being explicit about it, that the human presence in any gathering of words was always elusive, existing as it did in the very tentative, sometimes self-doubting plays of sound.

We found it convenient to use canonical texts for what seem to me obvious reasons: first, because of the concentrated uses of language normally found in them and, second, because there is no better way to show that the grand cognitive achievements claimed for these same canonical works in other literature courses simply are not there. But a lot of it was also given to writings of no clear literary status, like samples of conversation, mottoes and aphorisms, or historical writings, as when the historian William Taylor, author of *Cavalier and Yankee* and a devoted member of the staff who had taught the earlier course at Amherst, led us through Parkman's *La Salle and the Discovery of the Great West.* We read letters, fragments from Simon Suggs (to complement *Adventures of Huckleberry Finn*), St. Thomas Aquinas (for his possible relevance to Joyce's *A Portrait of the Artist*), and writings by authors as marginal to the then-established canon as Edwin Muir and Sarah Orne Jewett. In choosing works for the introductory lectures and exercises, Brower preferred selections, like sketches from Jewett's *The Country of the Pointed Firs,* that discouraged any kinds of magnification, or pieces that failed of the kinds of coherence most teachers look for. One year he began the course with an exercise on a short poem by Edwin Muir which, as an exasperated newcomer to the staff complained, simply "doesn't come together." This only confirmed the wisdom of the choice for Brower, who said simply, "Well, let's see what they can do with it." "Do with it," not "get out of it." The question he liked to ask on this and other occasions was, again, simply "What is it like to read this poem?"—the very hardest of questions, and not one likely to encourage a search for coherent patterns.

Any kind of close reading in the fifties and sixties came to be called New Criticism, no matter how different was Blackmur from Richards, or Empson from Leavis, or Burke from Tate; literary-critical histories of the period have still not made the requisite distinctions, in part because they are concerned with what got into publication almost to the exclusion of what went on in the classrooms with teachers who published little or not at all. Because I had studied with Cleanth Brooks at Yale for a year after Amherst, had taught from Brooks and Warren's *Understanding Poetry* at Williams College for two years after that, and had spent a year around Leavis's *Scrutiny* (all this before Hum 6), the term New Criticism seemed to me then, as it does now, exasperatingly inexact. It needed and needs to be localized. The term designated for me an ideological mutation of I. A. Richards[8] that was occurring not at all in Hum 6, but rather to the south of it at Yale. It had emerged before that still further south, at Vanderbilt, home of the Fugitive group that included Robert Penn Warren, John Crowe Ransom, and Allen Tate, and in the *Southern Review,* published at Baton Rouge, Louisiana, from 1935 to 1942. The term New Criticism was Ransom's, from a title of his in 1941. There was a heady mixture in this New Criticism of science-bashing, of Christianity (Fall of Man variety), and a lot of covertly political emphasis on how a successful poem or story achieves a workable coherence and organism that nicely holds together all the tensions within it. It was to be inferred, I came to suspect, that the virtues found in a good poem were to be found also in your ideal agrarian community. The New Criticism's self-appointed enemy was the rationality and abstraction of northern, big-city capitalism. T. S. Eliot's description of his train trip into the south from New England at the beginning of *After Strange Gods*—the lectures at the University of Virginia that became the 1934 book he apparently later wanted to forget (in part for its anti-Semitism)—is a good indication of his alliance with some of the cultural mythologies of New Criticism. Still another clue to this ideological affiliation exists in Eliot's essay of 1923 entitled "*Ulysses,* Order, and Myth." It is there that he talks about "the panorama of futility and anarchy which is contemporary history" and suggests that it can be given order—"order" was a New Critical buzzword—by the mythic method of

Joyce's novel and, though he is too discreet to mention it, of another work of the same year, his own *The Waste Land*.

At Amherst, Eliot was never to be the dominant presence he became at Yale during the ascendency there of its New Criticism—which helps explain why the negative assessments of Eliot from Harold Bloom (Yale Ph.D., 1955) are more emphatic than my own—or even at Harvard, where Matthiessen wrote his early and influential *The Achievement of T. S. Eliot.* When he found himself teaching *The Waste Land,* for example, Brower could never read aloud the ending, "Shanti shanti shanti," without showing evident distaste.

The Amherst people had a great poet-critic of their own, Robert Frost, and Frost was quite open, though the Amherst group has never sufficiently picked up on this, about his attachments to William James and Emerson. Frost was far too astute to box himself in by attacking Eliot head-on in public, and their final meetings in London in 1957 were affectionate and admiring. However, . . . Eliot was the likely target of the urbanely disdainful remark in Frost's letter to *The Amherst Student* in 1935 that "Anyone who has achieved the least form to be sure of it, is lost to the larger excruciations." And Louis Untermeyer reports his saying in 1940 that "Eliot and I have our similarities and our differences. We are both poets and we both like to play. That's the similarity. The difference is this: I like to play euchre. He likes to play Eucharist." To put this somewhat differently, Frost never yearned for Eliot's "still point." He expected, again, no more than momentary stays against confusion; for him "confusion" resided not so much in "the futility and anarchy which is contemporary history" as in all of history at any time. "The background is hugeness and confusion," as he puts it in the *Amherst Student* letter, "shading away from where we stand into black and utter chaos; and against the background any small man-made figure of order and concentration." The "order" is manmade and temporary.

Eliot's exaltation of the so-called mythic method—along with

Joyce's endorsements, however skittish, of charts of mythic and other correspondences for each of his chapters—can be shown to have had a profoundly damaging effect on the readings not only of *The Waste Land, Ulysses,* and other modernist works, but on the reading of literature in general. The damage is epitomized in such influential codifications as Joseph Frank's 1945 essay in *Sewanee Review* called "Spatial Form in Modern Literature," where it is proposed that Eliot, Pound, Proust, Joyce, and Djuna Barnes "ideally intend the reader to apprehend their work spatially, in a moment of time, rather than as a sequence." Readers have of course always done that to some extent with any text, and, to keep their sanity, people regularly do something like it to the events of their lives, reassembling them into what Barthes called "stenographic space."[9] The *act* of reading, however, is not at all the same as remembering the text thereafter or reassembling it. It is an experience in time and not in space; we read, we know "what it is like to read," in sequence. Spatial reading represents an unfortunate triumph of the eye over the ear.

This distinction between eye and ear was especially important to Frost. As he admitted when writing to John Cournos in July 1914, he chose to "cultivate . . . the hearing imagination rather than the seeing imagination though I should not want to be without the latter." Earlier that same year he had written to another correspondent, John Bartlett, "The ear is the only true writer and the only true reader. I have known people who could read without hearing the sentence sounds and they were the fastest readers. Eye readers we call them. They get the meaning by glances. But they are bad readers because they miss the best part of what a good writer puts into his work." Beginning in 1916, when he first joined the Amherst faculty, and during yearly visits of some duration thereafter for most of his life, Frost was a seminal figure at Amherst, not only while Brower was teaching there but while Brower was himself a student. (He graduated summa cum laude in 1930.) Frost remembered hearing the undergraduate Brower read aloud an Elizabethan poem and saying on the spot, "I give you an

A for life." "Goodness sake," he remarked, "the way his voice fell
into those lines." Many of the Hum 6 staff had also been at
Amherst while Frost was around, including me, William Taylor,
Thomas Edwards, William Pritchard, and Neil Hertz. So were the
poets David Ferry, Richard Wilbur, and James Merrill. Ferry
wrote an undergraduate dissertation on Stevens in 1948, and Merrill a dissertation on Proust in 1947, both supervised by Brower.

What I take to be the strongest years of Amherst English were
in the decade before Brower's departure for Harvard in 1953. The
department then included, as I have mentioned, Armour Craig
and Theodore Baird, who were as close to Frost as Brower was,
Craig possibly more so. Craig's few published essays on nineteenth-
century English fiction and his teaching of it anticipated by two
decades the now familiar critical focus on how precariously its
structure sustains the moral and social rhetorics of judgment
through to the crucial endings of works like *Vanity Fair* or *Dombey
and Son* or *Middlemarch*. In 1966, what would now be called a deconstructive reading of *Adventures of Huckleberry Finn* in my *A
World Elsewhere* illustrated the kind of thing Craig showed us how
to do long before the term "deconstruction" was used to describe
it. Craig was then and still is a devoted reader of Kenneth Burke,
nearly as much as of Frost and, I assume, of Wittgenstein. (It is
pertinent in that regard that James Guetti, yet another Amherst
graduate, has recently been showing the importance of Wittgenstein to contemporary literary criticism.) As for Burke, Craig in
the early fifties considered changing the vocabulary of English
19–20, which had derived from Richards as well as Frost, so as to
feature Burke's pentad, in *A Grammar of Motives,* of "act," "scene,"
"agent," "agency," and "purpose."

The antipathy among Amherst people to any such proliferation
of metalanguage fortunately prevailed, however. And even if the
terminology had been adopted it would not have made the emphasis less Frostian, since Frost's insistence on the dramatic, on the
drama of and among words, anticipates what Burke's was to be,
even in detail. In a letter to L. W. Payne, Jr., in March 1936, Frost

repeats his earlier claims that "I've just found out what makes a piece of writing good. . . . it is making the sentences talk to each other as two or more speakers do in drama." This presages Burke's repeated argument that a sentence may itself epitomize literature conceived as symbolic action. As he would have it, somebody is always doing something in a sentence to somebody else; that is, the grammatical elements "talk" to one another. Similarly, Burke's pentad has all the ingredients called for by Frost in his preface to *A Way Out* in 1929: "Everything written is as good as it is dramatic. It need not declare itself in form, but it is drama or it is nothing. By whom, where, and when is the question."

It is in line with this that Brower's lifelong regard for Leavis, whom he first met at Cambridge University in 1932, is best understood. Leavis was the brilliant champion in English criticism of the 1930s and 1940s of what he liked to call "the dramatic use of language."[10] His repeated emphasis on that phrase has never, I think, been rightly understood. By "dramatic" he means to refer, as do Frost and Burke (whose term is "dramatistic") to the way words and sentences "talk to each other," the way they undo and reconstitute each other beyond the grasp of critical interpretations that look for unity and order. Ultimately, morality for Leavis had less to do with attitudes, though there is an excessive attitudinizing morality in him, than with the way one uses words. To focus in this manner on the dramatic is to look in writing for some active consent to a chastening fact: that words exist independently of the uses to which anyone, specifically including the reader, wants to put them. No matter how powerful the writer or the reader may be, his or her relation to words on a page is of necessity dialogic, a recognition that scarcely awaited the current Bakhtinian hoopla.[11] The struggle for verbal consciousness must not be left out of art, as Lawrence said in 1920, and that includes the art of reading. Frost, Burke, and Leavis, all of them central to the kinds of reading asked for by Baird and Craig at Amherst and later by Brower and his staff at Harvard, share a conviction that, as Frost puts it in a letter in 1938 to R. P. T. Coffin, "poetry is the renewal of words forever and ever." That sentiment obviously informs the title of my own *The Renewal of Literature,* no less than its subtitle, *Emersonian Reflections.*

Emerson is a nourishing source for the kind of reading whose pedagogical career I have tried to describe, a claim that will disturb only the most benighted of Francophile theoreticians. Given that Brower was first of all a classicist, that de Man (though his translation of *Moby-Dick* into Flemish appeared in 1945) knew essentially nothing about American literature, and that Wittgenstein and Leavis, who were friends of a sort in Cambridge in the early 1930s, have been brought into these equations, I cannot be supposed to think that Emersonian "reflections" occur only in Concord, Massachusetts. Among the many indications that Emerson did not regard himself or his country as specific to time and place is the remark in his Journals for March–April 1847 that "A good scholar will find Aristophanes & Hafiz & Rabelais full of American history." It can as aptly be said that a good scholar will find Emerson full of de Man, Derrida, and Barthes, just as, quite differently, he is full of Frost and Burke.

The most vital of these differences has to do with the vexed question of self-presence in writing and reading. For Emerson, writing and reading do not, merely because of the deconstructive tendencies inherent in language, dissolve human presence; human presence comes into existence *in* writing and reading thanks to these traceable actions by which, through troping, deconstructive tendencies are acknowledged and contravened. There exists a crude and over-emphatic perception of the assumed antagonism between deconstruction in language, on the one hand, and, on the other, the possible shaping, in language, of Emersonian selves. After all, why do words even need to be renewed, as Emerson insists they do, if not in recognition of their deconstructive potential? How, indeed, can something so problematic and fragile as Emersonian self-presence be understood except in the context of its opposite—the self-abandonment which for him is the only sure antidote to conformity, including conformity to one's own rhetoric?

In calling attention to Brower's vocal unassertiveness—as if he were heeding Emerson's warnings in "Self-Reliance"—and to the low-keyed precision of the readings he offered in class and in his writing, I want to suggest a consonance between this way of reading literary works and the kind of elusive self-presence that is to be found in them if we but listen for inflections of sound. A word so big and, by now, so prejudicial as "phonocentrism" grotesquely magnifies the true image of voice in writing; voice just as often is trying to marginalize itself, to evade those invitations to self-assertion that exist all around it in literary and social blandishments. To expect that the self in literature is an entity or a center is as credulous as to expect to find an actual pole when you get to the northern and southern extremities of the world. The poles are long since fallen, including, as Cleopatra and Shakespeare know, the soldier's pole.

My own rhetoric about absent or fallen poles raises once again the question of whether the word "subversive" is appropriate to Hum 6. The term has perhaps become too grandiose for the course I have been describing; the Glendowers of literary theory are forever using it, as if at its mention "the frame and huge foundation of the earth / Shaked like a coward." Meanwhile, the people I have associated with this course, from the Hum 6 staff all the way back to Emerson, harbored no such illusions as are now abroad about the power of reading or of writing, especially in criticism. Reading and writing are activities which for them require endless scruple. That is how the activity of reading begins, how it is carried on, and why, so long as the words are in front of you, it should never end. It need never be broken off out of some guilty feeling that the activity of reading is not sufficiently political or socially beneficial. It is to be understood as a lonely discipline that makes no great claims for itself. Reading conducted under such a regimen can be subversive only to the extent that it encourages us to get under and turn over not systems and institutions, but only words. The words most susceptible to subversion tend to be found in the works called literature because in literature they are quite consciously meant to be susceptible. And yet any words can be gotten under and turned over, including those in philosophical works and in all kinds of social and political writing. As we congratulate ourselves on subversive readings of nonliterary language, however, it should be kept in mind that the talent for such reading is often acquired by work done with literature itself, even while it is literature that is nowadays frequently under attack as being in league with some of the least commendable of our social arrangements. Criticism should remember Emerson's admonition in "The Conservative"—"The past has baked your loaf, and in the strengths of its bread you would break up the oven"—and begin to calm down.

Joyce Appleby, Lynn Hunt, and Margaret Jacob

Appleby is professor of history at the University of California at Los Angeles and the author of *Economic Thought and Ideology in Seventeenth-Century England* (1978), *Capitalism and a New Social Order: The Republican Vision of the 1790s* (1984), and *Liberalism and Republicanism in the Historical Imagination* (1992). Hunt is Annenberg Professor of History at the University of Pennsylvania, the author of *Politics, Culture, and Class in the French Revolution* (1984) and *The Family Romance of the French Revolution* (1992), and the editor of *The New Cultural History* (1989) and *The Invention of Pornography: Obscenity and the Origins of Modernity, 1500–1800* (1993). Jacob is professor of history at the New School for Social Research and the author of *The Newtonians and the English Revolution, 1689–1720* (1976), *The Radical Enlightenment: Pantheists, Freemasons, and Republicans* (1981), *The Cultural Meaning of the Scientific Revolution* (1988), and *Living the Enlightenment: Freemasonry and Politics in Eighteenth Century Europe* (1991).

from **The Future of History**

in *Telling the Truth About History* (1994)

TALK ABOUT THE FUTURE OF HISTORY pivots around the question of how best to deploy the passion to know. Focusing that passion is the investigators' belief that the past can reveal an aspect of what it is to be human. The desire to touch the past is a yearning to master time, to anchor oneself in worldliness, to occupy fully one's own historical context by studying its antecedents. Given the immediacy of human passion, the present is always implicated in the study of the past. Lived experience alters the questions historians ask, foreclosing some research agendas while inspiring new ones. This sensitivity of historians to the lived moment is particularly visible at times of deep and significant historical change such as the world is witnessing now.

The Cold War riveted international affairs to the foreign policies of the United States and the Soviet Union. For almost a half century, it determined identities, magnified anxieties, and permeated every intellectual enterprise. All that has now abruptly ended. The future of history, like the future of much else in the world, can now be imagined in markedly different ways. A new republic of learning is possible because bunkerlike positions staked out on the treacherous landscape of battle can be abandoned, because old absolutisms have fallen, taking down with them many of the absolutist elements within Western democracies. New thinking is possible, even required. A part of this new thinking will include a return to the intellectual center of the Western experience since the seventeenth century, to scientific knowledge and its philosophical foundations, revitalized and reconceptualized. . . .

Hope for the future republic of learning derives from the

capacity of the human sciences to offer criticism, both of natural science and of themselves. Historians and sociologists of science and technology are increasingly documenting the impact that the Cold War has had on the natural sciences. Just as physicians are never good at examining themselves, so historians may have difficulty assessing how the practice of history has also been affected by the ideological warfare of the past forty years. Indeed despairing of objectivity as an ideal may have a great deal to do with the fact that most historians now writing have spent all of their professional lives in the shadow of the Cold War. It is time to come out of the trenches.

The scholarship of the postwar generation has led to a thoroughly argued and historically grounded appreciation for the social construction of knowledge. Cynics have claimed that this approach to knowledge proves the omnipresence of ideologies, not truth, in all human learning. They fail to grasp the actual message that the social approach to knowledge formation offers—that all scientific work has an essentially social character. The system of peer review, open refereeing, public disputation, replicated experiments, and documented research—all aided by international communication and the extended freedom from censorship—makes objective knowledge possible. Research programs must be established and findings constantly tested. These involve social processes which leave traces to be encoded within the resulting knowledge, necessitating even more decoding of inherited knowledge.[1] The official secrecy and mimetic authoritarian styles of big-money science further disfigure the state of the sciences just as surely as the retreat into relativism undermines the will to know in the human sciences. By declaring knowledge a by-product of each speaker's situation, relativism turns every consensual group into a universe unto itself, while propagating the idea that truths just emerge from the place where one is coming from or the language one happens to use. It permits a mental segregation among researchers and a privileging of ironic discourse, an effect not so different from scientific publications that may only be read by people with security clearances.

If knowledge and the discourses it generates offer power, then the issue of access to it becomes vitally important. Just as the barriers to free access within science must now, urgently, be dismantled, so too the accessibility of history to the peoples of this nation must change. Far from diluting or distorting knowledge, democratic practices have toughened and seasoned the truths that have been generated since the eighteenth century. Demanding that all research be open recalls a part of Western history, the importance of the Enlightenment's principal legacy, the freedom to communicate and the forum of civil society that makes truth possible.

History will flourish in a revitalized public arena. It will do so, we would suggest, because relativism and the intellectual postures that feed into it will recede, departing in the company of the alienation engendered by the rigidities of the Cold War. So too the traditionalist critics of the democratizing of the academy will increasingly sound like a background chorus singing old Cold War tunes.

Since the eighteenth century all Western reform movements have depended upon the existence of a relatively unfettered, uncensored domain of public discourse. In the seventeenth century every inch of that space had to be fought for, and only gradually was it wrested from the hands of clerical and governmental officials whose censorship silenced voices and stifled curiosity and wonder about nature and society. Scientific and technological knowledge prospered because of the struggle for freedom of press and association, but during the protracted Cold War, significant segments of scientific knowledge became the property of security agencies. Large areas of scientific learning were, and still are, configured by the need for defense and domination rather than humanitarian needs. This sequestering ironically has eased the move away from science as humanists have made the "linguistic turn." The wonder the science once evoked in students has been

Limited development of talent because of insult of unpaid education. Even military loses—smart bombs should've been here long ag...

replaced by boredom, suggesting that the authoritarian style of much science teaching may be traceable to Big Science and its postwar alliance with military needs.[2]

Mystifying, ignoring, decrying, or relativizing scientific knowledge makes trivial that which is central to Western cultures. Perhaps because of the development of the history of science as a separate field, general history teaching largely ignores the scientific realm of social life, that arena where people might still display their wonder about nature and their efforts to satisfy an aroused scientific curiosity. The size of the gap between science and the humanities operates as an obstacle to the renewal of both. Leaving the history of specialized bodies of knowledge to a variety of subdisciplines may work for the history of music or art—although there too, general historical knowledge loses a vital piece of the human spirit—but consigning science and technology to that status in this particular culture severs a tap root. Teaching science to examine its biases as well as its truths, its arrogance as well as its elegance, would enrich the public as well as scientists and humanists because both participate in similar systems of knowledge construction and both are utterly dependent upon the vitality of civil society for the rigor, originality, and competitiveness of their theories and practices. Similarly, where democratic ideals and practices have faltered in either the community of the arts or that of the sciences, their critics rightly sound the alarm and proclaim the need for renewal within the republic of learning.

The democratic practice of history here advocated needs a philosophical grounding compatible with its affirmations. We find that grounding in a combination of practical realism and pragmatism, that is, in an epistemological position that claims that people's perceptions of the world have some correspondence with that world and that standards, even though they are historical products, can be made to discriminate between valid and invalid assertions.[3] The intellectual spirit of democratic scholarship celebrates a multiplicity of actors, diversely situated and skeptical of authority. They are seekers of a workable truth communicable within an improvable society. Sometimes the public might even venerate its scientists and savants, considering their accomplishments the work of sheer genius, but this would not put them off-limits to searching examinations or historical analysis.

Within Western philosophical traditions sympathetic to democracy only pragmatism promotes the criticism and debate, dissent and irreverence vital to the kind of history we are advocating, yet pragmatism makes a distinction we consider crucial: all knowledge can be provisional, in theory, without eliminating the possibility of some truths prevailing for centuries, perhaps forever. And one of the responsibilities of history is to record both the survival and reformulation of old truths.

Pragmatism has been available as an approach to learning since the 1870s, when Charles Peirce published a now classic set of papers. . . . [4] Peirce laid out a philosophy of mind that emphasized the empirical as the very foundation for rationality. Here empiricism stands for systematic investigation and rigorous experimentation, confident of the objectivity of the objects of analysis. The past easily qualifies as one such subject insofar as it resides in the artifacts that survive from it. The no-holds-barred approach of the pragmatist permits any claim about any object to be questioned, but rejects the relativism inherent in questioning all claims on principle. Its measured relativism springs from the knowledge of facts and theories that have failed to survive extended examination; it is not a philosophical position premised on categorical doubt. In addition, the pragmatist asks about the purpose of a knowledge claim. What goal will be achieved when modernity is debunked? If combined with dedication to the moral ends of action and a prophetic sense of the necessity for improvement, pragmatic empiricism can well serve a democratic agenda.

Pragmatism appealed to the great philosopher John Dewey, who embarked in the 1920s on a critical inspection of American education. In Dewey's mind, pragmatism's reliance upon the outcome of experiments to determine the truth of philosophical propositions supported the highest aspirations of democracy. Pragmatism's passion for constantly reforming the aims and methods of scientific inquiry supported a liberal society's moral obligation to develop and redevelop the fullest capacity of each member of society.

Practical realism works well with pragmatism, for both of these theories require a commitment to a knowable world outside, one which people experience as they check and alter what they say about it. Realists accept the objectivity of objects and consider the objects' frequent resistance to accurate representations as an invitation to further investigation. Because pragmatism endorses the democratic practice of truth-seeking, it accepts the babel of tongues in the day-to-day practice of knowing, learning, and teaching. In this arena, objects and the inquiring subjects they attract help keep the playing field level because, while the struggle to establish a truth is being waged, no privileged perspectives are recognized. Rather than grounding truth on first principles, pragmatists make truth's attainment a matter of self-correcting endeavors where any factual claim can be called into question, although not in the manner of the relativist who calls propositions into question, all at once.

Because its notion of truth emerges from a consensus of practitioners, pragmatists are exposed to tyranny from that group. What if the vast majority of investigators in a relevant field were to decide that all women are inferior or that one ethnic group failed to measure up to the standards of others? Pragmatism does not offer within its system of verification a formal set of criteria for determining that science directed to invidious distinctions is ultimately evil and frequently bunk. Indeed, pragmatism only works if democratic institutions are strong and functioning daily. Nor can the purpose to which knowledge is put be left to the decisions of any single group of knowledge seekers. Here the problem of exclusion bears directly on the fostering of relativism which occurs when any natural or social science is conducted in secrecy. If the playing field is restricted, leaving those excluded by virtue of race or class or gender to gape from the sidelines, then the pragmatic game devolves into entertainment for intellectuals, not the site for testing knowledge appropriate to the needs of a working democracy. With an absence of first principles, pragmatists can easily become relativists when the relevance of truth to the needs of society becomes more and more remote and anti-intellectual governments sponsor that remoteness.

For these reasons, pragmatism is only a provisional philosophy, but one that can be immensely useful for its endorsement of practice, verifiability, rationality, and progress achievable by reasonably well educated people. Pragmatism leaves unquestioned the consequence of the convergence of the popular will with the scientist's drive for knowledge. Assuming a commonality of interests without demonstrating their existence, pragmatism depends on democracy. Hence pragmatism is implicated in democracy's flaws, the principal one being exposure to the unchecked power of a majority when that majority acts capriciously.

This problem is as old as the American republic and has prompted a succession of astute observations about the nature of popular government. In his famous *Federalist No. 10*, James Madison set forth with wonderful clarity the dilemma of the majority being the greatest threat to its own political system. He began with factions, which he defined as groups acting against the rights of others or the long-term interests of the whole. Minority factions could be disruptive, but only majority factions, Madison shrewdly pointed out, could do mortal damage to republican government, for only they could seize control of the agencies of government. Two correctives to this threat presented themselves to Madison: elimination of the cause of majority faction or control of its effects. Naming freedom an essential component in the galvanizing of the passions and interests which animate majority faction, Madison rejected the idea of getting rid of the causes as a cure worse than the disease and concentrated instead upon managing its effects.[5]

The best government money can buy.

Madison made the Constitution, then being considered for ratification, his solution to majority faction because it would enlarge the scope of national governance and thereby increase the number of interests in the nation, making it unlikely that any one group could command the unchecked force of a majority. Approaching politics as a predicament, the drafters of the Constitution were determined to erect barriers to the exercise of arbitrary power. Madison boldly proclaimed that "ambition must be made to check ambition." It "may be a reflection on human nature, that such devices should be necessary," he continued, but "what is government itself, but the greatest of all reflections on human nature?"[6] As weapons against abuses of power, resorts to ambition and competition have some justification, but they have also undermined Americans' faith in a public arena where collective goals can be discussed. *Conformity of scabs submitting to upper class goals*

Alexis de Tocqueville, visiting the United States in the 1830s, saw a different majoritarian threat from the one that had preoccupied the revolutionary generation. For him the unchecked power of the majority in the United States sapped the individual's capacity to act independently by silently encouraging Americans to conform to majority taste, whether in ethics, in politics, or in philosophical views. Pervasive and invisible, Tocqueville's tyranny of the majority worked on individuals with an efficacy unknown in absolute monarchies. Without knowing it—even while extolling their freedom and autonomy—Americans, Tocqueville observed, conformed to a limited range of aspirations, preferring the psychological comfort of equal treatment over the emotional risks of genuine independence from the herd.[7]

Both of these analyses bear on the problem of creating, testing, and spreading knowledge in a democracy. They also expose the risk present in pragmatism's reliance upon the public to scrutinize the production of knowledge. Madison worried that majority factions could crush individual rights through the exercise of majority rule, and Tocqueville feared that majority opinion would eclipse the desire to soar beyond conventions, both results espe-

Factions within aristocracy

cially threatening to original scholarship. The history of American race relations amply supports their fears. White Americans have repeatedly acted as a majority faction toward blacks, using both informal violence and formal statutes to curtail the free exercise of their powers. At present a lesser threat to individual freedom has surfaced in the form of political correctness. Political correctness refers to a wall of sympathy raised to ward off challenges to policies directed at minorities. In an effort to protect minority students, some would declare off-limits debates that bear on issues affecting their concerns. Critics of "p.c." have a point when they focus on the dangers of limiting public discussion, since the curtailment of spirited, open dissent threatens the very democratic practices that affirmative action was created to serve.

Political correctness patronizes people by assuming that their interests are too fragile for public scrutiny. Political pluralism sells them short by ignoring the deliberative component of democratic decision-making. Both aggravate the problems of nurturing knowledge in a democracy. By accepting the proposition that bargaining among separate interest groups determines public policy, pluralism legitimates the competition for public resources. It is relativism in action; "truth" belongs to the winners. Opposed to both is a conception of a republic where lawmakers are informed by particular needs, but attentive to the general well-being. Such a republic can only come into existence when there is a popular supportive ethic. As Madison's and Tocqueville's critiques indicate, despair at achieving a consensus about the good of the whole entered American discourse early. An even deeper skepticism about the concept of a public good, transcendent of the nation's parts, pushed Americans toward the muscular masculinity of interest-group competition, a kind of arm-wrestling approach to politics which has stifled debate and limited public access for those without sufficient clout to push their way into the bargaining arena. Pragmatism, dependent as it is upon exhaustive testing of knowledge claims, has offered a reasoned support of public debate, but its deference to practice over principle has left democracy without an adequate defense against majority factions and majority tyrannies, not to mention the silent influence of well-financed interest groups.

Democracy and history always live in a kind of tension with each other. Nations use history to build a sense of national identity, pitting the demands for stories that build solidarity against open-ended scholarly inquiry that can trample on cherished illusions. Here the pressing question is which human needs should history serve, the yearning for a self-affirming past, even if distortive, or the liberation, however painful, that comes from grappling with a more complex, accurate account? Skepticism offers a way of resolving this tension by rejecting all truths, but in doing so it flies in the face of the common experience of knowing. Consider the outrage felt when a remembered experience is misrepresented. Where does this passionate sense of violation come from if truth is such a chameleon?

In important ways historians support the long-term goals of democratic societies when they insistently and honestly reconstruct past experience. They work for greater social inclusiveness because they bear witness to the records that have been suppressed. Having a history enables groups to get power, whether they use a past reality to affirm their rights or wrest recognition from those powerful groups that monopolize public debate. History doesn't just reflect; it provides a forum for readjudicating power and interests. If historical accounts remain in some sense interim reports, it is because the meaning of human experience can never be exhausted. *By ignoring the wage slavery of the majority and naming it as the op-presso*

A recent example of historical scholarship shaping public perceptions of a contemporary issue occurred when the Supreme Court deliberated on the constitutionality of the Pennsylvania abortion law in 1992.[8] Then the court had at its disposal a short history of abortion in America which gave an account of responses to unwanted pregnancies spanning more than three centuries. This historical record gave clear evidence that abortions had been well known and had been practiced without serious regulation in the United States until the late nineteenth century, when the practice met with new overt strictures. Knowing about the relevant past in this instance subtly shifted one's perspective. Historical knowledge proved satisfying because it quickened the sense of being linked to the past. Unexpectedly women and men discovered a common tie to the world of long-dead ancestors. Suddenly the burden of dealing with contemporary crises was lessened by the awareness that whatever people might do, they are not the first, nor probably the last, who will be forced to wrestle with this human problem. *using defective and deceptive logic*

This didactic function of history has long been recognized. Voltaire gave classic expression to it when he referred to history as philosophy teaching by example. Less frequently talked about is the derangement felt when the established consensus about national history breaks down, as it did in the last several years of the USSR. Soviet scholars had so slavishly served the state that they had written histories with little foundation in the widely shared documentation about the Russian Revolution and its aftermath. As a consequence of *glasnost,* comparisons could be made between the official Soviet histories and competing accounts of the same events written in the West. Painfully aware of these discrepancies, Mikhail Gorbachev placed a ban on teaching the once-official history to Russian youth until scholars could catch up with the pace of reform. And then he boldly canceled the Soviet Union's national high school history exams, because, as he said with startling candor, there was no point in testing the students' knowledge of lies. Here is exposed the linkage of truth, power, and meaning. However much skeptics deride the possibility of historical truth, when it confronts absolute falsehood the potency of a provisional accuracy becomes salient.

In the West we associate "party line" history with totalitarian governments, but even where there is academic freedom there are public repercussions when the delicate balance between consensual interpretations and open inquiry is upset. This was demonstrated in France during the celebration of the bicentennial of the French Revolution in 1989, only in this case it was not political but rather academic orthodoxy that generated a crisis. Disputes about the causes and character of the revolutionary events of '89 and '93 became so heated and so well publicized that French educational authorities deleted questions about the French Revolution from the secondary school examinations that year.

The similarity between the examples from the Soviet Union and France can be traced to the critical role their revolutions played in modern nation building. If the historical accounts of these momentous events are muddied, then the nation's collective identity is put at risk. For the United States, nation-building started with the ideals that justified independence and then gave cohesion to an aggregation of transplanted people establishing homes in a conquered land. Giving heterogeneity a good name, the nation's unifying creed endorsed the inclusiveness of an open society while falling far short of creating one in practice. Pragmatic initially without philosophers, Americans developed democratic practices which promoted experimentation, invention, and education. A century later a formal theory of pragmatism emerged which depended upon the rules and civility of an open republic and a commitment to the knowability of nature and hence to scientific truth. Today the nation's democratic creed as well as its pragmatic tradition rely upon a consensus of beliefs about reality and the possibility of arriving at common goals.

Bibliography

The collected works of Peirce, James, Holmes, and Dewey are available in the following editions (some of which are still being compiled):

Dewey, John. *The Early Works 1882–1898*. Ed. Jo Ann Boydston. 5 vols. Carbondale: Southern Illinois University Press, 1967–1972.

———. *The Middle Works 1899–1924*. Ed. Jo Ann Boydston. 15 vols. Carbondale: Southern Illinois University Press, 1976–1983.

———. *The Later Works 1925–1953*. Ed. Jo Ann Boydston. 17 vols. Carbondale: Southern Illinois University Press, 1981–1991.

Holmes, Oliver Wendell. *The Collected Works of Justice Holmes: Complete Public Writings and Selected Judicial Opinions of Oliver Wendell Holmes*. Ed. Sheldon M. Novick. 5 vols. Chicago: University of Chicago Press, 1995–.

James, William. *The Works of William James*. Ed. Frederick H. Burkhardt. 19 vols. Cambridge, Mass.: Harvard University Press, 1975–1988.

Peirce, Charles Sanders. *The Writings of Charles S. Peirce: A Chronological Edition*. Comp. by the editors of the Peirce Edition Project. 30 vols. Bloomington: Indiana University Press, 1982–.

The following paperback anthologies are recommended:

Jane Addams on Education. Ed. Ellen Condliffe Lagemann. New Brunswick, N.J.: Transaction, 1994.

The Social Thought of Jane Addams. Ed. Christopher Lasch. Indianapolis: Bobbs-Merrill, 1965.

The Philosophy of John Dewey. Ed. John J. McDermott. 2 vols. Chicago: Chicago University Press, 1981.

Dewey, John. *The Political Writings.* Ed. Debra Morris and Ian Shapiro. Indianapolis: Hackett Publishing, 1993.

The Essential Holmes: Selections from the Letters, Speeches, Judicial Opinions, and Other Writings of Oliver Wendell Holmes, Jr. Ed. Richard A. Posner. Chicago: University of Chicago Press, 1992.

James, William. *Selected Writings.* Ed. Graham Bird. New York: Everyman's Classic Library, 1995.

The Writings of William James: A Comprehensive Edition. Ed. John J. McDermott. Chicago: University of Chicago Press, 1977.

Mead, George Herbert. *Selected Writings.* Ed. Andrew J. Reck. Chicago: University of Chicago Press, 1981.

The Essential Peirce: Selected Philosophical Writings. Ed. Nathan Houser and Christian Kloesel. 2 vols. Bloomington: Indiana University Press, 1992–.

Here are some works on pragmatists and pragmatism:

Apel, Karl-Otto. *Charles S. Peirce: From Pragmatism to Pragmaticism.* Trans. John Michael Krois. Atlantic Highlands, N.J.: Humanities Press International, 1995.

Baker, Liva. *The Justice from Beacon Hill: The Life and Times of Oliver Wendell Holmes.* New York: HarperCollins, 1991.

Barzun, Jacques. *A Stroll with William James.* New York: Harper & Row, 1983.

Brent, Joseph. *Charles Sanders Peirce: A Life.* Bloomington: Indiana University Press, 1993.

Conklin, Paul K. *Puritans and Pragmatists: Eight Eminent American Thinkers.* Bloomington: Indiana University Press, 1968.

Cotkin, George. *William James: Public Philosopher.* Baltimore: Johns Hopkins University Press, 1990.

Davis, Allen Freeman. *American Heroine: The Life and Legend of Jane Addams.* New York: Oxford University Press, 1973.

Deegan, Mary Jo. *Jane Addams and the Men of the Chicago School.* New Brunswick: Transaction Books, 1988.

Diggins, John Patrick. *The Promise of Pragmatism: Modernism and the Crisis of Knowledge and Authority.* Chicago: University of Chicago Press, 1994.

Dykhuizen, George. *The Life and Mind of John Dewey.* Ed. Jo Ann Boydston. Carbondale: Southern Illinois University Press, 1973.

Feffer, Andrew. *The Chicago Pragmatists and American Progressivism.* Ithaca: Cornell University Press, 1993.

Fisch, Max H. *Peirce, Semeiotic, and Pragmatism.* Ed. Kenneth Laine Ketner and Christian J. W. Kloesel. Bloomington: Indiana University Press, 1986.

Gordon, Robert W., ed. *The Legacy of Oliver Wendell Holmes, Jr.* Stanford: Stanford University Press, 1992.

Grey, Thomas C. "Holmes and Legal Pragmatism." *Stanford Law Review* 41 (1989), 787–870.

Hollinger, David. *In the American Province: Studies in the History and Historiography of Ideas.* Bloomington: Indiana University Press, 1985.

Howe, Mark DeWolfe. *Justice Oliver Wendell Holmes: The Shaping Years, 1841–1870.* Cambridge, Mass.: Harvard University Press, 1957.

————. *Justice Oliver Wendell Holmes: The Proving Years, 1870–1882.* Cambridge, Mass.: Harvard University Press, 1963.

Joas, Hans. *George Herbert Mead: A Contemporary Re-examination of His Thought.* Trans. Raymond Meyer. Cambridge, Mass.: MIT Press, 1985.

Kuklick, Bruce. *The Rise of American Philosophy: Cambridge, Massachusetts, 1860–1930.* New Haven: Yale University Press, 1977.

Morris, Charles. *The Pragmatic Movement in American Philosophy.* New York: George Braziller, 1970.

Murphy, John P. *Pragmatism: From Peirce to Davidson.* Boulder: Westview Press, 1990.

Myers, Gerald E. *William James: His Life and Thought.* New Haven: Yale University Press, 1986.

Perry, Ralph Barton. *The Thought and Character of William James.* 2 vols. Boston: Little, Brown, 1935.

Ryan, Alan. *John Dewey and the High Tide of American Liberalism.* New York: W. W. Norton, 1995.

Scheffler, Israel. *Four Pragmatists: A Critical Introduction to Peirce, James, Mead, and Dewey.* New York: Humanities Press, 1974.

Smith, John E. *Purpose and Thought: The Meaning of Pragmatism.* Chicago: University of Chicago Press, 1984.

Thayer, H. S. *Meaning and Action: A Critical History of Pragmatism.* Indianapolis: Bobbs-Merrill, 1968.

Washington, Johnny. *Alain Locke and Philosophy: A Quest for Cultural Pluralism.* Westport: Greenwood Press, 1986.

Westbrook, Robert B. *John Dewey and American Democracy.* Ithaca: Cornell University Press, 1991.

White, G. Edward. *Justice Oliver Wendell Holmes: Law and the Inner Self.* New York: Oxford University Press, 1993.

White, Morton G. *Social Thought in America: The Revolt Against Formalism.* New York: Viking Press, 1949.

Wiener, Philip P. *Evolution and the Founders of Pragmatism.* Cambridge, Mass.: Harvard University Press, 1949.

The principal works of the contemporary pragmatists represented in this volume are listed in the headnotes to their selections. Other contemporary discussions and applications include the following:

Anderson, Charles W. *Pragmatic Liberalism.* Chicago: University of Chicago Press, 1990.

Brint, Michael, and William Weaver, eds. *Pragmatism in Law and Society.* Boulder: Westview Press, 1991.

Cavell, Stanley. *Conditions Handsome and Unhandsome: The Constitution of Emersonian Perfectionism.* Chicago: University of Chicago Press, 1990.

Dickstein, Morris, ed. *The Pragmatist Revival.* Durham: Duke University Press, 1997.

Gunn, Giles. *Thinking Across the American Grain: Ideology, Intellect, and the New Pragmatism.* Chicago: University of Chicago Press, 1992.

Hollinger, Robert, and David Depew, eds. *Pragmatism: From Progressivism to Postmodernism.* Westport: Praeger, 1995.

Joas, Hans. *Pragmatism and Social Theory.* Chicago: University of Chicago Press, 1993.

Kloppenberg, James. "Pragmatism: An Old Name for Some New Ways of Thinking?" *The Journal of American History* 83 (1996), 100–138.

McDermott, John J. *Streams of Experience: Reflections on the History and Philosophy of American Culture.* Amherst: University of Massachusetts Press, 1986.

Mitchell, W. J. T., ed. *Against Theory: Literary Studies and the New Pragmatism.* Chicago: University of Chicago Press, 1985.

Mulvaney, Robert J., and Philip M. Zeltner, eds. *Pragmatism: Its Sources and Prospects.* Columbia: University of South Carolina Press, 1981.

Orrill, Robert, ed. *The Condition of American Liberal Education: Pragmatism and a Changing Tradition.* New York: College Entrance Examination Board, 1995.

Rajchman, John, and Cornel West, eds. *Post-Analytic Philosophy.* New York: Columbia University Press, 1985.

Rosenthal, Sandra B. *Speculative Pragmatism.* Peru, Ill.: Open Court, 1986.

Saatkamp, Herman J., Jr. *Rorty and Pragmatism: The Philosopher Responds to His Critics.* Nashville: Vanderbilt University Press, 1995.

Seigfried, Charlene Haddock. *Pragmatism and Feminism: Reweaving the Social Fabric.* Chicago: University of Chicago Press, 1996.

————, ed. Feminism and Pragmatism Special Issue. *Hypatia,* 8/2 (Spring 1993).

Shusterman, Richard. *Pragmatist Aesthetics: Living Beauty, Rethinking Art.* Oxford: Blackwell, 1992.

Sunstein, Cass R. *Legal Reasoning and Political Conflict.* New York: Oxford University Press, 1996.

Symposium on the Renaissance of Pragmatism in American Legal Thought. *Southern California Law Review* 63 (1990), 1569–1854.

Notes

An Introduction to Pragmatism

1. G. K. Chesterton, *Orthodoxy* (New York: John Lane, 1908), 62.

2. Bertrand Russell, "Pragmatism" (1909), in *Philosophical Essays,* 2d ed. (London: Allen and Unwin, 1966), 109.

3. Gertrude Himmelfarb, *On Looking into the Abyss: Untimely Thoughts on Culture and Society* (New York: Knopf, 1994), 17.

4. John Searle, "Rationality and Realism: What Is at Stake?" *Daedalus* 122 (Fall 1992), 72.

5. John Dewey, "A Short Catechism Concerning Truth" (1909), in *The Middle Works 1899–1924, Volume 6: 1910–1911,* ed. Jo Ann Boydston. (Carbondale: Southern Illinois University Press, 1978), 11.

6. William James, "Philosophical Conceptions and Practical Results," in *Pragmatism,* ed. Frederick H. Burkhardt (Cambridge, Mass.: Harvard University Press, 1975), 259.

7. Ibid., 268.

8. James, *Pragmatism,* 42 (original in italics).

9. James, "Philosophical Conceptions and Practical Results," 258.

10. *Collected Papers of Charles Sanders Peirce,* ed. Charles Hartshorne and Paul Weiss (Cambridge, Mass.: Harvard University Press, 1931–1935), vol. 5, par. 12.

11. Henry James to Elizabeth Boott, January 24, 1872, in *Henry James Letters, Volume 1: 1843–1875,* ed. Leon Edel (Cambridge, Mass.: Harvard University Press, 1974), 267.

12. William James to Henry James, November 24, 1872, in *The Correspondence of William James, Volume 1: William and Henry 1861–1884,* ed. Ignas K. Skrupskelis and Elizabeth M. Berkeley (Charlottesville: University Press of Virginia, 1992), 177.

13. "Toward a Logic Book, 1872–73," in *The Writings of Charles S. Peirce: A Chronological Edition, Volume 3: 1872–1878,* ed. Christian J. W. Kloesel (Bloomington: Indiana University Press, 1986), 14–108.

14. *Collected Papers of Charles Sanders Peirce,* vol. 5, par. 13.

15. *The Letters of William James,* ed. Henry James (Boston: Atlantic Monthly Press, 1920), vol. 1, 147–48.

16. Oliver Wendell Holmes to Frederick Pollock, September 1, 1910, in *Holmes-Pollock Letters: The Correspondence of Mr. Justice Holmes and Sir Frederick Pollock 1874–1932,* ed. Mark DeWolfe Howe (Cambridge, Mass.: Harvard University Press, 1941), vol. 1, 167.

17. Oliver Wendell Holmes to Harold Laski, November 29, 1923, in *Holmes-Laski Letters: The Correspondence of Mr. Justice Holmes and Harold Laski 1916–1935,* ed. Mark DeWolfe Howe (Cambridge, Mass.: Harvard University Press, 1953), vol. 1, 565.

18. Oliver Wendell Holmes, "Codes, and the Arrangement of the Law" (1870), in *The Collected Works of Justice Holmes: Complete Public Writings and Selected Judicial Opinions of Oliver Wendell Holmes,* ed. Sheldon M. Novick (Chicago: University of Chicago Press, 1995), vol. 1, 212–13.

19. Oliver Wendell Holmes, *The Common Law* (Boston: Little, Brown, 1881), 1.

20. Ibid.

21. Oliver Wendell Holmes to Elmer Gertz, March 1, 1899, quoted in Liva Baker, *The Justice from Beacon Hill: The Life and Times of Oliver Wendell Holmes* (New York: HarperCollins, 1991), 172–73.

22. Oliver Wendell Holmes to Morris Cohen, September 6, 1920, quoted in *Portrait of a Philosopher: Morris R. Cohen in Life and Letters,* ed. Leonora Cohen Rosenfield (New York: Harcourt, Brace and World, 1962), 330.

23. John Dewey, *Experience and Nature,* in *The Later Works 1925–1953, Volume 1: 1925,* Ed. Jo Ann Boydston (Carbondale: Southern Illinois University Press, 1981), 312.

24. Oliver Wendell Holmes to Frederick Pollock, May 15, 1931, in *Holmes-Pollock Letters,* vol. 2, 287.

25. John Dewey, "The Bearings of Pragmatism upon Education" (1908–09), in *The Middle Works 1899–1924, Volume 4: 1907–1909,* 180 (original in italics).

26. John Dewey, *The School and Society* (1899), in *The Middle Works 1899–1924, Volume 1: 1899–1901,* 12.

27. John Dewey, "Ethical Principles Underlying Education," in *The Early Works 1882–1898, Volume 5: 1895–1898,* ed. Jo Ann Boydston (Carbondale: Southern Illinois University Press, 1972), 62.

28. John Dewey, "The Ethics of Democracy" (1888), in *The Early Works 1882–1898, Volume 1: 1882–1888,* 232.

29. "Biography of John Dewey," ed. Jane M. Dewey, in *The Philosophy of John Dewey,* ed. Paul Arthur Schilpp and Lewis Edwin Hahn (LaSalle, Ill.: Open Court Press, 1939), 26. This brief "biography" appears to have been largely dictated by Dewey to his daughters.

30. George Herbert Mead, *Mind, Self, and Society from the Standpoint of a Social Behaviorist,* ed. Charles W. Morris (Chicago: University of Chicago Press, 1934), 164.

31. George Herbert Mead, "The Mechanism of Social Consciousness," *The Journal of Philosophy, Psychology, and Scientific Methods* 9 (1912), 406.

32. William James, *A Pluralistic Universe,* ed. Frederick H. Burkhardt (Cambridge, Mass.: Harvard University Press, 1977), 146. (I have reversed the order of the sentences.)

33. James, *Pragmatism,* 125.

34. Alain LeRoy Locke, *Race Contacts and Interracial Relations: Lectures on the Theory and Practice of Race,* ed. Jeffrey C. Stewart (Washington, D.C.: Howard University Press, 1992), 97.

35. *Abrams v. United States,* 250 U.S. 616, 630 (1919).

36. Bruce A. Kimball, "Toward Pragmatic Liberal Education," in Robert Orill, ed., *The Condition of American Liberal Education: Pragmatism and a Changing Tradition* (New York: College Entrance Examination Board, 1995).

37. Richard Rorty, *Philosophy and the Mirror of Nature* (Princeton: Princeton University Press, 1979), 7–8.

Some Consequences of Four Incapacities

Published in *The Journal of Speculative Philosophy* 2 (1868), 140–57.

The Fixation of Belief

Published in *The Popular Science Monthly* 12 (November 1877), 1–15.

1. [English Scholastic philosopher and scientist (1214–1294).]
2. [The remark about the English philosopher Francis Bacon (1561–1626) is attributed to the English physician William Harvey (1578–1657).]
3. Not quite so, but as nearly so as can be told in a few words. [The German astronomer Johannes Kepler (1571–1630) devised a series of laws, known as Kepler's laws, that prescribe the orbits of the planets. Peirce, whose earliest scientific work was on astronomical observation, later regretted this passage, which he regarded as an inaccurate account of Kepler's actual scientific practice.]
4. [The French chemist Antoine Lavoisier (1743–1794), a founder of modern chemistry, the field in which Peirce had his graduate training.]
5. ["Read, read, read, work, pray, and read again."]
6. [The German physicist Rudolph Julius Emanuel Clausius (1822–1888) and the Scottish physicist James Clerk Maxwell (1831–1879). Peirce is referring to the kinetic theory of gases, a key instance of the scientific application of statistics, which renders behavior that is unpredictable on an individual level (for example, the movement of any single molecule of gas), lawlike when considered at the level of the mass (the movement of a whole cloud).]
7. I am not speaking of secondary effects occasionally produced by the interference of other impulses.
8. [Peirce is alluding to the doctrine of papal infallibility, which had been affirmed in 1870 by the First Vatican Council, under Pope Pius IX.]
9. ["The Fixation of Belief" was the first of six essays by Peirce published in *The Popular Science Monthly* under the heading "Illustrations

of the Logic of Science." The others were "How to Make Our Ideas Clear" (reprinted here, pp. 26–48), "The Doctrine of Chances" (March 1878), "The Probability of Induction" (April 1878), "The Order of Nature" (June 1878), and "Deduction, Induction, and Hypothesis" (August 1878).]

How to Make Our Ideas Clear

Published in *The Popular Science Monthly* 12 (January 1878), 286–302).

1. ["The Fixation of Belief," reprinted here, pp. 7–25.]
2. [The man is Peirce himself. He was married to Harriet Melusina Fay in 1862, but she left him in 1876, two years before this essay was published; they were divorced in 1883.]
3. [Figure 2 is Figure 1 rotated 45 degrees to the left.]
4. [As a trope; that is, metaphorically.]
5. Possibly the velocities also have to be taken into account.
6. [Charles Hartshorne and Paul Weiss, Peirce's first editors, identify this work as Gustav Kirchhoff, *Vorlesungen über mathematische Physik: Mechanik* (*Lectures on Mathematical Physics: Mechanics,* 1876).]
7. ["The Fixation of Belief."]
8. [All are nineteenth-century French scientists who established methods for measuring the speed of light. Metrology (the science of measurement) was the area of Peirce's most notable accomplishments as a practicing scientist in astronomy and geodesy.]
9. Fate means merely that which is sure to come true, and can nohow be avoided. It is a superstition to suppose that a certain sort of events are ever fated, and it is another to suppose that the word fate can never be freed from its superstitious taint. We are all fated to die.
10. [William Cullen Bryant, "The Battle-Field" (1837).]
11. [Thomas Gray, "Elegy Written in a Country Churchyard" (1750).]
12. ["The Doctrine of Chances," published in the same series in March 1878.]

A Guess at the Riddle

An unfinished manuscript, unpublished in Peirce's lifetime; published in *The Essential Peirce: Selected Philosophical Writings, Volume 1 (1867–1893)*, ed. Nathan Houser and Christian Kloesel (Bloomington: Indiana University Press, 1992), 245–79.

Evolutionary Love

Published in *The Monist* 3 (January 1893), 176–200.

1. [Claude Adrien Helvétius (1715–1771) was a French *philosophe,* and Cesare Bonesana Beccaria (1738–1794) was an Italian jurist; both influenced the English utilitarian Jeremy Bentham (1748–1832).]
2. ["God is love," which Peirce quotes earlier in the essay.]
3. ["The Law of Mind" was published in *The Monist* in July 1892. "Synechism" is defined there as "the tendency to regard continuity . . . as an idea of prime importance in philosophy." The illustration is from mathematics and involves the theory of infinitesimals, according to which, for example, no collection of points on a line can ever fill up the line so as to leave no room for other points—since there is always a point between any two points. Philosophically, Peirce considered this an argument against the belief that there exist ultimate elements into which things are divisible, including ideas, which, he said, "tend to spread continuously and to affect certain others which stand to them in a peculiar relation of affectibility."]
4. [Joseph Brent, Peirce's biographer, identifies the "Master in glomery" as Thomas J. Montgomery, a Wall Street businessman who had given Peirce a rubber check in exchange for a chemical bleaching process Peirce had developed.]
5. [Peirce's term for evolution by creative love, as described earlier in the essay.]

A Definition of Pragmatism

An unfinished and untitled manuscript, unpublished in Peirce's lifetime; published in *Peirce on Signs: Writings on Semiotic by Charles Sanders Peirce,* ed. James Hoopes (Chapel Hill: University of North Carolina Press, 1991), 246–48.

1. [Peirce was drafting a review of Herbert Nichols, *A Treatise on Cosmology* (1904).]
2. [William James introduced the term "pragmatism," which he credited to Peirce, in a lecture delivered in 1898. Most of Peirce's later writings on pragmatism were motivated by the desire to distinguish his understanding of the concept from the use made of it by James and James's disciples. Peirce is very likely responding here to James's review of *Studies in Logical Theory,* by John Dewey and some of his colleagues (the so-called Chicago School), in *The Psychological Bulletin* 1 (1904), 1–5, and to Dewey's review of *Humanism: Philosophical Essays,* by the Oxford pragmatist F. C. S. Schiller, also in *The Psychological Bulletin* 1 (1904), 335–40.]

Habit

Published as "The Laws of Habit," *The Popular Science Monthly* 30 (February 1887), 433–51; reprinted as chapter 4 in William James, *The Principles of Psychology* (New York: Holt, 1890), vol. 1, 104–27, which is the text used here.

1. [The first step that costs.]
2. [James is referring to *The Emotions and the Will* (1859; 3d ed. 1875), by the Scottish psychologist Alexander Bain (1818–1903). Peirce, many years later, traced his own formulation of pragmatism in part to Bain's definition of belief, in this work, as (in Peirce's paraphrase) "that upon which a man is prepared to act."]
3. [*A System of Logic* (1843; 8th ed. 1872); Mill is quoting Novalis.]
4. [Joseph Jefferson (1829–1905) was an American actor who performed in his own adaptation of "Rip van Winkle."]

The Will to Believe

Originally published in *The New World* 5 (June 1896), 327–47; reprinted in William James, *The Will to Believe and Other Essays in Popular Philosophy* (New York: Longmans, Green, 1897), 1–31, which is the text used here.

1. [Leslie Stephen, *The Life of Sir James Fitzjames Stephen* (1895).]
2. [James is referring to the Norwegian explorer Fridtjof Nansen, whose expedition lasted from 1893 to 1896.]
3. [James is referring to the discussion in Book One of *A Treatise of Human Nature* (1739–40), by the Scottish philosopher David Hume (1711–1776).]
4. [Blaise Pascal, *Pensées de M. Pascal sur la religion et sur quelques autres sujets* (*Thoughts on Religion and on Some Other Subjects,* 1670).]
5. [It will make you believe and stupefy you.]
6. [Arthur Hugh Clough, "With Whom Is No Variableness, Neither Shadow of Turning" (1869).]
7. [Thomas Henry Huxley, in the symposium "The Influence upon Morality of a Decline in Religious Belief," *The Nineteenth Century* 1 (1877), 331–58, 531–46. Square brackets are James's.]
8. [William Clifford, "The Ethics of Belief," in *Lectures and Essays,* ed. Leslie Stephen and Frederick Pollock (1879). James's brackets.]
9. [James is referring to Arthur Balfour, *The Foundations of Belief* (1895), which argued that since naturalism, which is distasteful morally and aesthetically, rests on principles that are undemonstrable, we have license to choose theism instead.]
10. Compare the admirable page 310 in S. H. Hodgson's *Time and Space* (London, 1865).
11. [The English churchman John Henry Newman (1801–1890), who became a cardinal of the Roman Catholic Church.]
12. [Our intellect's conformity with reality. James is paraphrasing the philosophy of Thomas Aquinas in this passage.]
13. [The aptitude for forcing certain assent.]
14. [Rest in cognition.]
15. [Being itself.]

16. [The German physicist Johann Carl Friedrich Zöllner (1834–1882) and the British mathematician Charles Howard Hinton (1853–1907).]

17. [Widespread agreement.]

18. [Limiting concept. The term is from Kant's *Critique of Pure Reason* (1781).]

19. [The English evolutionist philosopher Herbert Spencer (1820–1903) and the German biologist August Weismann (1834–1914).]

20. Compare Wilfrid Ward's essay "The Wish to Believe," in his *Witnesses to the Unseen,* Macmillan, 1893.

21. ["The heart has reasons reason does not understand."]

22. [In "The Sovereignty of Ethics," in *Lectures and Biographical Sketches* (1884).]

23. [For forcing my assent.]

24. [*Discours laïques* (1877).]

25. Since belief is measured by action, he who forbids us to believe religion to be true, necessarily also forbids us to act as we should if we did believe it to be true. The whole defence of religious faith hinges upon action. If the action required or inspired by the religious hypothesis is in no way different from that dictated by the naturalistic hypothesis, then religious faith is a pure superfluity, better pruned away, and controversy about its legitimacy is a piece of idle trifling, unworthy of serious minds. I myself believe, of course, that the religious hypothesis gives to the world an expression which specifically determines our reactions, and makes them in a large part unlike what they might be on a purely naturalistic scheme of belief.

26. *Liberty, Equality, Fraternity,* 2d ed. (London, 1874), p. 353.

What Pragmatism Means

Originally the second in a series of lectures James delivered at the Lowell Institute in Boston in November and December 1906, and then at Columbia University in January and February 1907. It was published as "A Defense of Pragmatism II: What Pragmatism Means" in *The Popular Science Monthly* 70 (April 1907), 351–64, and reprinted under the heading

"Lecture II" in William James, *Pragmatism: A New Name for Some Old Ways of Thinking* (New York: Longmans, Green, 1907), 43–81, which is the basis for the text used here.

1. Translated in the *Revue Philosophique* for January 1879 (vol. 7). [Reprinted here, pp. 26–48. Peirce did not use the term "pragmatism" in that essay, or anywhere else in print, until James had introduced it in "Philosophical Conceptions and Practical Results" (see n. 2).]

2. [The lecture was entitled "Philosophical Conceptions and Practical Results." It was published in the Berkeley *University Chronicle* 1 (September 1898), 287–310, and is reprinted in *Pragmatism,* ed. Frederick H. Burkhardt (Cambridge, Mass.: Harvard University Press, 1975), 257–70.]

3. "Theorie und Praxis," *Zeitsch. des Oesterreichischen Ingenieur u. Architecten-Vereines,* 1905, 4: 6. I find a still more radical pragmatism than Ostwald's in an address by Professor W. S. Franklin: "I think that the sickliest notion of physics, even if a student gets it, is that it is 'the science of masses, molecules and the ether.' And think that the healthiest notion, even if a student does not wholly get it, is that physics is the science of the ways of taking hold of bodies and pushing them!" (*Science,* January 2, 1903).

4. [The English philosopher Shadworth Hollway Hodgson (1832–1912) was a longtime friend of James. "Known as" is a term from Hodgson's *Philosophy and Experience* (1885).]

5. [Giovanni Papini (1881–1956), whose essays on pragmatism were collected in *Pragmatismo: (1903–1911)* (1920).]

6. [Lecture VI, "Pragmatism's Conception of Truth," reprinted here, pp. 112–31.]

7. [European scientists and logicians, all contemporaries of James.]

8. [The Oxford philosopher and champion of pragmatism Ferdinand Canning Scott Schiller (1864–1937). The writings James has in mind are collected in Schiller's *Humanism: Philosophical Essays* (1903) and *Studies in Humanism* (1907).]

9. [The reference is to the so-called Chicago School—John Dewey, who taught at the University of Chicago from 1894 to 1904, and sev-

eral of his colleagues, who collected their work in *Studies in Logical Theory* (1903), a volume dedicated to James.]

10. [The English chemist William Ramsay (1852–1916), who discovered helium in uranium ore.]

11. [James is referring to "Lecture V: Pragmatism and Common Sense," "Lecture VI: Pragmatism's Conception of Truth," and "Lecture VII: Pragmatism and Humanism."]

12. [No footprints lead back.]

13. ["Pragmatism's Conception of Truth."]

Pragmatism's Conception of Truth

Published under the heading "Lecture VI" in William James, *Pragmatism: A New Name for Some Old Ways of Thinking* (New York. Longmans, Green, 1907), 197–236.

1. [The Scottish physicist James Clerk Maxwell (1831–1879).]

2. [The Oxford philosopher and champion of pragmatism Ferdinand Canning Scott Schiller (1864–1937).]

3. [In his *Scientific Papers,* ed. W. D. Niven (1890).]

4. [In things.]

5. [Before the thing.]

6. [Gotthold Ephraim Lessing, "Hänschen Schlau" ("Sly Hans," 1753), slightly misquoted. In James's version: "Said Sly Hans to Cousin Fritz, 'How comes it, Cousin Fritz, that it always happens that it's the rich people in the world who have the most money?'"]

7. [In action.]

8. [James is referring to Søren Kierkegaard (1813–1855).]

9. A. E. Taylor, *Philosophical Review,* vol. 14, p. 288 [1905].

10. H. Rickert, *Der Gegenstand der Erkenntniss* [(*The Object of Knowledge*), 1892], chapter titled "Die Urtheilsnothwendigkeit." [The German philosopher Heinrich Rickert (1863–1936) was a teacher of Martin Heidegger.]

11. [In the essay "Self-Reliance" (1841).]

12. I am not forgetting that Professor Rickert long ago gave up the whole notion of truth being founded on agreement with reality. Reality, according to him, is whatever agrees with truth, and truth is founded solely on our primal duty. This fantastic flight, together with Mr. Joachim's candid confession of failure in his book *The Nature of Truth,* seems to me to mark the bankruptcy of rationalism when dealing with this subject. Rickert deals with part of the pragmatistic position under the head of what he calls "Relativismus." I cannot discuss his text here. Suffice it to say that his argumentation in that chapter is so feeble as to seem almost incredible in so generally able a writer. [The references are to the German philosopher Heinrich Rickert, whose *Der Gegenstand der Erkenntnis* James cited in note 10, and the English philosopher Harold Joachim (1868–1938), who confessed, in *The Nature of Truth* (1906), the inability of Idealist philosophy to produce a satisfactory theory of truth. James did discuss Rickert's treatment of the pragmatist position in his sequel to *Pragmatism, The Meaning of Truth* (1909), in the chapter called "Abstractionism and 'Relativismus.'"]

A Pluralistic Universe

This passage was originally part of the last of the Hibbert Lectures, delivered at Manchester College, Oxford, in 1908–9, and published as "Pluralism and Religion," *The Hibbert Journal* 6 (1908), 721–28. It appears in "Conclusions" in William James, *A Pluralistic Universe: Hibbert Lectures at Manchester College on the Present Situation in Philosophy* (New York: Longmans, Green, 1909), 303–31, which is the basis for the text used here.

1. [The phrase is from Benjamin Paul Blood, *The Flaw in Supremacy* (1893). Blood (1832–1919) was an American mystic whose writings were admired, and sometimes quoted, by James.]
2. [A many in small.]
3. [In an earlier chapter, "Bergson and Intellectualism," James had used the example of "a heavy log which takes two men to carry it. First A

and B take it. Then C takes hold and A drops off; then D takes hold and B drops off, so that C and D now bear it; and so on. The log meanwhile never drops, and keeps its sameness throughout the journey. Even so it is with all our experiences. Their changes are not complete annihilations followed by complete creations of something absolutely novel."]

4. [Oneness.]

5. [Disordered.]

6. ["Synechism" was Charles Peirce's term for his theory of continuity: see p. 482, n.3.]

7. ["Radical empiricism" was the name James gave to his own philosophical position; he regarded it as logically unconnected to pragmatism: "One may entirely reject it and still be a pragmatist," as he wrote in the preface to *Pragmatism*. He introduced the term in the preface to *The Will to Believe* (1897); some of his essays on the subject were published after his death as *Essays in Radical Empiricism* (1912). In the preface to *The Meaning of Truth* (1909), he defined radical empiricism as the view that "the parts of experience hold together from next to next by relations that are themselves parts of experience. The directly apprehended universe needs, in short, no extraneous trans-empirical connective support, but possesses in its own right a concatenated or continuous structure."]

8. [Primary condition.]

Lecture I: Early Forms of Liability

This passage was originally part of the first of the twelve lectures on the common law Holmes delivered at the Lowell Institute in Boston in November and December 1880; it was published in Oliver Wendell Holmes, Jr., *The Common Law* (Boston: Little, Brown, 1881), 1–38.

Lecture III: Torts—Trespass and Negligence

This passage was originally part of the third of the twelve lectures on the common law Holmes delivered at the Lowell Institute in Boston in November and December 1880; it was published in Oliver Wendell Holmes, Jr., *The Common Law* (Boston: Little, Brown, 1881), 77–129.

1. [I.e., a trial court judge.]
2. 7 *American Law Review* 654 et seq., July 1873. [The reference is to Holmes's own article "The Theory of Torts."]

Privilege, Malice, and Intent

Published in *The Harvard Law Review* 8 (1894), 1–14; reprinted in Oliver Wendell Holmes, *Collected Legal Papers* (New York: Harcourt, Brace and Howe, 1920), 117–37, which is the text used here.

1. [The emergence of the "external standard" was a major theme of *The Common Law.* It refers to the development (in Holmes's view of legal history) of a legal standard that evaluates conduct in light of its probable consequences as they would appear to a reasonable person, rather than by reference to the defendant's state of mind.]
2. [A common law maxim generally interpreted as: Every person should use his or her own property so as not to injure that of another.]

The Path of the Law

Originally a lecture delivered at the Boston University School of Law, January 8, 1897; first published in *The Harvard Law Review* 10 (1897), 457–78, and, under the title "Law and the Study of Law," in *Juridical Review* 9 (1897), 105–31. Reprinted in Oliver Wendell Holmes, *Collected Legal Papers* (New York: Harcourt, Brace and Howe, 1920), 167–202, which is the text used here.

1. [The Swiss-born zoologist and geologist Louis Agassiz (1807–1873) taught at Harvard from 1848 on. William James was one of his students.]

2. [The mill acts required payment of compensation for flooding a neighbor's lands—in effect, a tax on building a mill.]

3. [An unauthorized assumption of the rights of ownership.]

4. [A civil wrong or injury not arising out of contract.]

5. [Edward Coke (1552–1634), whose commentaries on English law were collected in the *Institutes* (1628).]

6. Roll. Rep. 368.

7. [A written agreement under seal. "Specific performance" means that the promise made in the contract must be fulfilled (here, that the lease be granted), as opposed to the payment of damages in lieu of fulfillment.]

8. [A system of justice according to fairness, outside the rule of common law. Equity courts no longer exist in the United States.]

9. See *Hanson v. Globe Newspaper Co.*, 159 Mass. 293, 302 [1893; Holmes, then a judge on the Massachusetts Supreme Judicial Court, wrote the opinion].

10. [Herbert Spencer, *Social Statics: Or, The Conditions Essential to Human Happiness* (1851). Holmes is citing Spencer's "first principle," which is restated many times in the book but which reads, in its initial formulation: "Every man has freedom to do all that he wills, provided he infringes not the equal freedom of any other man." This is the principle to which Holmes was later alluding in the famous sentence in his dissent, attacking the doctrine of "freedom of contract," in *Lochner v. New York* (1905): "The Fourteenth Amendment does not enact Mr. Herbert Spencer's Social Statics."]

11. [Always, everywhere, and by all.]

12. [The codes of medieval European law.]

13. [A man who knows the principles of law generally accepted by the courts.]

14. [From the start; in this case, when a defendant who has entered another's land innocently or with permission subsequently abuses his privilege, the act of entering becomes an illegal trespass retroactively.]

15. *Commonwealth v. Rubin*, 165 Mass. 453 [1896].

16. Havelock Ellis, *The Criminal*, 41, citing Garofalo. See also Ferri, *Sociologue Criminelle*, passim. Compare Tarde, *La Philosophie Pénale*.

17. An example of the law's refusing to protect the plaintiff is when he is interrupted by a stranger in the use of a valuable way, which he has travelled adversely [i.e., without permission] for a week less than the period of prescription [i.e., the period after which such adverse use confers a right to use or possession]. A week later he will have gained a right, but now he is only a trespasser. Example of privilege I have given already. One of the best is competition in business.

18. [The reference is to James Barr Ames, "Specialty Contracts and Equitable Defenses," *Harvard Law Review* 9 (1895), 49–59.]

19. [A specialty is a contract under seal.]

20. [A promise, not under seal, to do something or to pay someone.]

21. [The inducement—something gained by one party or lost by the other—formally required to make a legally enforceable contract.]

22. [Holmes is referring to the opinion in the English case of *Master v. Miller*, 4 T. R. 320 (1791).]

23. [Melville Madison Bigelow (1846–1921), then dean of the Boston University School of Law; James Barr Ames (1846–1910) and James Bradley Thayer (1831–1902) both at Harvard Law School. Frederick Pollock and F. W. Maitland, *A History of English Law Before the Time of Edward I* (1895).]

24. [Holmes is referring to his friend James Fitzjames Stephen (1829–1894), whose *History of the Criminal Law in England* was published in 1883; Frederick Pollock and Robert Samuel Wright, *An Essay on Possession in the Common Law* (1888); the English jurist John Austin (1790–1859); the English political philosophers Thomas Hobbes (1588–1679) and Jeremy Bentham (1748–1832); and the English jurists Thomas Erskine Holland (1835–1926) and Frederick Pollock (1845–1937).]

25. [*First Book of Jurisprudence* (1896). Pollock and Holmes were lifelong friends; their correspondence is collected in the two volumes of *Holmes-Pollock Letters,* ed. Mark DeWolfe Howe (1941).]

26. [English writer on law Henry de Bracton (d. 1268).]

27. [The law of prescription covers cases in which a lapse of time entails the loss of a right, as when someone acquires a right of way by continued unchallenged use, or when a creditor loses the right to recover

by remaining silent too long—just as, under the statute of limitations, the state loses its power to prosecute after a certain period.]

28. [I.e., without permission.]

29. [Holmes is referring to Henry Sumner Maine, *Ancient Law* (1861).]

30. [A favorite saying of the celebrated French actress Rachel (born Elizabeth Félix, 1821–1858)—attributed to her in, for example, Nina H. Kennard's biography *Rachel* (1886).]

31. *Phil. Des Rechts,* sec. 190 [1821].

Ideals and Doubts

Published in *Illinois Law Review* 10 (1915), 1–4; reprinted in Oliver Wendell Holmes, *Collected Legal Papers* (New York: Harcourt, Brace and Howe, 1920), 303–7, which is the text used here.

Natural Law

Published in *The Harvard Law Review* 32 (1918), 40–44; reprinted in Oliver Wendell Holmes, *Collected Legal Papers* (New York: Harcourt, Brace and Howe, 1920), 310–16, which is the text used here. Holmes notes that the essay was suggested by his reading of François Geny, *Science et technique en droit positif privé* (Paris, 1915).

1. "Ideals and Doubts" [1915; an excerpt is reprinted here, pp. 170–72].

Abrams v. United States

250 U.S. 616, 624, Holmes, J., dissenting.

1. [Jacob Abrams and four other men had been convicted under the Espionage Act for distributing several thousand pamphlets critical of American war policies. The pamphlets, thrown from a factory window in Manhattan, warned workers that participation in the war effort would help the United States and its allies crush the Bolshevik

revolution in Russia. The fourth count in the indictment, to which
Holmes refers a few sentences later, charged a conspiracy to incite interference with the production of materials necessary to the prosecu-
tion of the war.]

2. [Holmes had argued earlier in the opinion that "a deed is not done
   with intent to produce a consequence unless that consequence is
   the aim of the deed" (627). The requirement that for speech to be
   punishable the intent to cause an illegal act must be the speaker's
   "proximate motive" is a distinctive element in Holmes's theory of
   free speech.]

3. [Expression intended to incite people to change the government by
   unlawful means.]

The Ethics of Democracy

Published in *University of Michigan Philosophical Papers* 1 (2d ser.), 1888.

1. [*Popular Government* (1885); Dewey is using the American edition,
   published in 1886. Maine's historical study of the law, particularly *Ancient Law* (1861), was an important influence on Holmes's *Common
   Law.*]

2. [The German theologian David Friedrich Strauss (1808–1874), author of *The Life of Jesus* (1835–36), as paraphrased by Maine.]

3. [Dewey is referring to the English political philosophers Thomas
   Hobbes (1588–1679) and Jeremy Bentham (1748–1832) and the English jurist John Austin (1790–1859).]

4. [Samuel J. Tilden was governor of New York. He ran for president
   on the Democratic ticket in 1876, losing a disputed election to
   Rutherford B. Hayes. The passage quoted by Dewey is from *The
   Writings and Speeches of Samuel J. Tilden,* ed. John Bigelow (1885).]

5. The only case in which such statements cease to represent facts is
   when a constitutional amendment is submitted to a people, and they
   are compelled to vote yes or no, with no possibility of modification
   or amendment. But this is only an argument against the plebiscitum,
   (for such this process really is) not against democracy.

6. [The Swiss political philosopher Johann Kaspar Bluntschli. His organic theory of the state appeared in *Allgemeines Staatsrecht* (1851–52; English trans., 1892).]

7. [James Russell Lowell, "Democracy" (1884), in *Democracy, and Other Addresses* (1887).]

Theories of Knowledge

Chapter 25 in John Dewey, *Democracy and Education* (New York: Macmillan, 1916), 388–401.

1. [A chapter entitled "Educational Values," in which Dewey argued against dividing the curriculum into subject matter concerned with "intrinsic value" (the arts) and subject matter concerned with "instrumental value" (practical or vocational fields). This kind of segregation, he thought, is "a result of the isolation of social groups and classes. Hence it is the business of education in a democratic social group to struggle against this isolation in order that the various interests may reinforce and play into one another."]

The Need for a Recovery of Philosophy

Published in John Dewey et al., *Creative Intelligence: Essays in the Pragmatic Attitude* (New York: Holt, 1917), 3–69.

1. [The French philosopher Henri Bergson (1859–1941), whose criticism of traditional empiricism appeared in *Essai sur les données immédiates de la conscience* (translated as *Time and Free Will*, 1889), *Matière et mémoire* (*Matter and Memory*, 1896), and *L'Évolution créatrice* (*Creative Evolution*, 1907). Bergson's "time philosophy" is closely allied with William James's radical empiricism; their names were frequently paired in contemporary discussions, and they had a substantial correspondence.]

2. [James uses this figure of speech throughout *Pragmatism;* see, for example, the exhortation to "bring out of each word its practical cash-value" on pp. 97–98 in "What Pragmatism Means," reprinted here.]

3. [Dewey is referring to George Santayana, who criticized pragmatism in these terms in the opening chapter of *Winds of Doctrine* (1913).]

Experience, Nature and Art

Chapter 9 in John Dewey, *Experience and Nature* (LaSalle, Ill.: Open Court, 1925; 2d ed., New York: W. W. Norton, 1929), 354–93.

1. [In *The Politics*.]
2. [A category found already fixed in nature.]
3. [A term coined by the English critic Clive Bell in *Art* (1913), where it is defined as "aesthetically moving form" and "the one quality common to all works of visual art." The concept is associated with the painter Roger Fry and with the aesthetics of the Bloomsbury circle.]

I Believe

Published in *I Believe: The Personal Philosophies of Certain Eminent Men and Women of Our Time,* ed. Clifton Fadiman (New York: Simon and Schuster, 1939), 347–54.

1. [Dewey's earlier essay is "What I Believe," *Forum* 83 (March 1930), 176–82.]
2. [The writers H. G. Wells (1866–1946) and George Bernard Shaw (1856–1950) were associated with the Fabians, an English reform movement.]
3. [The National Industrial Recovery Act (1933) was the cornerstone of the New Deal. Dewey did not support Roosevelt and was generally dismissive of New Deal economic policy.]
4. [Dewey is referring to the English evolutionist philosopher Herbert Spencer (1820–1903).]

A Function of the Social Settlement

Published in *Annals of the American Academy of Political and Social Science* 13 (May 1899), 323–45.

1. [Benjamin Disraeli (1804–1881); his novel *Sybil: Or, The Two Nations* was published in 1845.]

2. [Samuel Augustus Barnett (1844–1913), English clergyman and founder of the social settlement movement.]

3. [John Dewey, *The Significance of the Problem of Knowledge* (Chicago: University of Chicago Press, 1897); reprinted in John Dewey, *The Early Works, 1882–1898, Volume 5: 1895–1898: Early Essays,* ed. Jo Ann Boydston (Carbondale: Southern Illinois University Press, 1972), 20–21, slightly condensed and paraphrased.]

4. [William James, "Philosophical Conceptions and Practical Results," the first use of the term "pragmatism" in print. Originally published in the Berkeley *University Chronicle* 1 (September 1898), 287–310; reprinted in *Pragmatism,* ed. Frederick H. Burkhardt (Cambridge, Mass.: Harvard University Press, 1975), 257–70. James is articulating what he calls "the principle of Peirce, the principle of pragmatism."]

The Mechanism of Social Consciousness

A talk delivered to the Western Philosophical Association, Chicago, April 5 and 6, 1912; published in *The Journal of Philosophy, Psychology, and Scientific Methods* 9 (1912), 401–6.

1. [James expressed his views on this subject most emphatically in "Does 'Consciousness' Exist?" *The Journal of Philosophy, Psychology, and Scientific Methods* 1 (1904), 477–91; reprinted in the posthumous collection *Essays in Radical Empiricism* (1912).]

A Contrast of Individualistic and Social Theories of the Self

This text is based on students' notes for Mead's course "Social Philosophy," which he taught at the University of Chicago from 1900 to 1930; the core of the material consists of notes taken in 1927. These were collated and edited by Charles W. Morris and published posthumously in

George Herbert Mead, *Mind, Self, and Society from the Standpoint of a Social Behaviorist* (Chicago: University of Chicago Press, 1934), 222–26.

1. Historically, both the rationalist and the empiricist are committed to the interpretation of experience in terms of the individual (1931).
   Other people are there as much as we are there; to be a self requires other selves (1924).

2. In defending a social theory of mind we are defending a functional, as opposed to any form of substantive or entitive, view as to its nature. And in particular, we are opposing all intracranial or intra-epidermal views as to its character and locus. For it follows from our social theory of mind that the field of mind must be co-extensive with, and include all the components of, the field of the social process of experience and behavior, i.e., the matrix of social relations and interactions among individuals, which is presupposed by it, and out of which it arises or comes into being. If mind is socially constituted, than the field or locus of any given individual mind must extend as far as the social activity or apparatus of social relations which constitutes it extends; and hence that field cannot be bounded by the skin of the individual organism to which it belongs.

3. The human being's physiological capacity for developing mind or intelligence is a product of the process of biological evolution, just as is his whole organism; but the actual development of his mind or intelligence itself, given that capacity, must proceed in terms of the social situations wherein it gets its expression and import; and hence it itself is a product of the process of social evolution, the process of social experience and behavior.

Philosophy as a Kind of Writing: An Essay on Derrida

Published in *New Literary History* 10 (1978–79), 141–60; reprinted in Richard Rorty, *Consequences of Pragmatism (Essays: 1972–1980)* (Minneapolis: University of Minnesota Press, 1982), 90–109, which is the text used here.

1. [The invisible things of God or of nature. The phrase is associated with the philosophy of Thomas Aquinas.]
2. [Prudence.]
3. [Scientific knowledge.]
4. [Eros.]
5. [Scholarly discipline.]
6. [Rorty's ellipsis.]
7. [Rorty is referring to the English analytic philosopher P. F. Strawson, the American political philosopher John Rawls, and the American philosopher Hilary Putnam, whose essay "Fact and Value" is reprinted here, pp. 338–62.]
8. On Derrida's relation to contemporary philosophy of language, and especially to Wittgenstein, see Newton Garver, Preface to Jacques Derrida, *Speech and Phenomenon, and Other Essays in Husserl's Theory of Signs,* trans. David B. Allison (Evanston: Northwestern University Press, 1972), and "Derrida on Rousseau on Writing," *Journal of Philosophy* 74 (1977): 663–73; Marjorie Green, "Life, Death and Language: Some Thoughts on Wittgenstein and Derrida," in *Philosophy in and out of Europe* (Berkeley and Los Angeles: University of California Press, 1976), pp. 142–54; John Searle's exchange with Derrida in the first two volumes of *Glyph* [1977]; Richard Rorty, "Derrida on Language, Being, and Abnormal Philosophy," *Journal of Philosophy* 74 (1977): 673–81.
9. [Rorty is referring to work in the philosophy of language by philosophers ranging from the German logician Gottlob Frege (1848–1925) to the contemporary American philosopher Donald Davidson. Derrida's early work was on the German phenomenologist Edmund Husserl (1859–1938).]
10. [Literally: calmness and unhiddenness. Heidegger uses *Gelassenheit* to mean "release" or "letting go," as a poet might be said to abandon control over the language of a poem; *Unverborgenheit* is used to name the quality of being unconcealed, an attribute of the truth of Being, as opposed to the cognitive truths of science and metaphysics.]

11. Derrida, *Of Grammatology,* trans. Gayatri Chakravorty Spivak (Baltimore: Johns Hopkins University Press, 1976), pp. 17–18.

12. Ibid., p. 158.

13. [J. L. Austin, *Sense and Sensibilia,* ed. G. J. Warnock (London: Oxford University Press, 1961), 2.]

14. [The contemporary American philosopher John Searle.]

15. [In "What Pragmatism Means," reprinted here, pp. 93–111.]

16. [*Of Grammatology,* 158; literally: "There is no outside-the-text," with a pun on the French word "hors-texte," meaning bookplate.]

17. [Origin.]

18. From "Differance," in Derrida, *Speech and Phenomena,* p. 146.

19. [The Swiss linguist Ferdinand de Saussure (1857–1913). His writings, collected in *Cours de linguistique générale* (*Course in General Linguistics,* 1916), were a major influence on structuralism in a variety of fields.]

20. *Of Grammatology,* p. 46.

21. See Wilfrid Sellars, *Science, Perception and Reality* (London and New York: Routledge and Kegan Paul, 1963), pp. 160 ff.

22. *Of Grammatology,* p. 6.

23. Cf. Martin Heidegger, *The Question of Being,* trans. William Kluback and Jean T. Wilde (New York: Twayne, 1958), a translation of *Zur Seinsfrage* (Frankfurt: Klostermann, 1959).

24. Heidegger, *On Time and Being,* trans. Joan Stambaugh (New York: Harper and Row, 1972), p. 24.

25. *Of Grammatology,* pp. 18–19.

26. Ibid., p. 167.

27. Ludwig Wittgenstein, *Philosophical Investigations* (New York and London: Macmillan, 1953), pt. 1, sec. 261.

28. [Cognized by means of things that have been made. The phrase is associated with Aquinas.]

29. [A Derridean amalgam of the homophonic French words for "difference" and "deferral." Derrida usually insists on the term's untranslatability, but it can be understood as the product of (1) the meaning of a signifier is a function of its difference from other signifiers (a premise of structuralism) and (2) the chain of significations never ends—e.g., by pointing to a referent "outside the text" or to a "tran-

scendental signified"—and meaning is therefore perpetually deferred (a premise of poststructuralism). The "trace" is the vestige within the sign of these deferred significations.]

30. *Speech and Phenomenon,* pp. 158–59.

31. [The reference is to Thomas S. Kuhn, *The Structure of Scientific Revolutions* (Chicago: University of Chicago Press, 1962), a text often cited by Rorty. Kuhn defines "normal science" as "research firmly based upon one or more past scientific achievements, achievements that some particular scientific community acknowledges for a time as supplying the foundation for its further practice."]

32. [The German-American logician Rudolf Carnap (1891–1970).]

33. [Dominatrix of the disciplines if no longer queen of the sciences.]

34. [The contemporary American analytic philosopher Willard Van Orman Quine.]

35. [Transcend.]

36. [Knowledge of knowledge—i.e., epistemology. The phrase is used by Plato and Aristotle.]

Postmodernist Bourgeois Liberalism

Published in *The Journal of Philosophy* 80 (1983), 583–89; reprinted in Richard Rorty, *Objectivity, Relativism, and Truth: Philosophical Papers, Volume 1* (Cambridge: Cambridge University Press, 1991), 197–202, which is the text used here.

1. [Ronald Dworkin, liberal legal philosopher whose work emphasizes the concept of rights; Roberto Unger, political philosopher and a founder of the Critical Legal Studies movement, which emphasizes the political bases of legal principles; Alasdair MacIntyre, moral philosopher and critic of Enlightenment thought; and Michael Oakeshott, conservative philosopher of politics and education. Selections from the writings of John Dewey are reprinted here, pp. 181–271.]

2. [Michael Walzer, *Spheres of Justice* (1983).]

3. [Ronald Dworkin, "What Justice Isn't" (1983), later reprinted in *A Matter of Principle* (Cambridge, Mass.: Harvard University Press, 1985),

214–20. Dworkin's sentence, in that text, reads: "We cannot leave justice to convention and anecdote."]

4. [Jean-François Lyotard, *The Postmodern Condition: A Report on Knowledge* (1979), trans. Geoff Bennington and Brian Massumi (Minneapolis: University of Minnesota Press, 1984), xxiv ("I define *postmodern* as incredulity toward metanarratives").]

5. [Rorty is referring to John Rawls, *A Theory of Justice* (1971), which posits a pre-social condition in which individuals choose the principles of a just society without knowing in advance what their own status within that society will be.]

6. [Rorty is referring to "Two Dogmas of Empiricism" (1951), reprinted in Willard Van Orman Quine, *From a Logical Point of View: Nine Logico-Philosophical Essays,* 2d ed. (Cambridge, Mass.: Harvard University Press, 1980), 20–46.]

7. *Liberalism and the Limits of Justice* (New York: Cambridge University Press, 1982), p. 179. Sandel's remarkable book argues masterfully that Rawls cannot naturalize Kant and still retain the meta-ethical authority of Kantian "practical reason." [Sandel is responding to the argument in Rawls's *A Theory of Justice* (1971); see note 5.]

8. [*Science and Metaphysics* (1968), chaps. 6 and 7. Sellars introduced the notion of "community intentions" in "Philosophy and the Scientific Image of Man" (1960), reprinted in his *Science, Perception and Reality* (New York: Humanities Press, 1963), 127–96; it plays an important role in Rorty's principal work of political philosophy, *Contingency, Irony, and Solidarity* (1989).]

9. [A school of American jurisprudence which emphasized the political and practical nature of judicial decision making. It is generally understood to derive from Holmes's essay "The Path of the Law" (reprinted here, pp. 145–69), and is associated with the work of Jerome Frank, Karl Llewellyn, and their followers.]

10. [The linguist Noam Chomsky, a critic of American foreign policy.]

11. *Reason, Truth and History* (New York: Cambridge University Press, 1981), p. 216. [An excerpt from another chapter of this book is reprinted here, pp. 338–62.] "Limousine Liberals" signifies acceptance of a contradiction, which blocks realization that they are agents of conservatives, who have bred a false alternative to their own power.

12. I discuss such redefinition in the Introduction to *Consequences of Pragmatism* (Minneapolis: University of Minnesota Press, 1982).

Fact and Value

Chapter 6 in Hilary Putnam, *Reason, Truth and History* (Cambridge: Cambridge University Press, 1981), 127–49.

1. For a non-technical account of Tarski's work see my *Meaning and the Moral Sciences*, pt. 1, lecture 1. [The reference is to Alfred Tarski, "The Concept of Truth in Formalized Languages," in *Semantics, Metamathematics* (1956).]

2. [The hypothesis that we are all brains which have been suspended in a vat of nutrients and hooked up to a computer programmed to produce the collective hallucination of a real world. Putnam argues, in his first chapter, that this hypothesis is self-refuting, on the ground that if we can consider whether it is true or false, it cannot be true.]

3. But I keep changing my mind about whether it would or not.

4. If they do make such predictions, then it does make this much difference: their view is no longer incoherent in the way we criticized in Chapter 1, since they are making a claim that could be justified (eventually), and hence one that does not require a view of truth as "transcendent" (or independent of justification) to be understood.

5. [Putnam's ellipsis.]

6. [Putnam's term for the so-called copy theory of truth—the view that a statement is true if it corresponds to a mind-independent reality. *Reason, Truth and History* is an attempt to stake out a mediating position between metaphysical realism and the "alternative" view that all truths are "hopelessly subjective." Putnam's name in this book for his position is "internal realism"; he later, in *The Many Faces of Realism* (LaSalle, Ill.: Open Court, 1987), renamed it "pragmatic realism."]

7. *Ethica Nicomachea*, bk. 1, chap. 3.

8. [Putnam is referring to the English churchman John Henry New-

man (1801–1890), who converted to Catholicism, and the German-American logician Rudolf Carnap (1891–1970).]

9. Routledge and Kegan Paul, 1970.

10. [American mathematician and logician (1906–1978).]

11. [*Ways of Worldmaking* (1978).]

12. An unintentionally funny version of the projection theory is cited by C. S. Lewis in *The Abolition of Man* (Macmillan, 1947). Lewis quotes a secondary school English text (which he does not identify, out of charity). "You remember that there were two tourists present [Lewis is talking about the well-known story of Coleridge at the waterfall]: that one called it 'sublime' and the other 'pretty'; and that Coleridge mentally endorsed the first judgment and rejected the second with disgust. Gaius and Titius [Lewis's pseudonyms for the unidentified authors of the text] comment as follows: 'When the man said *That is sublime,* he appeared to be making a remark about the waterfall. . . . Actually he was not making a remark about the waterfall, but about his own feelings. What he was saying was really *I have feelings in my mind associated with the word "Sublime,"* or shortly, I have sublime feelings.' " [Square brackets and ellipsis in the original.]

13. [*Moral Luck* (1981).]

14. David Wiggins in "Truth, Invention, and the Meaning of Life," *Proceedings of the British Academy,* vol. 62, 1976.

Against Theory

Published in *Critical Inquiry* 8 (Summer 1982), 723–42; reprinted in *Against Theory: Literary Studies and the New Pragmatism,* ed. W. J. T. Mitchell (Chicago: University of Chicago Press, 1985), 11–30, which is the text used here.

1. E. D. Hirsch, Jr., *Validity in Interpretation* (New Haven, Conn., 1967), pp. 216, 219. Our remarks on Hirsch are in some ways parallel to criticisms offered by P. D. Juhl in the second chapter of his *Interpretation: An Essay in the Philosophy of Literary Criticism* (Princeton, N.J., 1980). Juhl's position will be discussed in the next section. All further cita-

tions to these works will be included in the text. [The section on Juhl's book has been omitted here.]

2. The phrase "piece of language" goes back, Hirsch notes, to the opening paragraph of William Empson's *Seven Types of Ambiguity,* 3d ed. (New York, 1955).

3. See Hirsch, *The Aims of Interpretation* (Chicago, 1976), p. 8.

4. John R. Searle, "Reiterating the Differences: A Reply to Derrida," *Glyph* 1 (1977): 202.

5. Wordsworth's lyric has been a standard example in theoretical arguments since its adoption by Hirsch; see *Validity in Interpretation,* pp. 227–30 and 238–40.

6. Searle, "Reiterating the Differences," p. 202.

7. In conversation with the authors, Hirsch mentioned the case of a well-known critic and theorist who was persuaded by new evidence that his former reading of a poem was mistaken but who, nevertheless, professed to like his original reading better than what he now admitted was the author's intention. Hirsch meant this example to show the importance of choosing intention over some other interpretive criterion. But the critic in Hirsch's anecdote was not choosing among separate methods of interpretation; he was simply preferring his own mistake. Such a preference is surely irrelevant to the theory of interpretation; it might affect what one does *with* an interpretation, but it has no effect on how one *gets* an interpretation.

8. The arguments presented here against theoretical treatments of intention at the local utterance level would apply, virtually unaltered, to accounts of larger-scale intentions elsewhere in Hirsch; they would apply as well to the theoretical proposals of such writers as M. H. Abrams, Wayne C. Booth, R. S. Crane, and Ralph W. Rader— all associated, directly or indirectly, with the Chicago School. Despite variations of approach and emphasis, these writers tend to agree that critical debates about the meaning of a particular passage ought to be resolved through reference to the broader structural intentions informing the work in which the passage appears. Local meanings, in this view, should be deduced from hypothetical constructions of intentions implicit, for example, in an author's choice of genre; these

Besides the author himself can create something
he didn't intend to, realize it is better, and let it stand.

interpretive hypotheses should in turn be confirmed or falsified by their success or failure in explaining the work's details. But this procedure would have methodological force only if the large-scale intentions were different in theoretical status from the local meanings they are supposed to constrain. We would argue, however, that all local meanings are always intentional and that structural choices and local utterances are therefore related to intention in exactly the same fashion. While an interpreter's sense of one might determine his sense of the other, neither is available to interpretation—or amenable to interpretive agreement—in a specially objective way. (Whether interpretations of intention at any level are best conceived as hypotheses is another, though a related, question.) [The Chicago School of criticism is associated with the work of the literary scholar Ronald S. Crane (1886–1967) and the philosopher Richard McKeon (1900–1985), both of whom came to the University of Chicago in the mid-1930s and whose teachings influenced several generations of literary critics.]

9. At least this is true of the present generation of theorists. For earlier theorists such as W. K. Wimsatt and Monroe C. Beardsley, the objective meanings sought by positive theory were to be acquired precisely by *subtracting* intention and relying on the formal rules and public norms of language. This, of course, is the view they urge in "The Intentional Fallacy" (*The Verbal Icon: Studies in the Meaning of Poetry* [Lexington, Ky., 1954], pp. 3–18).

10. Negative theory rests on the perception of what de Man calls "an insurmountable obstacle in the way of any reading or understanding" (*Allegories of Reading* [New Haven, Conn., 1979], p. 131). Some theorists (e.g., David Bleich and Norman Holland) understand this obstacle as the reader's subjectivity. Others (like de Man himself and J. Hillis Miller) understand it as the aporia between constative and performative language, between demonstration and persuasion. In all cases, however, the negative theorist is committed to the view that interpretation is, as Jonathan Culler says, "necessary error" (*The Pursuit of Signs* [Ithaca, N.Y., 1981], p. 14). [Bleich and Holland are asso-

ciated with "reader-response" criticism; de Man, Miller, and Culler
are associated with deconstruction.]

11. Stanley Fish, *Is There a Text in This Class?: The Authority of Interpretive
    Communities* (Cambridge, Mass., 1980), p. 370; all further citations to
    this work will be included in the text.

12. Fish calls his account "a general or metacritical belief" (*Is There a Text
    in This Class?,* p. 359; cf. pp. 368–70).

13. In one respect Fish's prescription is unusual: it separates the two the-
    oretical goals of grounding practice and reaching objective truth. It
    tells us what is true and how to behave—but not how to behave in or-
    der to find out what is true.

Pragmatism, Pluralism, and the Healing of Wounds

An address delivered to the Eastern Division Meeting of the American
Philosophical Association, December 29, 1988; published as an appendix
in Richard J. Bernstein, *The New Constellation: The Ethical-Political Horizons of Modernity/Postmodernity* (Cambridge, Mass.: MIT Press, 1992),
323–39.

1. Alasdair MacIntyre, "Epistemological Crisis, Dramatic Narrative and
   the Philosophy of Science," *Monist* 60 (1977), p. 461.

2. [Josiah Royce (1855–1916) was a friend and Harvard colleague of
   William James. He developed a philosophy he termed "pragmatic absolutism."]

3. Charles Sanders Peirce, "Questions Concerning Certain Faculties
   Claimed for Man," "Some Consequences of Four Incapacities," and
   "Grounds of Validity of the Laws of Logic." These papers are in-
   cluded in volume 5 of Charles S. Peirce's *Collected Papers,* ed. Charles
   Hartshorne and Paul Weiss (Cambridge, Mass.: Harvard University
   Press, 1932–1935). [An excerpt from "Some Consequences of Four
   Incapacities" is reprinted here, pp. 4–6.]

4. Charles S. Peirce, *Collected Papers,* vol. 5, p. 264.

5. Wilfrid Sellars, "Empiricism and the Philosophy of Mind," in *Minnesota Studies in the Philosophy of Science,* 1, ed. Herbert Feigl and

506   Notes to Pages 387–394

Michael Scriven (Minneapolis: University of Minnesota Press, 1956), p. 300 [reprinted in Sellars's *Science, Perception and Reality* (New York: Humanities Press, 1963), 127–96. Bernstein is referring to two essays by the analytic philosopher Willard Van Orman Quine: "Two Dogmas of Empiricism" (1951), in *From a Logical Point of View,* 2d. ed. (Cambridge, Mass.: Harvard University Press, 1980), 20–46, and "Ontological Relativity" (1968), in *Ontological Relativity and Other Essays* (New York: Columbia University Press, 1969), 26–68.]

6. Peirce, *Collected Papers,* vol. 5, p. 265 ["Some Consequences of Four Incapacities"].

7. Ibid.

8. See Hans Joas, *G. H. Mead: A Contemporary Re-examination of His Thought* (Cambridge, Mass.: MIT Press, 1985).

9. John Dewey, *Experience and Nature, The Later Works 1925–1953,* vol. 1, ed. Jo Ann Boydston (Carbondale: Southern Illinois University Press, 1981), p. 43. [A chapter of this book is reprinted here, pp. 233–64.]

10. William James, *A Pluralistic Universe* (Cambridge, Mass.: Harvard University Press, 1977), p. 26. [An excerpt from this book is reprinted here, pp. 132–35.]

11. The following paragraphs are adapted from the introduction of my book, *Philosophical Profiles* (Philadelphia: University of Pennsylvania Press, 1986), pp. 2–5.

12. [English mathematician and philosopher Alfred North Whitehead (1861–1947), who taught at Harvard after 1924.]

13. Richard Rorty, "Philosophy in America Today," in his *Consequences of Pragmatism* (Minneapolis: University of Minnesota Press, 1982), p. 215.

14. [The English philosophers Gilbert Ryle and J. L. Austin, influenced in part by the later work of Ludwig Wittgenstein, principally *Philosophical Investigations* (1953).]

15. "Philosophy in America Today."

16. [In "The Need for a Recovery of Philosophy" (1917), an excerpt from which is reprinted here, pp. 219–32.]

17. [Bernstein is referring to Thomas S. Kuhn, *The Essential Tension* (1977), Jürgen Habermas, *Theorie des kommunikativen Handelns* (*The Theory of Communicative Action,* 1981; English trans., 1984), and Karl-

Otto Apel, *Transformation der Philosophie* (*Towards a Transformation of Philosophy*, 1973; English trans., 1980).]

18. William James, "A World of Pure Experience," *Journal of Philosophy, Psychology, and Scientific Methods* 1 (1904), p. 533 [reprinted in James's *Essays in Radical Empiricism* (1912)].

19. [The distinction is between a morality which locates the source of obligation in an abstract and universal sphere, as when we say that our conscience requires us to violate a social more (*Moralität*), and an ethics grounded in the practices of an actual community (*Sichlichkeit*). The first term is associated with Kant, the second with Hegel.]

20. [The Anglo-Austrian philosopher of science Karl Popper (1902-1994) and the French historian Michel Foucault (1926-1984).]

21. Alasdair MacIntyre, *Whose Justice? Which Rationality?* (Notre Dame: University of Notre Dame Press, 1988). See especially chap. 19, "Tradition and Translation."

22. Richard Rorty, *Philosophy and the Mirror of Nature* (Princeton: Princeton University Press, 1979), p. 316. [Bernstein's review of this book is reprinted in his *Philosophical Profiles,* 21-57.]

23. Karl Popper, "Normal Science and Its Dangers," in Imre Lakatos and Alan Musgrave, eds., *Criticism and the Growth of Knowledge* (Cambridge: Cambridge University Press, 1970), p. 56.

24. [The reference is to Donald Davidson, "On the Very Idea of a Conceptual Scheme," in *Inquiries into Truth and Interpretation* (Oxford: Clarendon Press, 1984), 183-98.]

25. [The concept of the "domination-free communication situation" is prevalent in Habermas's work; see, for an example, "Further Reflections on the Public Sphere," in *Habermas and the Public Sphere,* ed. Craig Calhoun (Cambridge, Mass.: MIT Press, 1992), 421-61.]

26. Hans-Georg Gadamer, *Text und Interpretation* (Munich: Finh, 1984). The English translation is from Fred R. Dallmayr, "Hermeneutics and Deconstruction," in *Critical Encounters* (Notre Dame: University of Notre Dame Press, 1987), p. 135.

27. Richard Rorty, "Pragmatism, Relativism, and Irrationalism," *Proceedings and Addresses of the American Philosophical Association* 53 (1980), p. 736 [reprinted in Rorty's *Consequences of Pragmatism,* 160-75].

28. John Courtney Murray, S.J., *We Hold These Truths* (New York: Sheed and Ward, 1960), p. 14.

Prophetic Pragmatism

From Chapter 6 in Cornel West, *The American Evasion of Philosophy: A Genealogy of Pragmatism* (Madison: University of Wisconsin Press, 1989), 211–39.

1. [West is referring to discussions earlier in his book of the pragmatic elements in the work of Emerson, Lionel Trilling, Reinhold Neibuhr, and the political philosopher Sidney Hook. Hook was a disciple of John Dewey; the other writers are not customarily classified as pragmatists.]

2. Raymond Williams, *Modern Tragedy* (Stanford: Stanford University Press, 1966), pp. 48–49.

3. Hans-Georg Gadamer, *Truth and Method* (New York: Seabury Press, 1975), pp. 245–341. Edward Shils, *Tradition* (Chicago: University of Chicago Press, 1981).

4. Williams, *Modern Tragedy*, pp. 83–84.

5. Antonio Gramsci, *Selections from the Prison Notebooks*, ed. and trans. Quintin Hoare and Geoffrey Nowell Smith (New York: International Publishers, 1971), p. 348.

6. Ibid., pp. 348, 349.

7. Ibid., p. 417. For an elaboration of this Gramscian viewpoint, see Cornel West, "Religion and the Left," *Prophetic Fragments* (Grand Rapids, Mich.: Eerdmans, 1988), pp. 13–21.

8. Edward Said, *The World, the Text, and the Critic* (Cambridge, Mass.: Harvard University Press, 1983), pp. 1–30.

9. For a prophetic pragmatist treatment of this matter, see Cornel West, "The Historicist Turn in Philosophy of Religion," in *Knowing Religiously*, ed. Leroy S. Rouner (Notre Dame: University of Notre Dame Press, 1985), pp. 36–51. See also Cornel West, "On Leszek Kolakowski's *Religion*," in *Prophetic Fragments*, pp. 216–21.

A Pragmatist Manifesto

Chapter 15 in Richard A. Posner, *The Problems of Jurisprudence* (Cambridge, Mass.: Harvard University Press, 1990), 454–69.

1. Obviously *rightness* here is being used in the second of two senses relevant to law: that is, with reference to substantive justice, justice in the individual case, rather than formal justice, which emphasizes systemic concerns such as adherence to precedent. The disvaluing of the second sense is a defining feature of critical legal studies and other radical theories of law.

2. [A major argument of *The Common Law* in particular. Two excerpts from this work are reprinted here, pp. 137–41.]

3. [In "The Path of the Law," reprinted here, pp. 145–69.]

4. And one mirrored on the practical level in the extraordinary diversity of interpretive approaches found in judicial opinions. It is difficult for even a supreme court to bring about uniformity of interpretive approach, because ordinarily the interpretive theory in a judicial opinion is just dictum. The case would, or at least plausibly could, have come out the same way on a different theory, making the particular theory articulated dispensable, and therefore dictum.

5. [The maxim that agreements or stipulations of the parties to a contract must be observed.]

6. [A contemporary movement in legal scholarship that emphasizes the political assumptions and consequences of ostensibly neutral legal language and procedure. It is sometimes understood as a descendant of the legal realism of the 1930s, which has, in turn, been understood to derive from Holmes's "Path of the Law."]

7. [Posner is referring to the English philosopher and political writer Edmund Burke (1729–1797).]

8. See, for example, Federal Judicial Center, *Report of the Study Group on the Case Load of the Supreme Court* (1972); Note, "Of High Designs: A Compendium of Proposals to Reduce the Workload of the Supreme Court," 97 *Harvard Law Review* 307 (1983); Arthur D. Hellman, "Caseloads, Conflicts, and Decisional Capacity: Does the Supreme Court Need Help?" 67 *Judicature* 28 (1983).

9. [Peirce's definition appears in "How to Make Our Ideas Clear," reprinted here, pp. 26–48; James's appears in "The Will to Believe," reprinted here, pp. 69–92, and "Pragmatism's Conception of Truth," reprinted here, pp. 112–31; Holmes's is implied in his opinion in *Abrams v. United States,* an excerpt from which is reprinted here, pp. 178–80.]

10. [Posner is referring to Thomas S. Kuhn, *The Structure of Scientific Revolutions* (1962) and *The Essential Tension* (1977).]

11. [Posner is referring to the views expressed in Karl Popper, *Logik der Forschung* (*The Logic of Scientific Discovery,* 1934; English trans. 1959).]

12. [Posner is referring to the view expressed in Ludwig Wittgenstein, *Philosophical Investigations* (1953).]

13. [The reference is to Jürgen Habermas, *Theorie des kommunikativen Handelns* (*The Theory of Communicative Action,* 1981; English trans. 1984).]

14. [Posner discusses Rorty's article "Unger, Castoriadis, and the Romance of a National Future" (1988), which is reprinted in Richard Rorty, *Essays on Heidegger and Others: Philosophical Papers, Volume 2* (Cambridge: Cambridge University Press, 1991), 177–92.]

15. See generally Sanford Levinson, *Constitutional Faith* (1988). One potentially constructive overlap is the lawyer's and the theologian's common interest in practical reason. In Chapter 2 I cited Cardinal Newman's *Grammar of Assent;* here I add Nicholas Rescher, *Pascal's Wager: A Study of Practical Reasoning in Philosophical Theology* (1985).

16. [*Farwell v. Boston & Worcester R.R.,* 45 Mass. 49 (1842); *West Virginia State Board of Education v. Barnette,* 319 U.S. 624 (1943).]

17. Holmes's prophecy of 1897 is in process of being fulfilled at long last: "For the rational study of the law the black-letter man may be the man of the present, but the man of the future is the man of statistics and the master of economics. . . . I look forward to the time when the part played by history in the explanation of dogma shall be very small, and instead of ingenious [historical] research we shall spend our energy on a study of the ends sought to be attained and the reasons for desiring them. As a step toward that ideal it seems to me that every

lawyer ought to seek an understanding of economics. . . . In the present state of political economy . . . we are called on to consider and weigh the ends of legislation, the means of attaining them, and the cost. We learn that for everything we have to give up something else, and we are taught to set the advantage we gain against the other advantage we lose, and to know what we are doing when we elect." "The Path of the Law," 10 *Harvard Law Review,* 457, 469, 474 (1897). [Square brackets are Posner's.] *Why Zero Sum?*

18. See C. Edwin Baker, "Scope of the First Amendment Freedom of Speech," 25 *UCLA Law Review* 964, 974–81 (1978).

19. As powerfully argued in Peter Munz, *Our Knowledge of the Growth of Knowledge: Popper or Wittgenstein?* (1985).

20. These are views propounded by Frederick Schauer. See *Free Speech: A Philosophical Inquiry* 32–33 (1982); "Liars, Novelists, and the Law of Defamation," 51 *Brooklyn Law Review* 233, 266 (1985). Schauer does note with approval that fallibilist theories of science support the epistemic case for a free market in ideas. See *Free Speech: A Philosophical Inquiry,* at 25. But on the whole he is skeptical about that case.

21. This argument is developed in Richard A. Posner, "Art for Law's Sake," 68 *American Scholar* 513 (1989).

22. While adhering to its earlier ruling upholding punishment of draft-card burning, the Supreme Court has now ruled that flag burning is constitutionally protected. See *Texas v. Johnson,* 109 S. Ct. 2533 (1989).

Reading Pragmatically

Published as "Hum 6, or Reading Before Theory," *Raritan* 9 (Spring 1990), 14–31; reprinted as chapter 4 in Richard Poirier, *Poetry and Pragmatism* (Cambridge, Mass.: Harvard University Press, 1992), 171–93, which is the text used here.

1. [Poirier is referring to the English critic William Empson, the author of *Seven Types of Ambiguity* (1930) and other works, and the American critic R. P. Blackmur, many of whose essays are collected in *The Lion and the Honeycomb* (1955).]

2. Kermode's brilliantly argued and persuasive discussions of the so-called canon are to be found most readily in his *History and Value* (Oxford: Clarendon Press, 1988), 108–27, and *An Appetite for Poetry* (Cambridge, Mass.: Harvard University Press, 1989), 189–207.

3. [Jacques Derrida, *Of Grammatology*; English translation 1976. Derrida's work is discussed here by Richard Rorty in "Philosophy as a Kind of Writing," pp. 304–28.]

4. [George Santayana (1863–1952), a student and colleague of William James in the Harvard philosophy department, and the contemporary philosopher, also at Harvard, Stanley Cavell.]

5. *In Defense of Reading* was published in 1962 (New York: Dutton), and obviously only those who had taught the course before that date were asked to contribute. The contributors, in order of appearance on the title page, were Reuben A. Brower, Paul de Man, William H. Pritchard, Neil Hertz, Anne Davidson Ferry, Thomas B. Whitbread, Stephen Kitay Orgel, Paul J. Alpers, Paul Bertram, Oswald Johnston, Thomas R. Edwards, Jr., William Youngren, G. Armour Craig, William R. Taylor, and Richard Poirier.

6. As this manuscript goes to the press, I am reading with admiration Russell B. Goodman, *American Philosophy and the Romantic Tradition*, in which he quotes Wittgenstein as saying: "I really want my copious punctuation marks to slow down the speed of reading. Because I should like to be read slowly. (As I myself read.)" The quotation is taken from *Culture and Value*, ed. G. H. von Wright and trans. Peter Winch (Chicago: University of Chicago Press, 1980), 16.

7. [Cleanth Brooks and Robert Penn Warren's *Understanding Poetry* (1938) was an influential textbook that provided New Critical guidelines, with an emphasis on "close reading" and attention to form, for teaching poetry.]

8. [Poirier is referring to Richards's *Principles of Literary Criticism* (1924) and *Practical Criticism* (1929), works that emphasize the experience of reading and that, as Poirier suggests, influenced the New Critics.]

9. [The French critic Roland Barthes (1915–1980).]

10. [Leavis's most sustained argument for this method of reading is *The Living Principle: "English" as a Discipline of Thought* (1975); Poirier else-

where mentions the chapter on T. S. Eliot's *Four Quartets* in that book as an instance of the kind of criticism he here calls pragmatic.]

11. [Poirier is referring to the Russian critic Mikhail Bakhtin (1895–1975), whose essays in *The Dialogic Imagination* (published in English translation in 1981) received considerable attention from Western critics.]

The Future of History

From Chapter 8 in Joyce Appleby, Lynn Hunt, and Margaret Jacob, *Telling the Truth About History* (New York: W. W. Norton, 1994), 271–309.

1. For part of this argument we are indebted to Helen Longino, *Science as Social Knowledge* (Princeton, N.J., 1991).

2. On the problems in science education, see Sheila Tobias's essay in W. Stevenson Bacon, ed., *Revitalizing Undergraduate Science* (Tucson, 1992).

3. For a general discussion of these issues as they apply to Charles Peirce, Hilary Putnam, and Richard Rorty, see Richard J. Bernstein, "The Resurgence of Pragmatism," *Social Research* 59 (1992), 825–26.

4. [Charles S. Peirce, "The Fixation of Belief" (reprinted here, pp. 7–25), "How to Make Our Ideas Clear" (reprinted here, pp. 26–48), "The Doctrine of Chances," "The Probability of Induction," "The Order of Nature," and "Deduction, Induction, and Hypothesis," all published in *The Popular Science Monthly*, November 1877 to August 1878.]

5. Federalist No. 10, in Edward Mead Earle, ed., *The Federalist* (New York, 1937), pp. 54–59. (Originally published in 1787–88.)

6. Earle, ed., *The Federalist*, p. 337.

7. Alexis de Tocqueville, *Democracy in America* (New York, 1835).

8. [*Planned Parenthood of Southeastern Pennsylvania v. Casey*, 505 U.S. 833 (1992).]

Index

Permissions Acknowledgments

The editor thanks Sam Cohen, Tamara Evans, Scott MacDonald, Hayden Pelliccia, Burton Pike, Richard Rorty, and Paul Stasi for their advice and assistance with the anthology, and John Brenkman, John Patrick Diggins, and Joan Richardson, with whom he has taught much of this material, for their intellectual stimulation and companionship.